MW00800909

Harley-Davidson Big Twins
Service and Repair Manual

by Curt Choate, Tom Schauwecker, Penny Cox, Mike Stubblefield and Alan Ahlstrand

Models covered
1200 FL: FL, FLH, FLHS, 1970 to 1980
1200 FX: FX, FXE, FXS, FXEF, 1970 to 1980
1340 FL: FLT, FLTC/U, FLH, FLHF, FLHR, FLHS, FLHT, FLHTC/U, 1978 on
1340 FXR: FXR, FXRS, FXRS-SP, FXRS-CONV, FXLR, FXRD, FXRT, 1982 on
1340 FX/Softail: FXB, FXD, FXE, FXDG, FXDL, FXDWG, FXDS-CONV, FXEF, FXS, FXSB, FXWG,
    FXST, FXSTC, FXSTS, FLST, FLST-SP, FLSTC, FLSTF, FLSTN, 1979 through 1999
1340 Dyna: FXD, FXDB, FXDC, FXDL, FXDS-CONV, FXDWG, 1991 through 1998

ABCDE
FGHIJ
KLMNO
PQR

ISBN **1 56392 536 2**

British Library Cataloguing in Publication Data
A catalogue record for this book is available from the British Library.

Library of Congress Control Number
Printed in the USA

Haynes Publishing
Sparkford, Nr Yeovil, Somerset BA22 7JJ, England

Haynes North America, Inc
861 Lawrence Drive, Newbury Park, California 91320, USA

04-272

Contents

LIVING WITH YOUR HARLEY-DAVIDSON BIG TWINS

Introduction

Daily (pre-ride) checks

MAINTENANCE

Routine maintenance and servicing

Contents

REPAIRS AND OVERHAUL

Engine, transmission and associated systems

Chassis and bodywork components

Electrical system

Wiring diagrams

REFERENCE

Index

Harley-Davidson
Milwaukee Magic

by Alan Ahlstrand

Milwaukee Magic

Late in the 1960s, on a typical warm summer California evening, a friend showed up at my house and announced, "Alan, if I can't make the payment, I'm coming to you for the money, because I'm *not* losing this bike."

He'd just traded his Suzuki X-6 - a 250cc 2-stroke twin with six-speed transmission, at that time being talked about as the new Harley-beater - for a new-to-him 1966 Sportster XLCH.

I'd ridden the Suzuki and laid it down on asphalt, so I wasn't invited onto the front seat of the Sportster. Instead, he gave complete instructions in back-seat riding technique for a torquey motorcycle without a sissy bar or grab strap for the passenger: "Put your hands around my waist and lock your fingers, or the bike will jet out from under you." Off we went,

ending up on newly-opened Highway 280 south of San Francisco, which was deserted at 2 a.m. Helmetless, ungoggled, dressed in jeans and t-shirts and unbridled by a sense of mortality, we cranked it up. After I'd had enough time to think "We're crazy, but yeee-haaa" more than once, he took one hand off the grip, turned around with one eye closed, the other half-closed and streaming tears, grinned, and held up one finger - we'd hit a hundred miles an hour.

Maybe the speedometer was optimistic, and it was really only 97.4 or so, but when the wind is shredding the shirt on your back and flapping your face like flags in a hurricane, the difference is academic.

Every Harley rider has done something like that - or will, when the time and place are right - and that Milwaukee magic has been the key to the company's modern success.

All of this started a century ago. In 1903

Arthur Davidson and William S. Harley finished a three-year project, building what amounted to a powered bicycle. The first Harley-Davidson engine had a single cylinder with a bore of 2-1/8 inches and a stroke of 2-7/8 inches, displacing 405 cc. The intake valve was not operated mechanically; rather, it was sucked open by the downward pull of the piston and pushed shut by the compressing fuel-air mixture on the piston's upward stroke, a design shared with contemporary automobile engines such as the Knox Porcupine. Power transmission was by a leather belt, assisted when necessary by bicycle pedals, a chain, sprockets and human effort. Braking was accomplished by pedaling backwards, bicycle-style. The front suspension was the leading-link design later to be improved and used in Springers, historic and modern. The rear suspension? There wasn't any - the bike's rigid, triangular rear frame section connected directly to the rear axle.

From 1903 to 1909, the company continued to grow, with steady improvements in the single-cylinder bike's design, steady increases in sales, and a move from the shed where the company started to a two-story factory in Milwaukee. In 1909 Harley's first V-twin, the model 5D, was introduced, and with it the company's enduring theme.

Despite diversions such as the Topper scooter and Aermacchi singles of the Sixties and Seventies, the theme continues to the present day. The heart of all Harleys, the key to what makes a motorcycle a Harley-Davidson, is the engine. The rest of the bike exists to keep the engine off the pavement. This function is performed in grand style, of course, with a near-infinite selection of customizing possibilities, but at the center of it all is a big-displacement, narrow-angle, uneven-firing, air-cooled V-twin that roars instead of wails. From the flatheads that succeeded the Model 5D, to the Knucklehead of 1936, to the Panhead of 1948, to the Shovelhead of 1966, to the Evolution of 1984, to the current Twin Cam 88, every important Harley-Davidson engine has fit that description.

(Actually, the only official designations in the list are Evolution and Twin Cam 88. Panhead, Knucklehead and Shovelhead were

The 1975 FLH1200 (Shovelhead)

informal names, based on the appearance of the cylinder heads and valve covers. For that reason, the Twin Cam 88 came dangerously close to being dubbed "Fathead.")

In addition to big piston displacement and a V-twin configuration, Harley engines share some unique characteristics. The angle between the cylinders, or "V," is 45 degrees. The crankshaft has one crankpin, with both connecting rods mounted on it. This means that the cylinders fire 90-degrees apart (at 315 and 405 degrees of crankshaft rotation). This uneven firing sequence gives the engine its signature "potato-potato" idle. In addition to being mounted on a single crankpin, the connecting rods are mounted knife-and-fork style rather than side-by-side. In this design, the bottom end of one connecting rod is an inverted Y, with the bottom end of the other connecting rod centered between the Y's branches. This allows the engine to be narrow from side to side, while the small angle between the cylinders allows it to be narrow front-to-rear.

The company continued producing new products under family ownership until 1969, when it was bought by the conglomerate AMF. The AMF years, 1969 to 1981, were widely regarded as the company's Dark Ages - sales dropped, along with the bikes' reputation for quality. My friend replaced his 1966 Sportster with a 1979 model, and then replaced a series of tachs and speedometers because the needles kept breaking off from vibration. This era ended with the company's rescue in a buyout by company executives, led by Vaughn Beals. This is one of the most successful employee buyouts in corporate history, if the company's stock price and sales are any indication - the stock has multiplied in value many times, and Harley-Davidson has for years maintained the biggest market share in the cruiser and touring bike categories.

That almost didn't happen - and Harley-Davidson nearly ended up in the recycling bin of history, as a nostalgic brand name that would-be entrepreneurs could paste onto yet another corporate startup attempt.

The buyout coincided with a downturn in the motorcycle market. Along with that, competition from Japanese bikes had become well established. The Suzuki X-6 wasn't a Harley-beater, but there were now plenty of four-cylinder Japanese 750s that were. Worse yet, the major Japanese manufacturers began to build V-twin cruisers. Faced with imminent doom, Harley-Davidson turned to the US government for help. This came in the form of a tariff, beginning in 1983, on Japanese-built motorcycles with displacements over 700 cc. The result was a sudden rash of Japanese bikes displacing 699cc, but it was enough to keep the company alive. Its fortunes even improved enough that it asked for an early end to the tariff in 1987.

The motorcycle market coasted along the bottom for several years, then finally began to

The 1974 XL1000 Sportster (Shovelhead)

The XL1200 Sportster (Evolution)

The 1993 FLSTC Heritage Softail (Evolution)

The 1993 XLH 883 Sportster Hugger (Evolution)

turn up significantly in the early 1990s. As the market revived, the audience was changing; motorcyclists were becoming older, richer, but more in need of a bad boy image (and increasingly, a bad girl image). They also needed bikes that were reliable and relatively comfortable to ride. Harley-Davidson had possessed the image for decades, even if Marlon Brando did ride a Triumph in "The Wild One." With the Evolution engine and improved quality control, the company was on its way to reliability. Comfort and simplicity had been evolving, and continued to do so.

Comfort and simplicity were no part of the Sportster XLCH, but in its day, the bike was enough of a thrill ride to make up for it. The kickstarter, operated in the wrong synchronicity with the twist-grip spark timing, could kick back and hurt you. The drum brakes stopped the bike far less capably than the engine made it go. The XLCH had no battery; its electrical system was powered by a magneto, which meant that the lights would dim if you let the engine idle. (Why no, officer, I wasn't speedshifting, I was just trying to keep the lights safely bright.)

The XLCH was intended for competition. Other Harleys were easier to ride, and had battery-based electrical systems. Electric start was introduced on the first Electra Glide in 1965. Final drive progressed from an exposed chain, to an enclosed chain, to a cogged belt that's still in use. Drum brakes were replaced by discs at front and rear. Rubber engine mounts were employed on touring bikes, and later on the Dyna. The hardtail look of early bikes was recreated with the Softail, but the Softail had a rear suspension. A well-designed sequential port fuel injection system was added as an option. Some models were designed with low seat heights to accommodate shorter riders.

The Evolution engine was a turning point in the company's history, even though it was essentially a refined top end on the Shovelhead bottom end. The iron cylinders and heads of the Shovelhead were replaced with aluminum components. The valve train's basic design was unchanged, with a single gear-driven camshaft, hydraulic lifters, pushrods and rocker arms. The change to aluminum at the top end eliminated a major source of oil leaks, at the joints of the cylinders and crankcase, because the parts now expanded and contracted at the same rate as they heated and cooled. The combination of mechanical improvement and Harley tradition was enthusiastically received by customers, first in the Big Twins for 1984 and then in the Sportster for 1986.

The Evolution engine was superseded by the Twin Cam 88, in the Touring and Dyna chassis for the 1999 model year and in Softails for 2000 (the Evo is still used in the Sportster). Unlike the Evolution, the Twin Cam 88 was a completely new design, even while it retained the basics of the traditional Harley

A hundred years old, and stronger than ever - 100th Anniversary models sport a distinctive logo

Past meets future - the Sportster is essentially unchanged, while the V-Rod is radically new

engine. Despite the name, the engine did not have overhead cams. The Twin Cam designation came about because the wide spacing between the large cylinder bores made a single camshaft impractical. The solution was to use one camshaft for each cylinder. The camshafts are mounted in a support plate on the right side of the engine, below the cylinders. The rear camshaft is driven by the crankshaft through a chain and sprockets mounted outside the camshaft support plate. The rear camshaft drives the front camshaft through a second chain and sprockets, mounted inside the camshaft support plate. As with earlier Harley engines, the camshafts operate the valves through hydraulic lifters, pushrods and rocker arms.

Engine vibration in Dyna and Touring models was handled by rubber engine mounts. In the Softail, where the engine is solidly mounted to the chassis, another solution was needed. This was the Twin Cam 88B, the balancer-equipped version of the engine that appeared in Softails in 2000. The Twin Cam 88B is the same as non-counterbalanced versions from the crankshaft up. A pair of balance shafts, one behind the crankshaft and one in front, are driven by the crankshaft through a chain and sprockets.

Thus Harley-Davidson ends its first century with a very good product line and very good prospects. What's in store for Harley's next century? Logically, the company's future cruisers and touring motorcycles should be variations of the V-Rod sport bike. The V-Rod is an attractive mix of Harley tradition and modern technology. Like traditional Harleys, the V-Rod has a V-twin engine. Unlike traditional Harleys, the V-Rod employs overhead cams, four-valve heads and liquid cooling to produce an impressive 115 horsepower. And yet, Harley customers have left V-Rods on the sales floor in record numbers while buying more Twin Cam 88s every year.

Modern Japanese bikes tend to have four-figure price tags and five-figure redlines; Harleys, traditional and V-Rod, are the other way around. Modern Harleys are well built and reliable, but so are their competitors. Why, in the face of those facts, do traditional Harleys continue to dominate their market? When Milwaukee magic applies, logic doesn't. It's as simple, and as complicated, as that.

Acknowledgements

Thanks to Michael Kuehner for letting us photograph his 1984 FXR (with custom paint, seat, fenders, front forks and air cleaner) for the front cover, and to Eugene Saar for arranging the photo shoot. Thanks also to Joe Del Negro and Ted Tossi of Cycle Imagery, Santa Cruz, California, for letting us photograph the 1989 Softail (with custom air cleaner) shown on the front cover. Thanks also to JIMS Tools, of Camarillo, California (www.jimsusa.com), for supplying the special tools used in some photographs. The introduction "Milwaukee Magic" was written by Alan Ahlstrand.

About this manual

The aim of this manual is to help you get the best value from your motorcycle. It can do so in several ways. It can help you decide what work must be done, even if you choose to have it done by a dealer; it provides information and procedures for routine maintenance and servicing; and it offers diagnostic and repair procedures to follow when trouble occurs.

We hope you use the manual to tackle the work yourself. For many simpler jobs, doing it yourself may be quicker than arranging an appointment to get the motorcycle into a dealer and making the trips to leave it and pick it up. More importantly, a lot of money can be saved by avoiding the expense the shop must pass on to you to cover its labor and overhead costs. An added benefit is the sense of satisfaction and accomplishment that you feel after doing the job yourself.

References to the left or right side of the motorcycle assume you are sitting on the seat, facing forward.

We take great pride in the accuracy of information given in this manual, but motorcycle manufacturers make alterations and design changes during the production run of a particular motorcycle of which they do not inform us. No liability can be accepted by the authors or publishers for loss, damage or injury caused by any errors in, or omissions from, the information given.

Buying spare parts

Once you have found all the identification numbers, record them for reference when buying parts. Since the manufacturers change specifications, parts and vendors (companies that manufacture various components on the machine), providing the ID numbers is the only way to be reasonably sure that you are buying the correct parts.

Whenever possible, take the worn part to the dealer so direct comparison with the new component can be made. Along the trail from the manufacturer to the parts shelf, there are numerous places that the part can end up with the wrong number or be listed incorrectly.

The two places to purchase new parts for your motorcycle - the accessory store and the franchised dealer - differ in the type of parts they carry. While dealers can obtain virtually every part for your motorcycle, the accessory dealer is usually limited to normal high wear items such as shock absorbers, tune-up parts, various engine gaskets, cables, chains, brake parts, etc. Rarely will an accessory outlet have major suspension components, cylinders, transmission gears, or cases.

Used parts can be obtained for considerably less than new ones, but you can't always be sure of what you're getting. Once again, take your worn part to the salvage yard for direct comparison.

Whether buying new, used or rebuilt parts, the best course is to deal directly with someone who specializes in parts for your particular make.

1 or 5	Market designation
HD	Harley-Davidson
1 or 4	Heavyweight or middleweight motorcycle
2 or 3 letters	Model designation
Single letter	Engine displacement
1 or 2	Introduction date or model
0 through 9 or X	Check digit
Single digit	Model year
Single letter	Location or manufacturer
Six digits	Sequential serial number

Vehicle Identification Number (VIN) details (typical)

Decoding the Vehicle Identification Number (VIN)

The frame serial number is stamped into the right side of the steering head and printed on a decal attached to the right frame downtube. An abbreviated frame serial number is stamped on the crankcase below the "V" of the cylinders. Both of these numbers should be recorded and kept in a safe place so they can be given to law enforcement officials in the event of a theft.

The frame serial number and engine serial number should also be kept in a handy place (such as with your driver's license) so they are always available when purchasing or ordering parts for your machine.

The Vehicle Identification Number (VIN) contains code letters and numbers that provide specific information about each motorcycle. The purpose of each letter or number is shown in the accompanying illustration. The letter and number codes are described below.

VIN key for pre-1980 models

Model	First Two Digits (Model)	Next Five Digits (Sequential Number)	Second Last Digit (Manufacturer)	Last Digit (Model) (Season)
FL or FLP	1A	10000 and up (5 digits)	Harley-Davidson	8 (1978)
FLH	2A			
FX	2C		H	
FXE	9D			
FXS	2F			
FLH-1200	2A			
FX-1200	2C			8
FXE-1200	9D	60000	H	(1978½)
FXEF-1200	5E	and		
FXEF-80	6E	up	H	9
FXS-1200	2F	10000		(1979)
FLH-80	3G	and		
FXE-80	6G	up		
FXS-80	7G			
FXWG-80	9G			
FLH-80 Classic	3H			
FLHS-80	5H			
FL-80	6H	10000	J	0
FLH-1200 Police	7H	and up		(1980)
FLH-1200 Shrine	8H			
FLH-80 Police	9H			
FLH-80 Shrine	1K			
FLT	5G	00001 and up	J	0 (1980)

Examples: 1979 FLH-1200, 2A12141H9
1980 FLH-1200, 2A12141JO

Model codes, 1981 and later

1981 through 1984 FL

AA	FLH-80
AB	FLHP-80 Police, chain
AC	FLH-80 Shrine, chain
AH	FLHP-80 Police, belt
AK	FLHS-80
AL	FLH-80 Shrine, belt

1981 through 1984 FX

BA	FXE-80
BE	FXWG-80
BD	FXB
BH	FXST
BG	FXDG

1985 and later FLT

DB	FLTC
DD	FLHTC (1984 and 1985)
DD	FLHT (1986 and later)
DE	FLHTC sidecar (1984 and 1985)
DE	FLHT sidecar (1986 and later)
DG	FLHT Shrine (1984 and 1985)
DG	FLHTC Shrine (1986 and later)
DH	FLTC sidecar
DJ	FLHTC
DK	FLHTC Shrine (1986 through 1989)
DK	FLTC Shrine (1995 and 1996)
DM	FLTC Ultra
DN	FLTC Ultra sidecar
DP	FLHTC Ultra
DR	FLHTC Ultra sidecar
DS	FLTC Ultra Shrine
DT	FLHTC Ultra Shrine
FA	FLHS
FB	FLHR-I
FC	FLHTCU-I
FD	FLHR

FE	FLHTCU-I
FF	FLHTC-I
FG	FLHTCU-I sidecar
FL	FLHTCU-I Shrine
FP	FLTR
FR	FLHTC-I
FS	FLTR-I

1985 and later FXR

EA	FXR
EB	FXRS
EC	FXRT
EE	FXRDG
EG	FXRS Sport
EH	FXRD
EL	FXLR
EM	FXRS-CONV

1985 and later FX/Softail

BH	FXST
BJ	FLST or FLSTC
BK	FXSTC
BL	FXSTS
BM	FLSTF
BN	FLSTN
BP	FXSTSB
BR	FLSTS
BT	FXSTB

1991 and later Dyna Glide

GA	FXDB Daytona
GB	FXDB Sturgis
GC	FXDC
GD	FXDL
GE	FXDWG
GG	FXDS CONV
GH	FXD

The VIN is printed on a decal on the right frame downtube; an abbreviated version is stamped in the crankcase forward of the front pushrods

The VIN is also stamped in the frame on or near the steering head

Professional mechanics are trained in safe working procedures. However enthusiastic you may be about getting on with the job at hand, take the time to ensure that your safety is not put at risk. A moment's lack of attention can result in an accident, as can failure to observe simple precautions.

There will always be new ways of having accidents, and the following is not a comprehensive list of all dangers; it is intended rather to make you aware of the risks and to encourage a safe approach to all work you carry out on your bike.

Asbestos

● Certain friction, insulating, sealing and other products - such as brake pads, clutch linings, gaskets, etc. - contain asbestos. Extreme care must be taken to avoid inhalation of dust from such products since it is hazardous to health. If in doubt, assume that they do contain asbestos.

Fire

● Remember at all times that gasoline is highly flammable. Never smoke or have any kind of naked flame around, when working on the vehicle. But the risk does not end there - a spark caused by an electrical short-circuit, by two metal surfaces contacting each other, by careless use of tools, or even by static electricity built up in your body under certain conditions, can ignite gasoline vapor, which in a confined space is highly explosive. Never use gasoline as a cleaning solvent. Use an approved safety solvent.

● Always disconnect the battery ground terminal before working on any part of the fuel or electrical system, and never risk spilling fuel on to a hot engine or exhaust.

● It is recommended that a fire extinguisher of a type suitable for fuel and electrical fires is kept handy in the garage or workplace at all times. Never try to extinguish a fuel or electrical fire with water.

Fumes

● Certain fumes are highly toxic and can quickly cause unconsciousness and even death if inhaled to any extent. Gasoline vapor comes into this category, as do the vapors from certain solvents such as trichloro-ethylene. Any draining or pouring of such volatile fluids should be done in a well ventilated area.

● When using cleaning fluids and solvents, read the instructions carefully. Never use materials from unmarked containers - they may give off poisonous vapors.

● Never run the engine of a motor vehicle in an enclosed space such as a garage. Exhaust fumes contain carbon monoxide which is extremely poisonous; if you need to run the engine, always do so in the open air or at least have the rear of the vehicle outside the workplace.

The battery

● Never cause a spark, or allow a naked light near the vehicle's battery. It will normally be giving off a certain amount of hydrogen gas, which is highly explosive.

● Always disconnect the battery ground terminal before working on the fuel or electrical systems (except where noted).

● If possible, loosen the filler plugs or cover when charging the battery from an external source. Do not charge at an excessive rate or the battery may burst.

● Take care when topping up, cleaning or carrying the battery. The acid electrolyte, even when diluted, is very corrosive and should not be allowed to contact the eyes or skin. Always wear rubber gloves and goggles or a face shield. If you ever need to prepare electrolyte yourself, always add the acid slowly to the water; never add the water to the acid.

Electricity

● When using an electric power tool, inspection light etc., always ensure that the appliance is correctly connected to its plug and that, where necessary, it is properly grounded. Do not use such appliances in damp conditions and, again, beware of creating a spark or applying excessive heat in the vicinity of fuel or fuel vapor. Also ensure that the appliances meet national safety standards.

● A severe electric shock can result from touching certain parts of the electrical system, such as the spark plug wires (HT leads), when the engine is running or being cranked, particularly if components are damp or the insulation is defective. Where an electronic ignition system is used, the secondary (HT) voltage is much higher and could prove fatal.

Remember...

✗ **Don't** start the engine without first ascertaining that the transmission is in neutral.

✗ **Don't** attempt to drain oil until you are sure it has cooled sufficiently to avoid scalding you.

✗ **Don't** grasp any part of the engine or exhaust system without first ascertaining that it is cool enough not to burn you.

✗ **Don't** allow brake fluid or antifreeze to contact the machine's paintwork or plastic components.

✗ **Don't** siphon toxic liquids such as fuel or hydraulic fluid by mouth, or allow them to remain on your skin.

✗ **Don't** inhale dust - it may be injurious to health (see Asbestos heading).

✗ **Don't** allow any spilled oil or grease to remain on the floor - wipe it up right away, before someone slips on it.

✗ **Don't** use ill-fitting wrenches or other tools which may slip and cause injury.

✗ **Don't** lift a heavy component which may be beyond your capability - get assistance.

✗ **Don't** rush to finish a job or take unverified short cuts.

✗ **Don't** allow children or animals in or around an unattended vehicle.

✗ **Don't** inflate a tire above the recommended pressure. Apart from overstressing the carcass, in extreme cases the tire may blow off forcibly.

✔ **Do** ensure that the machine is supported securely at all times. This is especially important when the machine is blocked up to aid wheel or fork removal.

✔ **Do** take care when attempting to loosen a stubborn nut or bolt. It is generally better to pull on a wrench, rather than push, so that if you slip, you fall away from the machine rather than onto it.

✔ **Do** wear eye protection when using power tools such as drill, sander, bench grinder etc.

✔ **Do** use a barrier cream on your hands prior to undertaking dirty jobs - it will protect your skin from infection as well as making the dirt easier to remove afterwards; but make sure your hands aren't left slippery. Note that long-term contact with used engine oil can be a health hazard.

✔ **Do** keep loose clothing (cuffs, ties etc. and long hair) well out of the way of moving mechanical parts.

✔ **Do** remove rings, wristwatch etc., before working on the vehicle - especially the electrical system.

✔ **Do** keep your work area tidy - it is only too easy to fall over articles left lying around.

✔ **Do** exercise caution when compressing springs for removal or installation. Ensure that the tension is applied and released in a controlled manner, using suitable tools which preclude the possibility of the spring escaping violently.

✔ **Do** ensure that any lifting tackle used has a safe working load rating adequate for the job.

✔ **Do** get someone to check periodically that all is well, when working alone on the vehicle.

✔ **Do** carry out work in a logical sequence and check that everything is correctly assembled and tightened afterwards.

✔ **Do** remember that your vehicle's safety affects that of yourself and others. If in doubt on any point, get professional advice.

● If in spite of following these precautions, you are unfortunate enough to injure yourself, seek medical attention as soon as possible.

1 Engine oil level check

Before you start:

Caution: Do not run the engine in an enclosed space such as a garage or workshop.

✔ On all models except the FXR, 1991 and later Dynas, and 1993 and later FLTs, the level should be checked with the motorcycle held upright. On these models, check the level with the motorcycle on its sidestand. In all cases, the motorcycle should be standing on level ground.

✔ Remove the oil filler plug/dipstick, located either under the seat or on the side of the oil tank, or on later models on the oil pan (take care to avoid scalding your hands) **(see illustration)**.

✔ Wipe the dipstick clean, identify the oil level marks and reinsert in the oil tank/pan. Withdraw the dipstick and read the oil level **(see illustration)**. If the level is near or below the lower mark, add the recommended oil to bring it up to the Full mark. (On Softails where there is no Full mark, fill to the base of the filler plug.)

✔ Reinstall the oil filler plug/dipstick.

Bike care:

● If you have to add oil frequently, you should check whether you have any oil leaks. If there is no sign of oil leakage from the joints and gaskets the engine could be burning oil (see *Troubleshooting*).

The correct oil

● Modern, high-revving engines place great demands on their oil. It is very important that the correct oil for your bike is used.

● Always top up with a good quality oil of the specified type and viscosity and do not overfill the engine.

Oil type..	H-D rating 360 or equivalent
Oil viscosity	
Shovelhead engine	
Normal 20 to 90-degrees F.............................	SAE 20W-50
Below 40-degrees F......................................	SAE 30
Above 40-degrees F	SAE 40
Above 80-degrees F	SAE 60
Evolution engine	
Below 40-degrees F (4-degrees C)...............	H.D. Multi-Grade, SAE 10W-40
Above 40-degrees F (4-degrees C)	H.D. Multi-Grade, SAE 20W-50
Above 60-degrees F (16-degrees C)	H.D. Regular Heavy, SAE 50
Above 80-degrees F (27-degrees C)	H.D. Extra Heavy, SAE 60

1 The Softail engine oil filler cap is in the oil tank on the right side of the bike.

2 The Dyna engine oil filler cap is on the right side, behind the rear cylinder.

3 Here's the engine oil filler cap on a Road King, between the exhaust pipe and side cover on the right side of the bike (other Touring models similar).

4 Rock the engine oil dipstick back-and-forth while pulling it out. Measure the oil level on the dipstick scale.

2 Suspension, steering and final drive checks

Suspension and Steering:
● Check that the front and rear suspension operate smoothly without binding.
● Check that the suspension is adjusted as required.
● Check that the steering moves smoothly from lock-to-lock.

Final drive:
● Check the drivebelt tension with the belt cold, the bike on the sidestand and the weight of the rider on the seat. Using a tension gauge is the best way to check, but the gauge isn't absolutely necessary. If belt tension is incorrect, adjust it (see Chapter 1). On later Dyna models, the belt is visible through a hole in the belt guard.
● On chain drive models (1970 through 1985), check the drive chain slack isn't excessive and adjust it if necessary (see Chapter 1).
● On chain drive models without an automatic oiler, lubricate the chain if it looks dry (see Chapter 1).

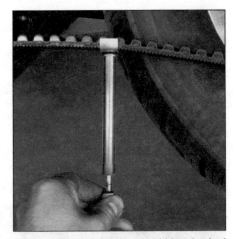

The rear drivebelt tension should be checked at the center of the upper run (Softail) or lower run (Dyna and Touring models), with the bike on the sidestand. Apply 10-pounds force to the belt (ideally, using a tension gauge) and measure the belt deflection.

3 Legal and safety checks

Lighting and signalling:
● Take a minute to check that the headlight, tail light, brake light, instrument lights and turn signals all work correctly.
● Check that the horn sounds when the switch is operated.
● A working speedometer graduated in mph is a statutory requirement in the UK.

Safety:
● Check that the throttle grip rotates smoothly and snaps shut when released, in all steering positions. Also check for the correct amount of freeplay (see Chapter 1).
● Check that the engine shuts off when the kill switch is operated.
● Check that sidestand return spring holds the stand securely up when retracted.

Fuel:
● This may seem obvious, but check that you have enough fuel to complete your journey. If you notice signs of fuel leakage - rectify the cause immediately.
● Ensure you use the correct grade unleaded fuel - see Chapter 4 Specifications.

4 Brake fluid level checks

> **Warning: Some early models used DOT 3 brake fluid. Later models use DOT 5. If you don't know which type your bike uses, have the brake hydraulic system drained and flushed before refilling. Refer to the manufacturer's fluid recommendation stamped on the reservoir cap or cover. Never mix DOT 3 and DOT 5 fluids or brake failure may occur.**

Before you start:

✔ Ensure the motorcycle is held vertical while checking the levels. Make sure the motorcycle is on level ground.

✔ Make sure you have the correct hydraulic fluid. Make sure you have the correct hydraulic fluid (see the Warning above). Never reuse old fluid.

✔ Wrap a rag around the reservoir being worked on to ensure that any spillage does not come into contact with painted surfaces.

Bike care:

● The fluid in the front and rear brake master cylinder reservoirs will drop slightly as the brake pads wear down.

● If any fluid reservoir requires repeated topping-up this is an indication of a hydraulic leak somewhere in the system, which should be investigated immediately.

● Check for signs of fluid leakage from the hydraulic hoses and components - if found, rectify immediately.

● Check the operation of both brakes before taking the machine on the road; if there is evidence of air in the system (spongy feel to lever or pedal), it must be bled as described in Chapter 7.

1 Check the front brake fluid level in the sight glass (if equipped) on top of the master cylinder. If the level is high enough, the sight glass will be dark. It lightens in color as the fluid level drops.

2 The rear master cylinder reservoir is tucked into the frame on some early models

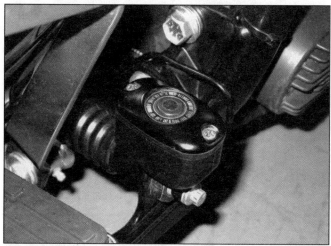

3 The rear master cylinder on later models is located near the brake pedal and has a sight glass. Fluid level is checked in the same way as for the front master cylinder.

4 If the fluid level is low in either master cylinder, remove the cover screws and lift off the cover and diaphragm. Top up to 1/8-inch (3 mm) from the gasket surface with the specified brake fluid, then reinstall the cover and diaphragm.

5 Tire checks

The correct pressures:
● The tires must be checked when **cold**, not immediately after riding. Note that low tire pressures may cause the tire to slip on the rim or come off. High tire pressures will cause abnormal tread wear and unsafe handling.
● Use an accurate pressure gauge.
● Proper air pressure will increase tire life and provide maximum stability and ride comfort.

Tire care:
● Check the tires carefully for cuts, tears, embedded nails or other sharp objects and excessive wear. Operation of the motorcycle with excessively worn tires is extremely hazardous, as traction and handling are directly affected.
● Check the condition of the tire valve and ensure the dust cap is in place.
● Pick out any stones or nails which may have become embedded in the tire tread. If

left, they will eventually penetrate through the casing and cause a puncture.
● If tire damage is apparent, or unexplained loss of pressure is experienced, seek the advice of a tire fitting specialist without delay.

Tire tread depth:
● Tires incorporate wear indicators in the tread. Identify the triangular pointer or 'TWI' mark on the tire sidewall to locate the indicator bar and replace the tire if the tread has worn down to the bar.

Tire pressures - psi (Bars)*

1970 through 1983
FL models (except FLT)
  Front 20 (1.4)
  Rear 24 (1.7)
FLT models
  Front 24 (1.7)
  Rear 26 (1.8)
FX models (except FXR/FXWG)
  Front 24 (1.7)
  Rear 26 (1.8)
FXWG models
  Front 30 (2.1)
  Rear 26 (1.8)
FXR models
  Front 24 (1.7)
  Rear 24 (1.7)

1984 and 1985
FLTC models
  Front 28 (1.9)
  Rear 36 (2.5)
FLFT/C, FXRS and FXRT models
  Front 30 (2.1)
  Rear 36 (2.5)
FXEF and FXSB models
  Front 30 (2.1)
  Rear 32 (2.2)

FXWG and FXST models
  Front 30 (2.1)
  Rear
    Early 1985 . . . . .28 (1.9)
    All others 32 (2.2)

1986 through 1990 (approximate)
FXR models
  Front 30 (2.1)
  Rear 36 (2.5)
FLT models
  Front 36 (2.5)
  Rear 36 (2.5)
FLST/C, FXEF, FXSB
  Front 36 (2.5)
  Rear 36 (2.5)
FXWG, FXST, FXST/C and FXSTS models
  Front 30 (2.1)
  Rear 32 (2.2)

1991-on
FXST/C, FXSTS, FXD Dyna models
  Front 30 (2.1)
  Rear 36 (2.5)
All others same as for 1986 through 1990

Pressure based on rider weighing 150 lbs (68 kg). Increase pressure in rear tire 2 psi (0.14 Bar) and in front tire 1 psi (0.7 Bar) for each additional 50 lbs (23 kg) of weight. Do not exceed maximum pressure

1 Check the tire pressures when the tires are **cold** and keep them properly inflated.

2 Measure tread depth at the center of the tire using a tread depth gauge.

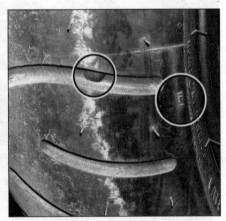
3 Tire tread wear indicator bar and its location marking (usually either an arrow, a triangle or the letters TWI) on the sidewall (arrow).

Chapter 1
Tune-up and routine maintenance

Contents

Degrees of difficulty

Easy, suitable for novice with little experience	**Fairly easy,** suitable for beginner with some experience	**Fairly difficult,** suitable for competent DIY mechanic	**Difficult,** suitable for experienced DIY mechanic	**Very difficult,** suitable for expert DIY or professional

Specifications

Recommended spark plugs

1970 through 1974	No. 3-4
1975 and 1976	No. 5-6
1977 through early 1978	No. 5A-6 or 5R-6
Late 1978 and 1979	No. 5A6A or 5R6A*
1980 through 1983	No. 5R6A or 5RL
1984 and later	No. 5R6A only

*Harley-Davidson No. 5A6 or 5R6 can be used in place of 5A6A or 5R6A if the plug is gapped at 0.038 to 0.043-inch (1.0 to 1.1 mm)

Spark plug gap

1970 through 1978	0.028 to 0.033 inch (0.7 to 0.8 mm)
1979 and later	0.038 to 0.043 inch (1.0 to 1.1 mm)

Contact breaker point gap

All models	0.018 inch (0.46 mm)

Ignition timing

Late 1978 through 1983
  Fully retarded .... 3-degrees BTDC
  Fully advanced .... 35-degrees BTDC
Early 1984
  Range .... 5 to 50-degrees BTDC
  Start... 5-degrees BTDC
  At fast idle .... 35-degrees BTDC
  At 1800 to 2800 rpm .... 50-degrees BTDC

Late 1984 and later

Range
  Through 1994 all, 1995 US .... 0 to 35-degrees BTDC
  1995 international, 1996-on all.. 0 to 42.5-degrees BTDC
Start .... TDC (0-degrees)

Idle speed

Tillotson carburetor.. 900 to 1000 rpm
Bendix carburetor .... 700 to 900 rpm
Keihin carburetor
  1976 through early 1978 .... 900 rpm
  Late 1978 through 1983 .... 800 to 900 rpm
  1984 through 1989
    FLT and FXR
      1984 through 1988 .... 900 to 950 rpm
      1989..1000 to 1050 rpm
    FX and Softail..1000 to 1050 rpm
  1990 through 1992
    FLT and FXR ....1000 rpm
    FX/Softail and Dyna ....1000 to 1050 rpm
  1993 and later (all) ....1000 to 1050 rpm

Drivetrain and suspension

Primary chain slack
  Cold.. 5/8 to 7/8 inch (16 to 22 mm)
  Hot.. 3/8 to 5/8 inch (9 to 16 mm)
Primary belt slack .... 3/8 to 1/2-inch (9 to 13 mm)
Final drive chain slack
  1970 through 1983 .... 1/2-inch (13 mm)
  1984 and later
    FX/Softail models
      FXST only .... 1-1/8 to 1-1/4 inch (28 to 32 mm)
      All others.. 1/2 to 5/8-inch (13 to 16 mm)
    FLT/FXR models .... 1/2-inch (13 mm)
Final drive belt slack
  Through 1983 .... 5/8 to 3/4-inch (16 to 19 mm)
  1984 through 1990
    FX/Softail models.. 5/8 to 3/4-inch (16 to 19 mm)
    FLT/FXR models .... 5/16 to 3/8-inch (8 to 9 mm)
    FLST/C, FXST/C models.. 3/8 to 1/2-inch (9 to 13 mm)
  1991 and later
    FLST/C/F/N, FXSTC/S models .... 3/8 to 1/2-inch (9 to 13 mm)
    FLT/FXR and Dyna models .... 5/16 to 3/8-inch (8 to 9 mm)

Brakes

Front brake lever freeplay
  Drum brake... 3/16-inch (4.5 mm)
  Disc brake .... None
Brake shoe thickness (minimum)... 0.100-inch (0.25 mm) or near rivets
Brake pad thickness (minimum) .... 1/16-inch (1.6 mm)
Rear brake pedal height setting .... See Chapter 6
Rear master cylinder freeplay.. See Chapter 6

Clutch

Foot control freeplay.. 1/8-inch (4 mm)
Lever freeplay
  1970 through early 1978 .... 1/4-inch (7 mm)
  Late 1978 through 1983 (except FLT/FXR) .... 1/16 inch (1.6 mm)

FLT/FXR models
 1980 through 1983 (at ball end) .... 1/4-inch (7 mm)
 Early 1984 (at bracket) .... 1/16-inch (1.6 mm)
 Late 1984 through 1989 (at bracket)... 1/8 to 3/16-inch (4.0 to 4.5 mm)
1990-on (at bracket) .... 1/16 to 1/8-inch (1.6 to 4.0 mm)
Clutch adjustment clearance
1970 through early 1979 release lever-to-starter motor......................... 3/8 to 5/8-inch(9 to 16 mm)
 Late 1979 through 1983 release lever-to-bearing extrusion
  on starter motor housing (except FLT/FXR)................................. 13/16-inch (21 mm)
Outer disc surface-to-spring collar inner edge.. 7/8 to 1-1/32-inch (22 to 25 mm)

Tire pressures - psi (Bars)*

1970 through 1983
FL models (except FLT)
 Front 20 (1.4)
 Rear 24 (1.7)
FLT models
 Front 24 (1.7)
 Rear 26 (1.8)
FX models (except FXR/FXWG)
 Front 24 (1.7)
 Rear 26 (1.8)
FXWG models
 Front 30 (2.1)
 Rear 26 (1.8)
FXR models
 Front 24 (1.7)
 Rear 24 (1.7)

1984 and 1985
FLTC models
 Front 28 (1.9)
 Rear 36 (2.5)
FLFT/C, FXRS and FXRT models
 Front 30 (2.1)
 Rear 36 (2.5)
FXEF and FXSB models
 Front 30 (2.1)
 Rear 32 (2.2)
FXWG and FXST models
 Front 30 (2.1)
 Rear
  Early 1985 .... 28 (1.9)
  All others 32 (2.2)

1986 through 1990 (approximate)
FXR models
 Front 30 (2.1)
 Rear 36 (2.5)
FLT models
 Front 36 (2.5)
 Rear 36 (2.5)
FLST/C, FXEF, FXSB
 Front 36 (2.5)
 Rear 36 (2.5)
FXWG, FXST, FXST/C and FXSTS models
 Front 30 (2.1)
 Rear 32 (2.2)

1991-on
FXST/C, FXSTS, FXD Dyna models
 Front 30 (2.1)
 Rear 36 (2.5)
All others same as for 1986 through 1990

*Pressure based on rider weighing 150 lbs (68 kg). Increase pressure in rear tire 2 psi (0.14 Bar) and in front tire 1 psi (0.7 Bar) for each additional 50 lbs (23 kg) of weight. Do not exceed maximum pressure molded into tire sidewall.

1

Torque specifications

Oil tank drain plug	120 inch-lbs (14 Nm)
Engine oil pan drain plug (FLT and Dyna models)	14 to 30 ft-lbs (19 to 41 Nm)
Spark plugs	18 to 22 ft-lbs (24 to 30 Nm)
Axle nuts (front and rear)	See Chapter 6

Transmission drain plug
Four-speed models	9 to 15 ft-lbs (12 to 20 Nm)

Five-speed models
FLT through 1982 and FXR	84 inch-lbs (9 Nm)
FLT, 1993 and later	14 to 30 ft-lbs (19 to 40 Nm)

Softails and Dynas
Through 1996	0.16 to 0.18 inch (4.0 to 4.5 mm) above surface of housing
1997 and later	14 to 30 ft-lbs (19 to 41 Nm)

Recommended lubricants and fluids

Engine oil

Shovelhead engine
Oil type	HD rating 360 or equivalent
Normal (20 to 90-degrees F	SAE 20W-50
Below 40-degrees F	SAE 30
Above 40-degrees F	SAE 40
Above 80-degrees F	SAE 60

Evolution engine
Oil type	H-D rating 360 or equivalent

Oil viscosity
Below 40-degrees F (4-degrees C)	H.D. Multi-Grade, SAE 10W-40
Above 40-degrees F (4-degrees C)	H.D. Multi-Grade, SAE 20W-50
Above 60-degrees F (16-degrees C)	H.D. Regular Heavy, SAE 50
Above 80-degrees F (27-degrees C)	H.D. Extra Heavy, SAE 60

Oil tank capacity
FLT	4 US qt, 3.3 Imp qt, 3.8 liters

Softail
With filter change	3 US qt, 2.5 Imp qt, 2.8 liters
Oil change only	2 US qt plus 14 fl oz, 1.67 Imp qt plus 14.6 Imp oz, 1.9 liters (1)

1. Do not overfill. Adding the full 3 quarts if the filter isn't changed will cause the oil tank filler cap to blow off.

Oil pan capacity
FLT	4 US qt, 3.3 Imp qt, 3.8 liters
FXR, Dyna	3 US qt, 2.5 Imp qt, 2.8 liters

Primary chaincase oil (wet clutch)

Type	Harley-Davidson Primary Chaincase Lubricant (part no. 99887-84)

Capacity (approximate)
1984 through 1990	1.5 US qt, 1.2 Imp qt, 1.4 liters
1991 and later	38 to 44 US fl oz, 40 to 47 Imp fl oz, 1124 to 1130 cc
Level	At bottom of clutch spring

Transmission oil

Type
1970 through 1983	Harley-Davidson Super Premium or equivalent 20W-50
1984 and later	Harley-Davidson Transmission Lubricant (part no. 99882-84)

Capacity (approximate)
FLT/FXR models through 1990	1 US pt, 17 Imp oz, 473 cc
All others	20 to 24 US fl oz, 21 to 25 Imp fl oz, 581 to 710 cc

Brake fluid

Type	DOT 3 (early models), DOT 5 (later models)

 Warning: *Do not mix fluid types. If not known, fully drain the fluid and have the system flushed before refilling. Refer to the manufacturer's fluid recommendation stamped on the reservoir cap or cover.*

Fork oil

Type
1970 through 1983	
FLT, FXR, FLHT and FXRS	Harley-Davidson Type E fork oil or equivalent
All others	Harley-Davidson Type B fork oil or equivalent
1994 and later (all models)	Harley-Davidson Type E fork oil or equivalent

Amount
  1970 through 1983
    Through 1972 FX, FXE and FXS
      Drain and fill .... 5-1/2 US fl oz, 5.7 Imp fl oz, 163 cc
      After overhaul .... 6-1/2 US fl oz, 6.8 Imp fl oz, 192 cc
    Through early 1977 FL and FLH
      Drain and fill .... 6-1/2 US fl oz, 6.8 Imp fl oz, 192 cc
      After overhaul .... 7 US fl oz, 7.3 Imp fl oz, 207 cc
    Late 1977 and later FLT, FLH and FLHS
      Drain and fill .... 7-3/4 US fl oz, 8.1 Imp fl oz, 229 cc
      After overhaul .... 8-1/2 US fl oz, 8.8 Imp fl oz, 251 cc
    1973 and later FXR, FXB, FXSB, FXE, FXEF and FXS
      Drain and fill .... 5 US fl oz, 5.2 Imp fl oz, 148 cc
      After overhaul .... 6 US fl oz, 6.2 Imp fl oz, 177 cc
    FXWG
      Drain and fill .... 9-1/4 US fl oz, 9.6 Imp fl oz, 274 cc
      After overhaul .... 10 US fl oz, 10.4 Imp fl oz, 296 cc
  1984 and later
    FXEF
      Drain and fill .... 5-1/2 US fl oz, 5.7 Imp fl oz, 163 cc
      After overhaul .... 6-3/4 US fl oz, 7.0 Imp fl oz, 200 cc
    FXSB
      Drain and fill .... 5-3/4 US fl oz, 6.0 Imp fl oz, 170 cc
      After overhaul .... 6-1/2 US fl oz, 6.8 Imp fl oz, 192 cc
    FLT
      Drain and fill .... 7-3/4 US fl oz, 8.1 Imp fl oz, 229 cc
      After overhaul .... 8-1/2 US fl oz, 8.8 Imp fl oz, 251 cc
    FXR and FXRS (1984 through 1987)
      Drain and fill .... 6-1/4 US fl oz, 6.5 Imp fl oz, 185 cc
      After overhaul .... 7 US fl oz, 7.3 Imp fl oz, 207 cc
    FXR and FXRS (1988 and later)
      Drain and fill .... 9.2 US fl oz, 9.6 Imp fl oz, 272 cc
      After overhaul .... 10.2 US fl oz, 10.6 Imp fl oz, 302 cc
    FXRD and FXRT (1984 through 1987)
      Drain and fill .... 7 US fl oz, 7.3 Imp fl oz, 207 cc
      After overhaul .... 7-3/4 US fl oz, 8.1 Imp fl oz, 229 cc
    FXRD and FXRT (1988 and later)
      Drain and fill .... 10-1/2 US fl oz, 10.9 Imp fl oz, 311 cc
      After overhaul .... 11-1/2 US fl oz, 12.0 Imp fl oz, 340 cc
    FXLR, FXDB, FXDC, FXDL and FXDS-CONV
      Drain and fill .... 9.2 US fl oz, 9.6 Imp fl oz, 272 cc
      After overhaul .... Not specified
    FXRSE and FXRS-SP
      Drain and fill .... 10-1/2 US fl oz, 10.9 Imp fl oz, 311 cc
      After overhaul .... 11-1/2 US fl oz, 12.0 Imp fl oz, 340 cc
    FXSTC, FXDWG
      Drain and fill .... 10.2 US fl oz, 10.6 Imp fl oz, 302 cc
      After overhaul .... 11.2 US fl oz, 11.7 Imp fl oz, 331 cc
    FLSTC/F/N
      Drain and fill .... 11.5 US fl oz, 12.0 Imp fl oz, 340 cc
      After overhaul .... 12.5 US fl oz, 13.0 Imp fl oz, 370 cc

Final drive chain

Conventional chain .... Harley-Davidson Chain Spray (part no. 99870-58) or
    High Performance Chain Lube Plus (part no. 99865-81)
O-ring chain .... High Performance Chain Lube Plus (part no. 99865-81) or
    API GL-5 gear lube SAE 80 or 90

Greasing points

Steering head bearings .... Harley-Davidson Special Purpose Grease or equivalent
Sidestand .... Loctite Aerosol Anti-Seize or equivalent
Swingarm pivot bearings .... Medium weight, lithium-based multi-purpose grease
Throttle grip .... Graphite grease
Cables and lever pivots .... Harley-Davidson Super Oil or equivalent
Brake pedal/shift lever pivots .... Medium weight, lithium-based multi-purpose grease
Compensating sprocket rubber dampers .... Harley Davidson Poly-Oil

1

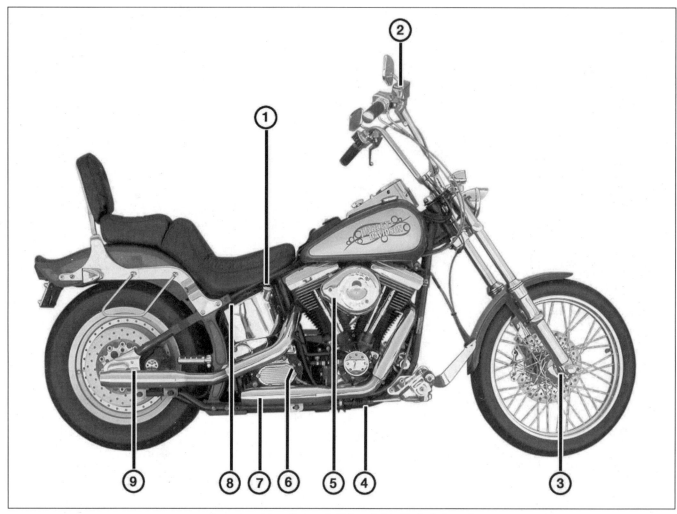

Component locations - right-hand side (Softail shown)

1   Oil tank filler cap
2   Front brake fluid reservoir
3   Fork drain plug
4   Rear brake fluid reservoir
5   Air cleaner
6   Transmission filler plug
7   Transmission drain plug
    (behind muffler)
8   Battery (under seat)
9   Right drivebelt adjuster (behind cover)

Component locations - left-hand side (Softail shown)

1   Front spark plug
2   Rear spark plug
3   Left drivebelt adjuster (behind cover)

4   Clutch cover
5   Primary inspection cover

6   Oil filter
7   Fork drain plug

1

1 Harley Big Twins Routine maintenance intervals

Note: *The pre-ride inspection outlined in the owner's manual covers checks and maintenance that should be carried out on a daily basis. It's condensed and included here to remind you of its importance. Always perform the pre-ride inspection at every maintenance interval (in addition to the procedures listed).*

Daily or before riding

Check the engine oil level
Check the fuel level and inspect for leaks
Check the operation of both brakes - also check the fluid level and look for leakage (disc brakes)
Check the tires for damage, the presence of foreign objects and correct air pressure
Check the throttle for smooth operation and correct freeplay
Check the operation of the clutch - make sure the freeplay is correct
Make sure the steering operates smoothly, without looseness and without binding
Check for proper operation of the headlight, taillight, brake light, turn signals, indicator lights, speedometer and horn
Make sure the sidestand returns to its fully up position and stays there under spring pressure
Make sure the engine STOP switch works properly
Lubricate the final drive chain (early models) and check play
Check deflection of the final drive belt

Every 300 miles

Lubricate the drive chain (chain drive models without automatic chain oiler) (see Section 3)
Check fluid levels (see Section 4)

Every 1000 miles

Service the air cleaner (see Section 5)
Adjust the drive chain or belt (see Section 3)
Adjust the brakes (see Section 6)
Check the hydraulic brake fluid level (see Pre-ride checks)
Inspect the brake discs and pads (see Section 6)
Check the adjustment of the clutch (see Section 7)
Check the fuel lines and fittings for leaks (see Section 8)
Inspect the hydraulic brake lines for leaks (see Section 9)
Inspect the oil lines for leaks (see Section 10)
Lubricate the clutch and front brake hand lever pivots (see Section 11)
Lubricate the clutch, throttle and choke cables (see Section 11)
Grease the speedometer drive gear (see Section 11)
Grease the rear brake pedal bearing (see Section 11)
Grease the foot shift lever bearing (see Section 11)
Grease the foot clutch pedal bearing (if equipped) (see Section 11)

Lubricate the seat post roller and bolt and the seat suspension bushings (see Section 11)

Lubricate the seat post roller and bolt and the seat suspension bushings (see Section 11)
Check the tightness and condition of all visible fasteners (see Section 12)
Inspect the tires for wear and proper inflation (see Section 13)
Check the tightness of the spokes, if applicable (see Section 13)
Adjust the primary chain or belt (if equipped) (see Section 14)
Change the engine oil and filter and clean the tappet oil screen (see Section 15)
Adjust the automatic chain oiler (if equipped) (see Section 16)

Every 2000 miles

Check and adjust the idle speed (see Section 17)
Check and adjust the throttle cable (see Section 18)
Check and adjust the choke cable (see Section 19)
Check the transmission oil level (see Section 4)
Check the battery electrolyte level (see Section 4)
Check the condition of the spark plugs (see Section 20)
Check the condition of the contact breaker points (if equipped) (see Section 21)
Check and adjust the ignition timing (see Section 22)
Clean the fuel filter screen on the fuel tank valve (see Section 23)
Adjust the final drive belt tension (see Section 24)
Grease the seat post and seat bar bearings (see Section 11)
Grease the swingarm pivot bearings (see Section 11)

Every 5000 miles

Replace the spark plugs (see Section 20)
Change the transmission oil and clean the magnetic drain plug (see Section 25)
Grease the internal spiral of the throttle sleeve and the speedometer and tachometer cables (see Section 18)
Inspect the shock absorbers and bushings (see Section 26)
Check the steering head and swingarm bearing free play (see Section 27)
Change the fork oil (see Section 28)
Grease the contact breaker point cam and ignition advance unit (see Section 21)

Every 10,000 miles

Adjust the primary belt (if equipped) (see Section 29)
Repack the wheel bearings (see Section 30)
Repack the swingarm bearings (tapered roller bearing models) (see Section 30)
Repack the steering head bearings (see Section 30)
Lubricate the belt drive compensating sprocket rubber dampers (see Section 31)
Adjust the Springer fork (see Section 32)

2 Introduction to tune-up and routine maintenance

1   This Chapter covers in detail the checks and procedures necessary for the tune-up and routine maintenance of your motorcycle. Section 1 includes the routine maintenance schedule, which is designed to keep the machine in proper running condition and prevent possible problems. The remaining Sections contain detailed procedures for carrying out the items listed on the maintenance schedule, as well as additional maintenance information designed to increase reliability.

2   Since routine maintenance plays such an important part in keeping the motorcycle in safe condition and operating at its optimum, this Chapter should be used as a comprehensive check list. For the rider who does all of the bike's maintenance, these lists outline the procedures and checks that should be done on a routine basis.

3   Maintenance and safety information is printed on decals in various locations on the motorcycle. If the information on the decals differs from that included here, use the information on the decal.

4   Deciding where to start or plug into the routine maintenance schedule depends on several factors. If you know your motorcycle's maintenance history, and if it has been maintained according to the manufacturer's standards, you may want to pick up routine maintenance as it coincides with the next mileage or calendar interval. If you have owned the machine for some time but have never performed any maintenance on it, then you may want to start at the nearest interval and include some additional procedures to ensure that nothing important is overlooked. If a major engine overhaul has just been done, then you may want to start the maintenance routine from the beginning. If you have a used machine and have no knowledge of its history or maintenance record, it may be a good idea to combine all the checks into one large service initially and then settle into the prescribed maintenance schedule. Note that

the procedures normally associated with ignition and fuel system tune-ups are included in the routine maintenance schedule. A regular tune-up will ensure good engine performance and help prevent engine damage due to improper carburetion and ignition timing.

5   The Sections detailing the maintenance and inspection procedures are written as step-by-step comprehensive guides to the performance of the work. They explain in detail each of the routine inspections and maintenance procedures in the checklist. References to additional information in applicable Chapters are also included and shouldn't be overlooked.

6   Before beginning any actual maintenance or repair, the machine should be cleaned thoroughly, especially around the oil filter, spark plugs, air cleaner, carburetor or fuel induction module, etc. Cleaning will help ensure that dirt doesn't contaminate the engine and will allow you to detect wear and damage that could otherwise easily go unnoticed.

Every 300 miles (500 km)

3 Drive chain - check, adjustment and lubrication

Check

1   A neglected drive chain won't last long and can quickly damage the countershaft and rear wheel sprockets. Routine chain adjustment and lubrication isn't difficult and will ensure maximum chain and sprocket life.

2   To check the chain, place the motorcycle upright with a rider sitting on it and shift the transmission into Neutral. Make sure the ignition switch is Off.

3   Check for the specified free play (slack) at the lower chain run, midway between the sprockets. On models with an enclosed chain, you'll have to remove the lower rubber boot from the chain housing to check the chain tension. The boot can be detached by removing the two screws and the mounting plate. Chains usually don't wear evenly, so rotate the rear wheel and check the free play in a number of places. As wear occurs, the chain will actually get longer, which means that adjustment usually involves removing some slack from the chain. In some cases where lubrication has been neglected, corrosion and galling may cause the links to bind and kink, which effectively shortens the chain's length. If the chain is tight between the sprockets, rusty or kinked, it's time to replace it with a new one.

4   After checking the slack, grasp the chain where it wraps around the rear sprocket (this won't be possible on enclosed chains) and try to pull it away from the sprocket. If more than 1/4-inch of play is evident, the chain is excessively worn and should be replaced with a new one.

Adjustment

5   Rotate the rear wheel until the chain is positioned where the least amount of slack is present.

6   Loosen the axle nut. On pre-1973 models, loosen the brake sleeve nut and brake anchor nut also. On 1973 through 1978 models, loosen the brake anchor castle nut after removing the cotter pin. Late 1978 through 1983 models must have the brake caliper anchor nut loosened to adjust the chain tension **(see illustration)**.

7   Turn the axle adjusting nuts on both sides of the rear wheel until the proper chain tension is attained. Be sure to turn both adjusting nuts the same amount to keep the rear wheel in alignment. If the adjusting nuts reach the end of their travel, the chain is probably excessively worn and should be replaced with a new one. An accurate method of checking the alignment of the rear wheel is to measure the center-to-center distance between the swingarm pivot bolt and the rear axle on both sides of the machine. When the distances are equal, the rear wheel (and thus the chain and sprockets) should be properly aligned.

8   Tighten the axle nut and the anchor bolt (the brake caliper anchor nut on rear disc brake models) and install new cotter pins where necessary. Recheck the tension of the drive chain.

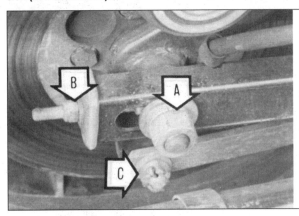

3.6 Loosen the axle nut (A) and the brake caliper anchor nut (C) before adjusting the chain tensioner (B) (typical)

1

3.10 Apply chain lubricant to the joints between the side plates and the rollers - not in the center of the rollers

3.11 Dislodge the spring clip with a screwdriver or needle-nose pliers and remove it from the master link pins

3.15 The closed end of the spring clip MUST face the direction of chain travel (arrow)

Lubrication

9   Many models produced through 1982 are equipped with automatic chain oilers; refer to Section 15 for maintenance and adjustment procedures. Some models have an enclosed chain. On these models the housing is full of oil, so the chain is constantly lubricated (refer to Section 4 to check oil level). The remaining models must have the chain manually lubricated as described below.

10   The best time to lubricate the chain is after the motorcycle has been ridden. When the chain is warm, the lubricant will penetrate the joints between the side plates, pins, bushings and rollers to provide lubrication of the internal load bearing areas. Use a good quality chain lubricant and apply it to the area where the side plates overlap - not the middle of the rollers. After applying the lubricant, let it soak in for a few minutes before wiping off any excess **(see illustration)**.

11   If the chain is extremely dirty, it should be removed and cleaned before it's lubricated. Remove the master link spring clip with pliers **(see illustration)**. Be careful not to bend or twist it. Slide out the master link and remove the chain from the sprockets. Clean the chain and master link thoroughly with solvent. Use a small brush to remove caked-on dirt. Wipe off the solvent, hang up the chain and allow it to dry.

12   Inspect the chain for wear and damage. Look for cracked rollers and side plates and check for excessive looseness between the links. To check for overall wear, lay the chain out on a clean, flat surface in a straight line. Push the ends together to take up all the slack between the links, then measure the overall length. Pull the chain ends apart as far as possible and measure the overall length again. Subtract the two measurements to determine the difference in the compressed and stretched lengths. If the difference, which is an indication of wear, is equal to or greater than 3-per cent of the chain's nominal length, it's excessively worn and should be replaced with a new one.

13   Check the master link, especially the clip, for damage. A new master link should be used whenever the chain is reassembled.

14   Check the sprockets for wear also. If the teeth have a hooked appearance, or are excessively worn or damaged, replace the sprockets with new ones. Never put a new chain on worn sprockets or a worn chain on new sprockets. Both chain and sprockets must be in good condition or the new parts will wear rapidly. Refer to Chapter 5 for sprocket removal and installation procedures.

15   Reposition the chain on the sprockets and insert the master link. This should be done with both ends of the chain adjacent to each other on the back side of the rear wheel sprocket. **Note:** *Make sure the closed end of the master link clip points in the direction of chain travel* **(see illustration)**.

16   Lubricate and adjust the chain as previously described.

---

4   Fluid levels- check

Engine oil

1   Engine oil level should be checked before every ride as described in *Daily (Pre-ride)* checks at the beginning of this manual, as well as at the specified maintenance intervals.

Brake fluid

2   Fluid level in the front and rear brake master cylinders should be checked before every ride as described in *Daily (pre-ride) checks* at the beginning of this manual, as well as at the specified maintenance intervals.

3   Also check the brake fluid for signs of contamination. If the fluid is contaminated, bleed all of it out and replace it with new fluid (see Chapter 6).

 Warning: Do not mix fluid types. If not known, fully drain the fluid and have the system flushed before refilling. Refer to *the manufacturer's fluid recommendation stamped on the reservoir cap or cover.*

Battery electrolyte

Warning: Be extremely careful when handling or working around the battery. The electrolyte is very caustic and an explosive gas is given off when the battery is charging.

4   On early models, to check the level of the electrolyte in the battery, remove the caps from the top of each cell **(see illustration)**. The electrolyte level should be up to the triangle or circle at the base of each cell. On later models, you'll have to remove the right side cover to get at the battery, which has a transparent case. The electrolyte level should be between the upper and lower level marks on the case **(see illustration)**.

5   To fill the battery, remove each cell cap and add enough distilled water to each cell to bring the level to the proper height - don't overfill it. Also, don't use tap water, except in

4.4a On some batteries the cell caps must be removed to check the electrolyte . . .

4.4b . . . while on others the electrolyte level is visible through the translucent case

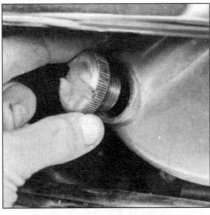

4.8 The transmission oil level should be at the bottom of the filler plug opening

an emergency, as it will shorten the service life of the battery. The cell holes are quite small so it may help to use a plastic squeeze bottle with a small spout to add the water.

6　Periodically, the battery should receive a thorough inspection (including a check of the specific gravity of the electrolyte). Refer to Chapter 7 for these procedures.

Transmission oil

7　Hold the motorcycle in an upright position throughout the inspection procedure.
8　Remove the oil filler plug and the oil

level plug **(see illustration)**. If there's only one plug, it serves as both the level and the filler plug. Some models have a dipstick attached to the oil filler plug. The oil level should be at the bottom of the plug opening or between the two marks on the dipstick.
9　If necessary, add enough oil of the recommended type to fill the transmission to the proper level - don't overfill it.
10　Install the oil level and filler plugs.

Enclosed drive chain oil

11　Hold the motorcycle in an upright position throughout the inspection procedure.

12　Remove the oil level plug at the rear of the drive chain enclosure, near the bottom. The oil level should be at the bottom of the plug opening.
13　If the oil level is low, reinstall the oil level plug.
14　Remove the saddlebag from the left side of the motorcycle and unscrew the oil fill plug from the top of the chain enclosure. Hold the motorcycle upright and remove the level plug again.
15　Add the proper grade of oil until it just begins to run out of the oil level hole. Don't add too much.
16　Install the two plugs and reinstall the saddlebag on the motorcycle.

Primary chaincase oil (wet clutch models)

Note: *Models with belt primary drive have no lubricant supply, and chain drive models with a dry clutch have an oil feed off the engine lubrication system.*
17　Check the level with the machine standing upright on level ground.
18　Remove the screws which secure the circular clutch cover in the primary chaincase. Remove the cover and its O-ring.
19　The oil should be level with the clutch cover opening on models through 1989, or level with the bottom of the clutch diaphragm spring from 1990 onwards.
20　Add oil if necessary and refit the cover and O-ring.

Every 1000 miles (1600 km)

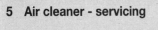

5　Air cleaner - servicing

1　In order to gain access to the air cleaner element, remove the plated cover attached to the air cleaner assembly by screws or

5.1 The air cleaner cover is secured with one or more Allen-head screws on most models

Allen head bolt(s) **(see illustration)**. This will expose the filter element and screen.
2　The air cleaner element used on 1970 and 1971 models is made of metal mesh. It should be removed, washed in a non-flammable solvent and saturated with clean engine oil after it's been allowed to dry. This type of service should be performed at least every 1000 miles and more frequently if the machine is used in very dusty conditions.
3　Later models have a foam-type filter. If a film of dirt has built up on the outer surface or if light spots appear on the surface, the filter should be cleaned and re-oiled. If the filter element is cracked, torn or distorted so it doesn't fit the screen, install a new one.
4　On 1972 through 1983 models, the plastic foam air filter element should be removed from the protective screen and washed in a non-flammable solvent, then allowed to dry. Next, immerse it in clean engine oil. Allow it to soak until the element is uniform in color. If necessary, work the oil into the filter with your hands. Wring out the filter to remove the excess oil, then replace the element on the screen so the three grooves face the screen. Install the cover with the retaining screws or bolts.
5　On 1984 through 1990 models, remove

the foam element from the screen and wash it with hot water and soap. After it's dry, apply 1-1/2 tablespoons of engine oil to it with an atomizer or work it into the filter by hand. Squeeze out any excess oil, then reinstall the filter, cover and bolt.
6　1991 and later models use a paper/wire mesh filter. To clean, wash in lukewarm water and a mild detergent. Let it dry naturally, or blow dry from the inside of the element out. Refit the element when completely dry. Take care when installing the filter on 1993 and later models that the crankcase breather connectors fit into the holes in the back of the element and over the bleed bolt heads.
7　Never run the machine without the air cleaner attached or without the air filter element in place. The carburetion or fuel injection is set up to take into account the presence of the air cleaner and will be affected if the settings aren't changed to compensate.
8　A clogged or split air cleaner element will also have an adverse effect on engine performance. It's better to give the air cleaner more frequent attention than necessary rather than to neglect it altogether. It's an item that shouldn't be ignored during the normal service routine.

1

6.11 The brake pad lining thickness (arrows) can be checked on most models without removing the caliper

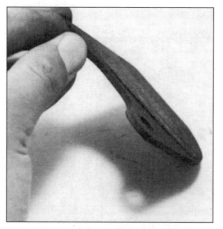

6.12 If the pads are allowed to wear to this extent, the disc(s) are at risk of damage

7.5 On models through early 1984, adjust the clutch cable at the bracket on the engine

6 Brake system - check and adjustment

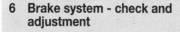

1   A routine general check of the brakes will ensure that any problems are discovered and remedied before the rider's safety is jeopardized.

2   Check the brake lever and pedal for loose connections, excessive play, bends, and other damage. Replace any damaged parts with new ones (see Chapter 6).

3   Make sure all brake fasteners are tight. On disc brake models, check the brake pads for wear as described below and make sure the fluid level in the reservoir is correct (see *Daily (pre-ride) checks* at the beginning of this manual). Look for leaks at the hose connections and check for cracks in the hoses. If the lever is spongy, bleed the brakes as described in Chapter 6.

4   Make sure the brake light operates when the front brake lever is depressed.

5   Make sure the brake light is activated when the rear brake pedal is depressed.

6   On disc brake models, neither brake light switch is adjustable. If a front switch fails to operate properly, replace it with a new one (see Chapter 8). If a rear switch, which detects hydraulic pressure in the rear brake line, fails to operate properly, bleed the rear brake (see Chapter 6). If that doesn't solve the problem, replace the switch with a new one (see Chapter 8).

Drum brake adjustment

7   On front drum brakes, the brakes should begin to drag when the lever has reached about 1/4 of its travel. If not, loosen the cable locknut and turn the adjusting nut to achieve the correct amount of play, then tighten the locknut. Check to make sure the brakes release completely.

8   Operate the pedal while rolling the bike forward. The brake linings should begin to make contact with the drum when the pedal

has been pressed 1-1/4 inches. Tighten or loosen the brake adjusting nut to achieve the specified travel.

Front drum brake inspection

9   The front brake assembly, complete with the backing plate, can be withdrawn from the front hub after the axle has been pulled out and the wheel removed form the forks. Refer to Chapter 6 for the recommended wheel removal procedure.

10   Examine the brake shoe linings. If they're thin or worn unevenly, they should be replaced with new ones.

Front disc brake inspection

11   The front brake pads, on some models, can be examined for wear by looking through the opening at the rear of the caliper **(see illustration)**. If in doubt about the condition of the brake pads, remove the caliper(s) and measure the thickness of the pads lining material. Refer to Chapter 6 for the caliper removal procedures.

12   Check the pads for wear, damage and looseness. Make sure the metal backing plate is flat and not distorted. If one pad has worn until the lining is less than 1/16-inch (1.6 mm) thick, replace both pads with new ones **(see illustration)**.

Rear drum brake inspection

13   Refer to Chapter 6 for the recommended wheel removal procedure to examine the condition of the rear drum brake linings. If the linings are worn unevenly or are worn to the specified service limit, they should be replaced with new ones.

Rear disc brake inspection

14   On some models the caliper must be disassembled to examine the condition of the rear brake pads, while other models merely require the caliper to be removed from the mounting bracket to gain access to the brake pads. Refer to Chapter 6 for the procedure required for your motorcycle.

Remove the brake pads and check their condition. The information in Step 12 also applies to the rear brake pads.

15   Check the condition of the caliper mounting pins and boots. Clean the boots and apply silicone grease to the pin sliding surfaces.

16   Check and lubricate the rear brake linkage.

7 Clutch - adjustment

Foot clutch control pedal

1   Place the foot pedal in the "heel down" (disengaged) position and check to make sure the clutch lever strikes the transmission case cover. The length of the foot pedal rod must be adjusted until it just covers the foot pedal bearing cover so the bearing cover doesn't bend the rod down.

2   Remove the clutch cover from the primary chaincase cover.

3   With the foot pedal in the "toe down" (engaged) position, loosen the clutch adjustment locknut. Use a screwdriver to turn the pushrod adjusting screw. The pushrod should be adjusted so there's about 1/8-inch of free play at the end of the clutch lever before the clutch disengages. Turn the screw counterclockwise for more lever movement, or to the right (clockwise) for less movement.

4   Hold the adjusting screw stationary and tighten the locknut.

Dry clutch models (through early 1984)

Clutch lever

5   If the free play at the clutch lever on the handlebar isn't as specified, it must be adjusted. Loosen the locknut on the adjusting sleeve (you'll have to keep the swivel nut

7.9 Remove the screws and detach the clutch cover from the primary chaincase

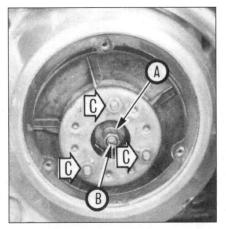

7.10 Clutch adjustment details (models through early 1984)

A   *Locknut*
B   *Adjusting screw*
C   *Nuts (for tightening clutch plate/discs)*

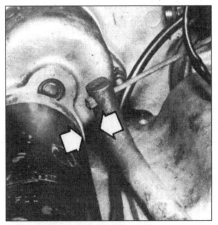

7.11 Measure the distance between the clutch release lever and the starter motor (1970 through 1978 models)

from turning on 1982, 1983 and early 1984 FLT and FXR models). Turn the adjusting sleeve either in or out of the mounting bracket until the desired free play is attained **(see illustration)**.
6   Tighten the locknut and recheck the free play adjustment.

Clutch

7   If the sleeve can't be adjusted enough to achieve the specified free play, the cable may be stretched beyond adjustment, requiring a new cable, or the clutch itself may need adjustment.
8   Loosen the locknut on the cable adjusting sleeve and screw the adjusting sleeve into the bracket as far as possible. On 1982, 1983 and early 1984 FLT and FXR models, the ball end of the cable must be removed from the release arm.
9   Remove the screws securing the clutch cover to the primary chaincase and detach the cover **(see illustration)**.
10   Loosen the locknut on the adjusting screw in the center of the clutch **(see illustration)**.
11   On 1970 through 1978 models, turn the adjusting screw until the clutch release lever is the specified distance from the starter motor housing **(see illustration)**. To move the lever

towards the rear, turn the adjusting screw clockwise. Turn the screw counterclockwise to move the end of the lever forward.
12   To adjust the clutch on late 1978 and later models (except FLT and FXR), turn the adjusting screw in until it makes contact with the pushrod, then back the screw out 1/8-turn.
13   Later FLT and FXR models (1980 through late 1984) are adjusted in a similar manner. Turn the adjusting screw clockwise until there's no free play in the release arm, then back the screw out 1/4-turn.
14   Tighten the locknut while holding the adjusting screw to keep it from moving.
15   Attach the clutch cable, if it was removed. Adjust the cable or rod until the recommended free play is achieved at the clutch lever or foot pedal.
16   Install the clutch cover on the chaincase with a new gasket coated with gasket sealer. The cover must be installed airtight.

Clutch discs

17   If the clutch still slips after the cable and clutch control are adjusted, the clutch discs

must be adjusted.
18   Remove the clutch cover from the chaincase **(see illustration 7.9)**.
19   Tighten the three nuts on the outside of the spring collar 1/2-turn at a time until the clutch holds **(see illustration 7.10)**. With the transmission in Neutral, crank the engine to see if the clutch is holding. DO NOT tighten the nuts any more than necessary to make the clutch hold. Measure the distance between the outer disc and the spring collar. If it's less than 7/8-inch, the clutch plates must be replaced with new ones.
20   Install the clutch cover (Step 16).

Wet clutch models (late 1984-on)

21   On 1986 and earlier models, disconnect the clutch cable from the transmission release lever. On 1987 and later models, loosen the locknut at the cable adjuster and turn the adjuster all the way in to provide slack in the cable **(see illustration)**.
22   Remove the clutch cover from the primary chaincase **(see illustration 7.9)**.
23   Loosen the locknut on the adjusting screw in the center of the clutch **(see illustration)**.

1

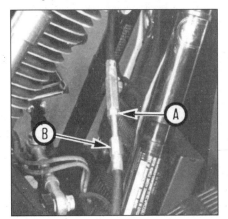

7.21 On 1987 and later models, the clutch cable adjuster is part of the cable housing

7.23 Clutch adjustment details - late 1984 and later

A   *Locknut*
B   *Adjusting screw*

7.25 Measure the gap between the inner face of the clutch adjuster plate (A) and the diaphragm spring edge (B) with a straightedge and feeler gauge(s) - the spring should be flat or very slightly concave, not bowed out (late 1984-on)

24   Turn the adjusting screw out (counter-clockwise) to provide clutch pushrod free play.

25   Place a straightedge across the face of the diaphragm spring, against the adjuster plate **(see illustration)**. Using a feeler gauge, measure the gap between the outer edge of the spring and the straightedge. If it's greater than 0.010-inch (0.25 mm) (which means the spring is convex, or bowed out at the center), the spring compression must be adjusted. This is done by repositioning the adjuster plate. If the spring is bowed out more than 0.010-inch (0.25 mm) in the center, the plate is moved to the next hole position to compress the spring more. If the spring is dished more than 0.010-inch (0.25 mm) at the center (concave), the plate is moved to relieve the compression. The recommended spring position is flat to 0.010-inch (0.25 mm) concave.

26   To make the adjustment, loosen the adjuster plate bolts in 1/4-turn increments until the spring tension is relieved, then remove them. Reposition the plate to compress or release the spring, as required, then install the bolts. **Note:** *If the spring can't be properly adjusted, the clutch plates must be removed and measured (Chapter 2B). If the thickness is within the specified limits, an additional steel plate can be added to the clutch assembly. If the spring is not properly adjusted, the clutch will fail prematurely.*

27   Tighten the adjuster plate bolts to 8 ft-lbs (11 Nm) in a criss-cross pattern, then recheck the clearance as described in Step 25.

28   If it's correct, remove the bolts once again (Step 26) and apply Loctite 222 to the threads, then reinstall them for the final time (Step 27).

29   Turn the adjusting screw in (clockwise) until the pushrod free play is removed.

30   Back out the adjusting screw 3/4-turn and tighten the locknut. Hold the screw to keep it from moving as the nut is tightened.

31   On 1986 and earlier models, reconnect the cable at the transmission and adjust it to produce the specified free play at the hand lever. **Note:** *On 1985 and 1986 FXWG and 1986 FXST models, loosen the locknut on the cable adjuster and turn the adjuster to position the release lever 13/16-inch (21 mm) from the transmission cover tower. Apply light pressure to the lever to eliminate pushrod freeplay.*

32   On 1987 and later models, squeeze the handlebar lever as far as possible three times, to set the ball and ramp release mechanism, then turn the adjuster in the cable to provide the specified free play at the hand lever. Tighten the adjuster locknut and make sure the rubber boot is repositioned.

8 Fuel system - check

⚠ *Warning: Gasoline is extremely flammable, so take extra precautions when you work on any part of the fuel system. Don't smoke or allow open flames or bare light bulbs near the work area, and don't work in a garage where a natural gas-type appliance (such as a water heater or clothes dryer) is present. If you spill any fuel on your skin, rinse it off immediately with soap and water. When you perform any kind of work on the fuel system, wear safety glasses and have a fire extinguisher suitable for a class B type fire (flammable liquids) on hand.*

1   The condition of the fuel system components, hoses and connections should be checked periodically to reduce the likelihood of a fuel leak developing. If the smell of gasoline is noticed while riding or after the motorcycle has been parked, the system should be checked immediately.

⚠ *Warning: If a fuel odor is detected, be sure to work in a well-ventilated area and don't allow open flames (cigarettes, appliance pilot lights, etc.) or unshielded light bulbs in or near the work area.*

2   Inspect the area around the fuel tank, fuel valve and underneath the carburetor or induction module for evidence of leaks and damage. Carefully inspect all fuel lines to make sure they're tightly connected to the fittings and not cracked or otherwise deteriorated. If so, they should be replaced immediately with new ones. Check all hose clamps to make sure they're tight.

3   If there's leakage from the fuel valve, make sure it's securely attached to the fuel tank. If a leak persists between the valve and tank, drain the tank (referring to Section 23, if necessary), remove the valve and apply thread sealing tape to the threads of the valve. If the leak is coming from the body of the valve, it'll have to be replaced with a new one.

4   If leakage is occurring at the carburetor (models so equipped), it indicates defective carburetor gaskets. The carburetor should be removed and disassembled as described in Chapter 3 to locate the problem.

5   Check all evaporative emission system hoses and components for damage and deterioration (later California models only).

9 Brake system - general check

1   A routine general check of the brakes will ensure that any problems are discovered and remedied before the rider's safety is jeopardized.

2   On early models, check the brake shoes for excessive wear and the lever, brake cable or rod and pedal for loose connections, excessive play, distortion and damage. Replace any damaged parts with new ones. Refer to Section 6 for the brake shoe wear check.

3   On disc brake systems, carefully examine the master cylinder, the hoses and the calipers for evidence of brake fluid leakage. Pay particular attention to the hoses. If they're cracked, abraded, or otherwise damaged, replace them with new ones. If leaks are evident at the master cylinder or caliper(s) they should be rebuilt by referring to the appropriate Sections in Chapter 6.

4   Check the disc brake lever/pedal for proper operation. It should feel firm and return to its original position when released. If it feels spongy, or if lever travel is excessive, the system may have air trapped in it. Refer to Chapter 6 and bleed the brakes.

5   Check the brake pads for excessive wear by referring to Section 6.

6   Examine the brake discs for cracks and evidence of scoring. Measure the thickness of each disc and compare it to the specifications on the disc. Any disc worn beyond the allowable limit must be replaced with a new one.

7   If the brake lever/pedal pulsates when the brakes are applied during operation of the machine, the disc(s) may be warped. Attach a dial indicator setup to the fork slider or swingarm and check the disc runout. If the runout is greater than specified in Chapter 6, replace the disc with a new one. If a dial indicator isn't available, a dealer service department or motorcycle repair shop can make this check for you.

8   Make sure both brake light switches operate properly.

10 External oil lines - check

1   Follow the external lines (if equipped) from the oil tank to the engine and check them for leaks.

11.3 Lubricating a cable with a pressure lube adapter (make sure the tool seats around the inner cable)

11.6 Use a grease gun to inject grease into the brake pedal fitting . . .

11.7 . . . the seat post fitting (not all models) . . .

2   Replace the lines if they're cracked or deteriorated. Use new hose clamps.

11 Lubrication - general

1   Since the controls, cables and various other components of a motorcycle are exposed to the elements, they should be lubricated periodically to ensure proper operation.
2   The clutch and brake lever pivots should be lubricated with light oil. Don't apply too much oil to the pivots, as the oil will attract dirt, which could cause the controls to bind.
3   The throttle, clutch, front drum brake and choke cables should be treated with a commercially available cable lubricant, which is specially formulated for use on motorcycle control cables. Small adapters for pressure lubricating the cables with spray can lubricants are available and work very well **(see illustration)**.
Caution: DO NOT lubricate the enrichener cable for the CV carburetor used on 1990 and later models.
4   Speedometer and tachometer cables should be removed from their housings and lubricated with a very light grease or cable lubricant.
5   If the throttle operates roughly, a light coat of grease should be applied to the inside of it, as described in Chapter 3.
6   The pivot points of the rear brake pedal, foot clutch control pedal, gear shift lever, footpegs and sidestand should all be lubricated with multi-purpose grease **(see illustration)**.
7   If applicable, lubricate the seat post, seat bar bearings, seat suspension bushings and the seat post roller and bolt **(see illustration)**.
8   Some models have a grease fitting installed in the swingarm. Use a hand-oper-

ated grease gun to fill the area between the bearings with grease at the recommended intervals.
9   On models equipped with a grease fitting on the shift lever or its linkage pivot points **(see illustration)**, grease the fittings at the recommended intervals.
10   On models equipped with a speedometer drive gear at the front wheel, grease the gear (see Chapter 8).

12 Fasteners - check

1   Since vibration of the machine tends to loosen fasteners, all nuts, bolts, screws, etc, should be periodically checked for tightness. **Note:** *DO NOT tighten the cylinder head bolts.*
2   If a torque wrench is available, use it along with the torque Specifications at the beginning of the appropriate Chapter.
3   Be sure of check the tightness of all the engine mounting bolts and the engine mount stabilizer(s) at the recommended intervals.

11.9 . . . and the shift lever fitting

13 Tires/wheels/spokes - general check

1   Routine tire and wheel checks should be made with the realization that your safety depends to a greet extent on their condition.
2   Check the tires carefully for cuts, tears, embedded nails or other sharp objects and excessive wear. Operation of the motorcycle with excessively worn tires is extremely hazardous, as traction and handling are directly affected. Check the tread depth at the center of the tire and replace worn tires with new ones when the tread is worn excessively.
3   Repair or replace punctured tires and tubes as soon as damage is noted. Don't try to patch a torn tire, as wheel balance and tire reliability may be impaired.
4   Check the tire pressures when the tires are cold and keep them properly inflated. Proper air pressure will increase tire life and provide maximum stability and ride comfort. Keep in mind that low tire pressures may cause the tire to slip on the rim or come off, while high tire pressures will cause abnormal tread wear and unsafe handling.
5   The cast alloy wheels used on some models are virtually maintenance free, but they should be kept clean and checked periodically for cracks, dented rims and other damage. Never attempt to repair damaged cast wheels; they must be replaced with new ones.
6   On machines equipped with wire spoked wheels, periodic checks are extremely important. Inspect the rims for dents and cracks. Check all spokes for damage (such as cracks and distortion) and make sure they're tight. To check spoke tightness, strike each one lightly with a screwdriver or other metal tool and listen to the sound that's produced. A crisp, ringing sound indicates a properly tensioned spoke. If a dull thud is produced, the spoke is loose.
7   A spoke wrench of the proper size should be used to tighten the loose spokes

1

13.7 Check the tension of the spokes periodically, but don't over-tighten them

14.4 On later models, remove the cover from the outer primary chaincase to check and adjust the chain tensioner

14.7 Loosen the bolt (arrow) and move the chain tensioner shoe up-and-down to adjust the primary chain

(see illustration). Also, lubricate the nipples (at the point where the spokes thread into them and at the rim) with light oil before tightening the spokes. Don't over-tighten them, as wheel concentricity, roundness and side play will be affected.

8   Refer to Chapter 6 for the procedures to follow for checking and truing wheels.

14 Primary chain - adjustment

1   Adjustment of the primary chain requires the removal of the primary chain cover on 1970 through early 1978 models. On these models, place a shallow drain pan under the primary chaincase and remove the eight screws securing the case.

2   On early models with footboards, the rear pivot bolt on the footboard must be removed to allow the footboard to move down for removal of the chaincase.

3   On some FX and FXE models, the gearshift lever must be removed from the pivot shaft. The shift lever is secured to the shaft by a pinch bolt and nut. When the pinch bolt and nut are removed, the lever can be separated from the splined shaft.

4   Models produced from late 1978-on have a removable inspection cover attached to the chaincase. Remove the screws and detach the cover **(see illustration)**.

5   Check the tension of the primary chain midway between the two sprockets. The chain probably will not wear evenly, so one section of chain may be tighter than another. Because of this the chain tension should be adjusted at its tightest spot. On engines with an electric starter, disconnect the wires to the spark plugs and ground them against the engine. Crank the engine over to make the primary chain move so the tension can be checked at various points on the chain.

6   Adjustment of the chain is controlled by a tensioning shoe, which is retained on a ser-rated back plate by a large center bolt.

7   With the chain at its tightest point, loosen the center bolt of the chain adjuster and move the tensioner shoe up-or-down **(see illustration)** until the desired tension is attained.

8   Tighten the center bolt and recheck the tension along the entire length of the chain.

9   Inspect the chain for broken, cracked or badly worn links. If the chain cannot be adjusted to the specified tension or if it exhibits any type of defect, it should be replaced with a new one as described in Chapter 2.

10   Carefully clean any gasket material and dirt off the primary chaincase and the inspection cover (on later models) or the chaincase cover (on early models). Attach new gaskets and install the primary case cover or inspection cover.

11   Tighten the screws securely. On early models, install the footboard and shift lever if they were removed.

12   Replenish any lost chaincase lubricant (wet clutch models) or engine oil (dry clutch models) if the chaincase cover was removed.

Every 2000 miles (3200 km)

15 Engine oil, filter and primary chaincase oil - change

1   Consistent routine oil and filter changes are the single most important maintenance procedure you can perform on a motorcycle. The oil not only lubricates the internal parts of the engine, but it also acts as a coolant, a cleaner, a sealant and a protectant. Because of these demands, the oil takes a terrific amount of abuse and should be replaced often with new oil of the recommended grade and type. Saving a little money on the difference in cost between good oil and cheap oil won't pay off if the engine is damaged.

2   Before changing the oil, warm up the engine so the oil will drain easily. Be careful when draining the oil - the exhaust pipes, the engine and the oil itself can cause severe burns. The drain plug is at the bottom of the oil tank **(see illustration)**.

3   Place a container below the oil tank to drain the used oil into. If required, a chute made out of sheet metal or cardboard can be used to guide the oil into the receptacle. This will prevent oil from spilling on the motorcycle. On 1993 and later FLT and 1991 and later Dyna models, the engine oil is held in an oil pan attached to the bottom of the transmission. Position a drain tray under the drain plug (forward most plug on the pan). It isn't necessary to drain the crankcase.

4   Remove the oil filler cap and dipstick, followed by the oil tank/pan drain plug.

5   On late 1978 and later models, the tappet oil screen must be removed and cleaned

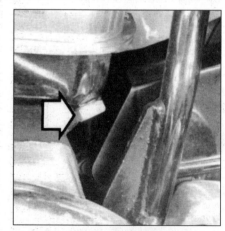

15.2 Typical oil tank drain plug location (arrow)

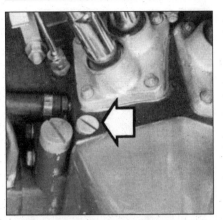

15.5a Remove the tappet oil screen plug (arrow) with a large screwdriver . . .

15.5b . . . then remove the screen and clean it with solvent (and compressed air, if available) - make sure the spring is in place before installing the plug

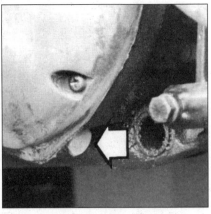

15.6 Remove the chaincase drain plug (arrow) to drain the oil out of the case

at every oil change. The screen is located near the rear cylinder tappet block on the cam case **(see illustrations)**.

6   Remove the primary chaincase drain plug on late 1978 and later models (except FXS/FXSB) and allow the oil to drain. The plug is located on the bottom of the inner chaincase or chaincase cover, below the clutch cover **(see illustration)**. Clean the magnetic drain plug, reinstall it and tighten securely.

7   On models equipped with a filter in the oil tank, lift the filter out of the tank after the oil is drained **(see illustration)**. The oil filter is housed in a cartridge and can be removed after detaching the filter clip and sealing washer from the upper end of the cartridge tube. The filter element should be replaced with a new one every time the oil is changed.

8   When replacing the element, make sure the O-ring is positioned correctly on the cartridge flange. The correct order of assembly within the cartridge is: Seal, spring, lower retainer, filter element, cap sealing washer and filter clip.

9   On late 1978 and later models so equipped, remove the plug from the air filter drain hose and allow the hose to drain.

10   Many models produced from 1980 on are equipped with a spin-on disposable oil

filter. Locate the filter and unscrew it from the engine. Use a filter wrench that fits over the end of the filter and is turned with a 3/8-inch drive ratchet to remove the filter. If a filter wrench isn't available and the filter can't be removed by hand, one last-ditch method of removing the filter is to pierce it with a long screwdriver and twist it off. The damage to the filter doesn't matter, since it'll be replaced with a new one anyway. If additional maintenance is planned for this time period, check or service another component while the oil is allowed to drain completely.

11   Prior to installing the new spin-on filter, coat the rubber seal with clean engine oil **(see illustration)**, then screw it into place. Tighten the filter by hand an additional 1/4 to 1/2-turn (3/4 to full turn on Dyna models) after the seal first makes contact with the mounting surface.

12   The oil tank should be flushed at least every other oil change. To flush it, install the drain plug and pour approximately one quart of kerosene into the tank. Agitate the kerosene by rocking the motorcycle from side-to-side. Remove the drain plug and allow the kerosene and displaced sludge to drain out. Cleaning on those models which have an oil pan under the transmission may

also be carried out by detaching the pan from the transmission (see Chapter 2A).

13   Be sure the seal is in good condition before final installation of the drain plug.

14   Pour the amount and type of oil listed in this Chapter's Specifications into the oil tank or pan. Insert the oil filter canister, on models so equipped, and replace the oil filler cap and dipstick.

15   Where applicable, refill the primary chaincase with the specified quantity and type of oil, and check the level.

16   Start the engine and allow it to run for about a minute. Check the oil filter and drain plug(s) for leaks. Check the oil level on the dipstick and, if necessary, add enough oil to bring the level to the recommended height.

16 Automatic drive chain oiler - maintenance and adjustment

1   Many early models are equipped with an automatic rear drive chain oiler **(see illustration)**. On some, but not all models, an extension of this system lubricates the primary drive chain where a dry clutch is fitted.

2   Turn the oiler adjusting screw in until it bottoms on the seat. **Note:** *Keep track of the*

1

15.7 Remove the oil filter assembly (if equipped) from the oil tank

15.11 Smear a film of clean oil onto the gasket surface

16.1 Automatic chain oiler adjustment screw (arrow)

17.3a The throttle stop screw (arrow, typical early model) is turned to change the idle speed (you may need a stubby screwdriver on some models) . . .

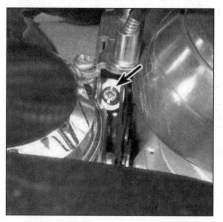

17.3b . . . while on later models with a Keihin CV carburetor, a long screwdriver will be needed to reach the screw (arrow)

18.13a Slide back the rubber boots for access to the throttle cable adjusters

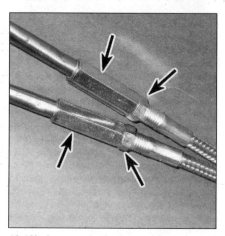

18.13b Loosen the locknuts (right arrows) and turn the adjusters (left arrows)

number of turns required to bottom the adjuster.

3   Completely unscrew the adjuster and blow the orifice out with compressed air.

4   Install the adjusting screw and turn it in until it bottoms, then back it out the required number of turns to its original position. The normal setting is 1/4-turn open.

5   The oiler should release two or three drops of oil per minute. Turn the adjusting screw in if less oil is desired; turn it out if more oil is needed.

17 Idle speed (carbureted models) - adjustment

1   The idle speed should be checked and adjusted if it's obviously too high or too low. Before adjusting the idle speed, be sure the ignition timing is set correctly and the spark plug gaps are correct.

2   The engine should be at normal operating temperature, which is usually reached after 10 or 15 minutes of stop and go riding. Place the motorcycle on the kickstand and make sure the transmission is in Neutral.

3   Turn the throttle stop screw until the specified speed is obtained **(see illustrations)**.

4   If a smooth, steady idle cannot be obtained, the fuel/air mixture may be incorrect. Refer to Chapter 3 for fuel/air mixture adjustment procedures.

18 Throttle operation/grip freeplay - check and adjustment

Check

1   With the engine stopped, make sure the throttle grip rotates easily from fully closed to fully open with the front wheel turned at vari-

ous angles. The grip should return automatically from fully open to fully closed when released. If the throttle sticks, check the throttle cables for cracks or kinks in the housings. Also, make sure the inner cables are clean and well lubricated.

2   Check for a small amount of freeplay at the grip and compare the freeplay to the value listed in this Chapter's Specifications.

Adjustment

Spiral throttle control

3   Early models use a spiral-type throttle control with a single throttle cable. It can be identified by the screw in the end of the grip (drum type throttle controls have an end cap, rather than an end screw).

4   When turned by hand and released, the throttle grip must return to the closed (idle) position. There should be 1/4-inch between the carburetor control clip and throttle control coil with the throttle closed. If not, or if the grip turns stiffly, the grip should be disassembled, cleaned and inspected (see Chapter 3).

Single cable, drum type throttle control

5   When turned by hand and released, the throttle grip must return to the closed (idle) position. If it doesn't return freely, back off the friction screw until it does.

6   If the throttle grip turns stiffly, or if backing off the friction screw doesn't cause it to return freely, it should be disassembled, cleaned and inspected (see Chapter 3).

7   Locate the throttle cable's connection at the carburetor. Watch it while turning the handlebars all the way from full left to full right lock. The inner cable should not pull on the carburetor lever as the handlebars are turned.

8   If it does, loosen the knurled round locknut on the cable adjuster (not the hex locknut on the elbow fitting). Turn the adjuster to change the cable's effective length, then tighten the locknut. Recheck as

described in Step 7.

9   Center the front wheel in the straight-ahead position and open the throttle all the way. The carburetor throttle lever should reach the full-open position as the grip reaches the end of its travel. If not, adjust the stop screw on the underside of the grip with a 2 mm Allen wrench. Don't allow the grip to have remaining travel when the carburetor is all the way open, or the cable will be damaged by the strain.

Dual cables (1981 and later models)

Note: *These motorcycles use two throttle cables - a throttle (pull) cable and an idle (push) cable.*

10   Start freeplay adjustments at the throttle end of the cables. Loosen the locknut on each cable where it leaves the handlebar. Turn the adjusters to eliminate all throttle grip play, but leave the locknuts loose for the time being.

11   While holding the throttle wide open, make sure the cam on the throttle pulley just touches its stop. If necessary, turn the adjuster on the throttle cable to change the position of the throttle pulley cam. Once this is done, tighten the throttle cable locknut.

20.6a Spark plug manufacturers recommend using a wire-type gauge when checking the gap - if the wire doesn't slide between the electrodes with a slight drag, adjustment is required

20.6b To check the gap, bend the side electrode only, as indicated by the arrows, and be very careful not to crack or chip the ceramic insulator surrounding the center electrode

21.2 The breaker point cover is retained by two screws (arrows)

21.3 Detach the primary wire (1) and remove the screws (2) securing the baseplate

12   Release the throttle grip and turn the handlebars all the way to full right lock.

13   Turn the idle cable adjuster at the handlebar while watching the cable housing at the carburetor or throttle body **(see illustrations)**. The adjustment is correct when the cable housing just touches the spring inside the cable tube on the cable bracket.

14   Make sure the throttle pulley returns to idle when the throttle grip is in the closed throttle position.

 Warning: Turn the handlebars all the way through their travel with the engine idling. Idle speed should not change. If it does, the cables may be routed incorrectly. Correct this condition before riding the bike.

19 Choke knob - check

1   Inspect the choke knob and cable. The choke should pull out easily and stay out by itself.

2   If the knob doesn't operate correctly, loosen the hex nut behind the mounting bracket. Hold the cable with a wrench on the cable flats and adjust the knob's tension with the plastic knurled nut behind the knob. If this doesn't help, check the plunger bushing for wear or damage and replace as necessary. Don't lubricate the cable.

20 Spark plugs - check and replacement

1   Make sure your spark plug wrench or socket is the correct size before attempting to remove the plugs.

2   Disconnect the spark plug caps. Clean any dirt from around the base of the plugs with compressed air, a damp cloth or a brush, then remove the plugs. Inspect the electrodes for wear. Both the center and side electrodes should have square edges and the side electrode should be of uniform thickness. Look for excessive deposits and a cracked or chipped insulator around the center electrode. Compare the spark plugs to the color spark plug photos on the inside back cover of this manual. Check the threads, the washer and the ceramic insulator body for cracks and other damage.

3   Inspect the electrodes for wear. Both the center and side electrodes should have square edges and the side electrodes should be of uniform thickness. Look for excessive deposits and a cracked or chipped insulator around the center electrode. Compare the spark plugs to the color spark plug photos on the inside back cover of this manual. Check the threads, the washer and the ceramic insulator body for cracks and other damage.

4   If the electrodes aren't excessively worn, and if the deposits can be easily removed with a wire brush, the plugs can be regapped and reused (if no cracks or chips are visible in the insulator). If in doubt concerning the condition of the plugs, replace them with new ones, as the expense is minimal.

5   Cleaning spark plugs by sandblasting isn't recommended, since grit from the sandblasting process may remain in the plug and be dislodged after it's installed in the engine, which obviously can cause damage and increased wear.

6   Before installing new plugs, make sure they're the correct type and heat range. Check the gap between the electrodes - they're not pre-set. For best results, use a wire-type gauge rather than a flat gauge to check the gap **(see illustration)**. If the gap must be adjusted, bend the side electrode

only and be very careful not to chip or crack the insulator nose **(see illustration)**.

7   Thread the plug into the head by hand. Tighten the plugs finger-tight (until the washers bottom on the cylinder head) then use a wrench to tighten them an additional 1/4-turn. Do not overtighten them.

8   Reconnect the spark plug caps.

21 Contact breaker points - check and replacement

1   If the contact breaker points are badly burned, pitted or worn, they should be replaced with a new set. This also applies if the fiber heel that rides on the breaker cam is badly worn.

2   To remove the points, detach the point cover **(see illustration)**, then remove the two screws that secure the base plate to the camshaft cover on the engine.

3   You'll also have to disconnect the primary wire **(see illustration)**.

4   Prior to removal, mark the base plate in relation to the distributor or camshaft cover

1

21.4 Remove the baseplate with the points attached

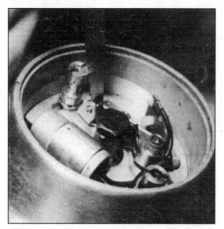

21.7 Check the point gap with a feeler gauge - if the gap is correct, the feeler gauge will just slide between the two contacts with a slight amount of drag

21.8 Lockscrew (1) and breaker point adjusting slot (2) locations

with a scribe or permanent felt-tip pen so the assembly can be installed in the same position. This will eliminate the need to retime the ignition after reassembly. Detach the base plate - the points will come out with the plate **(see illustration)**.

5   Pull the condenser terminal off the terminal post, unhooking the moving contact point return spring at the same time. Lift off the moving contact point and release the fixed contact by removing the single screw through the mounting base. Note the arrangement of the insulators and other washers to prevent them from being replaced in the wrong order.

6   Install the points in the reverse order of removal. Make sure the insulators are installed in the correct positions. It's a good idea to place a small amount of distributor cam tube on the pivot pin prior to installation of the moving contact point.

7   Check and adjust the point gap with a feeler gauge when the points are completely opened by one of the cam lobes **(see illustration)**.

8   Loosen the lock screw on the base

plate of the fixed contact point and move the point by inserting a screwdriver into the adjusting slot and turning it (see **illustration**). Adjust the points until the specified gap is obtained, then retighten the lock screw and recheck the gap.

9   Turn the engine over until the points are completely opened by the other cam robe and check the gap. The gap should be exactly the same for both cam lobes. If it isn't, the cam is defective and must be replaced with a new one.

22 Ignition timing (carbureted models) - check and adjustment

Note: *Ignition timing is not adjustable on fuel injected models.*

1   A timing light is the best and most accurate way to check the ignition timing, since it's done with the engine running. The timing light leads should be attached to the appropriate spark plug wire (start with the front one) and to the battery terminals. It's a good idea to replace the plug in the left

22.1 Install the special clear plastic plug in the crankcase inspection hole before running the engine to check the timing

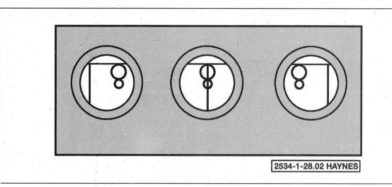

22.2a Here are the 1970 through 1978 timing marks - they should be centered in the opening

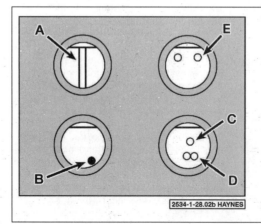

22.2b Timing marks (late 1979 and later)

1   *Front cylinder advance mark (late 1979 through early 1980) or front cylinder TDC mark (late 1980-on)*

2   *Front cylinder TDC mark(late 1979 through early 1980)*

3   *Front cylinder advance mark (late 1980 through 1994 all; 1995 US)*

4   *"Lazy 8" rear cylinder advance mark (some models)*

5   *Front cylinder advance mark (1995 international; 1996-on all)*

22.3a On later models with electronic ignition, drill out the rivet heads and remove the outer screw . . .

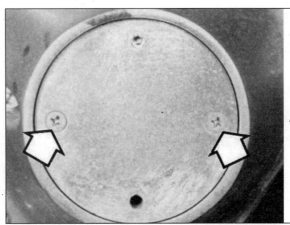

22.3b . . . then remove the screws (arrows) and detach the inner cover and gasket to get at the sensor plate

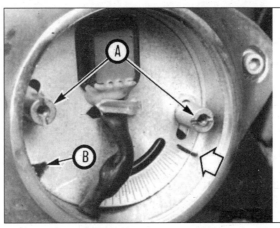

22.4 Mark the sensor plate (arrow), then loosen the screws (A) and insert a screwdriver into the slot (B) to change the position of the plate – move the plate a little at a time and recheck the timing

crankcase with the special clear plastic factory Timing Mark View Plug (part no. HD-96295-65C) **(see illustration)**, otherwise oil spray will be a problem when the engine is running. Make sure the plug doesn't touch the flywheel.

2   Run the engine at approximately 2000 rpm (1300 to 1500 rpm on 1984 and later models) and observe the timing marks through the crankcase opening **(see illustrations)**. The front cylinder timing mark should appear stationary in the opening. As the engine is revved up, the advance mark should move into view.

3   On early models, remove the point cover as described in Section 18 to get at the breaker plate. On later models, drill out the rivet heads **(see illustration)** and detach the outer cover, then remove the screws and take off the inner cover and gasket to get at the sensor plate **(see illustration)**. Mark the sensor plate and cover with a felt-tip pen or a scribe to ensure the sensor plate (ignition timing) can be returned to its original position if desired.

4   Adjustments can be made by loosening the contact breaker point base plate or electronic ignition sensor plate screws and rotating the plate very carefully, in small increments, with a screwdriver inserted in the slot provided **(see illustration)**. The ignition timing will change as the plate is moved. **Note:** *When checking the ignition advance on later carbureted models, be sure to check the Vacuum Operated Electric Switch (VOES) also. With the engine idling, unplug the VOES hose from the carburetor and plug the carburetor fitting. The timing should retard - the engine speed should decrease. When the hose is reattached to the carburetor, the engine speed should increase (the timing should advance). If it doesn't, check the VOES wire connection at the ignition module and the VOES ground wire connection. If they appear to be okay, the VOES may be defective and should be replaced with a new one.*

23 Fuel filter (carbureted models) - cleaning and replacement

1   Make sure the fuel control valve is in the Off position. Remove the air cleaner assembly, detach the hose from the carburetor fitting and drain the contents of the fuel tank into a gasoline container.

2   Unscrew the gland nut on the valve from the bottom of the fuel tank **(see illustration)**. The screen-type filter is attached to the fuel control valve **(see illustration)**.

3   Thoroughly clean the filter. It can be removed from the valve to be cleaned or replaced if it's damaged.

4   If the valve itself leaks, it's not practical to attempt to repair it. The complete unit should be replaced with a new one.

5   Apply thread sealant to the threads before installing the valve on the fuel tank.

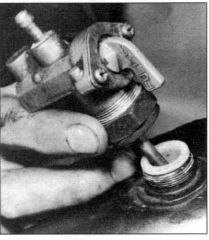

23.2a Loosen the large nut and remove the fuel valve from the tank . . .

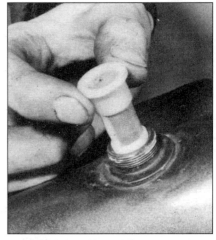

23.2b . . . to gain access to the screen-type filter for cleaning

1

24.7a On Softails, loosen the locknut (left arrow) and turn the drivebelt adjuster (right arrow)

24.7b On Dynas, remove the clip from the end of the axle and loosen the axle nut (left arrow), then turn the adjuster (right arrow)

24 Final drive belt - check, adjustment and inspection

Check

1   Drive belt tension should be checked, and adjusted if necessary before every ride as described in *Daily (pre-ride) checks* at the beginning of this manual, as well as at the specified maintenance intervals.

2   The tension should be checked and adjusted with the bike on the ground and weight equivalent to the rider on the seat. The belt should be cold, so don't check tension or make the adjustment right after the bike has been ridden.

3   Harley-Davidson recommends using a tension gauge to prevent the belt from being set too loose. This can allow the belt to jump one or more sprocket teeth, which will damage the belt.

4   To check belt tension, apply 10 lbs. (4.54 kg) upward pressure on the center of the lower belt run (at the point of the viewing window if equipped) and measure the amount the belt moves. Write this measurement down.

5   Roll the bike to change the belt position and repeat the measurement along every few inches of the belt. Do this along the entire belt until you locate the tightest point (where the belt moves least). At this point, compare the measurement to the range listed in this Chapter's Specifications.

6   If the belt is not within the specified range, adjust it.

Adjustment

7   Pull the cotter pin or clip out of the axle nut, then loosen the nut **(see illustrations)**.

8   Turn the belt adjuster bolts (at the rear of the swingarm, one on each side of the bike) in equal amounts until the belt tension is correct, then tighten the locknuts. Be sure to tighten or loosen the adjusters evenly so the rear wheel isn't cocked sideways.

9   Check the belt tension.

10   Tighten the rear axle locknut to the initial torque listed in this Chapter's Specifications, then install the cotter pin. If necessary, tighten the nut just enough to align the holes so the cotter pin can be installed, but don't exceed the maximum torque listed in this Chapter's Specifications.

 Warning: Overtightening the nut could cause the rear wheel bearings to seize, resulting in loss of control of the motorcycle.

Inspection

11   Place the transmission in neutral and support the bike with the rear wheel off the ground. Rotate the rear wheel slowly and check each belt and sprocket tooth for wear or damage. The following conditions don't require belt replacement, but the belt should be given frequent, complete inspections:

a) *Hairline cracks in the internal portion of the belt teeth (if the cracks don't penetrate the outer layer of the tooth - the layer that contacts the sprocket)*

b) *Minor chips in the internal tooth material at the ends of teeth*

c) *Frayed fabric along the edges, with strands of cord exposed*

d) *Bevel wear of the outer edge of the belt*

e) *Stone damage in the middle of the belt*

12   The following conditions require belt replacement:

a) *Cracks that penetrate the outer layer of a tooth*

b) *Missing teeth*

c) *Hook (uneven) wear of teeth*

d) *Outer layer of teeth worn through*

e) *Stone damage on the edge of the belt*

13   Check the sprocket teeth for chips and other damage, especially if the damaged area has sharp edges. If the damage is severe enough that it has left a pattern on the belt, replace the belt and sprockets.

14   If teeth are missing or heavily damaged, replace the belt and sprockets.

15   Check the chrome surface of the sprockets for wear. If you can't tell whether the chrome has worn off, drag a sharp tool (knife tip or nail) across the surface in the valley between two teeth. If the chrome is good, it won't be visibly scratched by the tool. If the chrome has worn away and the aluminum is exposed, the tool will leave a shiny scratch. In this case, replace the belt and sprockets.

Every 5000 miles (8000 km)

25 Transmission oil - change

1   Remove the drain plug from the bottom of the transmission and allow the oil to drain completely into a shallow pan. On later models (with the engine oil pan mounted under the transmission), note that the transmission oil drain plug threads into the oil pan casting; it is the rearmost of the two drain plugs.

2   Clean the magnetic drain plug of any metallic particles; if significant amounts are found, the transmission should be dismantled for detailed inspection.

3   When all of the oil is drained, reinstall the drain plug. Be careful not to over-tighten it.

4   Remove the oil filler plug and the oil level plug, if equipped, from the right rear side of the transmission.

5   Hold the motorcycle in an upright position while filling the transmission. Pour in the specified grade of oil until the desired level is reached. On models with an oil level hole,

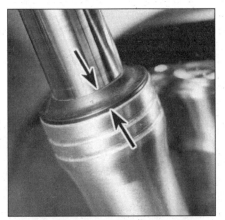

26.3 Check above and below the fork seals (arrows) for signs of leakage

28.2 Unscrew the cap from the top of the fork leg

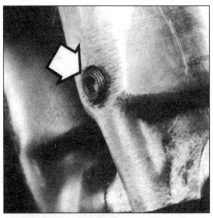

28.3 Remove the drain plug from the bottom of the fork leg - it's an Allen screw (shown) or a Phillips screw

allow the oil to flow out of the hole until the level is at the bottom of the hole.

6   Install the oil filler plug and the oil level plug, if equipped.

26 Suspension - inspection

1   The suspension components must be maintained in top operating condition to ensure rider safety. Loose, worn or damaged suspension parts decrease the vehicle's stability and control.

2   While standing alongside the motorcycle, lock the front brake and push on the handlebars to compress the forks several times. See if they move up-and-down smoothly without binding. If binding is felt, the forks should be disassembled and inspected as described in Chapter 5.

3   Carefully inspect the area around the fork seals for any signs of fork oil leakage **(see illustration)**. If leakage is evident, the seals must be replaced as described in Chapter 5.

4   Check the tightness of all suspension nuts and bolts to be sure none have worked loose.

5   Inspect the shocks for fluid leakage and tightness of the mounting nuts. If leakage is found, the shocks should be replaced.

6   Carefully raise the motorcycle and support it securely with the rear wheel off the ground. Make sure it can't fall off the support to either side. Grab the swingarm on each side, just ahead of the axle. Rock the swingarm from side-to-side. There should be no discernible movement at the rear. If there's a little movement or a slight clicking can be heard, make sure the pivot bolts and locknut are correctly torqued. If the pivot bolts are tight, but movement is still noticeable, then the swingarm will have to be removed and the bearings replaced, repacked and adjusted as described in Chapter 5.

7   Check the tightness of all rear suspension nuts and bolts.

8   Check all air suspension lines and fittings for damage and distortion. Make sure all fittings are tight.

27 Steering head bearings - check

1   The steering head is equipped with tapered roller-type bearings, which seldom require servicing. In extreme cases, worn or loose steering head bearings can cause steering wobble that's potentially dangerous.

2   To check the bearings, lift the motorcycle and support the machine so the front wheel is in the air.

3   Point the wheel straight ahead and slowly move the handlebars from side-to-side. Dents or roughness in the bearing races will be felt and the bars won't move smoothly.

4   Next, grasp the fork legs and try to move the wheel forward and backward. Any looseness in the steering head bearings will be felt. Refer to Chapter 5 for bearing maintenance and repair procedures.

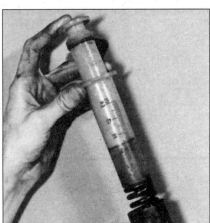

28.6 Fill the fork leg with the specified amount of fork oil (a baby bottle or measuring cup will make it easier to measure the amount accurately)

28 Fork oil - change

1   Support the motorcycle securely with the front wheel off the ground.

2   Remove the cap from the top of one of the fork legs **(see illustration)**.

3   Remove the drain plug from the bottom of the fork leg (near the axle), that the cap was removed from **(see illustration)**.

4   Allow the oil to drain for a few minutes, then pump the forks up-and- down to force the remainder of the oil out.

5   Install the drain plug in the bottom of the fork leg.

6   Fill the fork with the specified amount of the recommended fork oil **(see illustration)**. If the fork has been disassembled, it will require additional fork oil.

7   Check the condition of the seal around the fork cap. If necessary, replace the seal with a new one **(see illustration)**. Attach the fork cap to the top of the fork leg.

8   Repeat Steps 2 through 7 for the other fork leg.

1

28.7 Replace the fork cap seal (arrow) if it's damaged

Every 10,000 miles (16,000 km)

29 Primary belt - adjustment

1   On models equipped with a primary drive belt, the tension should be checked every 10,000 miles. Only models produced from late 1981 through 1983 have belts that are adjustable. Earlier models have non-adjustable belts that must be replaced if they're stretched excessively.
2   Remove the screws securing the primary case cover to the engine and detach the cover with the gasket. On FXB/FXSB models, note the location of the one short screw.
3   Loosen the four bolts securing the primary case to the crankcase after cutting the safety wire. Pay attention to the way the safety wire is routed to ensure correct reassembly.
4   There are four nuts that secure the transmission to the transmission mounting plate that must be loosened, followed by the bolt securing the transmission to the frame tab.
5   Loosen the two starter motor nuts.
6   On most models there's a hole in the housing through which a screwdriver can be inserted to pry against the housing, increasing tension on the belt. Check the tension on the belt and increase or decrease it as necessary until the free play is within the specified limit.
7   On models without the hole drilled in the case, the tension must be adjusted by carefully prying between the alternator rotor and the primary case.
8   With the screwdriver held in place, apply tension to the belt. Tighten the two inside bolts to the specified torque, followed by the two outside bolts.
9   Install new safety wire through the inside bolts.

Caution: Extensive damage within the primary case could occur if the motorcycle is operated without safety wire installed.
10   Tighten the four transmission-to-transmission mounting plate nuts to the specified torque. Tighten the transmission-to-frame tab bolt to the specified torque.
11   Tighten the starter motor nuts.
12   Clean any gasket material and dirt off the mating surfaces of the primary chaincase cover and the crankcase. Install the primary chaincase cover with a new gasket. On FXB/FXSB models, be sure to install the one shorter screw in the proper location.
13   After the primary belt is adjusted, it may be necessary to adjust the clutch cable, the rear brake pedal free play, the shifter linkage and the secondary drive belt as described in the appropriate Sections. All of these adjustments should be checked before the motorcycle is operated.

30 Wheel, swingarm and steering head bearings - repack

1   The wheel bearings should be removed, inspected and repacked with grease (see Chapter 6).
2   The swingarm bearings and steering head bearings should be removed, inspected and repacked with grease (see Chapter 5).

31 Compensating sprocket rubber dampers - lubrication

Belt primary drive models only

1   Remove the primary drive belt and compensating sprocket (see Chapter 2B).
2   With the compensating sprocket removed, it can be disassembled to lubricate

the two sets of rubber dampers with Harley-Davidson POLY-OIL (part no. 99860-81).
3   Reassemble the compensating sprocket and install it with the primary drive-belt as described in Chapter 2.

32 Springer fork rocker bearings - adjustment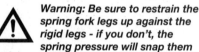

Caution: This procedure requires the spring load to be taken off the rockers by disconnecting the spring forks. This can be done without removing the forks from the motorcycle.
1   Refer to Chapter 5 and perform the first five Steps in Springer fork removal.
2   Detach the spring fork legs from the rockers (see Chapter 5 if necessary).

⚠️ *Warning: Be sure to restrain the spring fork legs up against the rigid legs - if you don't, the spring pressure will snap them forward with extreme force, which could cause serious injuries!*
3   Loosen the jam nuts and bearing retainers on the rockers.
4   Move the RIGHT rocker UP against the rigid fork. Move the LEFT rocker BACK against the rigid fork.
5   Slowly tighten the bearing retainers until contact is felt, then tighten each one an additional (one) flat - mark the flats if necessary.
6   Hold each retainer so it can't move and tighten the jam nuts to 95 to 105 ft-lbs (129 to 142 Nm). **Note:** *Approximately 1/16 inch (1.6 mm) of the retainer will protrude past the jam nut when everything is installed and tightened correctly. The rockers may not feel like they're tightened equally, but it doesn't matter - they'll equalize within a few miles of riding. If it feels like there's metal-to-metal contact, the spherical bearings in the rocker(s) must be replaced.*
7   Reattach the spring fork legs to the rockers, then put everything back together.

Every 30,000 miles (48,000 km)

33 Fuel filter (fuel injected models) - replacement

The filter on fuel injected models is mounted inside the tank. It should be replaced at the specified maintenance interval (see Chapter 3).

Chapter 2 Part A
Engine

Contents

Degrees of difficulty

Easy, suitable for novice with little experience	**Fairly easy,** suitable for beginner with some experience	**Fairly difficult,** suitable for competent DIY mechanic	**Difficult,** suitable for experienced DIY mechanic	**Very difficult,** suitable for expert DIY or professional

2A

Specifications

General

Engine type	45-degree V-twin, four-stroke
Bore	
1200 cc	3.438 inches (87.3 mm)
1340 cc	3.498 inches (88.8 mm)
Stroke	
1200 cc	3.968 inches (100.8 mm)
1340 cc	4.250 inches (108.0 mm)
Displacement	
1200 cc	73.66 cubic inches
1340 cc	81.6 cubic inches

Oil pressure

All models	12 to 35 psi (0.83 to 2.42 Bars)

Valves

Margin width limit .... 0.031 inch (0.787 mm)

Seat width

    Shovelhead engine .... 0.050 to 0.090 inch 1.270 to 2.286 mm)

    Evolution engine

        Standard .... 0.040 to 0.062 inch (1.016 to 1.575 mm)

        Service limit .... 0.090 inch (2.286 mm)

Valve stem protrusion from cylinder head boss

    Shovelhead engine (late 1978-on) .... 1.600 to 1.645 inch (40.64 to 41.78 mm)

    Evolution engine

        Standard .... 1.990 to 2.024 inch (50.55 to 51.41 mm)

        Service limit .... 2.034 inches (51.66 mm)

Valve-to-guide clearance

    Shovelhead engine

        1970 through early 1981 (intake)

            Standard .... 0.002 to 0.004 inch (0.051 to 0.102 mm)

            Service limit .... 0.002 to 0.006 inch (0.051 to 0.152 mm)

        1970 through early 1981 (exhaust)

            Standard .... 0.0035 to 0.0055 inch (0.089 to 0.140 mm)

            Service limit .... 0.0035 to 0.0075 inch (0.089 to 0.191 mm)

        Late 1981-on (with valve guide seal) - intake

            Standard .... 0.0009 to 0.0026 inch (0.023 to 0.066 mm)

            Service limit .... 0.0009 to 0.0035 inch (0.023 to 0.089 mm)

        Late 1981-on (with valve guide seal) - exhaust

            Standard .... 0.0014 to 0.0031 inch (0.036 to 0.079 mm)

            Service limit .... 0.0014 to 0.0040 inch (0.036 to 0.102 mm)

    Evolution engine

        Intake

            Standard .... 0.0008 to 0.0026 inch (0.020 to 0.066 mm)

Service limit .... 0.0035 inch (0.089 mm)

        Exhaust

            Standard .... 0.0015 to 0.0033 inch (0.038 to 0.084 mm)

            Service limit .... 0.004 inch 90.102 mm)

Valve stem taper limit .... 0.0015 inch (0.038 mm)

Valve stem face (or tip) eccentricity limit .... 0.002 inch (0.051 mm)

Valve spring free length

    Shovelhead engine (inner)

        1970 through early 1982 .... 1.30 to 1.36 inch (33 to 34.5 mm)

Late 1982-on .... 1.50 to 1.56 inch (38 to 40 mm)

    Shovelhead engine (outer)

        1970 through early 1982 .... 1.90 to 1.96 inch (48 to 50 mm)

        Late 1982-on .... 1.72 to 1.78 inch (44 to 45 mm)

    Evolution engine

        Inner .... 1.926 to 1.996 inch (48.920 to 50.968 mm)

        Outer .... 2.105 to 2.177 mm(53.467 to 55.296 mm)

Valve spring tension/length (late 1978-on)

    Shovelhead engine (intake)

        Late 1978 through early 1982

            Open .... 69 to 81 lbs @51/64 inch (31 to 37 kg @20.2 mm)

            Closed .... 20 to 26 lbs @ 1-3/16 inch (9 to 12 kg @ 30 mm)

        Late 1982-on

            Open .... 77 to 87 lbs @ 3/4-inch (35 to 40 kg @ 19 mm)

            Closed .... 32 to 40 lbs @ 1-3/16 inch (15 to 18 kg @ 30 mm)

    Shovelhead engine (exhaust)

         Late 1978 through early 1982

            Open .... 179 to 195 lbs @15/16 inch (81 to 89 kg @ 24 mm)

            Closed .... 104 to 120 lbs @ 1-3/8 inch (47 to 54 kg @ 35 mm)

        Late 1982-on

            Open .... 182 to 204 lbs @ 15/16-inch (83 to 93 kg @ 24 mm)

            Closed .... 76 to 94 lbs @ 1-3/8 inch (35 to 43 kg @ 35 mm)

Evolution engine

    Intake

        Open .... 98 to 112 lbs @1.107 to 1.213 inch (44 to 51 kg @ 28 to 31 mm)

        Closed... 38 to 49 lbs @ 1.577 to 1.683 inch (17 to 22 kg @ 40 to 43 mm)

    Exhaust

        Open .... 183 to 207 lbs @ 1.282 to 378 inch (83 to 94 kg @ 33 to 35 mm)

        Closed... 72 to 92 lbs @ 1.751 to 1.848 inch (33 to 42 kg @ 44 to 47 mm)

Rocker arms

Shovelhead engine
Shaft-to-rocker arm bushing clearance
  Standard .... 0.0005 to 0.002 inch (0.013 to 0.051 mm)
  Service limit.. 0.0005 to 0.0035 inch (0.013 to 0.089 mm)
End clearance.. 0.004 to 0.025 inch (0.102 to 0.635 mm)
Evolution engine
Shaft-to-rocker arm bushing clearance
  Standard .... 0.0005 to 0.002 inch (0.013 to 0.051 mm)
  Service limit.. 0.035 inch (0.089 mm)
Rocker arm-to-bushing clearance .... 0.002 to 0.004 inch (0.051 to 0.107 mm)
Shaft-to-cover bore clearance
  Standard .... 0.0007 to 0.0022 inch (0.018 to 0.056 mm)
  Service limit.. 0.0035 inch 90.089 mm)
End clearance
  Standard .... 0.003 to 0.013 inch (0.076 to 0.330 mm)
  Service limit.. 0.025 inch (0.635 mm)

Cylinder head warpage limit (Evolution engine)

All Evolution models .... 0.006 inch (0.152 mm)

Cylinders (Evolution engine)

Bore
Diameter limit (without overbore) .... 3.501 inch (88.93 mm)
Taper limit... 0.002 inch (0.05 mm)
Out-of-round limit.. 0.003 inch (0.08 mm)
Gasket surface warpage limit
  Top (cylinder head) .... 0.006 inch (0.15 mm)
  Base .... 0.008 inch (0/20 mm)

Pistons and rings

Piston-to-bore clearance
Shovelhead engine
  Standard
    1970 through early 1978......................... 0.001 to 0.002 inch (0.025 to 0.050 mm)
    Late 1978-on... 0.002 to 0.0025 inch (0.050 to 0.063 mm)
  Service limit.. 0.002 to 0.005 inch (0.050 to 0.127 mm)
Evolution engine
  Standard
    KSG piston (late 1985-on) .... 0.00075 to 0.00175 inch (0.019 to 0.044 mm)
    All others.. 0.00055 to 0.00165 inch (0.014 to 0.042 mm)
  Service limit.. 0.0053 inch (0.135 mm)
Compression ring side clearance
Shovelhead engine
  Standard .... 0.004 to 0.005 inch 90.102 to 0.127 mm)
  Service limit.. 0.004 to 0.006 inch 90.102 to 0.152 mm)
Evolution engine
  Standard
    Top ring .... 0.002 to 0.0045 inch (0.050 to 0.114 mm)
    Second ring .... 0.0016 to 0.041 inch (0.040 to 0.104 mm)
  Service limit (both) .... 0.006 inch (0.152 mm)
Oil control ring side clearance
Shovelhead engine
  Standard .... 0.003 to 0.005 inch (0.076 to 0.127 mm)
  Service limit.. 0.003 to 0.006 inch (0.076 to 0.152 mm)
Evolution engine
  Standard .... 0.0016 to 0.0076 inch (0.041 to 0.193 mm)
  Service limit.. 0.008 inch (0.20 mm)
Ring end gap
Compression rings
  Shovelhead engine
    Standard.. 0.010 to 0.020 inch (0.254 to 0.508 mm)
    Service limit .... 0.010 to 0.031 inch (0.254 to 0.787 mm)
  Evolution engine
    Standard.. 0.007 to 0.020 inch (0.178 to 0.508 mm)
    Service limit .... 0.030 inch (0.762 mm)
Oil ring rail
  Shovelhead engine .... 0.010 to 0.045 inch (0.254 to 1.143 mm)
  Evolution engine .... 0.009 to 0.052 inch (0.23 to 1.32 mm)

2A

Connecting rods

Piston pin-to-connecting rod clearance
   Shovelhead engine
      Standard .... 0.0008 to 0.0012 inch (0.020 to 0.030 mm)
      Service limit .... 0.0008 to 0.0020 inch (0.020 to 0.051 mm)
   Evolution engine
      Standard .... 0.0003 to 0.0007 inch (0.008 to 0.018 mm)
      Service limit .... 0.001 inch (0.025 mm)
Big end side play
   Standard.. 0.05 to 0.025 inch (0.13 to 0.54 mm)
   Service limit .... 0.030 inch (0.76 mm)
Big end radial clearance
   Shovelhead
      Standard .... 0.001 to 0.0015 inch (0.025 to 0.038 mm)
      Service limit .... 0.001 to 0.0017 inch 90.025 to 0.043 mm)
   Evolution engine
      Standard .... 0.0004 to 0.0017 inch (0.010 to 0.043 mm)
      Service limit .... 0.002 inch (0.05 mm)

Tappets

Tappet-to-guide clearance
   Standard.. 0.001 to 0.002 inch (0.025 to 0.050 mm)
   Service limit .... 0.003 inch (0.076 mm)
Guide-to-crankcase clearance (Evolution engine)
Roller radial fit
   Standard.. 0.0005 to 0.001 inch (0.013 to 0.025 inch)
   Service limit .... 0.0015 inch (0.038 mm)
Roller end clearance
   Shovelhead engine
      Standard .... 0.008 to 0.010 inch (0.203 to 0.254 mm)
      Service limit .... 0.008 to 0.025 inch (0.203 to 0.635 mm)
   Evolution engine (service limit) .... 0.015 inch (0.381 mm)

Gearcase

Breather gear end play
   Shovelhead engine
      1970 through early 1978 .... 0.001 to 0.005 inch (0.025 to 0.127 mm)
      Late 1978 through 1983.. 0.001 to 0.016 inch (0.025 to 0.406 mm)
   Evolution engine
      Minimum .... 0.001 to 0.011 inch (0.025 to 0.280 mm)
      Maximum .... 0.016 inch (0.406 mm)
Camshaft-to-bushing clearance
   Standard.. 0.0008 to 0.0018 inch (0.020 to 0.046 mm)
   Service limit .... 0.003 inch (0.076 mm)
Camshaft-to-bearing clearance
   Shovelhead engine... 0.0005 to 0.0030 inch (0.013 to 0.076 mm)
   Evolution engine
      Standard .... 0.0005 to 0.0025 inch (0.013 to 0.064 mm)
      Service limit .... 0.005 inch (0.127 mm)
Camshaft end play
   1970 through early 1978 .... 0.001 to 0.005 inch (0.025 to 0.127 mm)
   Late 1978 through 1987 .... 0.001 to 0.016 inch (0.025 to 0.406 mm)
   1988-on .... 0.001 to 0.050 inch (no spacer) (0.025 to 1.270 mm)
Oil pump drive shaft-to-bushing clearance
   Shovelhead engine
      Standard .... 0.0008 to 0.0012 inch (0.020 to 0.030 mm)
      Service limit .... 0.0008 to 0.0025 inch (0.020 to 0.064 mm)
   Evolution engine
      Standard .... 0.0004 to 0.0025 inch (0.010 to 0.064 mm)
      Service limit .... 0.0035 inch (0.089 mm)

Flywheel/crankshaft assembly

Maximum runout at rim
   Shovelhead engine
      1970 through early 1978... 0.003 inch (0.076 mm)
      Late 1978-on... 0.006 inch (0.152 mm)
   Evolution engine... 0.015 inch (0.381 mm)

Maximum runout at shaft
    Shovelhead engine
        1970 through early 1978 .... 0.001 inch (0.025 mm)
        Late 1978-on .... 0.002 inch (0.051 mm)
    Evolution engine .... 0.003 inch (0.076 mm)
Flywheel assembly end play
    Shovelhead engine
        1970 through 1981 .... 0.001 to 0.006 inch (0.025 to 0.152 mm)
        1982-on .... 0.001 to 0.004 inch (0.025 to 0.107 mm)
    Evolution engine
        Standard .... 0.001 to 0.005 inch (0.025 to 0.13 mm)
        Service limit .... 0.006 inch (0.152 mm)
Timing side (pinion shaft) bearing axial play
    Shovelhead engine
        Standard .... 0.0004 to 0.0008 inch (0.010 to 0.020 mm)
        Service limit
            1200 cc .... 0.0008 to 0.0020 inch (0.020 to 0.051 mm)
            1340 cc .... 0.0004 to 0.0020 inch (0.010 to 0.051 mm)
    Evolution engine .... 0.0002 to 0.0009 inch (0.005 to 0.023 mm)
Gearcase cover bushing-to-mainshaft clearance
    Shovelhead engine
        Standard .... 0.0005 to 0.0012 inch (0.013 to 0.030 mm)
        Service limit .... 0.0005 to 0.0025 inch (0.013 to 0.064 mm)
    Evolution engine
        Standard .... 0.001 to 0.0025 inch (0.025 to 0.064 mm)
        Service limit .... 0.0035 inch (0.089 mm)
Sprocket shaft bearing
    Inner race-to-shaft .... 0.0002 to 0.0015 inch (0.005 to 0.038 mm)
    Outer race-to-crankcase .... 0.0012 to 0.0032 inch (0.030 to 0.081 mm)

Torque specifications

Upper engine mounting bracket
    Through 1990 .... 35 to 40 ft-lbs (47 to 54 Nm)
    1991 and 1992 .... 22 to 28 ft-lbs (30 to 39 Nm)
    1993-on
        At cylinder head .... 28 to 35 ft-lbs (38 to 48 Nm)
        At frame .... 28 to 32 ft-lbs (38 to 43 Nm)
Front and rear mounting bolts .... 33 to 38 ft-lbs (47 to 52 Nm)
Rocker arm cover
    Shovelhead engine .... 12 to 15 ft-lbs (16 to 20 Nm)
    Evolution engine
        1/4-inch bolts .... 120 to 156 inch -lbs 914 to 18 Nm)
        5/16-inch bolts .... 15 to 18 ft-lbs (20 to 24 Nm)
Rocker arm shaft (acorn) locknut .... 12 to 18 ft-lbs (16 to 24 Nm)
Rocker arm shaft end cap (1980 and 1981 only)
Cylinder head bolts
Shovelhead engine .... 55 to 75 ft-lbs (75 to 102 Nm)
    Evolution engine (1984 FXST models only)
        Step 1 .... 84 to 108 inch-lbs (9 to 12 Nm)
        Step 2 .... 15 to 17 ft-lbs (20 to 23 Nm)
        Step 3 .... 24 to 26 ft-lbs (33 to 35 Nm)
    Evolution engine (all other models)
        Step 1
            Bolt 1 only .... 84 inch-lbs (9 Nm)
            All others .... 84 to 108 inch-lbs (9 to 12 Nm)
        Step 2 .... 12 to 14 ft-lbs (16 to 19 Nm)
        Step 3 .... Tighten an additional 90-degrees (1/4-turn)
Cylinder barrel base nuts .... 32 to 40 ft-lbs (43 to 54 Nm)
Oil pump cover nuts/bolts
    Shovelhead engine
        Plastic gasket .... 45 to 50 inch-lbs (5 to 6 Nm)
        White paper gasket .... 50 to 60 inch-lbs (6 to 7 Nm)
        Black paper gasket .... 90 to 120 inch-lbs (10 to 14 Nm)
    Evolution engine .... 90 to 120 inch-lbs (10 to 14 Nm)
Tappet guide bolts
    Shovelhead engine
        1970 through early 1978 .... 120 inch-lbs (14 Nm)
        Late 1978-on .... 65 to 105 inch-lbs (7 to 12 Nm)

Tappet guide bolts (continued)

Evolution engine

Through 1990 .... 90 to 120 inch-lbs (10 to 14 Nm)

1991-on .... 12 to 15 ft-lbs (16 to 20 Nm)

Crankshaft timing (pinion) gear nut.. 35 to 45 ft-lbs (47 to 61 Nm)

Flywheel sprocket shaft nut

1970 through early 1978 .... 400 ft-lbs (540 Nm)

Late 1978 through early 1981 .... 300 to 440 ft-lbs (400 to 596 Nm)

Late 1981-on.. 290 to 320 ft-lbs (393 to 434 Nm)

Pinion shaft nut

Late 1978 through early 1981 .... 120 to 160 ft-lbs (163 to 217 Nm)

Late 1981-on.. 140 to 170 ft-lbs (190 to 231 Nm)

Crank pin nut

1980 and early 1981 .... 150 to 250 ft-lbs (203 to 339 Nm)

Late 1981-on.. 180 to 210 ft-lbs (244 to 285 Nm)

Crankcase stud nuts

1970 through early 1978 .... 22 to 26 ft-lbs (30 to 35 Nm)

Late 1978 through 1983.. 12 to 15 ft-lbs (16 to 20 Nm)

Crankcase bolts/nuts

Shovelhead engine.. 22 to 26 ft-lbs (30 to 35 Nm)

Evolution engine

Through 1990.. 15 to 19 ft-lbs (20 to 26 Nm)

1991-on (see text)... 15 to 17 ft-lbs (20 to 23 Nm)

Gearcase cover screws .... 90 to 120 inch-lbs (10 to 14 Nm)

Tappet screen plug

Shovelhead engine.. 90 to 160 inch-lbs (10 to 18 Nm)

Evolution engine .... 90 to 120 inch-lbs (10 to 14 Nm)

1 General information

The engine used in the models covered by this manual is a large capacity, 45-degree V-twin, mounted inline with the frame. In this Chapter, the early engine (through 1984) with cast-iron heads and cylinders is referred to as the Shovelhead engine, while the later engine (1985-on) with aluminum heads and cylinders, as will as redesigned rocker boxes, is called the Evolution engine - the term used by the factory. Actually, the Evolution engine was first installed in 1984 FXST models and the Shovelhead engine was used in all other 1984 models, so there was some overlap of engine types and model years.

Aluminum alloy castings are used throughout the engine, with the above-mentioned exception of the cylinder barrels and heads on Shovelhead engines, which were cast-iron. The engine has overhead valves actuated by hydraulic tappets and pushrods from the camshaft mounted in the gearcase at the right-hand side of the engine. The tappets on Shovelhead engines are two-piece. The Evolution engine has one-piece tappets (with larger rollers than the Shovelhead engine) and hollow, one-piece pushrods that feed oil to the rocker arm shafts, eliminating the need for external oil lines. A gear-type oil pump, driven off the crankshaft, provides pressurized oil to the main engine components.

An electric starter is standard on most models. The early FX models were equipped with a kickstarter, but they can be equipped with an electric starter as well.

Service procedures for the clutch, primary drive and transmission are covered in Part B of this Chapter.

2 Cylinder compression - check

1 Among other things, poor engine performance may be caused by leaking valves, incorrect valve clearances, a leaking head gasket, or worn pistons, rings and/or cylinder walls. A cylinder compression check will help pinpoint these conditions and can also indicate the presence of excessive carbon deposits in the cylinder heads.
2 The only tools required are a compression gauge and a spark plug wrench. Depending on the outcome of the initial test, a squirt-type oil can may also be needed.
3 Run the engine until it reaches normal operating temperature. Place the motorcycle on the sidestand or prop it securely upright. Remove the spark plugs (see Chapter 1, if necessary). Work carefully - don't strip the spark plug hole threads and don't burn your hands.

2.5 A compression gauge with a threaded fitting for the spark plug hole is preferred over the type that requires hand pressure to retain the seal

4 Disable the ignition by unplugging the primary wires from the coils (see Chapter 4). Be sure to mark the locations of the wires before detaching them.
5 Install the compression gauge in one of the spark plug holes **(see illustration)**. Hold or block the throttle wide open.
6 Crank the engine over for five to seven revolutions (or until the gauge reading stops increasing) and observe the initial movement of the compression gauge needle as well as the final total gauge reading. Repeat the procedure for the other cylinder and compare the results to the value listed in this Chapter's Specifications.
7 If the compression in both cylinders built up quickly and evenly to the specified amount, you can assume the engine upper end is in reasonably good mechanical condition. Worn or sticking piston rings and worn cylinders will produce very little initial movement of the gauge needle, but compression will tend to build up gradually as the engine spins over. Valve and valve seat leakage, or head gasket leakage, is indicated by low initial compression which does not tend to build up.
8 To further confirm your findings, add a small amount of engine oil to each cylinder by inserting the nozzle of a squirt-type oil can through the spark plug holes. The oil will tend to seal the piston rings if they are leaking. Repeat the test for the other cylinder.
9 If the compression increases significantly after the addition of the oil, the piston rings and/or cylinders are definitely worn. If the compression does not increase, the pressure is leaking past the valves or the head gasket. Leakage past the valves may be due to insufficient valve clearances, burned, warped or cracked valves or valve seats, or valves that are hanging up in the guides.
10 If compression readings are considerably higher than specified, the combustion chambers are probably coated with excessive carbon deposits. It is possible (but not very likely) for carbon deposits to raise the compression enough to compensate for the effects of leakage past rings or valves.

Remove the cylinder heads and carefully decarbonize the combustion chambers (see Section 10).

3 Operations possible with the engine in the frame

The components and assemblies listed below can be removed without having to remove the engine from the frame. If, however, a number of areas require attention at the same time, removal of the engine is recommended.

It's not necessary to remove the engine from the frame unless the crankcases have to be separated to gain access to the crankshaft, connecting rods or bearings. If only the cylinder heads and related valvetrain components (including the camshaft and tappets), or the pistons, rings or barrels require attention, the work can be done with the engine in the frame, provided the various disassembly procedures outlined in this Chapter are modified slightly. However, if major work or a complete overhaul is necessary, remove the engine from the frame.

Operations that can be completed with the engine in the frame include removal and installation of the:

Alternator
Starter motor
Transmission and related components
Clutch and primary drive components
Cylinder heads and cylinder barrels
Camshaft and drive gear
Oil pump and related components
Tappets and pushrods
Rocker arms and shafts
Valves, springs, seals and guides
Rocker box gaskets
Cylinder head and base gaskets

This does not, however, apply to the main crankcase assembly, which is split vertically and cannot be separated until the engine is out of the frame. Conversely, the crankcase assembly must be bolted together before it can be reinstalled in the frame.

2A

4 Operations requiring engine removal

It is necessary to remove the engine/transmission assembly from the frame and separate the crankcase halves to gain access to the crankshaft, connecting rods and bearings.

5 Major engine repair - general note

1 It is not always easy to determine when or if an engine should be completely overhauled, as a number of factors must be considered.

2 High mileage is not necessarily an indication that an overhaul is needed, while low mileage, on the other hand, does not preclude the need for an overhaul. Frequency of servicing is probably the single most important consideration. An engine that has regular and frequent oil and filter changes, as well as other required maintenance, will most likely give many miles of reliable service. Conversely, a neglected engine, or one which has not been broken in properly, may require an overhaul very early in its life.

3 Exhaust smoke and excessive oil consumption are both indications that piston rings and/or valve guides are in need of attention. Make sure oil leaks are not responsible before deciding that the rings and guides are bad. Refer to Section 2 and perform a cylinder compression check to determine for certain the nature and extent of the work required.

4 If the engine is making obvious knocking or rumbling noises, the connecting rod and/or main bearings are probably at fault.

5 Loss of power, rough running, excessive valve train noise and high fuel consumption rates may also point to the need for an overhaul, especially if they are all present at the same time. If a complete tune-up does not remedy the situation, major mechanical work is the only solution.

6 An engine overhaul generally involves restoring the internal parts to the specifications of a new engine. During an overhaul the piston rings are replaced and the cylinder walls are bored and/or honed. If a rebore is done, then new pistons are also required. The crankshaft and connecting rods are replaced as a complete assembly if problems are found with any of them. Generally the valves are serviced as well, since they are usually in less than perfect condition at this point. While the engine is being overhauled, other components such as the carburetor (if equipped) and starter motor can be rebuilt also. The end result should be a like-new engine that will give as many trouble-free miles as the original.

7 Before beginning the engine overhaul, read through all of the related procedures to familiarize yourself with the scope and requirements of the job. Overhauling an engine is not all that difficult, but it is time consuming. Plan on the motorcycle being tied up for a minimum of two weeks. Check on the availability of parts and make sure that any necessary special tools, equipment and supplies are obtained in advance.

8 Most work can be done with typical shop hand tools, although a number of precision measuring tools are required for inspecting parts to determine if they must be replaced. Often a dealer service department or motorcycle repair shop will handle the inspection of parts and offer advice concerning reconditioning and replacement. As a general rule, time is the primary cost of an overhaul so it doesn't pay to install worn or substandard parts.

9 As a final note, to ensure maximum life and minimum trouble from a rebuilt engine, everything must be assembled with care in a spotlessly clean environment.

Note: *These engines use a number of O-rings, some of them very close to each other in size. Make sure O-rings are labeled when you buy them, or else have the parts supplier label them for you. Don't remove the labels until you're ready to install the O-rings.*

6 Engine - removal and installation

Warning: The engine is VERY heavy. Engine removal and installation should be done with the aid of at least one strong assistant, though two are preferable, to avoid damage or personal injury that could occur if the engine is dropped. A hydraulic floor jack should be used to support and lower the engine if possible (they can be rented at low cost).

HAYNES HINT *Where options are given for removal of components not essential for engine removal, such as the starter motor or alternator rotor, bear in mind that although these do not weigh much by themselves, they add to the weight of the engine, and anything that can be removed to reduce the overall weight is a bonus.*

Removal

1 Because of its size and weight, at least two people must be available for this task, preferably with a third person to steady the cycle while the engine is lifted in and out. An engine hoist is recommended, if available. If the cylinder heads and barrels are removed first, one person may manage to lift the engine out of the frame.

2 Since the motorcycle isn't normally equipped with a centerstand, the initial disassembly should be done with the machine resting on the sidestand, unless some form of rigid stand is available (like the ones used in many repair shops). Since the lower frame tubes are close together, the machine won't be too stable if it's supported on them. If the machine is on the sidestand, be sure it's on level ground and the wheels are chocked so it won't roll.

3 Disconnect the negative cable from the battery.

4 Drain the fuel tank (carbureted models) or relieve fuel system pressure (fuel injected models) (see Chapter 3).

5 Refer to Chapter 3 and remove the fuel tank. **Note:** *On FLT and FXR models (1985-on), rocker box, tappet block and camshaft repairs can be accomplished at this point without continuing the engine removal procedure.*

6 On models so equipped, detach the passenger seat (see Chapter 7).

7 Place a drain pan under the crankcase and remove the primary chaincase (wet clutch models) and transmission drain plugs, allowing the oil to drain. This task is easier if the engine is warm so that the oil flows more freely.

8 Drain the engine oil tank by removing the drain plug and directing the oil via a metal chute into a container. On 1993 and later FLT and 1991 and later Dyna models (which have an engine oil pan on the bottom of the transmission), remove the drain plug and allow the oil to drain into the pan along with the transmission and primary chaincase oil.

9 When all of the oil has drained, replace and tighten all the drain plugs after checking the sealing washers to make sure they're clean and in good condition. Note that the chaincase plug is magnetic; any metal particles that have collected should be cleaned off. Tighten the drain plugs now, otherwise this point may be overlooked during reassembly.

10 Remove the pivot pin securing the footboards (if equipped), by unscrewing the thin nut and driving the pin out. Remove the bracket supporting the rear of the right-hand footboard. It's held in place with a single bolt.

11 On models with a kickstarter, loosen the pinch bolt and pull the kickstarter off the shaft.

12 The upper cylinder head bracket must be removed from the engine (on models fitted with a stabilizer bar don't loosen the stabilizer jam nuts). Pay attention to the installed locations of the washers and be sure to reinstall them in the same positions during installation. It may be helpful to draw a sketch to refresh your memory if the motorcycle will be apart for an extended period of time. On models where the bracket also retains the ignition switch, tape the switch/bracket to the upper frame tube so disconnection of the wires is unnecessary.

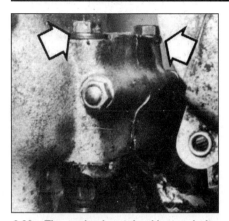

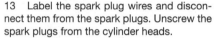

6.33a The engine is retained by two bolts at the rear end . . .

6.33b . . . and two bolts at the front

6.34 Lift the engine out from the right side of the frame

13 Label the spark plug wires and disconnect them from the spark plugs. Unscrew the spark plugs from the cylinder heads.

14 Remove the air cleaner assembly from the engine (see Chapter 3).

15 Disconnect the throttle cable(s) and the choke control cable from the carburetor or induction unit (see Chapter 3). On carbureted Evolution models, detach the VOES (Vacuum Operated Electrical Switch) hose from the carburetor.

16 Remove the carburetor or induction unit. On carbureted models, remove the intake manifold (see Chapter 3). Stuff clean rags into the intake ports in the heads to prevent dirt or debris from entering.

17 Remove the exhaust system (see Chapter 3).

18 On 1985 and later FLT/FXR models, remove the large center bolt from the front engine mount and the bolt from the outer end of the front stabilizer. Remove both front engine mount bolts and detach the mounting plate and stabilizer assembly. **Note:** *With the external components removed from the engine to this extent, it's possible to remove the cylinder heads and barrels (see Section 10). If more extensive repairs are required, continue with the remaining engine removal steps.* On 1985 and later FX/Softail models, an access hole has been provided in the frame to remove the left rear rocker cover bolt. A rolled up paper tube should be inserted into the hole first and pushed down until it touches the engine to prevent dropping the bolt into the frame as it's removed. Also, you may have to compress the rear intake valve spring to provide enough clearance for removal of the lower rocker cover (use special tool no. HD-3464 1 to compress the spring). On some other models, the rear bolts in the rear cylinder rocker cover can't be removed separately - loosen them all the way, then detach the box from the head with the bolts in the holes.

19 On later FLT/FXR models (1984-on), remove the left footboard and rear bracket or the footrest brackets. On FXR models, remove the shift lever.

20 Remove the screws securing the primary chaincase cover and separate the cover from the engine. If the cover is stuck, don't pry it loose. Instead, tap around the edges with a soft-face hammer. If necessary, remove the shift lever from the shaft to allow the cover to be removed. The pedal is secured on a splined shaft with a pinch bolt. **Note:** *On FX/Softail models (1985-on), remove the compensating sprocket shaft nut so the sprocket can come off the shaft as the engine is removed. On FLT/FXR models, remove the adjuster bolt as well.*

21 Remove the clutch and sprocket assemblies as described in Section 35. Disconnect the final drive chain/belt as described in Chapter 5.

22 Remove the bolts securing the primary chaincase to the engine and gearbox, accessible from the front and rear face of the chaincase; they will be locked in place with tab washers or safety wire.

23 Loosen the four bolts or nuts attaching the inner primary chaincase to the transmission (see Chapter 2B).

24 Unplug the rectifier/regulator (left-hand side of the engine) and the breaker point or sensor plate primary wires (right-hand side of the engine). Removal of the rectifier/regulator isn't necessary, but since it's in close proximity to the engine, it may be accidentally damaged. See Chapter 8 for removal procedures.

25 Disconnect its wire(s), and unscrew the oil pressure switch from oil pump cover (early models) or crankcase (later models) (see Chapter 8 if necessary). **Note:** *If the motorcycle has an Evolution engine, the oil lines must be disconnected from the pump and crankcase as well.*

26 On models with an automatic chain oiler, disconnect the chain oiler hose from the oil pump. Label the remaining oil lines and disconnect them from the oil pump or the back of the primary chaincase and oil tank. It may help to draw a sketch of the oil line connections to help during reassembly.

27 Remove the crankcase breather line from the oil pump.

28 The alternator rotor (magnet ring) must be removed on all early models except FLT

and FXR. Refer to Chapter 8 for the removal procedure.

29 The rear brake master cylinder assembly on FL models should be disconnected from the frame and pivoted down, out of the way. On FX models, the right-hand footrest and the brake pedal assembly must be removed (see Chapter 7). **Note:** *If you're working on an FX model with an Evolution engine, that doesn't have forward foot controls, remove the right-hand footrest, the brake pedal and the master cylinder assembly.*

30 On late 1978 through 1983 four-speed models, the starter and housing must be removed along with the primary chaincase. Label the wires to the starter to assist in reassembly. Refer to Chapter 8, if necessary, for the starter motor removal procedure.

31 Remove the speedometer drive cable from the crankcase on early models.

32 On models with an Evolution engine, detach the clutch cable from the engine bracket or detach the bracket from the engine.

33 Remove the two rear and the two front engine mounting bolts **(see illustrations)**. Make sure all electrical wires and control cables have been disconnected from the engine and are out of the way. Note: *On FXRT models, the front cylinder upper rocker cover must be removed, along with the two bolts from the lower fairing support bracket. Raise the right side of the fairing about one-inch and support it with wood blocks.*

34 The engine is very heavy and there's little room for maneuvering it out of the frame. An engine hoist would be very helpful, but it's not absolutely necessary **(see illustration)**. The engine should be lifted out of the frame to the right side.

Installation

35 As was evident during engine removal, there's very little clearance available for maneuvering the engine into the frame. You should have three persons available for this operation - two to lift the engine and locate it correctly, while the third person steadies the frame. Lift the engine in from the right-hand

2A

side of the machine.

36 When the engine is in position, install the two front and two rear engine mounting bolts, being careful not to damage the threads as they're tapped into place. Move the engine as necessary to align the bolt holes.

37 Install and tighten the nuts. Install the cylinder head support bracket and tighten the retaining nuts and the main bolt. Note the washer positioned between the frame lug and bracket - it shouldn't be left off or the stress will strain the bracket and frame.

38 Reverse the removal procedure for the remaining components. Note the following points:

a) Use new gaskets at all exhaust pipe connections.

b) Adjust the drive chain or belt, throttle cable(s) and clutch cable following the procedures in Chapter 1.

c) Fill the engine oil tank (and primary chaincase oil if applicable), and check the oil level (see Chapter 1).

7 Engine disassembly and reassembly - general information

1 Before disassembling the engine, clean the exterior with a degreaser and rinse it with water. A clean engine will make the job easier and prevent the possibility of getting dirt into the internal areas of the engine.

2 In addition to the precision measuring tools mentioned earlier, you will need a torque wrench, a valve spring compressor, oil gallery brushes (see illustration), a piston ring removal and installation tool and a piston ring compressor. Some new, clean engine oil of the correct grade and type, some engine assembly lube (or moly-based grease) and a tube of RTV (silicone) sealant will also be required.

3 An engine support stand made from short lengths of 2 x 4's bolted together will facilitate the disassembly and reassembly procedures. The perimeter of the mount should be just big enough to accommodate the engine crankcase. If you have an automotive-type engine stand, an adapter plate can be made from a piece of plate, some angle iron and some nuts and bolts.

4 When disassembling the engine, keep "mated" parts together (including gears, cylinders, pistons, etc. that have been in contact with each other during engine operation). These "mated" parts must be reused or replaced as an assembly.

5 Engine/transmission disassembly should be done in the following general order with reference to the appropriate Sections.

> Remove the cylinder heads
> Remove the cylinders
> Remove the pistons
> Remove the camshafts
> Remove the oil pump
> Remove the primary drive housing (see Chapter 2B)
> Remove the alternator rotor/stator coils and starter jackshaft (see Chapter 8)
> Separate the crankcase halves
> Remove the crankshaft and connecting rods

6 Reassembly is accomplished by reversing the general disassembly sequence.

8 Top Dead Center (TDC) - locating

1 Various procedures in this manual require placing one of the pistons at TDC on its compression stroke.

2 Remove the spark plugs (see Chapter 1).

3 Rotate the crankshaft as follows: With the primary cover installed, support the bike with the rear wheel off the ground. Place the transmission in fourth or fifth gear and turn the rear wheel in the forward direction.

7.2 A selection of brushes is required for cleaning holes and passages in the engine components

4 Slip a screwdriver into the removal slot of the spring cap retainer on the intake pushrod (this is the pushrod closest to the center of the engine, on either front or rear cylinder). Push down on the screwdriver and pry outward to remove the spring cap retainer (see Section 10).

5 Lift the lower pushrod cover to expose the intake lifter. Place a finger on the lifter so you can feel it rise and fall, then rotate the crankshaft as described above. Let the intake lifter rise, then fall, indicating that the intake valve has closed, which means the piston has traveled downward on the intake stroke.

6 Place a finger over the spark plug hole and turn the engine as described above. This will cause air pressure to build up against your finger as the piston rises on the compression stroke. Keep turning until the pressure stops building, then look into the spark plug hole with a flashlight. Turn the engine back and forth slightly while watching the top of the piston, which will go up and down slightly. Center the piston at the top of its stroke.

9.1a Detach the oil line between the rocker boxes (Shovelhead engine) . . .

9.1b . . . and the line between the crankcase and head (Shovelhead engine)

10.3 Carefully lift the rocker box off the studs (Shovelhead engine)

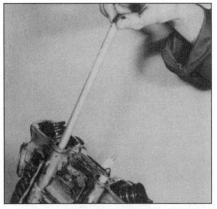

10.4a Remove the pushrods and mark them so they can be returned to their original locations

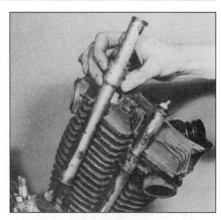

10.4b Once the rocker box has been detached, the pushrod tube can be removed as a complete unit

9 External oil lines (Shovelhead engine) - removal and installation

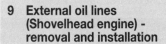

1 Unscrew the fittings and remove the oil lines, taking care not to damage them **(see illustrations)**.
2 Install new rubber seals on the oil lines.

Caution: Be sure the seals seat correctly, or oil flow to the cylinder heads may be cut off.

3 Position the oil lines and tighten the fitting nuts securely, but don't overtighten them and strip the threads.
4 Run the engine and check for leaks.

10 Cylinder heads, rocker arms, pushrods and lifters - removal and installation

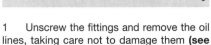

Removal

Shovelhead engine

1 Begin by removing the intake manifold (if it's still in place). It's secured by two clamps. Loosen both clamp screws and pull the intake manifold out of the head fittings. Note that on early models there's an O-ring inside each port, to ensure an airtight joint.
2 Remove the rocker boxes. Begin by unscrewing the fittings and removing the small diameter external oil lines, which are easily damaged (see Section 9).
3 Each rocker box is secured by several nuts, which should be loosened in 1/4-turn increments. Make sure the valves of the cylinder involved are closed, to avoid stress on the casting from an open valve (place the cylinder at TDC compression as described in Section 8). Mark the rocker boxes so they can't be interchanged and remove them **(see illustration)**.
4 The pushrods should be lifted out of the tubes and clearly marked to make sure they're replaced in their original locations

(see illustration). The pushrod tubes can then be detached, each as a complete assembly **(see illustration)**.
5 Each cylinder head is retained by five bolts, which will be very tight **(see illustration)**. Loosen them in 1/4-turn increments, following a criss-cross pattern, until they can be removed by hand. If the cylinder head isn't free after the bolts have been removed, tap it lightly with a soft-face hammer in an attempt to break the seal. Don't attempt to pry it off, or fins will be broken. There's no point in marking the cylinder heads, since they cannot be interchanged.
6 On late 1981 and early 1982 models, remove the clamp and oil hose from the fitting on each cylinder.
7 **Note:** *The hydraulic tappets/cam followers are installed in pairs in two separate tappet guides, secured at the top of the case by four small bolts. On Shovelhead engines, each tappet is a two-piece assembly (separate tappet and cam follower) and they may fall apart as they're removed.* Use a scribe and mark the position of the tappet guide on the case to ensure proper alignment during installation.

8 Remove the bolts securing the guide, then fashion a U-shaped tool from a large paper clip, engage the tool in the tappets to hold them in place and lift the tappets and guide out as an assembly **(see illustration)**. It may be necessary to tap around the edge of the guide with a soft-faced mallet to break the gasket seal. Be careful not to drop the tappets out the bottom of the guide, into the case.
9 Label the components or store them so they will be reinstalled in the same locations.
10 Remove the pushrod tube seals and washers from the top of each tappet guide.
11 Remove all traces of the old gasket and sealant from the guide and crankcase.
12 Repeat the procedure for the remaining guide.

Evolution engine

13 Push down on the front pushrod tube spring retainer, then remove the keeper and pull the upper tube out of the recess in the underside of the cylinder head (it's a good idea to start with the front head). Repeat the procedure for the remaining pushrod tube.
14 Remove the Allen-head screws and

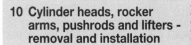

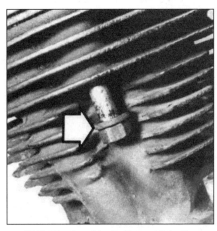

10.5 The head bolts thread into the bottom of the cylinder head

10.8 Don't let the tappets fall into the case as the guide is removed

2A

10.14 Remove the Allen-head screws (arrows) and detach the upper rocker arm cover (Evolution engine) . . .

10.15 . . . then lift off the middle rocker arm cover and gasket (arrow) (Evolution engine)

10.16 Remove the four large bolts (arrows), then with the valves completely closed, tap out the rocker shafts from the left side (Evolution engine)

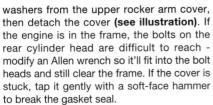

washers from the upper rocker arm cover, then detach the cover (see illustration). If the engine is in the frame, the bolts on the rear cylinder head are difficult to reach - modify an Allen wrench so it'll fit into the bolt heads and still clear the frame. If the cover is stuck, tap it gently with a soft-face hammer to break the gasket seal.

15   Remove the middle rocker arm cover (see illustration). Remove and discard all rocker cover gaskets and use new ones during reassembly.

16   Turn the crankshaft until both valves in the affected head are closed, then remove the large bolts retaining the lower rocker arm cover (see illustration).

17   Carefully tap the rocker arm shafts out of the lower rocker arm cover (from the left side), then lift out the rocker arms and remove the pushrods and tubes (the pushrods must not be interchanged or turned end-for-end, so make sure they're marked!). Make sure the parts are marked or stored in marked containers - they must be returned to their original locations during reassembly.

18   Remove the lower rocker arm cover-to-cylinder head bolts (see illustration). There are two Allen-head bolts and three hex-head bolts.

19   Detach the lower rocker arm cover and gaskets. Discard the gaskets and use new ones during reassembly.

20   Loosen the cylinder head bolts in 1/8-turn increments, following a criss-cross pattern. If they aren't loosened gradually, the head, cylinder or crankcase studs may be distorted. Remove the bolts and any washers installed under them (on 1988 and later models, washers aren't used).

21   Carefully lift off the cylinder head, then remove the gasket and O-rings around the dowel sleeves. Discard the gasket and O-rings and use new ones during installation.

22   Refer to Steps 7 through 11 above to remove the tappets and guides. Note that Evolution engines use one-piece tappet and roller assemblies.

Inspection

Pushrods

23   Check the ends of the pushrods where they ride in the tappets and the rocker arms (see illustration). Check for distortion by rolling them on a flat surface such as a pane of glass. If wear or distortion is evident, new pushrods should be installed.

Rocker arms

24   To disassemble a rocker box on Shovelhead engines, unscrew the rocker arm shaft end caps found on the right-hand side of each rocker box (see illustrations).

25   Check the rocker arm bushings and the shafts for evidence of excessive wear and damage (see illustrations).

26   Measure the outside diameter of the shaft (where it rides in the bushings) and the inside diameter of the rocker arm bushings. Subtract the diameter from the bushing diameter to obtain the clearance. If it's excessive, install new parts or have the bushings in the rocker arm(s) replaced by a dealer service department or other qualified shop.

27   Check each rocker arm where it con-

10.18 Remove and label the rocker arms, then remove the three hex bolts and two Allen bolts to detach the lower rocker arm cover (Evolution engine)

tacts the pushrod and valve stem. If cracks, scuffing or breakthrough in the case hardened surface are evident, install a new rocker arm.

10.23 Check the pushrod ends for wear and make sure the oil holes (Evolution engine) are clear

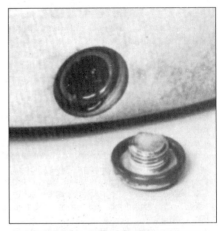

10.24a On Shovelhead engines, remove the rocker shaft end cap . . .

10.24b ... and unscrew the acorn nut from the other end

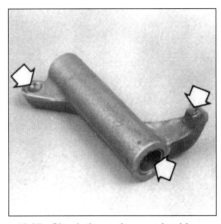

10.25a Check the rocker arm bushings, pushrod recesses and valve stem pads for wear and damage (arrows)

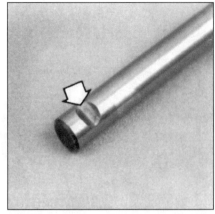

10.25b Check the rocker shafts for wear on the friction surfaces - the Evolution engine shafts have a cutout (arrow) for the bolt to pass through

Lifters

28 Make sure the rollers on the lifters turn freely, with no play on their pins. If you find either problem, replace the lifter.

29 Measure the diameter of the lifters and lifter bores, using a micrometer and bore gauge. Calculate the difference and compare it to the value listed in this Chapter's Specifications. If it's beyond the specified range, replace the lifters or the crankcase, whichever is worn.

30 Check the lifters for worn pushrod sockets. Make sure the plunger inside the lifter is fully in contact with the lifter C-clip. Operate the plunger inside the lifter and make sure it moves freely. Replace the lifter if problems are found.

31 Place the lifters in clean engine oil and keep them in a covered container until they're reinstalled.

Installation

Shovelhead engine

32 If the rocker boxes have been disassembled, they should now be reassembled, keeping the parts in their original locations. Oil the rocker shafts prior to insertion and

install new sealing washers behind the acorn nuts. Use new O-rings behind the caps on the other end.

33 Place a new rocker box gasket over the studs in the cylinder head. To prevent the heel of each rocker arm from contacting the valve springs when the rocker box is attached to the cylinder head, place the inverted rocker box on the workbench and lower the cylinder head into position. Hold the two components together, invert them and install the nuts. Tighten the nuts in I/4-turn increments, following a criss-cross pattern, to the recommended torque.

34 Install the cylinder heads. Use new cylinder head gaskets (no sealant) and tighten the bolts in a criss-cross pattern in three steps.

35 Separate the components of each pushrod tube by removing the keeper from the upper portion of each tube. Replace the tube seals with new ones. Reassemble each pushrod tube, without the keeper, in the retracted position and insert them into the guide block recesses.

36 The pushrods should be installed in the following sequence. Rotate the crankshaft until the front cylinder exhaust tappet is just

10.37 Install each pushrod tube separately - make sure the pushrods are returned to their original locations

beginning to move. There's now sufficient clearance to install the rear cylinder exhaust pushrod. If necessary, loosen the pushrod adjustment locknut and screw in the adjuster to shorten the pushrod. Rotate the crankshaft until the front cylinder intake tappet is just beginning to move and install the rear cylinder intake pushrod. Repeat the procedure to install the front cylinder pushrods.

37 Rotate the crankshaft until one valve is completely open. The counterpart of this valve on the other cylinder is now completely closed and the tappet clearance can be checked accurately. Loosen the pushrod adjuster locknut and screw in the adjuster until there's perceptible play. Slowly unscrew the adjuster until the play is just eliminated. Mark the adjuster with a piece of chalk and then screw it down exactly four (4) turns. If the hydraulic tappet is dry (such as during reassembly), turn the adjusting screw down until the tappet is completely compressed. Mark the position, then turn the adjuster up exactly 1-3/4 turns on 1970 through early 1978 models, or exactly 1-1/2 turns on late 1978 through 1983 models. Tighten the locknut. Extend the pushrod tube so the upper and lower ends of the tube are located against the seals and then install the keeper **(see illustration)**.

38 Repeat the procedure for the remaining three pushrods.

39 Install the rocker oil feed line that runs from the crankcase to the rear rocker box and also the rocker box connection oil feed line. Use new rubber seals at each union.

40 Install the intake manifold (make sure the clamps are completely tight to prevent air leaks). Install new O-rings.

Evolution engine

Note: *Before beginning this procedure, clean the cylinder head bolt threads, then lubricate them with clean engine oil and thread the bolts onto the studs to make sure they don't bind.*

2A

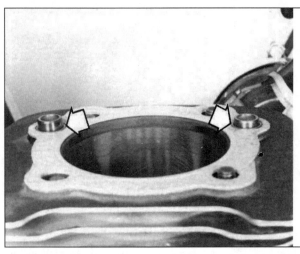

10.41 On Evolution engines, position the O-rings (arrows) over the dowel sleeves first, then install the head gasket and make sure it's aligned properly

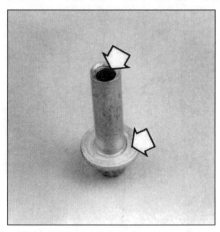

10.43 Clean and lubricate the threads and underside of each head bolt (arrows) before installing them (Evolution engine)

41 Install new O-rings over the dowel sleeves, then position the new head gasket on the cylinder barrel **(see illustration)**. No sealant is required on the head gaskets.

42 Make sure the bolt holes in the head are clean, then carefully lower it onto the cylinder - the dowel sleeves must enter the holes and align the head.

43 Lubricate the threads and the underside of each bolt head with engine oil **(see illustration)**.

44 Slip the washers over the bolts (where applicable), then install the bolts finger-tight.

Caution: The procedure for tightening the cylinder head bolts is extremely critical to prevent gasket leaks, stud failure and cylinder or head distortion.

45 Refer to the accompanying illustration

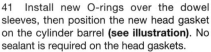

FRONT CYLINDER

REAR CYLINDER

2534-2a-10.18 HAYNES

10.45 Cylinder head bolt tightening/loosening sequence (Evolution engine)

and tighten bolt number one to 7 ft-lbs (9 Nm) **(see illustration)**. Tighten the remaining bolts to 7 to 9 ft-lbs (19 to 21 Nm) following the sequence shown.

46 Tighten each bolt to 12 to 14 ft-lbs following the sequence in **illustration 10.45**. **Note:** *On 1984 FXST models, tighten the bolts to 15 to 17 ft-lbs (20 to 23 Nm).*

47 Mark each bolt and the cylinder head with a felt-tip pen **(see illustration)**.

48 Turn each bolt, in the recommended sequence, an additional 90-degrees (1/4-turn) **(see illustration)**. **Note:** *On 1984 FXST models, don't turn the bolts 90-degrees. Instead, tighten them to 24 to 26 ft-lbs (33 to 35 Nm).*

49 Install the rocker cover gaskets with the sealant beads facing UP **(see illustration)**.

50 Squirt oil through the opening in the top of the timing case so the timing gears and camshaft lobes are liberally coated with it.

51 Place new gaskets in position over the openings in the case

52 Lubricate the components of each tappet and guide block. On Shovelhead engines, the tappets must be installed with the machined faces and the oil holes facing

in **(see illustration)**.

53 To prevent the tappets from falling into the gearcase during reassembly, pinch the two tappets together as the guide block is lowered into position. **Note:** *The guide blocks are marked FRONT and REAR to indicate which cylinder they belong with* **(see illustration)**.

54 Install and tighten the four bolts that retain each tappet guide block. You'll need a 12-point socket on some models to tighten the bolts. **Note:** *On Evolution engines, a tappet guide alignment tool must be threaded into the bolt hole nearest the tappet oil feed hole, then the other three bolts can be installed and tightened. Remove the guide tool, install the fourth bolt and tighten it securely.*

55 Install the hydraulic tappet oil screen and spring in the opening in the top of the case using a new sealing washer (see the oil change procedure in Chapter 1, if necessary).

56 On late 1981 and early 1982 models, attach the oil hose and secure it in position

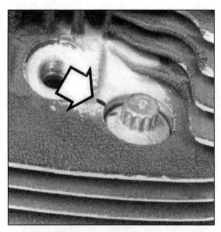

10.47 After the head bolts are all at the specified torque, make a mark on each bolt head flange and extend it onto the head (arrow)

10.48 Turn each head bolt an additional 90-degrees (1/4-turn) in an uninterrupted motion - this must be done exactly as described to prevent head gasket leaks

10.49 Position the new rocker cover gaskets on the cylinder head (arrows) with the sealant beads facing up

10.63a Position new gaskets (arrows) in the lower rocker arm cover grooves . . .

with a hose clamp.

57 Install new seals and assemble the pushrod tubes, then slip the pushrods into the tubes and install them in their original locations. Make sure they're seated in the tappets. **Note:** *The pushrods are color coded to ensure correct installation (rear exhaust -*

10.63b . . . then install the middle rocker arm cover and a new gasket (arrow) - use Gaska-cinch to hold the gaskets in the grooves if necessary

10.52 The oil hole in the tappet (arrow) MUST face in (Shovelhead engine)

purple; rear intake - blue; front intake - yellow; front exhaust - green). Don't turn the pushrods end-for-end; they must be mated with the rocker arm or tappet just like they were originally.

58 Make sure tappets for the cylinder being reassembled are on the cam lobe base circles (turn the crankshaft if necessary to reposition them).

59 Lubricate the rocker arm faces with moly-based grease, assemble the rocker arms and shafts in the lower rocker arm cover and slip all the bolts through the holes. The cutouts in the shafts must be positioned so the bolts will pass through the cover and the cutouts and retain the shafts.

60 Position the lower rocker arm cover on the head and thread all the bolts into place finger-tight. Make sure the pushrods are engaged in the rocker arm recesses.

61 Tighten the bolts in 1/4-turn increments, following a criss-cross pattern, to the specified torque. This will allow the tappets to bleed down slowly.

62 Make sure the pushrods spin freely.

63 Position new gaskets in the lower rocker arm cover **(see illustration)**, then install the middle rocker arm cover and a

10.64 Rubber umbrella valve location in rear cylinder (1993 and later models)

10.53 The guide blocks are marked FRONT and REAR so they can be installed in the correct cylinder

new gasket **(see illustration)**.

64 On 1993 and later models, check the breather passage from the rubber umbrella valve in the inner corner of each middle rocker cover to the bleed bolt hole on the side of the head - it should be unrestricted. If the rubber valve is damaged replace it **(see illustration)**.

65 Install the upper rocker arm cover and screws. Tighten the screws after making sure the middle rocker arm cover is positioned evenly on all sides.

11 Valves/valve seats/valve guides - servicing

1 Because of the complex nature of this job and the special tools and equipment required, servicing of the valves, the valve seats and the valve guides (commonly known as a valve job) is best left to a professional.

2 The home mechanic can, however, remove and disassemble the head, do the initial cleaning and inspection, then reassemble and deliver the head to a dealer service department or properly equipped motorcycle repair shop for the actual valve servicing. Refer to Section 12 for those procedures.

3 The dealer service department will remove the valves and springs, recondition or replace the valves and valve seats, replace the valve guides, check and replace the valve springs, spring retainers and keepers (as necessary), replace the valve seals with new ones and reassemble the valve components.

4 After the valve job has been performed, the head will be in like-new condition. When the head is returned, be sure to clean it again very thoroughly before installation on the engine to remove any metal particles or abrasive grit that may still be present from the valve service operations. Use compressed air, if available, to blow out all the holes and passages.

2A

12.7a Compress the springs with a valve spring compressor, then remove the keepers (arrows) with a magnet or needle-nose pliers

12 Cylinder head and valves - disassembly, inspection and reassembly

1   As mentioned in the previous Section, valve servicing and valve guide replacement should be left to a dealer service department or motorcycle repair shop. However, disassembly, cleaning and inspection of the valves and related components can be done (if the necessary special tools are available) by the home mechanic. This way no expense is incurred if the inspection reveals that service work is not required at this time.

2   To properly disassemble the valve components without the risk of damaging them, a valve spring compressor is absolutely necessary. This special tool can usually be rented, but if it's not available, have a dealer service department or motorcycle repair shop handle the entire process of disassembly, inspection, service or repair (if required) and reassembly of the valves.

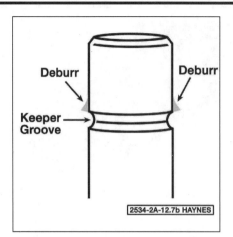

12.7b If the valve binds in the guide, deburr the area above the keeper groove

Disassembly

3   Remove the cylinder head from the engine (see Section 10).

4   Before the valves are removed, scrape away any traces of gasket material from the head gasket sealing surface. Work slowly and do not nick or gouge the soft aluminum of the head. Gasket removing solvents, which work very well, are available at most motorcycle shops and auto parts stores.

5   Carefully scrape all carbon deposits out of the combustion chamber area. A hand held wire brush or a piece of fine emery cloth can be used once the majority of deposits have been scraped away. Do not use a wire brush mounted in a drill motor, or one with extremely stiff bristles, as the head material is soft and may be eroded away or scratched by the wire brush.

6   Before proceeding, arrange to label and store the valves along with their related components so they can be kept separate and reinstalled in the same valve guides they are removed from (again, plastic bags work well for this).

7   Compress the valve spring on the first valve with a spring compressor, then remove the keepers and the retainer from the valve assembly **(see illustration)**. Do not compress the springs any more than is absolutely necessary. Carefully release the valve spring compressor and remove the springs and the valve from the head. If the valve binds in the guide (won't pull through), push it back into the head and deburr the area around the keeper groove with a very fine file or whetstone **(see illustration)**.

8   Repeat the procedure for the remaining valves. Remember to keep the parts for each valve together so they can be reinstalled in the same location.

9   Once the valves have been removed and labeled, pull off the valve stem seals with pliers and discard them (the old seals should never be reused), then remove the spring seats.

10   Next, clean the cylinder head with solvent and dry it thoroughly. Compressed air will speed the drying process and ensure that all holes and recessed areas are clean.

11   Clean all of the valve springs, keepers, retainers and spring seats with solvent and dry them thoroughly. Do the parts from one valve at a time so that no mixing of parts between valves occurs.

12   Scrape off any deposits that may have formed on the valve, then use a motorized wire brush to remove deposits from the valve heads and stems. Again, make sure the valves do not get mixed up.

Inspection

HAYNES HINT *Refer to Tools and Workshop Tips in the Reference section for details of how to read a micrometer and dial gauges.*

13   Inspect the head very carefully for cracks and other damage. If cracks are found, a new head will be required.

14   Using a precision straightedge and a feeler gauge, check the head gasket mating

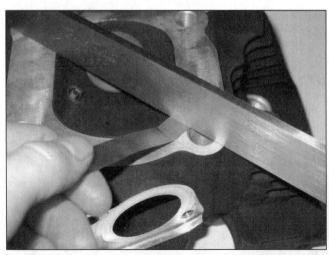

12.14 Lay a precision straightedge across the cylinder head and try to slide a feeler gauge of the specified thickness (equal to the maximum allowable warpage) under it

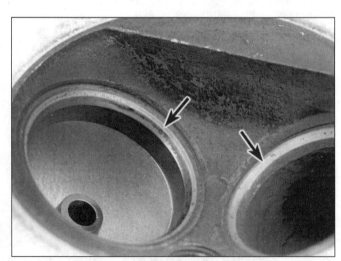

12.15a Check the valve seats (arrows) in each head - look for pits, cracks and burned areas

12.15b Measuring the valve seat width

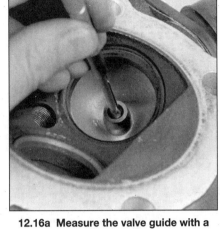

12.16a Measure the valve guide with a small hole gauge . . .

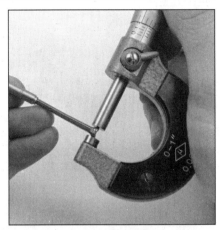

12.16b . . . then measure the gauge with a micrometer

surface for warpage. Lay the straightedge lengthwise, across the head and diagonally (corner-to-corner), intersecting the head bolt holes. Try to slip a feeler gauge of the same thickness as the warpage limit listed in this Chapter's Specifications under it, on either side of the combustion chamber **(see illustration)**. If the feeler gauge can be inserted between the head and the straightedge, the head is warped and must either be machined or, if warpage is excessive, replaced with a new one.

15   Examine the valve seats **(see illustration)**. If they are pitted, cracked or burned, the head will require valve service that is beyond the scope of the home mechanic. Measure the valve seat width and compare it to this Chapter's Specifications **(see illustration)**. If it is not within the specified range, or if it varies around its circumference, valve service work is required.

16   Clean the valve guides to remove any carbon buildup, then measure the inside diameters of the guides (at both ends and the center of the guide) with a small hole gauge and a 0-to-1-inch micrometer **(see illustrations)**. If the guides exceed the maxi-

mum value given in the Chapter's Specifications, they must be replaced. The guides are measured at the ends and at the center to determine if they are worn in a bell-mouth pattern (more wear at the ends). If they are, guide replacement is an absolute must.

17   Carefully inspect each valve face for cracks, pits and burned spots **(see illustration)**. Check the valve stem and the keeper groove area for cracks **(see illustration)**. Rotate the valve and check for any obvious indication that it is bent. Check the end of the stem for pitting and excessive wear. The presence of any of the above conditions indicates the need for valve servicing.

18   Measure the valve stem diameter and replace if it exceeds the minimum value listed in this Chapter's Specifications **(see illustration)**. Also check the valve stem for bending. Set the valve in a V-block with a dial indicator touching the middle of the stem. Rotate the valve and note the reading on the gauge. If the stem runout exceeds the value listed in this Chapter's Specifications, replace the valve.

19   Check the end of each valve spring for wear and pitting. Measure the free length

12.17a Check the valve face and margin for wear and cracks

(see illustration) and compare it to this Chapter's Specifications. Any springs that are shorter than specified have sagged and should not be reused. Stand the spring on a flat surface and check it for squareness **(see illustration)**.

2A

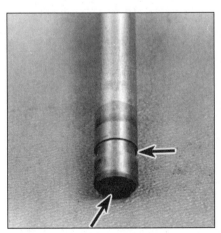

12.17b Look for wear on the end of the valve stem and make sure the keeper groove isn't distorted in any way

12.18 Measure the valve stem diameter with a micrometer

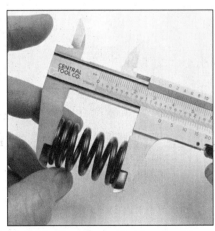

12.19a Measure the free length of the valve springs

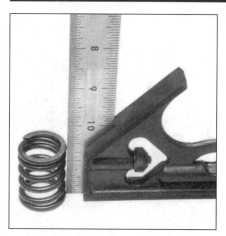

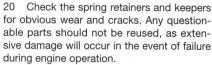

12.19b Check the valve springs for squareness

20   Check the spring retainers and keepers for obvious wear and cracks. Any questionable parts should not be reused, as extensive damage will occur in the event of failure during engine operation.

21   If the inspection indicates that no service work is required, the valve components can be reinstalled in the head.

Reassembly

22   Before installing the valves in the head, they should be lapped to ensure a positive seal between the valves and seats. This procedure requires fine valve lapping compound (available at auto parts stores) and a valve lapping tool. If a lapping tool is not available, a piece of rubber or plastic hose can be slipped over the valve stem (after the valve has been installed in the guide) and used to turn the valve.

23   Apply a small amount of fine lapping compound to the valve face **(see illustration)**, then slip the valve into the guide. **Note:** *Make sure the valve is installed in the correct guide and be careful not to get any lapping compound on the valve stem.*

24   Attach the lapping tool (or hose) to the valve and rotate the tool between the palms

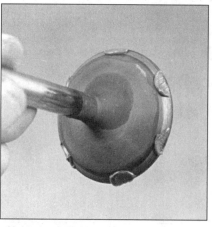

12.23 Apply the lapping compound very sparingly, in small dabs, to the valve face only

of your hands **(see illustration)**. Use a back-and-forth motion rather than a circular motion. Lift the valve off the seat and turn it at regular intervals to distribute the lapping compound properly **(see illustration)**. Continue the lapping procedure until the valve face and seat contact area is of uniform width and unbroken around the entire circumference of the valve face and seat **(see illustrations)**.

25   Carefully remove the valve from the guide and wipe off all traces of lapping compound. Use solvent to clean the valve and wipe the seat area thoroughly with a solvent soaked cloth. Repeat the procedure for the remaining valves.

26   Lay the spring seats in place in the cylinder head, then install new valve stem seals on each of the guides. Use an appropriate size deep socket to push the seals into place until they are properly seated. Don't twist or cock them, or they will not seal properly against the valve stems. Also, don't remove them again or they will be damaged.

27   Coat the valve stems with assembly lube or moly-based grease, then install one of them into its guide. Next, install the spring

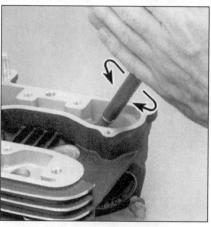

12.24a Rotate the lapping tool or hose back-and-forth between the palms of your hands

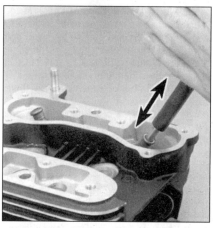

12.24b Lift the tool and valve periodically to redistribute the lapping compound on the valve face and seat

seats, springs and retainers, compress the springs and install the keepers. When compressing the springs with the valve spring compressor, depress them only as far as is absolutely necessary to slip the keepers into place. Apply a small amount of grease to the

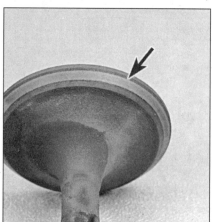

12.24c After lapping, the valve face should exhibit a uniform, unbroken contact pattern (arrow). . .

12.24d . . .and the seat should be the specified width (arrow) with a smooth, unbroken appearance

12.27 A small dab of grease will help hold the keepers in place on the valve spring while the valve is released

13.3 Carefully lift off the cylinder (after removing the base nuts on Shovelhead engines) - don't let the piston strike the crankcase

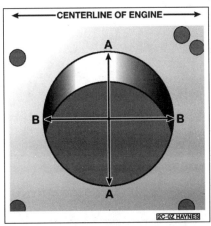

13.6 Measure the cylinder diameter in two directions, at the top, center and bottom of travel

13.14 A piston ring compressor . . .

keepers **(see illustration)** to help hold them in place as the pressure is released from the springs. Make certain that the keepers are securely locked in their retaining grooves.

28   Support the cylinder head on blocks so the valves can't contact the workbench top, then very gently tap each of the valve stems with a soft-faced hammer. This will help seat the keepers in their grooves.

29   Once all of the valves have been installed in the head, check for proper valve sealing by pouring a small amount of solvent into each of the valve ports. If the solvent leaks past the valve(s) into the combustion chamber area, disassemble the valve(s) and repeat the lapping procedure, then reinstall the valve(s) and repeat the check. Repeat the procedure until a satisfactory seal is obtained.

13 Cylinders - removal, inspection and installation

Removal

1   Before you start, obtain four six-inch lengths of 1/2-inch inside diameter tubing for each cylinder. You'll need these to slip over the studs.

2   Following the procedure given in Section 10, remove the cylinder head and pushrods (the lifters don't have to be removed). Make sure the crankshaft is positioned at Top Dead Center (TDC) for the cylinder you're working on (see Section 8).

3   If you're working on a Shovelhead engine, remove the four cylinder base nuts. On all models, lift the cylinder straight up just until you can stuff clean shop towels around the piston, in the space between the cylinder and crankcase **(see illustration)**. If the cylinder is stuck, tap around its perimeter with a soft-faced hammer. Don't attempt to pry between the cylinder and the crankcase, as you will ruin the sealing surfaces.

4   Lift the cylinder straight off the studs. Remove the cylinder base gasket.

Inspection

Caution: Don't attempt to separate the liner from the cylinder.

5   Check the cylinder walls carefully for scratches and score marks.

6   Using the appropriate precision measuring tools, check each cylinder's diameter 1/2-inch down from the top, halfway down the ring travel area, and at the bottom of the ring travel area, parallel to the crankshaft axis **(see illustration)**. Next, measure each cylinder's diameter at the same three locations across the crankshaft axis. Compare the results to this Chapter's Specifications. If the cylinder walls are tapered, out-of-round, worn beyond the specified limits, or badly scuffed or scored, have them rebored and honed by a dealer service department or a motorcycle repair shop. If a rebore is done, oversize pistons and rings will be required as well. Oversize pistons are listed in this Chapter's Specifications. Remove the torque plates after taking the measurements.

7   Lay a straightedge across the cylinder top surface and measure any gap between the straightedge and surface with a feeler gauge. Repeat the measurement on the cylinder bottom gasket surface. If either surface is warped beyond the limit listed in this Chapter's Specifications, replace the cylinder and piston.

8   If they are in reasonably good condition and not worn to the outside of the limits, and if the piston-to-cylinder clearances can be maintained properly (see Section 14), then the cylinders do not have to be rebored; honing is all that is necessary.

9   To perform the honing operation you will need the proper size flexible hone with fine stones, or a "bottle brush" type hone, plenty of light oil or honing oil, some shop towels and an electric drill motor. Harley-Davidson recommends a bottle-brush type hone with 240-grit stones. Hold the cylinder

block in a vise (cushioned with soft jaws or wood blocks) when performing the honing operation. Mount the hone in the drill motor, compress the stones and slip the hone into the cylinder. Lubricate the cylinder thoroughly, turn on the drill and move the hone up and down in the cylinder at a pace which will produce a fine crosshatch pattern on the cylinder wall with the crosshatch lines intersecting at a 60-degree angle - the angle is important to obtain good ring seating. Be sure to use plenty of lubricant and do not take off any more material than is absolutely necessary to produce the desired effect. Do not withdraw the hone from the cylinder while it is running. Instead, shut off the drill and continue moving the hone up and down in the cylinder until it comes to a complete stop, then compress the stones and withdraw the hone. Wipe the oil out of the cylinder and repeat the procedure on the remaining cylinder. Remember, do not remove too much material from the cylinder wall. If you do not have the tools, or do not desire to perform the honing operation, a dealer service department or motorcycle repair shop will generally do it for a reasonable fee.

10   Next, the cylinders must be thoroughly washed with warm soapy water to remove all traces of the abrasive grit produced during the honing operation. Be sure to run a brush through the bolt holes and flush them with running water. After rinsing, dry the cylinders thoroughly and apply a coat of light, rust-preventative oil to all machined surfaces.

Installation

11   Lubricate the cylinder bore, piston and rings with plenty of clean engine oil.

12   Install the new cylinder base gasket on the cylinder.

13   Slowly rotate the crankshaft until the piston is at top dead center.

14   Attach a piston ring compressor to the piston and compress the piston rings **(see illustration)**. A large hose clamp can be used instead - just make sure it doesn't scratch the piston, and don't tighten it too much.

2A

13.15 . . . makes installation of the cylinders much easier

14.3a Using a sharp scribe, scratch the cylinder position (front or rear) into the piston crowns - if there isn't an arrow mark pointing to the front, make one

14.3b Wear eye protection and pry the circlip out of the groove with a pointed tool

15 Install the cylinder over the piston and carefully lower it down until the piston crown fits into the cylinder liner (see illustration). Push down on the cylinder, making sure the piston doesn't get cocked sideways, until the bottom of the cylinder liner slides down past the piston rings. A wood or plastic hammer handle can be used to gently tap the cylinder down, but don't use too much force or the piston will be damaged.

18 Remove the piston ring compressor or hose clamp, being careful not to scratch the piston. Raise the piston enough to remove the support tool.

19 The remainder of installation is the reverse of removal. If you're working on a Shovelhead, tighten the cylinder base nuts to the torque listed in this Chapter's Specifications.

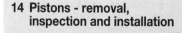

14 Pistons - removal, inspection and installation

1 The pistons are attached to the connecting rods with piston pins that are a slip fit in the pistons and rods.

2 Before removing the pistons from the rods, stuff a clean shop towel into each crankcase hole, around the connecting rod. This will prevent the circlips from falling into the crankcase if they are inadvertently dropped.

Removal

3 Using a sharp scribe, scratch the position of each piston (front or rear cylinder) into its crown. Each piston should also have an arrow pointing toward the front of the engine (see illustration). If not, scribe an arrow into the piston crown before removal. Support the piston and remove the circlip with needle-nose pliers or a pointed tool (see illustration). Push the piston pin out with fingers (see illustration). If the pin won't come out, fabricate a piston pin removal tool from threaded stock (stud), nuts, washers and a piece of pipe (see illustration).

4 Push the piston pin out from the opposite end to free the piston from the rod. You may have to deburr the area around the groove to enable the pin to slide out (use a triangular file for this procedure). Repeat the procedure for the other piston.

14.3c Push the piston pin part-way out, then pull it the rest of the way

Inspection

5 Before the inspection process can be carried out, the pistons must be cleaned and the old piston rings removed.

6 Using a piston ring installation tool, carefully remove the rings from the pistons (see illustration). Do not nick or gouge the pistons in the process.

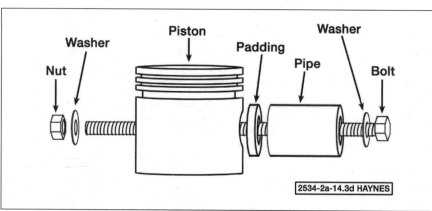

14.3d The piston should come out with hand pressure - if it doesn't, this tool can be fabricated from readily available parts

14.6 Remove the piston rings with a ring removal and installation tool

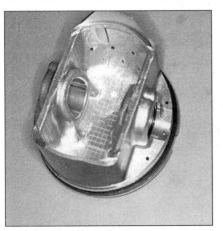

14.11 Check the piston pin bore and the piston skirt for wear, and make sure the internal holes are clear

14.13 Measure the piston ring-to-groove clearance with a feeler gauge

7   Scrape all traces of carbon from the tops of the pistons. A hand-held wire brush or a piece of fine emery cloth can be used once most of the deposits have been scraped away. Do not, under any circumstances, use a wire brush mounted in a drill motor to remove deposits from the pistons; the piston material is soft and will be eroded away by the wire brush.

8   Use a piston ring groove cleaning tool to remove any carbon deposits from the ring grooves. If a tool is not available, a piece broken off the old ring will do the job. Be very careful to remove only the carbon deposits. Do not remove any metal and do not nick or gouge the sides of the ring grooves.

9   Once the deposits have been removed, clean the pistons with solvent and dry them thoroughly. Make sure the oil return holes below the oil ring grooves are clear.

10   If the pistons are not damaged or worn excessively and if the cylinders are not rebored, new pistons will not be necessary. Normal piston wear appears as even, vertical wear on the thrust surfaces of the piston and slight looseness of the top ring in its groove. New piston rings, on the other hand, should always be used when an engine is rebuilt.

11   Carefully inspect each piston for cracks around the skirt, at the pin bosses and at the ring lands **(see illustration)**.

12   Look for scoring and scuffing on the thrust faces of the skirt, holes in the piston crown and burned areas at the edge of the crown. If the skirt is scored or scuffed, the engine may have been suffering from overheating and/or abnormal combustion, which caused excessively high operating temperatures. The oil pump should be checked thoroughly. A hole in the piston crown, an extreme to be sure, is an indication that abnormal combustion (pre-ignition) was occurring. Burned areas at the edge of the piston crown are usually evidence of spark knock (detonation). If any of the above problems exist, the causes must be corrected or the damage will occur again.

13   Measure the piston ring-to-groove clearance by laying a new piston ring in the ring groove and slipping a feeler gauge in beside it **(see illustration)**. Check the clearance at three or four locations around the groove. Be sure to use the correct ring for each groove; they are different. If the clearance is greater than specified, new pistons will have to be used when the engine is reassembled.

14   Check the piston-to-bore clearance by measuring the bore (see Section 13) and the piston diameter. Make sure that the pistons and cylinders are correctly matched. Measure the piston across the skirt on the thrust faces at a 90-degree angle to the piston pin, about 1/2-inch (13 mm) up from the bottom of the skirt **(see illustration)**. Subtract the piston diameter from the bore diameter to obtain the clearance. If it is greater than specified, the cylinders will have to be rebored and new oversized pistons and rings installed. If the appropriate precision measuring tools are not available, the piston-to-cylinder clearances can be obtained, though not quite as accurately, using feeler gauge stock. Feeler gauge stock comes in 12-inch lengths and various thicknesses and is generally available at auto parts stores. To check the clearance, select a piece of feeler gauge stock equal to the piston-to-cylinder clearance listed in this Chapter's Specifications. Slip the gauge into the cylinder alongside of the piston. The cylinder should be upside down and the piston must be positioned exactly as it normally would be. Place the feeler gauge between the piston and cylinder on one of the thrust faces (90-degrees to the piston pin bore). The piston should slip through the cylinder (with the feeler gauge in place) with moderate pressure. If it falls through, or slides through easily, the clearance is excessive and a new piston will be required. If the piston binds at the lower end of the cylinder and is loose toward the top, the cylinder is tapered, and if tight spots are encountered as the feeler gauge is placed at different points around the cylinder, the cylinder is out-of-round. Repeat the procedure for the remaining piston and cylinder. Be sure to have the cylinders and pistons checked by a dealer service department or a motorcycle repair shop to confirm your findings before purchasing new parts.

15   Apply clean engine oil to the pin, insert it into the piston and check for freeplay by rocking the pin back-and-forth. If the pin is loose, new pistons and pins must be installed.

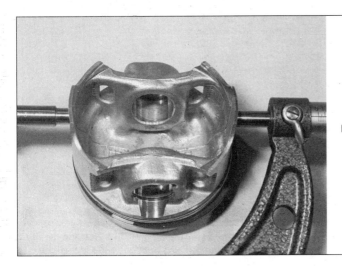

14.14 Measure the piston diameter with a micrometer

2A

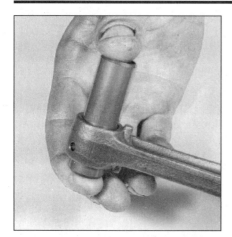

14.16 Slip the piston into the rod and try to rock it back-and-forth to check for looseness

14.18a On Shovelhead engines, the cast rib on the pin boss must be on the right-hand side of the engine (arrow)

14.18b Make sure both piston pin circlips are securely seated in the piston grooves

16   Repeat Step 15, this time inserting the pin into the connecting rod **(see illustration)**. If the pin is loose, measure the pin diameter and the pin bushing bore in the connecting rod (or have this done by a dealer service department or machine shop). Replace the piston and pin if the pin is worn; have the pin bushing pressed out and a new one pressed in if it's worn.

17   Refer to Section 15 and install the rings on the pistons.

Installation

18   Install the piston in its original location (front or rear cylinder) with the arrow pointing to the front of the engine. On Shovelhead engines, there's a raised rib on the underside of the piston pin boss; this must be on the right-hand side of the engine **(see illustration)**. Lubricate the pin and the rod bore with clean engine oil. Install a new circlip in the piston groove on one side of the piston (don't reuse the old circlips). Push the pin into position from the opposite side and install a new circlip. Compress the circlips only enough for them to fit in the piston. Make sure the circlips are properly seated in

the grooves **(see illustration)**.

19   Repeat the procedure to install the other piston.

15 Piston rings - installation

1   Before installing the new piston rings, the ring end gaps must be checked.

2   Lay out the pistons and the new ring sets so the rings will be matched with the same piston and cylinder during the end gap measurement procedure and engine assembly.

3   Insert the top (No. 1) ring into the bottom of the cylinder and square it up with the cylinder walls by pushing it in with the top of the piston **(see illustration)**. The ring should be about one inch above the bottom edge of the cylinder. To measure the end gap, slip a feeler gauge between the ends of the ring and compare the measurement to the Specifications.

4   If the gap is larger or smaller than specified, double check to make sure that you

have the correct rings before proceeding.

5   If the gap is too small, it must be enlarged or the ring ends may come in contact with each other during engine operation, which can cause serious damage. The end gap can be increased by filing the ring ends very carefully with a fine file **(see illustration)**. When performing this operation, file only from the outside in.

6   Excess end gap is not critical unless it is greater than 0.040 in (1 mm). Again, double check to make sure you have the correct rings for your engine.

7   Repeat the procedure for each ring that will be installed in the first cylinder and for each ring in the remaining cylinder. Remember to keep the rings, pistons and cylinders matched up.

8   Once the ring end gaps have been checked/corrected, the rings can be installed on the pistons.

9   The oil control ring (lowest on the piston) is installed first. It is composed of three separate components. Slip the expander into the groove, then install the upper side rail **(see illustration)**. Do not use a piston ring installation tool on the oil ring side rails as they may be damaged. Instead, place one

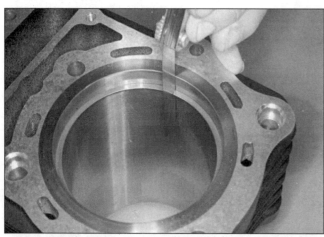

15.3 Check the piston ring end gap with a feeler gauge -measure at the bottom of the ring travel area if the cylinder looks worn

15.5 If the end gap is too small, clamp a file in a vise and file the ring ends (from the outside in only) to enlarge the gap slightly

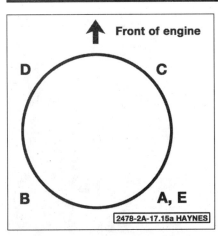

15.9 When installed, the piston ring gaps should be positioned as shown (120-degrees apart, and no closer than 10-degrees to the piston thrust surface)

A Top ring
B Oil ring expander
C Oil ring rail
D Second ring
E Oil ring expander

end of the side rail into the groove between the spacer expander and the ring land. Hold it firmly in place and slide a finger around the piston while pushing the rail into the groove. Next, install the lower side rail in the same manner.

10 After the three oil ring components have been installed, check to make sure that both the upper and lower side rails can be turned smoothly in the ring groove.

11 Install the second compression ring (middle ring) next. Do not mix the top and middle rings.

12 To avoid breaking the ring, use a piston ring installation tool and make sure that the identification mark is facing up. Fit the ring into the middle groove on the piston. Do not expand the ring any more than is necessary to slide it into place.

13 Finally, install the top compression ring in the same manner. Make sure the identifying mark is facing up.

14 Repeat the procedure for the remaining piston and rings. Be very careful not to con-

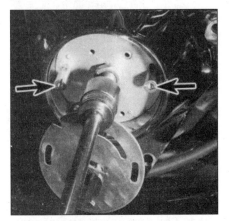

16.4b Service tool in position - note use of sensor plate screws (arrows)

16.3 The gearcase cover screws are different lengths - insert them in a cardboard template to keep track of where they go

fuse the middle and top rings.

15 Once the rings have been properly installed, stagger the end gaps, including those of the oil ring side rails (see illustration 15.9).

---

16 Gearcase cover, camshaft and timing gears - removal, inspection and installation

Removal

Caution: If the timing cover is not being removed as part of a general engine overhaul procedure, valve train pressure on the camshafts must be relieved (by removing the pushrods and tappets) before the timing cover or camshafts are disturbed.

1 Unscrew the tappet oil screen plug and lift out the O-ring, the spring and the oil screen from the top of the gearcase (refer to the oil change procedure in Chapter 1).

2 Remove the ignition components from the gearcase cover as described in the previous Section. Remove the tappets and guides as described in Section 10.

3 Remove the screws securing the gearcase cover to the crankcase (see illus-

16.4a Service tool necessary for gearcase removal - 1993 and later

tration). There are three different length screws used. Mark the screws in some way or draw a sketch to ensure installation of the correct length screw in each hole during reassembly.

HAYNES HiNT *Sketch the shape of the gearcase on a piece of cardboard, then mark the screw locations on the sketch. Poke holes in the location marks and put the screws into the holes to keep track of where they go.*

4 If care is exercised, it may be possible to tap around the edge of the gearcase cover with a soft-faced hammer to break the gasket seal, but it is recommended that a puller be used in order to remove the cover safely. A puller can be obtained through Harley-Davidson dealers (see illustrations), or could be fabricated by using the ignition sensor plate as a template. The puller is inserted in the same way as the sensor plate and the center bolt tightened down onto the camshaft end, thus pulling the gearcase off as it is tightened.

Caution: Do not pry the gearcase off - such action will destroy its finish and could incur breakage.

5 Remove the breather gear and spacer from the left side of the gearcase (see illustration).

16.5 Remove the crankcase breather gear and spacer from the gearcase bore

16.6 Carefully remove the camshaft, the shim (if equipped) and thrust washer from the gearcase

16.8 Unscrew the special nut (or plain nut) securing the timing gear

16.9 A two-jaw puller can be used to remove the timing gear from the end of the crankshaft on 1992 and earlier models

6   Carefully slide the camshaft out of the gearcase, along with the thrust washer and shim **(see illustration)**.

7   Lock the crankshaft to keep it from turning by inserting a tight fitting rod through the small end of one of the connecting rods. Place two pieces of wood across the opening in the crankcase. Carefully turn the crankshaft until the rod bears down on the two pieces of wood. If the engine isn't disassembled, apply the rear brake with the transmission in gear to keep the crankshaft from turning.

8   Unscrew the nut securing the timing gear to the crankshaft. On models through 1992 it has a left-hand thread (turn clockwise to loosen); the nut has only two flats and must be removed with an open-end wrench **(see illustration)**. On 1993 and later models a plain 6-sided nut is used, with a conventional right-hand thread.

9   On models through 1992 the timing gear is pressed onto the crankshaft, so a puller will be required to draw the gear off the shaft **(see illustration)**. On 1993 and later models the gear is a slip fit on its splines.

10   On models through 1992 remove the Woodruff key from the crankshaft, followed by the timing gear spacer **(see illustrations)**. On all models, remove the oil pump drive gear and its Woodruff key from the crankshaft.

Inspection

11   The timing gears are unlikely to require attention unless the engine has very high mileage or there has been a lubrication failure. Wear will be evident in the form of excessive backlash between the individual gears, with a characteristic "clacking" noise. If the gears are worn, the timing gear and camshaft must be replaced as a matched set. The dealer where you purchase the parts will make sure they're compatible.

12   The cam lobes should be checked for wear and damage in the form of pit marks, scuffing or flaking of the case hardened surfaces **(see illustration)**. Wear will be particularly evident on the flanks of the lobes, at the point where they begin to lift the tappets. If there's any doubt about the condition of the cam lobes, the camshaft should be replaced

as a precaution.

13   If the cam is worn or damaged, more than likely the tappets will require attention too. Check the rollers (which, if worn, can be replaced with a roller kit). Make sure the tappet guide itself isn't worn, causing the tappet to tilt and create additional mechanical noise. The pushrods should be examined and replaced if the ends are worn or damaged or if they're bent (see Section 10).

14   The needle roller bearings in the gearcase should be replaced if they don't turn smoothly or if damage or wear is evident. This also applies to all bushings. Replacement of the bearings should be done by a dealer service department (especially in the case of bushings, which may have to be reamed to size after installation). Don't forget the gearcase (timing) cover bushings. They're pegged in position and require expert attention when replacement is necessary.

Installation

15   Place the inner Woodruff key in the keyway on the crankshaft and slide the oil pump

16.10a Pry the Woodruff key out of the crankshaft and store it in a safe place

16.10b Slide the timing gear spacer (1992 and earlier models) and oil pump drive gear (all models) off the shaft

16.12 Check the camshaft lobes, gear teeth and bearing journals (arrows) for wear, damage and gear discoloration

16.15 Slide the oil pump drive gear (and timing gear spacer on 1992 and earlier models) into position . . .

16.16 . . . then install the timing gear

16.17 Insert the timed breather into the crankcase bore

drive gear into position **(see illustration)**. **Note:** *On early 1985 through 1992 Evolution engines, the chamfer on the oil pump drive gear must face IN. After the timing gear nut is tightened, make sure the timing gear spacer has noticeable end play.*

16   Install the spacer and outer Woodruff key (models through 1992) and replace the timing gear with the timing marks facing out **(see illustration)**. Lock the crankshaft, then install and tighten the timing gear nut. **Note:** *If the timing gear is replaced with a new one, the camshaft must be replaced as well because the gears must be matched for the correct clearance. When you purchase the new parts, the dealer should be able to supply them in matched sets.*

17   Slide the timed breather into position in the timing case **(see illustration)**. Before proceeding with reassembly, the timed breather end play should be checked and, if necessary, adjusted. Install a new timing case gasket and position the timed breather spacer on the end of the breather. Place a straightedge across the gasket and measure

the gap between the straightedge and the spacer with a feeler gauge. Subtract 0.006-inch (0.152 mm) from the measurement to find the end play, which should be within the specified limits. If the end play is incorrect, substitute a thrust washer of a different thickness. The washers are available in 0.110, 0.115, 0.120, and 0.125-inch (2.80, 2.92, 3.04 and 3.17 mm) sizes.

18   Lubricate the camshaft needle bearing and the plain bushings in the gearcase cover.

19   Rotate the flywheel until the left-hand mark on the timing gear face is at 12 o'clock.

20   Install the special thrust washer in the rear of the crankcase so the camshaft needle bearing is covered **(see illustration)**.

21   Place the shim (not used on 1988 and later model Evolution engines) on the inner end of the camshaft and install the camshaft so the timing marks align **(see illustration)**.

22   Place the timed breather spacer in position **(see illustration)**.

23 Lubricate the lip of the camshaft seal and install the gearcase cover, together with a

16.20 Insert the needle bearing and position the thrust washer as shown before installing the camshaft (and shim)

new gasket **(see illustration)**.

24   Install the cover screws and tighten them evenly, in a criss-cross pattern.

25   The camshaft end play must be

2A

16.21 Align the valve timing marks on the gears exactly as shown here (arrows)

16.22 Don't forget to install the timed breather spacer (apply a dab of grease to hold it in place while the cover is installed)

16.23 Install a new cover gasket over the dowel sleeves, then lubricate the cover bushings and seal and install the cover

16.25 Check the camshaft end play with feeler gauges before permanently bolting the gearcase cover in place

17.5 Oil pump line connections (arrows)

17.8a The oil pump gears seldom wear, but they must be replaced as sets if damage occurs

checked **(see illustration)**. If it's outside the specified limit, it must be adjusted by installing different shims. Shims are available in increments of 0.005-inch (0.127 mm) from 0.050 to 0.095-inch (1.27 to 2.41 mm).

17 Oil pump - removal, inspection and installation

Removal

1   Unless it's absolutely necessary, the oil pump should not be disassembled. The pump components are thoroughly lubricated, so wear is progressive and occurs very slowly over a long period of time. Damage to the pump is usually caused by metal or carbon particles passing through the gears, chipping or scoring them. In extreme cases, the gears may jam, causing the Woodruff key on the pump driveshaft to shear off.
2   **Note:** This procedure describes removal of the oil pump with the engine in the frame. If the engine has been removed, ignore the Steps that don't apply. Removal of the pump while the engine is in the frame can be done by removing the individual components, leaving the driveshaft in the case. Removal of the driveshaft requires removal of the gearcase cover (see Section 16) for access to the snap-ring. The gears must be marked as they're removed so they will be reinstalled in their original positions to maintain the original clearances.
3   Remove the right front footrest and mounting bracket to gain access to the oil pump (see Chapter 7). On some models, additional working space can be gained if the exhaust system is removed (see Chapter 3).
4   Drain the oil tank or oil pan (as applicable) as described in Chapter 1.
5   Disconnect all oil lines from the pump, labeling them first to ensure correct reconnection. The hose clamps installed at the factory are crimped aluminum, and can be

removed with the blade of a screwdriver or by cutting them off with wire cutters **(see illustration)**. On models with a front-mounted oil filter (1992 and later) it will be necessary to disconnect the steel oil line union from the pump lower adapter.
6   On early models with a pump mounted oil pressure switch, disconnect the wire(s) from the switch terminals.
7   Remove the bolts that pass through the pump body and, on some models, the two nuts. They must be loosened a little at a time (in 1/4-turn increments) to prevent distortion of the cover. Detach the cover and gasket.
8   The exposed gears provide the oil pressure **(see illustration)**. Remove the circlip from the end of the main feed drive gear and withdraw the gear and Woodruff key **(see illustration)**. Store the key and gear as a matched set.
9   Slide the feed driven gear off the idler shaft. **Note:** Don't allow the pump driveshaft to shift into the gearcase - it could cause dislocation of the drive gear Woodruff key, necessitating gearcase cover removal.
10   Remove the remaining bolts or nuts securing the pump body to the engine. Pull the pump body off the driveshaft and the scavenge drive gear.
11   Remove the scavenge drive gear and the Woodruff key, keeping them together, then withdraw the scavenge driven gear.
12   Generally, you don't have to remove the pump driveshaft unless the Woodruff key in the gearcase has been sheared. Check the condition of the key by rotating the crankshaft. If the driveshaft doesn't rotate consistently, the key is damaged and the driveshaft must be removed. In this case, remove the gearcase cover (see Section 16) for access to the snap-ring. Don't lose the snap-ring as it comes off the shaft **(see illustration)**.

 The snap-ring is difficult to remove because access is blocked by the gearcase wall. If possible, use a pair of external snap-ring pliers with 90-degree offset

jaws. If this type of tool isn't available, it's possible to spring the snap-ring out of position with a small screwdriver.
13   Unscrew the large plug at the top of the pump body and remove the relief valve assembly. Note how the parts are installed and which way they're facing during removal, to be sure they're installed properly during reassembly **(see illustrations)**.
14   Remove the smaller plug, followed by the anti-siphon valve spring and steel ball **(see illustrations)**.
15   Unscrew the plug from the rear of the pump body **(see illustration)**.
16   On models so equipped, the automatic drive chain oiler must be removed next. Turn the adjusting screw in as far as possible, counting the number of turns. Write the number down to be sure the adjusting screw will be in the correct position when it's reinstalled. Remove the adjusting screw.

Inspection

17   Clean all of the oil pump components with solvent and allow them to dry. Use compressed air to blow out all of the oil passages in the pump body and cover to be sure all oil, solvent and obstructions are removed. Do not mix up the gears or the tolerances in the pump will be affected.

17.8b Each pump gear is located on the shaft with a Woodruff key

17.12 Use offset snap-ring pliers to remove the circlip from the oil pump drive shaft (which will free the driven gear)

17.13a Unscrew the large plug to gain access to . . .

17.13b . . . the pressure relief valve plunger

17.14a The smaller threaded plug retains . . .

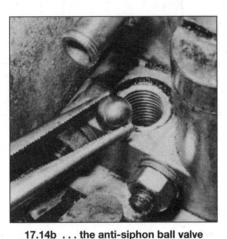

17.14b . . . the anti-siphon ball valve

17.15 Remove the oil passage plug to simplify cleaning of the oil passages

18 Inspect the pump gears for scoring and fractured teeth. If damage or wear is evident, the gears should be replaced with new ones. Intermeshing gears must always be replaced as a matched set.

19 Check the condition of the Woodruff keys. Be sure they fit in the gears and in the shaft keyways. Although slight play in the keys is permissible, it may indicate wear. When in doubt, replace them with new ones

and install a new shaft also.

20 Check the relief and anti-siphon valves and seats for pitting and other damage. Damaged seats cannot be easily repaired, so if damage is evident, a new pump body should be installed.

21 It's not unusual to have oil leakage at the cover-to-pump body joint and, more rarely, at the pump-to-gearcase joint. This condition is usually due to overtightened or

unevenly tightened bolts, causing distortion. Due to the small area of the mating surfaces, only a small amount of distortion will cause a leak. If the cover is distorted, a small amount of material may be removed by rubbing the cover on a piece of very fine (400 to 600 grit) emery paper spread over a perfectly flat surface. A surface plate or plate glass (not window glass) is ideal for the lapping operation. This method of resurfacing cannot be used for the pump body. If the mating surfaces on the pump body are altered, the manufacturer's tolerances will be changed, possibly causing the gears to lock.

22 Leakage at the unions on the oil pump body can be stopped by removing them and applying thread sealant or teflon tape to the threads. Do not apply too much sealant because there is danger of blocking an oil passage.

Assembly and installation

23 Reassemble and install the pump by reversing the disassembly and removal procedure using new gaskets, a new oil seal and circlip. Note that the driven gear should be installed before the Woodruff key, and make sure the snap-ring seats securely in its groove **(see illustrations)**.

2A

17.23a Position the oil pump driven gear, THEN install the Woodruff key (arrow)

17.23b Secure the pump gear with the circlip (arrow)

24 Inspect each gasket to be sure it doesn't block off any of the oil holes or obstruct the free movement of the oil pump gears. DO NOT use any gasket cement at any of the joints.

25 During reassembly, tighten the pump mounting bolts evenly, in 1/4-turn increments, and make sure the components rotate freely after each tightening sequence.

26 Jamming of the pump during reassembly can often be traced to the new gaskets interfering with the gears. If this happens, use a razor knife to trim the gasket until clearance is obtained.

27 Don't overtighten the pump bolts and nuts. The plastic gasket material will squeeze out under excessive pressure and prevent correct sealing.

28 Connect the oil lines to the pump in their original positions and secure them with new hose clamps.

29 Connect the wire(s) to the oil pressure switch (pump-mounted switch).

30 Fill the oil tank/oil pan with the recommended amount and type of oil (see Chapter 1).

18 Oil tank - removal and installation

1993-on FLT and 1991-on Dyna models

1 Drain the engine and transmission oil (see Chapter 1).

2 Disconnect the hose which runs from the oil pump to the oil pan union, having made note of its fitted position and routing (on certain models there may be identification marks on the hose ends). Discard hose clips; new ones must be fitted on installation.

3 On Dyna models remove the oil filler top section (two bolts) and pull the dipstick housing out of its O-ring in the pan.

4 On FLT models, release the dipstick housing and gasket from the transmission case (four bolts).

5 Loosening them evenly, remove all nine Dyna models) or twelve (FLT models) oil pan bolts. On FLT models access holes are provided in the frame crossmember for the awkwardly-positioned bolts. If stuck firmly in place, tap around the joint with a soft-faced mallet to release the gasket - do not lever with a screwdriver.

6 Maneuvering the oil pan past the crossmember on FLT models will be difficult due to limited clearance. Do not force it free; either remove the rear wheel and swingarm so that it can be removed rearwards, or disconnect the engine front mounting and raise the engine using a jack to obtain the necessary clearance.

7 Once removed, peel off the old gasket and clean the pan interior thoroughly.

8 Apply a smear of sealant to the oil pan gasket face and position the gasket on the

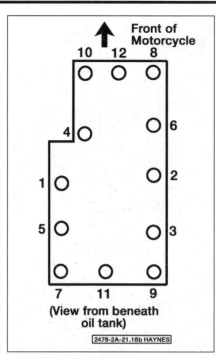

18.9 Oil pan bolt TIGHTENING sequence, late FLT models - viewed from below the motorcycle

pan. Lift the pan up against the transmission case and fit the retaining bolts loosely while taking care that the gasket remains in place.

9 Tighten all bolts evenly until the specified torque of 7 to 9 ft-lbs (9 to 12 Nm) is reached; on FLT models following the sequence **(see illustration)**.

10 Refit the dipstick assembly using new O-rings (Dyna models) or a new gasket (FLT models). If components were removed for access on FLT models, reinstall them.

11 Reinstall the pump-to-oil pan hose and secure with a new clamp.

12 Reinstall both drain plugs and replenish the engine and transmission oils.

All others

13 All models except the 1993-on FLT and 1991-on Dyna use an oil tank mounted above and behind the engine. Depending on model, it's mounted on the right side of the bike or centered in the frame.

14 Remove the seat (see Chapter 7). Where necessary, remove exhaust and electrical components that block access to the oil lines or mounting fasteners.

15 Label and disconnect the oil lines. Cover the disconnected ends of the lines (plastic bags and rubber bands will work) to keep out dirt.

16 Remove the mounting bolts or nuts and lift the tank out of the frame.

17 Inspect the rubber mounting grommets (if equipped) and replace them if they're cracked or deteriorated.

18 Installation is the reverse of the removal Steps.

19 Oil filter mount (1992 and later models) - removal and installation

1 On later models the oil filter is mounted on the crankcase front portion. Steel lines, running under the gearcase, connect the filter mount to the oil pump and tank/pan. The filter can be serviced as described in Chapter 1.

Removal

2 Drain the engine oil as described in Chapter 1.

3 Disconnect the oil lines at their unions with the mount and pump connectors. The mount is secured to the crankcase by two bolts and washers.

Installation

4 Install in the reverse order of removal, replacing all O-rings and seals with new ones. Tighten the filter mount bolts to 13 to 17 ft-lbs (18 to 23 Nm).

20 Crankcase - disassembly and reassembly

Disassembly

1 Check the end play of the crankshaft/flywheel assembly before the crankcases are split. Attach a dial indicator to the case with the stem in contact with the end of the crankshaft. Pull the crankshaft to the drive side of the engine as far as possible.

2 Zero the dial indicator, then push the crankshaft completely over to the timing side. The total end play should be within the tolerance given in the Specifications section of this Chapter. Greater play indicates the need for new drive side main bearings. If the play is greater than the specified amount, but the drive side main bearings are in good condition, shims (early models) or a thicker bearing spacer ring (later models) may be installed during reassembly.

3 Remove the nut from one end of each crankcase stud, and remove the bolts. Tap the studs out of the crankcase with a drift punch, having marked them so that they can be returned to their original holes in the casing on reassembly.

4 Tap around the edge of the right-hand crankcase with a soft-face hammer until the gasket seal is broken. Don't pry the two cases apart by inserting screwdrivers or tools between the mating surfaces or damage will result, causing oil leaks. After the seal has been broken, lift the right-hand crankcase half off the timing side main bearing.

5 The drive side crankshaft is a press fit in two tapered roller main bearings and the oil seal collar. Because of this, the flywheel

20.7 Install the flywheel (inner) tapered roller main bearing and spacer ring on the left-hand mainshaft

20.8a Support the crankshaft securely on blocks of wood . . .

20.8b . . . then carefully lower the left side crankcase over the bearing

assembly must be pressed out of the left crankcase half, leaving the oil seal, oil seal collar and outer (sprocket side) tapered roller bearing in the crankcase and the flywheel side (inner) tapered roller bearing on the crankshaft. Removal of the flywheel assembly requires a press, which will enable a controlled amount of pressure to be applied to the crankshaft end. Many automotive and motorcycle repair shops use this type of press and will carry out the operation for a nominal fee.

6   After crankshaft removal, position a large drift punch on the inner race of the sprocket side (outer) tapered roller bearing and drive the bearing, oil seal collar and oil seal out from the inside of the crankcase half. A piece of pipe with an outside diameter the same size as the bearing inner race will also work.

Reassembly

7   Install the timing side main bearing cages and rollers on the right- hand main shaft and the flywheel side (inner) tapered roller main bearing and inner race spacer ring on the left-hand main shaft **(see illustration)**. The tapered roller main bearing inner race should be driven into place with a length of

pipe or the appropriate special tool.
8   Support the flywheel assembly securely on wooden blocks so the right-hand main shaft is facing down **(see illustration)**. Lubricate the tapered roller main bearing with clean engine oil and position the left side crankcase over the shaft **(see illustration)**. Make sure the connecting rods don't damage the crankcase mouths when the crankcase is lowered into position.
9   Install the outer tapered roller main bearing in a manner similar to that used for installing the inner bearing **(see illustrations)**. Make sure the outer bearing is completely seated against the inner race spacer ring and make sure there's a small amount of end play in the flywheel assembly. If there is no end play, the tapered bearings are under preload. This condition must be rectified by pressing the flywheel assembly out of the bearing and installing one or more shims between the bearing spacer and one of the bearing inner races (early models) or by fitting a different thickness bearing spacer ring (later models). Shims are available in a variety of sizes. Adjust the end play to the specified limit.
10   Place the oil seal collar on the shaft so the widest diameter faces in **(see illustra-**

20.9a Slip the outer (sprocket side) tapered roller main bearing onto the mainshaft

tion). Drive the collar onto the shaft, using a length of pipe with an inside diameter slightly larger than the main shaft. Lubricate the sealing lip of the crankshaft oil seal and slide it over the main shaft and oil seal collar with the spring side facing in on dry-clutch models or facing out on wet-clutch models **(see illustration)**. Be careful to keep it square with the bore and tap it completely into the

2A

20.9b . . . and drive it into place with a piece of pipe and a hammer - don't continue to pound on it once it's seated

20.10a Install the oil seal collar on the mainshaft

20.10b Grease the lip of the oil seal before installing it (installed direction for wet-clutch models shown)

case. Make sure the flywheel assembly rotates freely in the crankcase half.

11   Invert the flywheel assembly, again blocking it securely on the workbench. Make sure the timing side main bearing spiral lock ring is in position and lubricate the bearing with clean engine oil.

12   Clean the mating surfaces of both crankcase halves and apply a non-hardening gasket sealant to the left-hand crankcase mating surface. Position the right-hand crankcase half over the mainshaft and lower it into position so the crankcase stud holes align.

13   On all models through 1990, insert the six crankcase studs and the two bolts, and install the stud washers and nuts. Note that the upper stud (between the crankcase mouths) may retain the speedometer drive cable clip or horn bracket on the left-hand side. On 1991 and later models, insert the three studs in their holes and secure their nuts lightly, then fit the bolts.

14   Before tightening the crankcase nuts/bolts ensure that the cylinder barrel surfaces are exactly aligned; tap the casting gently to bring into alignment if necessary.

15   On all models through 1990 tighten the fasteners evenly in a criss-cross pattern to 15 to 19 ft-lbs (20 to 26 Nm). On 1991 and later models, all fasteners should be tightened evenly to 10 ft-lbs (14 Nm) in a criss-cross pattern, and then after the cylinder barrels and heads have been installed, tightened to 15 to 17 ft-lbs (20 to 23 Nm). **Note:** *At all times during tightening make sure that the flywheel assembly is able to revolve freely.*

16   Before continuing, pad the crankcase mouths with clean rags to prevent dirt and other foreign matter from entering.

21 Crankcase components - inspection and servicing

1   After thorough cleaning, the crankcases should be examined for cracks and other signs of damage that may ultimately cause failure. Minor cracks can be repaired by welding, but if more extensive damage is apparent, replacement is recommended.

2   Note that crankcases are always supplied as a matched pair and should never be replaced any other way. This is important - the crankcases are line bored in pairs, so the bearing housings are aligned correctly. Replacement of only one half will result in a mismatch, which may cause the crankshaft to run out of line and absorb a surprising amount of power.

3   Make sure the mating surfaces are undamaged, otherwise oil leaks will be inevitable after reassembly. If there's any doubt about their ability to seal, use a liquid gasket sealer during reassembly.

4   Check the bearing housings to make sure they're undamaged. If they have worn

as the result of a bearing rotating, it's possible to repair using a special bearing sealant such as red Loctite during reassembly. This can be used successfully only if the amount of wear is small.

5   Now is the opportunity to retap any of the threads, if they require attention. Most damage is caused by over-tightening the drain plugs. If necessary, threaded holes can be repaired by installing Helicoil thread inserts, which will permit the original drain plug to be reused. Most dealers can perform this type of repair.

Oil seals - inspection and replacement

6   Even after very careful examination it's difficult to determine whether an oil seal can be reused, especially if it has been disturbed during disassembly. Because an oil seal failure will necessitate another teardown at a later date, it's recommended that all the oil seals be replaced with new ones during an overhaul, as a precautionary measure.

7   Oil seals are very easily damaged during reassembly. Always be very careful when installing shafts and grease the lips of the seals.

8   The most important oil seals on the engine are the ones on the drive side of the crankshaft assembly and in the gearcase cover, sealing the camshaft journal.

22 Crankshaft and connecting rods - inspection

1   The crankshaft and connecting rods are replaced as an assembly, even by dealer service departments. Removing the crankshaft from the left case half for crankshaft or bearing replacement requires a press and several special tools and should be done by a dealer service department or other qualified shop.

2   Remove the engine and separate the crankcase halves (see Sections 6 and 20).

3   Measure side clearance of the connecting rods with a feeler gauge. If it's not within the limits listed in this Chapter's Specifications, replace the crankshaft and connecting rods as an assembly.

4   While an assistant supports the connecting rods, spin the crankshaft and check for roughness, looseness or noise in the bearings that support the left side. If problems are found, have the bearings replaced by a dealer service department or other qualified shop.

5   Installation is the reverse of the removal steps.

23 Initial start-up after overhaul

1   Make sure the engine oil level is correct,

then remove the spark plugs from the engine. Place the engine STOP switch in the Off position and disconnect the primary wires from the ignition coil.

2   Turn on the key switch and crank the engine over with the starter until the oil pressure indicator light goes off (which indicates that oil pressure exists). Reinstall the spark plugs, connect the wires and turn the switch to On. **Note:** *If the oil pressure light won't go out on models with a screw-on oil filter, remove the filter (see Chapter 1). Hold the filter with the open end upright and pour oil into the center hole until the filter is full. Let the oil settle, then top it off again (you may need to do this twice). Reinstall the filter (a small amount of oil may leak out when you install it).*

3   Make sure there is fuel in the tank, then turn the fuel tap to the On position and operate the choke.

4   Start the engine and allow it to run at a moderately fast idle until it reaches operating temperature.

> ⚠ **Warning:** *If the oil pressure indicator light doesn't go off, or it comes on while the engine is running, stop the engine immediately.*

5   Check carefully for oil leaks and make sure the transmission and controls, especially the brakes, function properly before road testing the machine. Refer to Section 24 for the recommended break-in procedure.

24 Recommended break-in procedure

1   Any rebuilt engine needs time to break-in, even if parts have been installed in their original locations. For this reason, treat the machine gently for the first few miles to make sure oil has circulated throughout the engine and any new parts installed have started to seat.

2   Even greater care is necessary if the engine has been rebored or a new crankshaft has been installed. In the case of a rebore, the engine will have to be broken in as if the machine were new. This means greater use of the transmission and a restraining hand on the throttle until at least 500 miles (800 km) have been covered. There's no point in keeping to any set speed limit - the main idea is to keep from lugging the engine and to gradually increase performance until the 500 mile (800 km) mark is reached. These recommendations can be lessened to an extent when only a new crankshaft is installed. Experience is the best guide, since it's easy to tell when an engine is running freely.

3   If a lubrication failure is suspected, stop the engine immediately and try to find the cause. If an engine is run without oil, even for a short period of time, severe damage will occur.

Chapter 2 Part B
Clutch, primary drive and transmission

Contents

Degrees of difficulty

Easy, suitable for novice with little experience	**Fairly easy,** suitable for beginner with some experience	**Fairly difficult,** suitable for competent DIY mechanic	**Difficult,** suitable for experienced DIY mechanic	**Very difficult,** suitable for expert DIY or professional

Specifications

Clutch

Type

1970 through early 1984	Dry, multiple-disc with coil springs
Late 1984-on	Wet, multiple-disc with diaphragm spring

Dry clutch

Spring adjustment (from edge of spring collar-to-outer disc surface)

Four-speed transmission	1-1/32-inch (26.194 mm)
Five-speed transmission	7/8 to 1-1/32 inch (22.225 to 26.194 mm)
Minimum friction disc lining thickness	1/32 inch (0.794 mm)

Clutch spring

Free length	1-45/64 inch (26.103 mm)
Tension (late 1978-on)	30 to 38 lbs @ 1-1/4 inch (14 to 17 kg @ 32 mm)

Wet clutch

Steel plate warpage limit

1984 through 1989	0.011 inch (0.279 mm)
1990-on	0.006 inch (0.152 mm)
Minimum steel plate thickness (pre-1990 models only)	0.044 inch (1.118 mm)

Minimum friction disc thickness

Pre-1990 models	0.078 inch (1.981 mm)
1990-on (pack of all discs)	0.661 inch (166.79 mm)

Primary drive

Primary chaincase vacuum (with vent hoses pinched closed)	25-inch (635 mm) of water minimum at 1500 rpm

Transmission

Four-speed

Mainshaft main drive gear
  End play
    1970 through 1981 .... 0.0025 to 0.0135 inch (0.064 to 0.343 mm)
    1982 through 1984 .... 0.010 to 0.025 inch (0.254 to 0.635 mm)
    1985-on .... 0.010 to 0.035 inch (0.254 to 0.889 mm)
  Bushing on mainshaft (loose)
    Standard .... 0.0018 to 0.0032 inch (0.046 to 0.081 mm)
    Service limit .... 0.004 inch (0.102 mm)
Mainshaft
  Runout limit .... 0.003 inch (0.076 mm)
  First gear end bearing
    In housing (through 1984)
      Loose .... 0.0013 to 0.020 inch (0.033 to 0.508 mm)
      Press fit .... 0.0001 inch (0.002 mm)
    In housing (1985-on)
      Loose .... 0.0013 to 0.020 inch (0.033 to 0.508 mm)
      Press fit .... 0.0007 inch (0.018 mm)
    On shaft (through 1984)
      Loose .... 0.001 to 0.0015 inch (0.025 to 0.038 mm)
      Press fit .... 0.0007 inch (0.018 mm)
    On shaft (1985-on)
      Loose .... 0.0006 to 0.0015 inch (0.015 to 0.038 mm)
      Press fit .... 0.0007 inch (0.018 mm)
  Housing in case (through 1984)
    Loose .... 0.0005 to 0.0009 inch (0.013 to 0.023 mm)
    Press fit .... 0.001 to 0.015 inch (0.025 to 0.038 mm)
  Housing in case (1985-on)
    Loose .... 0.001 to 0.003 inch (0.025 to 0.076 mm)
    Press fit .... 0.0015 inch (0.038 mm)
  Third gear (through 1984)
    End play
      Standard .... 0.000 to 0.017 inch (0 to 0.432 mm)
      Service limit .... 0.000 to 0.020 inch (0 to 0.508 mm)
    Gear on shaft (loose)
      Standard .... 0.0012 to 0.0023 inch (0.030 to 0.058 mm)
      Service limit .... 0.0012 to 0.0030 inch (0.030 to 0.076 mm)
    Bushing in gear .... Press fit
  Third gear (1985-on)
    End play .... 0.005 to 0.021 inch (0.127 to 0.533 mm)
    Gear on shaft (loose)
      Standard .... 0.0016 to 0.0021 inch (0.041 to 0.053 mm)
      Service limit .... 0.003 inch (0.076 mm)
  Shifter fork clutch gear spacing (late 1978-on) .... 0.100 to 0.110 inch(0.2540 to 0.2794 mm)
Countershaft
  Runout limit .... 0.003 inch (0.076 mm)
  Drive gear end bearing (loose)
    Standard
      1970 through early 1978 .... 0.0005 to 0.0019 inch (0.013 to 0.048 mm)
      Late 1978-on .... 0.00025 to 0.002 inch (0.006 to 0.051 mm)
    Service limit .... 0.0005 to 0.002 inch (0.013 to 0.051 mm)
  First gear end bearing
    Standard
    Service limit
  Gear end play
    Standard
      1970 through early 1978 .... 0.007 to 0.012 inch (0.178 to 0.305 mm)
      Late 1978-on .... 0.004 to 0.012 inch (0.102 to 0.305 mm)
    Service limit .... 0.004 to 0.015 inch (0.102 to 0.381 mm)
  First gear
    Bushing on shaft (loose)
      Standard .... 0.000 to 0.0015 inch (0 to 0.038 mm)
      Service limit .... 0.000 to 0.002 inch (0 to 0.051 mm)
    Bushing in gear (loose)
      Standard .... 0.0005 to 0.0025 inch (0.013 to 0.064 mm)
      Service limit .... 0.0005 to 0.0030 inch (0.013 to 0.076 mm)

Second gear
  End play
    Standard .... 0.003 to 0.017 inch (0.076 to 0.432 mm)
    Service limit .... 0.003 to 0.020 inch (0.076 to 0.508 mm)
  Bushing on shaft (loose)
    Standard .... 0.000 to 0.0015 inch (0 to 0.038 mm)
    Service limit .... 0.000 to 0.002 inch (0 to 0.051 mm)
  Bushing in gear (loose)
    Standard .... 0.0005 to 0.002 inch (0.013 to 0.051 mm)
    Service limit .... 0.0005 to 0.0025 inch (0.013 to 0.064 mm)
Shifter fork clutch gear spacing
  1970 through early 1978
    First and second .... 0.080 to 0.090 inch (2.032 to 2.286 mm)
    Third and fourth .... 0.100 to 0.110 inch (2.540 to 2.794 mm)
  Late 1978-on
Gear backlash
  Standard .... 0.003 to 0.006 inch (0.076 to 0.152 mm)
  Service limit .... 0.003 to 0.010 inch (0.076 to 0.254 mm)
Shifter cam end play (through early 1979 models)
  Standard .... 0.005 to 0.0065 inch (0.127 to 0.165 mm)
  Service limit .... 0.005 to 0.007 inch (0.127 to 0.178 mm)

Five-speed

Mainshaft
  Runout... 0.000 to 0.003 inch (0 to 0.076 mm)
  End play .... None
First gear end bearing (press fit)
  In housing
    Standard .... 0.0001 inch (0.002 mm)
    Service limit .... 0.0001 to 0.0005 inch (0.002 to 0.013 mm)
  On shaft
    Standard .... 0.0007 inch (0.018 mm)
    Service limit .... 0.0007 to 0.0010 inch (0.018 to 0.025 mm)
Housing in case
  Standard .... 0.0010 inch (0.025 mm)
  Service limit .... 0.0010 to 0.0015 inch (0.025 to 0.038 mm)
First gear
  End play .... 0.0037 to 0.0339 inch (0.094 to 0.861 mm)
  Clearance .... 0.000 to 0.0080 inch (0 to 0.203 mm)
Second gear
  End play .... 0.0037 to 0.0329 inch (0.094 to 0.836 mm)
  Clearance .... 0.000 to 0.0800 inch (0 to 2.032 mm)
Third gear
  End play .... 0.005 to 0.042 inch (0.127 to 1.067 mm)
  Clearance .... 0.0003 to 0.0019 inch (0.008 to 0.048 mm)
Fourth gear
  End play .... 0.005 to 0.031 inch (0.127 to 0.787 mm)
  Clearance .... 0.0003 to 0.0019 inch (0.008 to 0048 mm)
Main drive gear (fifth)
  Bearing fit in transmission case
    Through 1983
      Tight.. 0.0009 inch (0.0023 mm)
      Loose.. 0.0020 inch (0.051 mm)
    1984-on
    Fit in bearing
      Through 1983
        Tight.. 0.0020 inch (0.051 mm)
        Loose.. 0.0009 inch (0.023 mm)
      1984-on
        Tight.. 0.0009 inch ((0.023 mm)
        Loose.. 0.0001 inch (0.002 mm)
  Fit on mainshaft .... 0.0001 to 0.0009 inch (0.002 to 0.023 mm)
  End play .... None
Shifter dog clearances
  Second-fifth
    Through 1983
      Minimum.. 0.025 inch (0.635 mm)
      Maximum... 0.139 inch (3.531 mm)

2B

Five-speed (continued)

1984-on	
Minimum	0.035 inch (0.899 mm)
Maximum	0.139 inch (3.531 mm)
Second-third	
Through 1983	
Minimum	0.021 inch 90.533 mm)
Maximum	0.164 inch (4.166 mm)
1984-on	
Minimum	0.035 inch (0.899 mm)
Maximum	0.164 inch (4.166 mm)
First-fourth	
Through 1983	
Minimum	0.030 inch (0.762 mm)
Maximum	0.152 inch (3.861 mm)
1984-on	
Minimum	0.035 inch (0.899 mm)
Maximum	0.152 inch (3.861 mm)
First-third (1984-on only)	
Minimum	0.035 inch (0.899 mm)
Maximum	0.157 inch (3.988 mm)
Side door bearing-to-side door	0.035 inch (0.899 mm)
Side door bearing-to-mainshaft	
Tight	0.0007 inch (0.178 mm)
Loose	0.0001 inch (0.002 mm)
Countershaft	
Runout	0.000 to 0.003 inch (0 to 0.076 mm)
End play	None
First gear	
End play	0.0050 to 0.0039 inch (0.127 to 0.099 mm)
Clearance	0.0003 to 0.0019 inch (0.008 to 0.048 mm)
Second gear	
End play	0.0050 to 0.0440 inch (0.127 to 0.118 mm)
Clearance	0.0003 to 0.019 inch (0.008 to 0.048 mm)
Third gear	
End play	0.0037 to 0.0329 inch (0.094 to 0.836 mm)
Clearance	0.0000 to 0.0080 inch (0 to 0.203 mm)
Fourth gear	
End play	0.0050 to 0.0390 inch (0.127 to 0.199 mm)
Clearance	0.0000 to 0.0080 inch (0 to 0.203 mm)
Fifth gear	
End play	0.0050 to 0.0440 inch (0.127 to 0.118 mm)
Clearance	0.0000 to 0.0080 inch (0 to 0.203 mm)
Shifter clutch clearance	
Second-third	
Through 1983	
Minimum	0.019 inch (0.483 mm)
Maximum	0.160 inch (4.064 mm)
1984-on	
Minimum	0.035 inch (0.889 mm)
Maximum	0.164 inch (4.196 mm)
First-third	
Through 1983	
Minimum	0.021 inch (0.533 mm)
Maximum	0.157 inch (3.988 mm)
1984-on	
Minimum	0.035 inch (0.889 mm)
Maximum	0.157 inch (3.988 mm)
Side door bearing-to-side door	0.0014 to 0.0010 inch (0.036 to 0.032 mm)
Side door bearing-to-countershaft	
Tight	0.0007 inch (0.118 mm)
Loose	0.0001 inch (0.025 mm)
Shifter cam assembly end play	0.001 to 0.004 inch (0.025 to 0.102 mm)
Transmission case outer surface-to-middle of center cam groove (through 1983 only)	3.043 inch (77.29 mm)
Outside machined surface of bearing support block-to-center cam groove nearest surface	1.992 to 2.002 inch (50.59 to 50.85 mm)

Shifter forks
    Taper .... 0.000 to 0.020 inch (0 to 0.508 mm)
    End play
        Shifter fork-to-cam groove .... 0.0017 to 0.0019 inch (0.043 to 0.048 mm)
        Shifter fork-to-gear groove .... 0.0010 to 0.0110 inch (0.025 to 0.279 mm)

Primary chaincase cover screws
1980 and later FLT/FXR models .... 84 to 108 inch-lbs (9 to 12 Nm)
1985 and later FX/Softail, 1991 and later Dyna models .... 108 to 120 inch-lbs (12 to 14 Nm)
All others .... 18 to 22 ft-lbs (24 to 30 Nm)

Primary chaincase-to-engine bolts
FLT/FXR models through 1992 .... 16 to 18 ft-lbs (22 to 24 Nm)
All others .... 18 to 22 ft-lbs (24 to 30 Nm)

Primary chaincase-to-transmission
1984 through 1992 FLT/FXR models
    5/16-inch bolts .... 13 to 16 ft-lbs (18 to 22 Nm)
    3/8-inch bolts .... 21 to 27 ft-lbs (28 to 37 Nm)
All others
    Nuts .... 30 to 35 ft-lbs (41 to 47 Nm)
    Bolts .... 18 to 22 ft-lbs (24 to 30 Nm)

1970 through early 1978 models only
Kickstarter lever pinch bolt .... 25 to 30 ft-lbs (34 to 41 Nm)
Starter cover .... 13 to 16 ft-lbs (18 to 22 Nm)
Starter crank gear nut .... 50 to 60 ft-lbs (68 to 81 Nm)
Mainshaft bearing retaining plate .... 72 to 120 inch-lbs (8 to 12 Nm)

Four-speed models only
Mainshaft ball bearing nut .... 50 to 60 ft-lbs (68 to 81 Nm)
Countershaft nut .... 55 to 65 ft-lbs (75 to 88 Nm)
Shifter fork nut
    1970 through early 1978 .... 25 ft-lbs (34 Nm)
    Late 1978-on .... 120 to 144 inch-lbs (14 to 16 Nm)
Shifter clutch nut (kickstart models only)
    1970 through 1975 .... 50 to 60 ft-lbs (68 to 81 Nm)
    1976-on .... 34 to 42 ft-lbs (46 to 57 Nm)
Mounting plate-to-transmission
    1970 through early 1978 .... 18 to 22 ft-lbs (24 to 30 Nm)
    Late 1978-on
        Nut .... 21 to 27 ft-lbs (28 to 37 Nm)
        Bolt .... 30 to 33 ft-lbs (41 to 45 Nm)
Top cover
    Screws (through early 1979) .... Not specified
    Bolts (late 1979-on) .... 13 to 16 ft-lbs (18 to 22 Nm)
Frame-to-transmission bolts (1985-on) .... 21 to 27 ft-lbs (28 to 37 Nm)
Clutch hub nut
    Through 1984 .... 50 to 60 ft-lbs (68 to 81 Nm)
    1985-on .... 35 to 50 ft-lbs (47 to 68 Nm)
Transmission sprocket nut
    1970 through early 1978 .... 140 to 150 ft-lbs (190 to 203 Nm)
    Late 1978 through early 1983 .... 105 to 120 ft-lbs (142 to 163 Nm)
    Late 1983-on .... 80 to 90 ft-lbs (108 to 122 Nm)
Sprocket nut lock screw (1985-on) .... 50 to 60 inch-lbs (6 to 7 Nm)
Compensating sprocket nut .... 80 to 100 ft-lbs (108 to 137 Nm)
Drain plug .... 15 ft-lbs (20 Nm)

Five-speed models only
Starter drive-to-chaincase .... 120 to 144 inch-lbs (14 to 16 Nm)
Mounting bolts .... 35 to 38 ft-lbs (47 to 52 Nm)
Mounting bracket-to-transmission .... 13 to 16 ft-lbs (18 to 22 Nm)
Side door mounting screws .... 13 to 16 ft-lbs (18 to 22 Nm)
Shifter arm screw .... 18 to 22 ft-lbs (24 to 30 Nm)
Shifter arm adjusting screw locknut .... 20 to 24 ft-lbs (27 to 33 Nm)
Countershaft-to-side door .... 27 to 33 ft-lbs (37 to 45 Nm)
Mainshaft-to-side door .... 27 to 33 ft-lbs (37 to 45 Nm)
Compensating sprocket nut .... 150 to 165 ft-lbs (203 to 224 Nm)

2B

Five-speed models only

Clutch hub nut
    Through 1989 .... 50 to 60 ft-lbs (68 to 81 Nm)
    1990-on .... 70 to 80 ft-lbs (68 to 81 Nm)
Side cover-to-side door... 84 to 108 inch-lbs (9 to 12 Nm)
Support block .... 84 to 108 inch-lbs (9 to 12 Nm)
Transmission sprocket nut
    Through 1983 .... 90 to 110 ft-lbs (122 to 150 Nm)
    1984 through 1994 .... 110 to 120 ft-lbs (150 to 163 Nm)
    1995-on
        First step .... 50 ft-lbs (68 Nm)
        Second step... 30 to 40-degrees additicnal, 45-degrees maximum
Transmission sprocket Allen-head bolt - through 1991 .... 50 to 60 inch-lbs (6 to 7 Nm)
Transmission sprocket lockplate bolts - 1992-on .... 84 to 108 inch-lbs (9 to 12 Nm)
Transmission drain plug
    FLT through 1992 and FXR .... 82 inch-lbs (9 Nm)
    FLT 1993-on .... 14 to 30 inch-lbs (19 to 40 Nm)
    FX/Softails and Dynas... 0.16 to 0.18 inch (4.0 to 4.5 mm) above surface of housing
Oil pan-to-transmission bolts .... 84 to 108 inch-lbs (9 to 12 Nm)

1 General information

This Part of Chapter 2 covers the components that transmit engine power from the crankshaft to the final drive chain or belt.

Power from the crankshaft is routed to the transmission via the primary drive chain or belt and clutch. The clutch on 1970 models is a dry type, with coil springs. The clutch on later models is of the wet, multi-plate type. The transmission is a four- or five-speed, constant-mesh unit. The clutch and primary drive chain or belt are contained in the primary drive housing on the left side of the engine. The transmission is mounted on the back of the engine.

A four-speed transmission was offered in all years covered by this manual and a five-speed was available beginning in 1980. A multi-plate, dry clutch with coil springs was used on all 1970 through early 1984 models, while a wet multi-plate clutch (with a large diaphragm spring) was introduced in late 1980 and modified for the 1990 model year. Access to the transmission is available after the primary drive components and clutch have been removed.

The transmissions used on these machines are contained in a separate aluminum case mounted behind the engine. Power to the transmission is transmitted via a multi-plate clutch and roller chain or cogged drive belt enclosed in a detachable

unit on the left side of the machine (known as the primary drive).

The selection of gears in the transmission is carried out by shifting forks. The forks slide the movable gears into and out of mesh with the various other gears. On four-speed models, the gear shifter unit is mounted on the outside of the transmission. Five-speed models have the shifter cam assembly bolted to the case, under the transmission top cover.

2 Primary drive and clutch components - removal

Primary drive components

1   Shift the transmission into gear. On some models the gear shift lever must be removed in order to remove the primary chaincase cover. On these models, the shift lever is secured to the splined shaft by a pinch bolt.
2   Remove the screws securing the primary chaincase cover. The screws should be loosened a little at a time in a criss-cross pattern.
3   Tap around the edge of the cover with a soft-face hammer to break the gasket seal. Detach the cover from the chaincase.
4   Lock the engine so the crankshaft can't turn. In order to do this, the transmission must be in gear and the drive sprocket must be held with a chain wrench or some other

tool. Another way to do this is to apply the rear brake while tile transmission is in gear or remove the spark plugs and bring the piston to the TDC position. Back the crankshaft up 1/8 of a revolution and fill the combustion chamber with nylon rope inserted through the spark plug hole. Be sure the end of the rope is still outside the engine.
5   Loosen the compensating sprocket nut. Same early models are equipped with a nut that requires a special peg wrench for removal and installation. Harley-Davidson special tool no. 94557-56 is recommended, but it's unlikely to be readily available. If the special tool isn't available, attach a U-bolt and use a large screwdriver or pry bar as a

2.5 The crankshaft must be locked in place to loosen the compensating sprocket nut

2.6a Remove the nut and cover, followed by . . .

2.6b . . . the collar (not used on all models) and the sliding cam

2.8 Unscrew the large center bolt (arrow) to free the chain tensioner assembly

lever. On other models the nut is very tight and will require a large wrench with a long handle in order to apply enough leverage to loosen it **(see illustration)**.

6 On primary chain models, unscrew the nut and remove the cover, the collar and the sliding cam **(see illustrations)**. The compensating sprocket and the shaft extension must remain in place until the primary chain is ready to come off (after the clutch is disassembled).

7 On belt primary drive models, remove the lockwasher and outer plate. The compensating sprocket assembly can remain in place until the belt is removed (after the clutch is disassembled). **Note:** *A setscrew secures the outer plate to the compensating sprocket. There's only one setscrew and its main purpose is to keep the outer plate aligned with the hub in case a puller must be used to remove the sprocket assembly. After the setscrew is removed, push the outer plate, the rubber dampers, the hub and the inner plate out of the sprocket.*

8 On primary chain models, remove the complete chain tensioner assembly by unscrewing the large center bolt that secures it to the rear of the crankcase **(see illustration)**.

Dry clutch (through early 1984 models)

9 The clutch spring backplate, the springs and the clutch pressure plate are removed as a unit. Because the two plates are under considerable pressure from the springs, a special procedure must be followed to ensure safe removal.

10 Remove the clutch adjusting screw locknut. Place a large washer, with an outside diameter larger than the center hole in the spring backplate, over the adjusting screw and reinstall the locknut **(see illustration)**.

11 Tighten the locknut until the springs are slightly compressed. The three spring tensioning nuts can now be removed and the plate spring assembly detached safely by

pulling it out of the clutch outer drum. The components should only be separated if one or more of them require replacement.

12 To separate them safely, insert three bolts through the original spring tensioning nut stud holes and attach a nut to each bolt. Tighten the nuts until the springs are compressed slightly, then remove the locknut and adjusting screw. Separate the parts by loosening the three nuts a little at a time. The bolts must have threads long enough to allow complete release of the spring pressure.

13 Remove the clutch plates, one at a time, noting their relative positions to simplify reassembly.

14 Grasp the clutch outer drum with one hand and the engine sprocket with the other and pull the two components off at the same time, along with the primary chain and chain tensioner **(see illustration)**.

15 On pre-1976 models, withdraw the clutch operating pushrod from the hollow transmission mainshaft. **Note:** *On belt drive models, remove the spacer(s) from behind the compensating sprocket. They're used for alignment of the sprockets and must be installed in their original locations during reassembly.*

2.10 Use a large washer (arrow) behind the adjusting screw locknut to compress the clutch springs

16 Remove the clutch hub nut after flattening the ears on the tab washer. Note that the nut has a left-hand thread and must be loosened in a clockwise direction.

17 The clutch hub is installed on a tapered portion of the transmission mainshaft and is located by a Woodruff key. As a result, the hub is very tight and a puller will be needed

2.14 Remove the primary drive assembly (and chain tensioner) as a unit

2B

2.17 A puller is required to remove the clutch hub from the transmission mainshaft

2.32a The shift linkage rod is secured by a circlip

2.32b Slide the pivot shaft out of the support bracket

to remove it **(see illustration)**. A puller that applies force with bolts at three points should be used. It should be positioned over the three longest studs projecting from the clutch hub so it can be held in place by the three spring tensioning nuts.

Caution: Before installing the puller, thread the hub nut onto the mainshaft approximately six turns to prevent the shaft threads from being damaged by the pressure of the bolt. The clutch push rod oil seal installed in the end of the nut must also be protected from the end of the bolt by a washer.

18 After removal of the clutch hub, pry the Woodruff key out of the shaft with a screwdriver.

Wet clutch (late 1984 and later models)

Caution: The clutch installed on 1990 and later models should not be disassembled by the home mechanic - a special tool is required to compress the diaphragm spring, which can fly out with extreme force if the tool isn't used. Have the clutch disassembled by a Harley-Davidson dealer service department.

19 On late 1984 through 1989 models proceed as follows: Loosen the adjuster plate bolts in 1/4-turn increments until the spring pressure is released, then remove them and detach the adjuster plate and diaphragm spring.
20 Remove the pressure plate. The steel clutch plates and friction discs can now be changed or inspected without additional disassembly. Remove the clutch plates and friction discs and keep them in order.
21 Remove the nut from the end of the transmission mainshaft. Note that it has left-hand threads!
22 Remove the pushrod threaded end piece.
23 Attach a puller to the clutch hub.
24 Refer to Step 14 above and remove the primary drive chain, the compensating

2.35 The rear of the inner primary chaincase is secured by studs (shown) (or bolts)

sprocket and the clutch drum/hub unit as an assembly. The clutch drum/hub unit must be removed from the transmission shaft with the puller - it won't slide off.
25 The clutch drum/hub unit shouldn't be disassembled unless the pilot bearing is defective. If the pilot bearing must be replaced, remove the circlips and press the clutch hub out of the bearing inner race.

Primary chaincase

26 On electric start models, the starter motor should now be detached and the starter solenoid disconnected. Carefully pry the rubber cap off the solenoid, which is mounted on the primary chaincase.
27 Disconnect the two large wires and the small wire. When loosening the main terminal nuts, make sure the terminal post is supported to prevent rotation and damage.
28 Working on the right-hand side of the machine, disconnect the single wire attached to the starter motor end cap. The wire is held by a nut.
29 Remove the bracket from the rear of the starter motor and then unscrew the two nuts that clamp the starter motor housing to the back of the primary chaincase (see Chapter 8 if necessary). The starter motor can now be withdrawn, leaving the starter secondary shaft in the primary chaincase.
30 On late 1978 and later models with a

four-speed transmission, remove the through bolts after the bracket is detached. Hold the starter motor at both covers to prevent it from falling apart and lift it out of position.
31 On all models, the inner primary chaincase can now be removed. Remove the gear shift lever, if not already done, and disconnect the pivot bracket chrome cover, which is retained by two screws.
32 Disconnect the shift linkage rod, at the operating arm, by removing the small circlip **(see illustration)**. Carefully ease the operating arm/pivot shaft out towards the rear of the pivot bracket **(see illustration)**. In some cases, removal of the chaincase inner front mounting bolt will be required to provide clearance for pivot shaft removal.
33 Loosen the bolts securing the transmission to the baseplate.
34 Remove the mounting bolts from the front section of the chaincase. On some models, two of the bolts are safety wired.
35 Remove the bolts securing the chaincase to the transmission **(see illustration)**. On five-speed models, two of the chaincase mounting bolts must be removed from the back side of the case and the other two bolts are secured with locking tabs and safety wire.
36 On models with an enclosed rear chain, remove the bolts securing the chain boot to

3.7 The clutch pushrod oil seal can be pried out of the hub nut

3.8 The bearing cage is secured by three spiral springs (arrows)

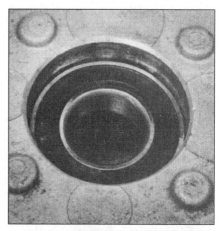

3.11a The modified outrigger bearing is pre-packed with grease and sealed

3.11b The original oil seal should also be installed

the primary chaincase.

37 Disconnect any oil lines or vent hoses that may be attached to the chaincase. Label them to be sure they're reinstalled in the proper place during reassembly.

38 Use a block of wood passed through from the right-hand side of the machine and a hammer to separate the chaincase from the transmission. **Note:** *On 1984 FLT/FXR models, the chaincase must be rotated clockwise around the transmission mainshaft to detach it.* The case is now free and can be lifted off.

39 If two washers fall off when the case is removed, be sure to install them on the two front transmission-to-primary case studs during reassembly.

3 Clutch components - inspection

Dry clutch

1 Check the condition of the clutch sprocket to make sure none of the teeth are chipped, broken off or badly worn.

2 Wash all of the clutch components, except the friction discs, and check the steel plates for warpage.

3 Visual inspection will show whether the clutch plate tangs are burred and whether corresponding indentations have formed in the slots they ride in. Burrs should be removed with a file, which can also be used to dress the slots square, provided the depth of the indentations isn't too great.

4 On pre-1981 models, the steel plates are equipped with a buffer device on the trailing edge of each slot. The buffer consists of a cage holding a spring loaded ball. If the cage is damaged or the ball no longer returns, the buffer unit must be replaced with a new one. The cage is held in position by two rivets - the heads can be ground off to allow removal with a punch.

5 Check the thickness of the friction discs. When the discs have worn thin, they

must be replaced. Always replace them as a complete set, even if some have not reached the service limit. Worn friction discs promote clutch slip.

6 Check the free length of the clutch springs and compare the results to the Specifications in this Chapter. Don't stretch the springs if they have compressed. They must be replaced when the service limit has been reached.

7 Check the clutch pushrod for distortion by rolling it on a sheet of glass. Heavy action is often caused by a bent rod, which may hang up. If oil has been leaking out along the mainshaft, check the condition of the clutch pushrod seal, which is mounted in the center of the clutch hub nut. The seal can be pried out and a new one driven in **(see illustration)**.

8 The bearing the clutch outer drum rides on is a single cage, double-row roller type and is mounted on the clutch hub boss. Check the fit of the clutch outer drum on the bearing. If radial play is evident, attention to the bearing is required **(see illustration)**.

9 If the bearing races are pitted or scored, they must be replaced, together with the main component they're attached to. To remove the bearing cage and rollers, pry the three spiral springs off the long clutch studs. Slide the bearing backing plate out of position. As the cage is removed, the rollers will fall free.

10 On some models, a journal ball bearing is installed in a housing in the rear of the primary chaincase to act as an outrigger bearing for the transmission mainshaft. This bearing is prone to lack of lubrication and failure. Check the bearing for up-and-down play and roughness when rotated. If the bearing requires replacement, the chaincase must be removed by separating it from the transmission and engine crankcase as described in the previous Section.

11 The outrigger bearing can be driven out, taking the oil seal with it. Heat the case to approximately 150-degrees F before attempting removal. A special ball bearing, prepacked with grease and incorporating an

oil seal, should be used as a replacement. This will prevent future failure due to lack of lubrication **(see illustrations)**.

Wet clutch

12 Clean all of the parts with solvent and dry them with compressed air (if available).

13 Check the friction discs for worn, checked and chipped linings. Look for grooves in the steel plates.

14 Check the steel plates for warpage with feeler gauges on a perfectly flat surface. Replace any that are warped beyond the specified limit.

15 Measure the thickness of the steel plates and friction discs. If they're thinner than specified, install new ones.

16 Check the diaphragm spring for cracks and damage.

17 Check the clutch hub keyway and Woodruff key for damage and distortion. Make sure the splines and slots in the hub and drum are smooth and undamaged. Check the tangs on the friction discs for burrs and wear.

18 See if the pilot bearing turns smoothly and make sure it isn't discolored from excessive heat.

2B

4 Primary drive components - inspection

1 Examine the teeth on the compensating (crankshaft) sprocket and the clutch drum. If any are chipped, hooked or broken, the sprocket must be replaced. It's a good idea to replace the clutch drum, the compensating sprocket and the primary chain or belt together as a matched set. A badly worn sprocket will cause the chain or belt to wear more rapidly and cause the engine to lose power.

2 Check the condition of the splines on the sliding cam and the shaft extension. If they're worn, the components should be replaced as a matched set. Although it's unlikely the sliding cam has worn to any great degree, it should be checked where it makes contact with the compensating sprocket.

3 The component most likely to wear is the sprocket spring, which will compress after extended use. Increased cam action is a sure sign the spring should be replaced.

4 On 1980 and early 1981 models with a primary drive belt, check the belt and measure the amount of play. The belt isn't adjustable, so if the play is over one-inch with 10 pounds of force applied to the top run of the belt at the midpoint, it must be replaced with a new one.

5 Check the belt carefully for oil and dirt deposits. Slight deposits can be removed with a shop towel. DO NOT clean the belt with solvent.

6 Check the belt for hardened or cracked back surface rubber, cracked or separated plies, worn, cracked or missing teeth and cracked or worn sides.

5 Primary drive and clutch - installation

1 If the gear shift linkage rod was disconnected, it should be reconnected before the inner primary chaincase is installed. Be sure the rod is facing the correct way or the clevis will bind on the selector box arm, causing difficult or missed shifts.

2 Place a new O-ring on the crankcase boss that mates with the inner chaincase (see illustration).

3 Apply red Loctite to the outer race of the transmission mainshaft ball bearing and install it in the chaincase bore. **Note:** *On late 1985 and later FLT/FXR models, the bearing is secured with two retaining rings, so Loctite isn't necessary. Later FX/Softail models don't have a bearing. However, a new seal must be installed and the splines on the transmission mainshaft should be wrapped with electrician's tape so the seal isn't damaged when the chaincase is installed.*

4 Refer to the *Caution* in Step 6 and then install the primary chaincase, pushing it into

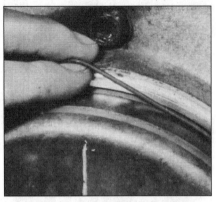

5.2 Place a new O-ring over the crankcase boss before installing the inner primary chaincase

position until it engages with the protruding studs or the bolt holes line up. On dry clutch models, connect the oil feed and return lines, using new hose clamps on their unions.

5 Install the bolts that secure the chaincase to the engine and tighten them to the specified torque in 1/4-turn increments. On some models, the two inside bolts must be locked together with safety wire **(see illustration)**. If the threads in the case and on the bolts are perfectly clean, thread-locking compound can be used instead of safety wire.

Caution: The engine and transmission mounting nuts/bolts must be loose when the inner chaincase is installed to prevent strain on the case and to allow it to self-align.

6 Install the chaincase-to-transmission nuts or bolts and locking tabs (if used), together with the oil breather orifice cover plate (if equipped). Note that the cover plate is installed with two washers on the inside of the plate, next to the chaincase. Tighten the nuts/bolts to the specified torque in /4-turn increments. Note that some later FLT/FXR models are equipped with locking tabs and the bolts have small holes in the heads - tie the bolts and tabs together with safety wire. Also, some models have locking tabs that must be bent up against the bolt heads.

7 Tighten the engine and transmission mounting nuts/bolts, then make sure the transmission mainshaft turns freely.

8 Apply grease to the clutch operating pushrod and insert it into the hollow transmission mainshaft.

5.5 Safety-wire or secure the two inner bolts with thread locking compound

9 Place the Woodruff key in position in the tapered section of the mainshaft and slide the clutch hub into position over the mainshaft. The Woodruff key will engage with the keyway in the clutch hub.

10 Install the tab washer and the clutch hub nut. Lock the mainshaft of the transmission to keep it from turning by shifting the transmission into First gear and applying the rear brake, then tighten the nut. Remember, the nut has left-hand threads. Bend the tabs on the lock washer over the nut to secure it.

Primary chain models

11 Install the compensating sprocket spacer (if used) and the shaft extension on the end of the crankshaft.

12 Lubricate the clutch bearing with clean engine oil. Assemble the compensating sprocket and the clutch outer drum on the workbench, so they're meshed with the primary drive chain. The chain should be installed with the tensioner assembly.

13 Lift the primary drive assembly and slide the compensating sprocket and clutch drum into place on the shafts.

Primary belt models

14 Lubricate the rubber dampers in the compensating sprocket with Harley-Davidson POLY-OIL. Assemble the clutch outer drum and the compensating sprocket on the workbench so they're meshed with the primary drive belt.

15 The clutch hub and compensating

Dimension Step "C"	Size	Part No.
0.234 to 0.304 in	0.060	24054-80
0.304 to 0.284 in	0.040	24053-80
0.284 to 0.264 in	0.020	24052-80
0.264 to 0.254 in	0.010	24051-80
0.254 to 0.244 in	0.000	None

5.15 Compensating sprocket spacer thickness table (primary belt drive models only)

2536-2b-5.15 HAYNES

5.18 Note the OUT mark on the steel clutch plates and install them correctly

5.19a Install the clutch spring tensioning nuts with the indentations facing IN

5.19b Tighten the spring tensioning nuts evenly until the correct clearance between the pressure plate and spring backplate is obtained

sprockets must be in alignment when they're installed. The alignment is altered by using different thickness spacers between the compensating sprocket and the alternator rotor. Place the spacers, removed during disassembly, over the crankshaft. If necessary, the spacer thickness can be determined as follows:

a) *Measure the distance from the alternator rotor hub outer surface to the primary chaincase gasket surface.*

b) *Measure the distance from the clutch hub friction surface to the primary chaincase gasket surface.*

c) *The difference between the two measurements (dimension step "C" in the table) must be looked up on the accompanying table* **(see illustration)** *to determine the correct thickness spacer(s) required to align the sprockets.*

16 Install the assembled components as a complete unit and slide the compensating sprocket and clutch drum into place on the shafts.

17 Install the inner plate, the hub, the rubber dampers and the outer plate in the compensating sprocket in the correct order. Secure the outer plate to the compensating sprocket with the set screw.

Dry clutch models

18 Replace the clutch plates one at a time, beginning with a steel plate, followed by a friction disc. Continue installing the plates, alternating between the two types. The steel plates are marked OUT on one side and should be installed accordingly **(see illustration)**. In addition, on models so equipped, the spring loaded buffers should be staggered in the outer drum.

19 Replace the spring/pressure plate assembly and install the three nuts with the indented face of each nut facing IN **(see illustration)**. Tighten the nuts evenly until the large washer on the adjusting screw becomes loose. Remove the locknut, discard the large washer and reinstall the locknut. Tighten or loosen the three nuts until the distance between the pressure plate and the

rear of the spring backplate is 1-1/32 inch (26 mm) **(see illustration)**.

Wet clutch models

20 Assemble the clutch plates and friction discs in the hub and drum assembly. Start and end with a steel plate.

21 Check the Woodruff key to make sure it's parallel with the transmission mainshaft taper and that it doesn't extend more than 0.119-inch above the shaft.

22 Install the compensating sprocket, the primary chain and the clutch drum/hub assembly at the same time. Align the key in the transmission mainshaft with the keyway in the clutch hub as it's installed on the shaft.

Caution: Make very sure the key is installed correctly - the clutch hub could be damaged if it isn't.

23 Apply two drops of red Loctite to the compensating sprocket nut and the clutch hub nut before installation. Install the hub nut and tighten it to the specified torque.

Caution: DO NOT overtighten it.

24 Install the pressure plate, the diaphragm spring and the adjuster plate in the clutch hub with the holes aligned. Make sure the spring is installed with the convex side out.

25 Apply purple Loctite to the bolt threads, then install the bolts and tighten them to 6.5 to 8 ft-lbs (9 to 11 Nm) in a criss-cross pattern.

26 Adjust the clutch as described in Chapter 1. **Note:** *If the retaining ring has been removed, make sure the beveled edge faces out when it's reinstalled.*

All models

27 Install the compensating sprocket and related components. Tighten the nut after locking the crankshaft as described in Section 2.

28 Install the chain tensioner center bolt so it engages with the sliding nut in the rear of the serrated adjuster plate. Adjust the chain tension as described in Chapter 1.

29 Adjust the tension of the primary drive

belt (if equipped) as described in Chapter 1.

30 On electric start models, the starter motor must be installed now to allow replacement of the clutch operating arm and adjustment of the clutch.

31 On late 1978 and later four-speed models, set the starter motor in position. The starter must be held at both covers during installation to prevent it from falling apart. Position the mounting bracket on the starter and insert the through-bolts.

32 On all other models, lubricate the starter secondary shaft bearing in the starter motor housing with grease. Place a new gasket over the starter motor retaining studs, then replace the oil seal holder plate with the raised edge facing the starter motor. Insert the starter driven gear into the housing attached to the front of the starter motor. Slide the starter motor into position so the splines on the secondary shaft engage with those in the driven gear. Push the starter motor until it's seated on the studs and install and tighten the two mounting nuts.

33 Attach the clutch operating arm to the shaft which runs into the transmission. Adjust the clutch as described in Chapter 1.

34 Connect the wires to the solenoid and place the rubber cap in position over them.

35 On five-speed models, coat the rear chain boots and their mating surfaces with RTV sealant. Place the boots in position and install and tighten the mounting bolts.

36 Install a new gasket on the primary chaincase, after checking the mating surfaces to make sure they're perfectly clean.

37 On models so equipped, replace the bronze washer on the end of the starter shaft.

38 On chain primary drive models, lubricate the primary drive chain with clean engine oil.

39 Carefully set the primary chaincase cover in position and install the mounting screws in their original locations. Tighten the screws a little at a time in a criss-cross pattern. Replenish the primary chaincase oil supply on wet clutch models.

2B

Models with chain primary drive and dry clutch only

40   In order to ensure the primary chaincase doesn't leak oil and, more importantly, so the automatic oil feed and return system functions correctly, the primary chaincase must be perfectly airtight.

41   Harley-Davidson recommends testing the chaincase with a vacuum gauge to check the seal. The vacuum should be 20-inches or more of water with the engine running at 1500 rpm and the breather pipe to the oil tank pinched closed. This test is impractical and in any case shouldn't be required if care has been taken during reassembly. A loss of vacuum and therefore failure of the chaincase lubrication may be due to the following defects:

a) *Leakage at the crankcase/chaincase O-ring*
b) *A damaged primary chaincase gasket*
c) *Damaged starter motor housing gasket or shaft O-ring*
d) *Leakage of air through the chaincase bearing or between the bearing inner race and the transmission mainshaft*

42   The defects listed probably won't prevent the feed of oil to the chaincase, but will prevent proper scavenging of the lubricant and cause a rise in the level.

43   Install the shift lever and secure it with the pinch bolt.

44   If nylon rope was inserted into the combustion chamber to lock the crankshaft, remove it now and reinstall the spark plug.

---

6   Transmission repair operations possible with the transmission in the frame

1   Attention to the kickstart mechanism, such as replacement of the ratchet and gear, can be carried out with the transmission in place, after removal of the outer cover. Replacement of the kickstart return spring can be carried out merely by detaching the kickstart lever and the spring cover plate.

2   Adjustment of the gear selector mechanism can be done without removing the transmission, but it requires removal of the clutch, primary drive and primary chaincase. The procedure for shifter adjustment is described in Section 9 of this Chapter.

---

7   Transmission - removal and installation

Removal

Four-speed models

1   The transmission can be removed from the frame with the engine still in place, but only after removal of the primary drive components and clutch, the starter motor (if equipped) and the battery and battery carrier (see Chapter 8 if necessary). With these major components removed to allow access to the transmission, continue as follows.

2   Remove the oil tank drain plug and allow all the oil to drain into a container.

3   Disconnect the oil tank breather hose, the return hose at the top of the tank and the oil feed line from the union at the oil pump. The hose clamps should be pried apart with a screwdriver and discarded.

4   Remove the oil tank filler cap and dipstick.

5   Remove the two nuts securing the oil tank to the rubber mounted support studs. Maneuver the oil tank off the studs and remove it from the machine to the left-hand side.

6   Remove the front right-hand footrest and mounting bracket. On some models, the footrest shaft also serves as the brake pedal pivot, and the brake operating pushrod must be withdrawn from the master cylinder as the assembly is removed.

7   Before disconnecting the final drive chain, flatten the tab washer ears securing the mainshaft sprocket nut and remove the nut. Note that the nut has a left-hand thread and must be removed in a clockwise direction **(see illustration)**. Remove the chain by removing the master link, then pull the transmission sprocket off the splines. On belt drive models, loosen the rear wheel adjusting nuts and remove the drive belt.

8   Disconnect the clutch cable from the release arm.

9   Remove the exhaust system components that are in the way of the transmission. On some models the entire exhaust system will have to be removed.

10   Separate the shift rod from the transmission. The shift rod is secured by either a cotter pin and clevis pin or by a bolt and nut.

11   Disconnect the wire for the Neutral indicator switch.

12   Remove the speedometer drive cable and housing from the transmission (not all models) (see Chapter 8).

13   Remove the bolt securing the transmission to the support bracket on the right side. Remove the bolts and screws attaching the transmission mounting plate to the frame.

14   Remove the transmission, with the mounting plate attached, out the left side of the frame.

Five-speed models

15   Drain the transmission oil (see Chapter 1). On 1993 and later FLT and 1991 and later Dyna models also drain the engine oil from the oil pan (see Chapter 1). On 1991 and later Dyna models, remove the oil pan (see Chapter 2A).

16   Remove the cover from the right side of the transmission. Note that the clutch cable can remain attached to its release arm.

17   Withdraw the pushrod end piece (complete with oil slinger on later models) from the mainshaft end. A snap-ring retains the

7.7 The transmission sprocket nut has left-hand threads

thrust bearing assembly to the pushrod end piece.

18   Disconnect the wires from the neutral switch. Detach the vent hose and on later models, engine oil hoses, from the transmission case.

19   Remove the bolts securing the top cover to the transmission and detach the top cover and gasket. Lift the shifter cam assembly out the transmission after unscrewing the four mounting bolts; take care not to lose the guide pins from the support blocks.

20   Remove the clutch and primary drive components as described in Section 2 (if not already done).

21   Mesh the gears in two speeds at a time to lock the transmission, then remove the locknuts and spacers.

22   Remove the mounting hardware from the side door of the transmission. Pull the side door, countershaft and mainshaft out of the transmission case as an assembly. Withdraw the main clutch pushrod from the mainshaft bore if necessary.

23   Label the oil hoses attached to the top of the transmission case and remove them. Plug the ends of the hoses.

24   Remove the oil filter from the bottom of the case (models through 1991).

25   On models with an enclosed drive chain, the rear chain boots must be disconnected from the primary chaincase. It may be necessary to use a Harley-Davidson special tool (part no. 97101-81) to accomplish this.

26   On chain drive models disconnect the master link and remove the chain from the sprocket. On belt drive models move the rear wheel forward in the swingarm to provide enough slack to maneuver the belt off the sprocket.

27   Lift the motorcycle and support it securely on blocks. Place a block of wood below the engine to support it.

28   Remove the nut and spacer from the swingarm pivot shaft on the right side of the frame.

29   On all models, remove the footrests from both sides of the motorcycle. On FXR models, the pivot shaft mounting brackets must also be removed.

8.2 Note the special breather screw in the top cover (four-speed)

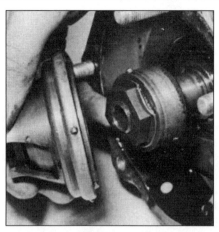

8.5 Pull the clutch release bearing off (four-speed)

8.6 Unscrew the end nut from the mainshaft (four-speed)

30 Tap the pivot shaft out of the swingarm from the right side of the motorcycle, using a large punch and a hammer. It isn't necessary to remove the nut and washer from the left side of the pivot shaft.

31 Separate the gear shifter rod from the shifter arm located at the top of the transmission.

32 Remove the two bolts and the washers

and nuts that secure the transmission to the engine.

33 Flatten back the tabs of their lockwashers, and remove the three or four bolts (as applicable) which retain the transmission case to the inner primary chaincase. On certain models the lower bolt is accessed from the rear side of the primary chaincase and also retains the engine ground strap.

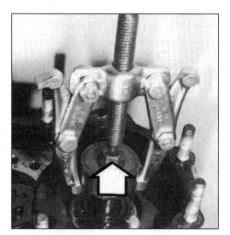

8.7 A puller will be needed to remove the bearing boss: note the bolt (arrow) inserted in the end of the mainshaft (four-speed)

8.10a Selector fork rod is secured by a screw (four-speed)

34 Lift the transmission case out of the frame.

35 The oil pan on 1993 and later FLT models may be detached from the transmission as described in Chapter 2A.

Installation

36 Installation is basically the reverse of removal.

---

8 Transmission - disassembly

Four-speed models

1 If the oil wasn't drained, do so now. Remove the drain plug from the bottom of the transmission until as much oil as possible has drained, then clean the drain plug and screw it back into the case.

2 Remove the screws retaining the top cover to the transmission. A special breather screw is also installed in the top cover. Note the location of the screw, then remove it **(see illustration)**. It must be installed in the same location during reassembly.

3 The top cover can now be lifted off, complete with the gear shifter assembly, and stored out of the way.

4 Remove the nuts securing the end cover to the transmission. On some models you'll also have to remove the battery carrier bracket. The cover is then free to be removed, complete with the kickstart shaft and spring (on models so equipped), and the clutch release shaft.

5 Pull the clutch release bearing off the end of the mainshaft **(see illustration)**. Position the transmission so the drive side end of the mainshaft is held securely in the jaws of a vise. Use wood blocks in the vise jaws to protect the mainshaft from damage.

6 Bend the ear of the tab washer, securing the end nut on the mainshaft, down and remove the nut and washer **(see illustration)**.

7 Remove the boss the clutch release bearing is attached to and to which the kickstart ratchet is attached (on kickstart models) from the tapered shaft end. The boss is a tight fit and will require a two or three-jaw puller to be used. When the puller is being attached, place a short bolt in the hollow end of the mainshaft to take the thrust of the puller screw **(see illustration)**.

8 After the boss has been removed, the kickstart ratchet gear engagement spring and bushing can be pulled off the shaft (kickstart models).

9 Pry the Woodruff key(s) from the end of the mainshaft with a small screwdriver. Store them in a safe place to prevent loss.

10 The shift fork shaft is a push fit in the case and is retained by a setscrew that passes through the top mating surface of the case. Remove the setscrew and carefully pull the shaft out **(see illustrations)**. Note the O-ring in the groove at the left end of the shaft.

2B

8.10b Slide the rod out and lift the forks out of the case (four-speed)

8.13 Flatten the tab washer, then remove the nut and the washer end plate (four-speed)

Don't lose the shift fork rollers, which are a loose fit on the fork pins.

11   Remove the four screws or Allen bolts holding the mainshaft bearing retainer plate to the inside wall of the transmission's outer compartment. The screws are very tight and may require an impact driver to loosen them.

12   Lift the retainer plate and the oil deflector (if equipped) out of the case.

13   Remove the countershaft end nut after flattening the tab washer on pre-1980 models. Remove the tab washer and the backing washer **(see illustration)**.

14   Remove the single screw passing through the speedometer driveshaft housing flange and pull the complete assembly out (if equipped).

15   Carefully drive out the countershaft with a brass punch.

16   Slide the needle roller bearing spacer washer out from between the countershaft First gear and the right-hand transmission wall. The complete countershaft gear cluster assembly can be lifted out as a unit. **Note:** *On early models, an uncaged needle roller bearing is installed in each end of the countershaft double gear. Be sure the needles don't fall out or, if they do, that the needles from one bearing don't get mixed up with those from the other. If loss or interchange of the 22 rollers in each bearing does occur, the two bearings must be replaced with new ones.*

17   After lifting the countershaft clusters out, remove the needle rollers and store them separately.

18   Using a soft-face hammer or a block of wood and a hammer (to protect the shaft end), drive the mainshaft out from the left side until the ball bearing just clears the large opening in the right transmission wall.

19   Using a scribe or awl, pry the circlip out of the groove in the mainshaft between the main drive gear and the mainshaft Third gear **(see illustration)**.

20   Withdraw the mainshaft, complete with the bearing and mainshaft double gear, while at the same time moving the circlip along the shaft.

21   Lift the mainshaft Third gear and the sliding dog clutch out of the transmission. Note that the dog clutch is installed with the

face stamped HIGH facing the main drive gear.

22   Push the main drive gear into the case and remove it from the top. On early models, the main drive gear runs on an uncaged needle roller bearing with 44 rollers. Remove the thrust washer from the bearing (if not already done), remove the 44 rollers and keep them in a safe place. Note the L-shaped key which engages with the drive gear splines and the keyway in the oil seal spacer.

5-speed models

23   Mount the transmission case securely in a vise equipped with soft jaws. If the sprocket nut has not already been loosened, place the drive chain/belt in position over the mainshaft (final drive) sprocket and secure the ends of the chain/belt to prevent the sprocket from turning. In the case of belt drives, be very careful not to bend the belt any more than necessary to hold the sprocket - the manufacturer advises not to form the belt into a loop smaller than 3 inches diameter, otherwise it may weaken.

24   On all models through 1991, flatten the ears on the tab washer securing the sprocket nut. The nut has left-hand threads so turn it clockwise to loosen it. Remove the retaining nut, tab washer, sprocket and sprocket spacer.

25   On 1992 and later models, remove the two lockscrews and slide off the locking plate **(see illustration)**. Unscrew and remove the sprocket nut, noting that it has a left-hand thread. Withdraw the sprocket and spacer.

26   In order to remove the main drive gear, a press is needed. Take the transmission case to a dealer service department or an automotive machine shop to have the gear removed.

---

9   Shifter assembly - overhaul

Four-speed transmission (1970 through early 1979)
Disassembly

1   Remove the three countersunk screws securing the shift arm to the dust cover. Remove the dust cover and the shift arm.

2   Remove the five long screws and the single short screws from the pawl carrier cover (they're retained by nuts behind the

8.19 Move the circlip out of the groove toward the right (four-speed)

8.25 Sprocket locking plate is secured by two screws (1992 and later models)

9.3a Remove the center screw and . . .

9.3b . . . the adapter plate from the cover (four-speed)

9.6 Remove the screw from the top cover to allow removal of the shift cam shaft (four-speed)

adapter plate). The pawl carrier cover, the carrier and the gasket are then free to be removed. **Note:** *The pawls in the carrier are spring-loaded. When the cover is removed the plungers may be released. Be sure to keep the two pawls and the springs separated, as well as the pawl carrier centralizer springs.*

3   The adapter plate and gasket can be separated from the cover after removing the single retaining screw **(see illustrations)**.

4   Disconnect the wire and unscrew the Neutral indicator switch from the cover.

5   The detent housing is secured by a tab washer. Bend the ears of the tab washer down, then unscrew the housing. Remove the housing, tab washer, spring and cam follower.

6   The shaft the shifter cam rotates on is secured by a single set screw **(see illustration)**. Remove the set screw from the left side of the cover and carefully tap the shaft out with a punch. When the shaft is removed, the shifter cam can be lifted out of the cover.

7   Removal of the shifter shaft isn't required unless the shaft bushing is worn. To remove the shaft, remove the cotter pin securing the shifter gear and pull the shaft out, leaving the gear and spring in the cover. These two remaining components will lift out.

Inspection

8   Clean all of the components, except the neutral indicator switch and gaskets, with solvent. Dry all of the parts with a clean, lint-free rag or compressed air (if available).

9   Work in clean, well lit surroundings so defects don't go undetected. Failure to notice damage or signs of advanced wear may necessitate another teardown at a later date, due to the premature failure of the part concerned.

10   Except in extreme cases, little wear will develop in the shifter components within the transmission itself, other than those described in the transmission inspection procedure. If the machine has covered a lot of miles, the shifter gear teeth and the teeth with which they mesh on the shifter cam may

wear, requiring replacement of both components.

11   The bushing the shifter shaft rides on and the bushing the pawl carrier rotates on may wear after extended periods of use. The pawl carrier bushing can be driven out of position with a tubular drift. The shouldered bushing in the cover must be drawn out with a puller because the shape of the casting obstructs access to it. A puller can be fabricated from a length of pipe, slightly wider than the bushing, a long threaded bolt and nut, and a pair of washers, one of which must be slotted and have a diameter slightly less than the smaller external diameter of the bushing.

12   Insert the bolt, head first, through the bushing. Slip the slotted washer over the bolt, from inside the case, to secure the bolt head.

13   Place the pipe over the shank of the bolt, followed by the second washer and the nut. Heat the case in an oven to about 300-degrees F before the bushing is removed. As the nut is tightened, the bushing will be drawn out of the case.

14   The new bushing can be installed in the case by reversing the bolt and pulling the bushing into position by tightening the nut

9.15 Check the tips of the pawls for wear (four-speed)

inside the case.

15   Inspect the tips of the two pawls and the cam follower **(see illustration)**. In order for these components to function properly, the tips must be fairly sharp. Worn components must be replaced with new ones.

16   Check the pawl return springs and the pawl carrier centralizer springs for distortion and loss of strength. Replace any suspect components as a matched set.

Reassembly

17   Lubricate the bushings in the cover with clean oil, then turn the cover over so the shifter gear and spring can be installed. Insert the shifter shaft so it engages with the shifter gear and spring. The shifter shaft can only be installed in one position. Align the scribed line on the shifter gear with the portion of the shaft boss adjacent to the extreme left-hand spline **(see illustration)**. Secure the shifter gear and spring to the shaft by inserting a new cotter pin through the radial hole in the shaft.

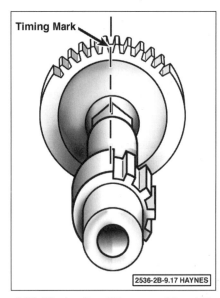

9.17 Aligning the shift gear and the shift shaft (the gear must be installed so the marked tooth gap aligns as shown)

2B

9.18a The relived tooth is for timing purposes (four-speed)

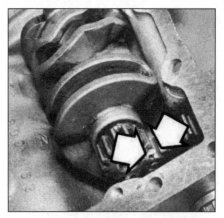

9.18b The shift gear and the shift cam gear must be timed (four-speed)

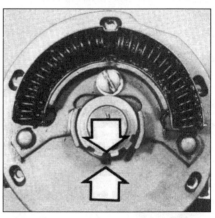

9.22 The adapter plate must be timed with the shifter shaft (four-speed)

18   The shifter cam must also be installed in the correct relationship to the shifter gear. When the shifter cam is installed, the slightly relieved (ground back) tooth must align with the scribed line on the shifter gear **(see illustrations)**.

19   Insert the shaft through the transmission cover and the shifter cam. Remember to install a new O-ring in the widest of the two grooves at the right end of the shaft before installing the shaft. Check the timing of the cam and gear and adjust it if necessary before securing the shaft with the setscrew inserted into the left-hand groove.

20   Position the adapter plate, and a new gasket, over the outer end of the shifter shaft. Loosely install the center screw to support the plate.

21   Install the cam follower, the spring, the tab washer and housing. Rotate the shifter cam so the cam follower engages any of the notches in the cam except the Neutral notch. First gear is when the shifter cam is in the extreme counterclockwise position, looking at the selector end.

22   Rock the shifter cam slightly to be sure the cam follower is perfectly seated. Rotate the adapter plate so the punched timing mark on the plate aligns exactly with the shifter shaft spline, which is second from the left **(see illustration)**.

23   Tighten the center screw securing the adapter plate and carefully check the alignment. **Note:** *Before continuing, be sure that all five positions of the shifter cam can be reached.* Installing the pawl carrier and the pawls and springs requires patience. The carrier is installed against the pressure of the pawl springs, together with the reluctance of the carrier centralizer spring to stay in place in the guides.

24   Install the carrier centralizer springs in the guide trough and lubricate them with grease.

25   Insert the two pairs of springs and pawls into the pawl carrier. Position the two pawls so the stepped portions face each other.

26   Lubricate the bronze bushing in the carrier as well as the pawls. Carefully place the

pawl carrier, slightly offset, in position over the shifter shaft boss.

27   Push the carrier towards the center position so the bronze bushing fits over the boss simultaneously with the centralizer projection (on the carrier) entering the gap between the two centralizer springs. The centralizer springs will probably try to spring out of position and the pawls will attempt to rotate in the pawl carrier. If this happens, take the pawl carrier off, reposition the pawls and springs and attempt the procedure again.

28   Position the pawl carrier cover on the adapter plate so the recessed portion is adjacent to the similarly shaped cutout in the adapter plate. Insert the shifter cover screws and attach and tighten the securing nuts.

29   Place the shifter arm/dust cover unit in position and install and tighten the three screws or Allen bolts.

30   The transmission cover is now ready to be attached to the main transmission case.

Four-speed transmission (late 1979-on)

Disassembly

31   Remove the five bolts securing the top cover to the transmission. The bolt directly above the final drive sprocket can only be loosened when removing the cover. To remove this bolt, the shift linkage must be disassembled.

32   Separate the cover from the transmission and remove the gasket.

33   Remove the two bolts securing the shifter shaft cover to the end of the transmission top cover.

34   Unscrew the bolt securing the shift lever to the transmission cover. Remove the shift linkage assembly from the transmission top cover.

35   With the shift linkage removed, the only remaining cover mounting bolt can be removed.

36   The shift linkage can be disassembled by removing the nut and washer that connects the linkage to the shifter shaft cover. On FX models, the two retaining rings on the

shift linkage must also be removed.

37   Drill a 1/4-inch hole in the plug in the top of the transmission cover and pry the plug from position. The plug must be replaced with a new one.

38   Reach into the top cover through the opening in the top and remove the snap-ring and washer securing the shifter cam and the pawl assembly.

39   Turn the cover over and remove the cam follower and spring from the corner of the cover. Remove the cam follower body from the transmission cover after bending the tabs of the lockplate out of the way and removing the retaining bolts.

40   Unscrew the four Allen bolts holding the pawl stops in position. Detach the pawl stops and spring from the cover.

41   Remove the neutral indicator switch from the cover.

Inspection

42   Clean all of the components, except the neutral indicator switch and gaskets, with solvent. Dry all of the parts with a lint-free rag or compressed air (if available). Work in clean, well lit surroundings so defects don't go undetected. Failure to notice damage or signs of advanced wear may necessitate another teardown at a later date, due to premature failure of the part concerned.

43   Inspect the tips of the cam follower and shifter pawls. In order for these components to function properly, the tips must be fairly sharp. Worn tips indicate the need for replacement with a new component.

44   Check the cam follower return spring and the pawl carrier spring for distortion and apparent weakening. Replace any defective components as a matched set.

45   Check the neutral indicator switch by depressing the plunger and releasing it. If the plunger doesn't spring back, the switch must be replaced with a new one.

Reassembly

46   Reassembly is the reverse of the disassembly procedure. Be sure to coat the pawl springs with multi-purpose grease before installation.

47 After the cam follower body is attached to the cover, bend the tabs of the lockplate up against the flats of the mounting bolts to lock them in place.

48 Coat the threads of the neutral indicator switch with thread sealant before installing it.

49 Be sure that the pawls engage with the teeth of the shifter cam gear when the pawl assembly is installed. Also be sure that the tab on the pawl carrier locates between the two springs before the washer and snap-ring are installed.

50 Coat the edges of the plug with gasket sealer and set the plug in place on top of the cover with the domed side of the plug facing up. Seat the plug by hitting the center with a ball-peen hammer.

51 Be sure to insert the transmission cover bolt into the left rear mounting hole before attaching the shifter linkage components.

Five-speed transmission

Disassembly

52 Remove the top cover from the transmission and the shifter cam.

53 Slide the support block off of the left side of the cam.

54 Remove the snap-ring from the right side of the shift cam with snap-ring pliers.

55 With the snap-ring removed, the outer thrust washer and the right support block can be slid off the shifter cam. Mark the outer thrust washer in some way so it's not mixed up with the inner thrust washer (where fitted).

Inspection

56 Clean all of the shifter components, except the bearings and the neutral indicator switch, with solvent. Dry all of the parts with a clean lint-free rag or, if available, with compressed air.

57 Work in clean, well lit surroundings so defects don't go undetected. Failure to notice damage or signs of advanced wear may necessitate another teardown at a later date, due to the premature failure of the part concerned.

58 Check that the plunger in the neutral indicator switch will spring back without binding after depressing it. If it binds it must be replaced with a new one.

59 Clean the bearings with a clean lint-free rag and examine them closely. If the bearings are pitted, grooved or worn, they will have to be replaced with new ones. The bearings must be pressed in and out of the support block. Be sure to install the bearings with the letters stamped in the bearings facing the outside of the support block when it is installed on the shifter cam.

60 Check the ends of the shifter cam. If they are pitted or grooved, the shifter cam and the bearings in the support blocks must be replaced with new ones. Make sure that the shaft inside the shifter cam is not loose. Check the shifter cam for wear and cracks and replace it with a new one if necessary.

Reassembly

61 Slide the inner thrust washer (not fitted from mid-1991) into position on the large end of the shifter cam. Install the right support block with the cam follower on the cam lobes.

62 Place the outer thrust washer on the end of the cam and secure the components with the snap-ring. Be sure the snap-ring is firmly seated in the groove and that the thrust washer(s) can spin after the snap-ring is installed.

63 Attach the left support block to the small end of the shifter cam and place the assembly in position in the transmission. Be sure to have the numbers on the support blocks facing down.

64 As the shifter cam is being lowered into position, engage the shifter forks in the slots. There are guide pins in the transmission case that the right support block (and from mid-1991, also left support block) must line up with.

65 Install the washers and bolts securing the support blocks and make sure the left support block is straight and does not bind on the bearing. This is especially important on early models, where the block is not located by guide pins. Tighten the mounting bolts to 7 to 9 ft-lbs (9 to 12 Nm).

Caution: Be careful not to overtighten the bolt nearest the neutral switch plunger - distortion may result.

66 Rotate the shifter cam and make sure all of the gears engage. Check the shifter cam alignment and shifter cam end play as described below.

67 If the neutral indicator switch was removed or replaced, apply thread sealing compound to its threads and tighten the switch to 3 to 5 ft-lbs (4 to 7 Nm). Check the gear engagement as described below.

68 Install the top cover on the transmission with a new gasket and tighten the cover bolts.

Shifter cam alignment

69 On all models through mid-1991 check the shifter cam alignment, and if necessary adjust by fitting a thicker or thinner inner thrust washer to the right support block. Refer to the appropriate paragraph below. Note that this check is not necessary on models from mid 1991 and later (identified by the omission of the inner thrust washer and 'pressed-in' neutral pin in shifter cam as opposed to cast ramp).

70 To align the shifter cam on models through 1983, the right side door and gasket must be removed. Refer to Section 7 for the removal procedure. Measure the distance the center of the groove is from the outer surface of the transmission case while the transmission is in 3rd gear. It should be 3.043 inch (77.29 mm). If the distance is wrong, the inner thrust washer must be replaced with a thicker or thinner one until the exact distance is obtained.

71 On 1984 to mid-1991 models, position the drum in neutral and take up any play against the right support block. Measure the distance from the outer machined surface of the right support block to the center cam groove's nearest edge. It should be 1.992 to 2.002 inch (50.59 to 50.85 mm); if not, replace the inner thrust washer with one of different thickness until the measurement falls within the specified range.

Shifter cam end play

72 Attach a dial indicator to the transmission case and measure the end play of the shifter cam. If it isn't within the 0.001 to 0.004 inch (0.025 to 0.102 mm) range, the outer thrust washer must be replaced with one of different thickness.

Gear engagement check

73 Shift the transmission into 3rd gear and check that the upper two pins on the shifter cam are perfectly centered in the slot of the shifter pawl. There should be 0.010 inch (0.254 mm) of clearance between the edges of the shifter pawl slot and the cam pin nearest that edge.

74 Adjust by loosening the locknut on the end of the transmission case and turning the adjusting screw until the desired clearance is obtained. Tighten the locknut to 20 to 24 ft-lbs (27 to 33 Nm) and recheck the clearance.

10 Transmission components - inspection

1 Give the transmission components a close visual examination for signs of wear and damage such as chipped or broken teeth, worn dogs or splines and bent selector arms. If the machine has had a tendency to jump out of gear, look carefully for worn dogs on the backs of the gears and similar wear on the projections on the dog clutches they engage. Check also for wear in the selector tracks in the shifter cam and the cam plate with which the detent pawl locates. In the former case, wear will be evident in the form of rounded corners or even a wedge-shaped profile. The corners of the cam plate tracks will wear first; all such wear is characterized by brightly polished surfaces.

2 The shifter arms usually wear across the fork that engages with a gear, causing a certain amount of sloppiness in the gear change. A bent shifter will immediately be obvious, especially if overheating has blued the surface.

3 All defective transmission components should be replaced. There is no satisfactory method of repairing them.

4 Don't forget to check the transmission mainshaft and countershaft. If it's suspected they're bent, the gear cluster must be stripped down and the shafts checked with a dial indicator. Neither one should have more than 0.003-inch (0.076 mm) runout. If this reading is exceeded, the shaft must be replaced.

2B

Four-speed transmission

5   After a thorough cleaning with solvent, check the mainshaft journal ball bearing for radial play and roughness when rotated. If either one is noted, install a new bearing. Removal of the bearing from the mainshaft can take place after the retaining nut has been unscrewed.

6   The two countershaft and single mainshaft needle roller bearings require a small amount of running clearance, as shown in the specifications. If additional play is evident, the bearings must be replaced. With the exception of the mainshaft needle roller bearing whose outer race is a press fit in the transmission case, the needle rollers on pre-1979 models run directly on the components they support and rotate on. If bearing wear is very advanced, damage may have occurred to the roller tracks on the components, requiring replacement. The sleeve gear bearing outer race may be driven or pressed out of the case after removing the oil seal collar and circlip. The case MUST be heated in an oven to approximately 300-degrees F before the race is driven out. Installation of the race should be carried out in a similar manner.

7   The clearance between the gears, bushings and shafts should be checked against the Specifications at the beginning of the Chapter. Replace any bushings that are outside the maximum clearance.

8   Oversize rollers are available to enable a selective fit between the components. Bushings and bearings should be replaced by a Harley-Davidson dealer service department with the necessary expertise and instruments for measurement of bearing play and bearing selection.

Five-speed transmission

9   Check the shifter fork shaft to be sure it's straight. If it's bent or damaged, it must be replaced with a new one. Using a small carpenter's square, check the shift forks to see if they're perfectly square on the shaft. If not, replace the shift forks.

10   Compare the shift forks to a new one. If the old forks have worn more than 0.020-inch, they must be replaced with new ones.

11   Make sure the bearings in the side door feel smooth when rotated and check to see if they're pitted or otherwise damaged. Replace the bearings with new ones if necessary. If the mainshaft or countershaft bearings in the side door must be replaced, they have to be pressed out of position and new ones pressed in. This should be done by a Harley-Davidson dealer service department or an automotive machine shop.

12   Check all of the bearings and oil seals in the transmission case for wear and damage. Replace any components that appear to be even slightly worn. When replacing oil seals, coat the lips of the seal with oil or grease and apply sealant or Loctite to the outside edge.

13   Check the condition of the springs on the shifter arm assembly. If the spring fails to hold the pawl on the cam pins, it must be replaced with a new one.

11 Kickstart components and clutch release shaft (four-speed models) - inspection

1   After removal of the transmission end cover, no further disassembly is required to determine the condition of the components. Apart from sudden failure of the kickstart return spring, the main area of wear occurs in the teeth of the kickstart gear and ratchet pinion and the teeth of the ratchet components. The latter type of wear will cause slipping. Worn teeth can't be reprofiled; the only remedy is replacement of the parts. The ratchet pinion is installed with a plain bushing, which can be driven out
if excessive play dictates replacement.

2   To remove the kickstart spindle, unscrew the nut after bending down the tab washer. Using a soft-face hammer, drive the spindle out, driving the kickstart gear off the shaft. As the spindle is withdrawn, the return spring will disengage automatically from the spindle. The spring can be removed after detaching the chrome cover, which is held in place by a single screw. Check the fit of the spindle in the two plain bushings. If wear is evident, the bushings can be driven out and new ones installed. An oil seal is installed between the two bushings - it must be replaced if the bushings are removed, or if oil leakage has occurred along the spindle.

3   Reassemble the kickstart mechanism as follows. Place the return spring in position with the thrust washer between the spring and case. The chamfered side of the thrust washer should face the spring. Lubricate the spindle and insert it through the bushings, attaching the inner end of the spring in the slotted spindle boss. Place the spindle end in the jaws of a vise and rotate the cover approximately one-turn in a clockwise direction to tension the spring (make sure the vise jaws are lined with some type of soft metal to avoid damage to the spindle). Connect the kickstart gear so the spindle is unable to unwind. Install the tab washer and nut, tighten the nut and bend the tab washer up to secure it.

4   In time, the clutch shaft bushings will wear, causing excessive movement of the shaft. To remove the shaft, dislodge the circlip from inside the case and pull the shaft out, leaving the release lever and thrust washer in the case. Remove the lever and thrust washer. The old bushings can be driven out and new ones installed.

12 Transaction - reassembly

Four-speed models

1   On pre-1978 models, insert the 44 needle rollers the main drive gear rides on into the transmission case. The needle rollers will be easier to keep in place if you apply heavy grease to the bearing race (see illustration). Later models have caged bearings.

2   Set the thrust washer in place over the bearings on the inside of the transmission case. Late 1978 and later models don't have a thrust washer between the inside of the transmission case and the main drive gear.

3   Install a new oil seal on the end of the main drive gear. Carefully slide the main drive gear into position, from the inside of the case. Make sure the uncaged bearings, on the earlier models, aren't disturbed or knocked out of place.

4   Slide the First and Second gears onto the mainshaft, followed by the bearing housing, the mainshaft bearing, the tab washer and the retaining nut.

5   Tighten the ball bearing retaining nut to the specified torque and lock it in position by bending over the ears of the tab washer.

6   Insert the partially assembled mainshaft into the transmission case until the Third gear, the bushing, the retaining washer, the circlip and the shifter (dog) clutch can be

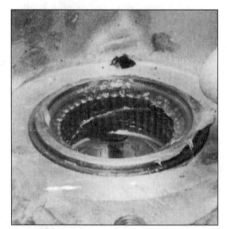

12.1 Secure the needle rollers in place with heavy grease (four-speed)

12.6a Be sure the circlip is correctly seated in the mainshaft groove (four-speed)

12.6b Note the HIGH mark on the shifter clutch (four-speed)

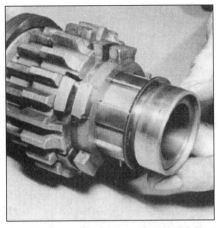

12.12a Install the shifter clutch and the washer, followed by . . .

12.12b . . . the First gear and bushing (four-speed)

installed on the mainshaft. Slide the circlip along the shaft until it can be seated in the groove **(see illustration)**. **Note:** *The shifter clutch must be installed with the side marked HIGH facing the main drive gear* **(see illustration)**.

7   Using a soft-face hammer, drive the mainshaft into the case until the shoulder of the bearing race is seated against the case.

8   On pre-1977 models with uncaged needle rollers on the countershaft, apply heavy grease to the countershaft gear and install the needle rollers. The lock ring and the bearing retaining washer must be installed on the countershaft gear before the bearings are placed in position.

9   On early models, attach the thrust washer on the left side of the countershaft gear in the recess. On late 1978 and later models, attach the caged needle bearings to the countershaft gear.

10   Coat the bearings with grease, then slide the bushing, the countershaft Second gear and the retaining washer onto the countershaft gear.

11   Secure the components on the countershaft gear with a new retaining ring.

12   Place the shifter clutch, the thrust washer, the First gear bushing and First gear in position on the countershaft gear **(see illustrations)**.

13   Make sure the uncaged needle rollers on early models are still in place **(see illustration)**.

14   Apply some grease to the countershaft end washers and place them in position on the inside of the transmission case. Carefully set the countershaft gear assembly in place in the case **(see illustration)**. With a new oil seal attached to the countershaft, insert the countershaft through the case and the countershaft gear assembly from the sprocket side of the case. **Note:** *The oil seal should be on the sprocket side of the case.*

15   Check the countershaft end play with a dial indicator. If the end play isn't within the specified limits, the end washer on the First gear end of the assembly can be exchanged for a washer of a different thickness to obtain the desired end play.

16   On pre-1980 models, position the mainshaft retaining plate so the V-shaped cutout is toward the right side of the shaft.

17   Place the oil deflector plate in position, on models so equipped, and secure the

retaining plate with the four screws.

18   Position the countershaft retaining plate with the flat side against the mainshaft retaining plate. Slide the tab washer over the countershaft and thread the retaining nut onto the shaft.

19   Tighten the retaining nut to the specified torque and bend the ears of the tab washer over the flats on the nut to secure it in position.

20   On 1980 and later models, position the retaining plate on the mainshaft so the extended corner of the plate engages the groove in the end of the countershaft.

21   Install and tighten the retaining plate mounting screws.

22   If the oil seal near the final drive sprocket was removed from the case, the new one should now be installed. Use a small file to clean up the case where the old oil seal was staked in place. On pre-1978 models, position a new cork seal over the main drive gear sleeve.

23   Lubricate the lips of the new oil seal and insert it into the case so the spring side of the seal is facing the main drive gear spacer. Carefully drive the oil seal into place. Be sure the seal enters the bore squarely.

24   When the seal is in place, use a cold chisel to stake it in two places, 180-degrees apart.

25   On pre-1978 models, install the L-shaped key so the longest portion locates in the main drive gear and the short end locates in the recess in the oil seal collar.

26   If new shift forks have been installed, or if the shift forks have been disassembled, they must be reassembled and adjusted so they're in the correct relationship to each other. This procedure requires shims 0.007 and 0.014-inch (0.18 and 0.36 mm) thick and a special transmission setting tool. The adjustment can't be done without the special tool, so it should be left to a Harley-Davidson dealer service department. The procedure is simple, but it's very important for the proper operation of the transmission.

27   Place the two fully assembled shift forks in the transmission so each one

2B

12.13 Make sure the needle rollers, in both ends of the countershaft gear, are in order (four-speed)

12.14 The thrust washer on the right end can be installed either before or after the countershaft assembly (four-speed)

engages with the channel on its respective shift (dog) clutch. **Note:** *The forks are not interchangeable. The fork with the larger diameter must engage the countershaft shifter clutch* **(see illustration).**

28   Check the condition of the O-ring attached to the groove in the left end of the shift fork shaft. Replace it with a new one if necessary.

29   Slide the shaft into position, engaging it with the shift forks, then install the setscrew used to secure the shaft. Be sure the narrow end of the setscrew engages the groove in the shaft.

30   Rotate the shift cam in the transmission cover so it's in the neutral position. Move the shift forks independently until the gears are also in neutral.

31   Thoroughly lubricate the gears in the transmission with oil and apply some lubricant to the channels in the shift cam.

32   Position a new transmission cover gasket on the case, over the two dowel pins.

33   Attach the shift fork roller to each fork pin. Lower the cover into place and make sure the shift fork rollers enter the channels in the shift cam.

34   Install and tighten the screws used to secure the cover to the transmission. Install the special breather bolt that fits in the right-hand side of the cover on some models.

35   Operate the shifter arm to see if each gear can be engaged - problems are usually caused by errors in one of the adjustment procedures.

36   On kickstart models, install the kickstarter gear and the thrust backing spring.

37   Place the Woodruff key(s) in position in the tapered end of the mainshaft. Attach the kickstart ratchet. On electric start models, a plain boss is installed in place of the ratchet.

38   Install the tab washer and the mainshaft nut. Lock the transmission and tighten the mainshaft nut to the specified torque. Bend the ears of the tab washer over the flats of the nut to lock it in place.

39   Attach the clutch thrust bearings and, on kickstart models, install the starter mechanism **(see illustration).**

40   Place a new gasket over the end cover studs and install the cover.

41   Insert the speedometer drive assembly, if equipped, into the side of the case, using a new gasket between the flange and the case. Tighten the retaining screw securely.

42   The transmission is now ready to install in the frame. Reverse the removal procedure, referring to Section 7.

43   Fill the transmission with the specified amount of oil or until the oil level is at the bottom edge of the plug hole.

Five-speed models

44   Position the sprocket spacer over the main drive gear, then slide the mainshaft (final drive) sprocket into position.

45   Place the tab washer (models through 1991 only) on the main drive gear. Install the nut, noting that it has left-hand threads and

12.27 Engage the shift forks with their respective shifter clutches (four-speed)

must be tightened counterclockwise to the specified torque. **Note:** *You'll have to hold the countershaft sprocket as described in Section 8 while the nut is tightened.* Lock the nut by bending over the ears of the tab washer (models through 1991) or by installing the lockplate and its retaining screws (models from 1992 and later).

46   The remainder of transmission reassembly must be done with the transmission case installed in the frame. Reverse the disassembly procedure in Section 8 for reassembly.

47   If the transmission won't fit in the swingarm, a special tool (H D-33805) is available to spread the swingarm cleveblocs.

48   When installing the swingarm pivot shaft through the swingarm and transmission from the left side, place the dowel pin holes in the plastic washers at the top. The chamfer on the washer for the right side must face out. Coat the pivot shaft with anti-seize compound before installation.

49   When installing the pivot shaft or the footrest mounting brackets, be sure the roll pins engage the locating hole in the rubber mount. Also make sure the flat on the pivot shaft registers with the flat on the rubber mount on the right.

50   Position the footrests so they'll fold up at a 45-degree angle to the rear before tight-

ening them.

51   On FLT models, the rear chain boots and the mating surfaces on the inner primary chaincase and transmission must be coated with RTV sealant. Tighten the mounting screws to 48 inch-lbs.

52   See if all of the gears can be engaged. If not, adjust the shifter as described in Section 9.

53   Lubricate the seal and screw the oil filter into place on the bottom of the transmission. Install the oil drain plug and fill the transmission to the recommended level.

54   When installing the final drive chain, make sure the closed end of the master link faces the direction of chain travel.

13 Clutch cable - replacement

1   Loosen the cable adjuster to provide as much slack as possible in the cable (see Chapter 1).

2   Remove the snap-ring from the underside of the cable retaining pin at the handlebar lever, then pull out the pin and disconnect the upper end of the clutch cable from the lever.

12.39 The clutch release cam must locate in the thrust bearing recess (four-speed)

3   Drain the primary chaincase oil (see Chapter 1).

4   If you're working on an early model without a small round clutch inspection cover in the primary chaincase cover, remove the primary chaincase cover (see Section 3). If you're working on a motorcycle that does have a clutch inspection cover, remove it.

5   On early models, free the cable from the bracket.

6   On later models, you'll need to disassemble the release mechanism **(see illustration)**. Note the location of the gap in the retaining ring so it can be reinstalled in the same location, then remove the retaining ring. Take the inner ramp and coupling out of the primary chaincase cover. Hold them together as you remove them so the coupling balls don't fall out.

7   Turn the inner ramp and disconnect the coupling from it, then detach the end of the cable from the coupling. Unscrew the cable

fitting from the transmission cover and remove its O-ring.

8   Before removing the cable from the bike, tape the lower end of the new cable to the upper end of the old cable. Slowly pull the lower end of the old cable out, guiding the new cable down into position. Using this method will ensure the cable is routed correctly.

9   Installation is the reverse of the removal steps, with the following additions:

a)   *Use a new O-ring on the clutch cable threaded fitting.*

b)   *Position the retaining ring gap as noted during removal.*

c)   *Use a new gasket on the clutch inspection cover (if equipped) and tighten its bolts to the torque listed in this Chapter's Specifications.*

d)   *Lubricate and adjust the clutch cable (see Chapter 1).*

e)   *Don't forget to refill the primary chaincase oil.*

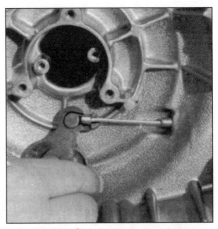

13.6 On later models the release mechanism must be disassembled to disconnect the clutch cable

2B

Notes

Chapter 3
Fuel and exhaust systems

Contents

Degrees of difficulty

| **Easy,** suitable for novice with little experience | | **Fairly easy,** suitable for beginner with some experience | | **Fairly difficult,** suitable for competent DIY mechanic | | **Difficult,** suitable for experienced DIY mechanic | | **Very difficult,** suitable for expert DIY or professional | |

Specifications

Carburetor

Type

1970	Tillotson
1971 through 1975	Bendix
1976 through 1989	Keihin non-CV
1990-on	Keihin CV

Adjustments

Idle speed	See Chapter 1
Fast idle speed	See Chapter 1
Float level	See text

Low speed mixture screw setting *(late 1977 through 1979 models only)*

FLH-80 (carburetor 27466 - 78)	3/4 turn open
FLH-1200 (carburetor 27467-78A)	1-1/8 turn open
FX-1200 (carburetor 27468-78A)	1-1/8 turn open

Fast idle speed

Late 1978 through 1983 models only	1500 rpm

3

Main jet sizes

Tillotson	0.049, 0.051, 0.053, 0.055, 0.057, 0.059, 0.061 and 0.063
Bendix	90, 95, 100, 105, 110, 115, 120 and 125
Keihin	
1976 through early 1978	1.60, 1.65, 1.70, 1.75, 1.80 and 1.85 mm
Late 1978 through 1983	150, 155, 160 and 165
1980 through 1985	160
1984 through 1989	155
FLT	
Early 1984	165
Late 1984 through 1986	175
1987	170
FXR	
1984 and 1985	160
1986	170
1987	165
FLT and FXR (1988 and 1989)	
California	140
All others	165
All other models	
1986 FXWG and FXST/C	170
1988 and 1989 California	140
All others	165
1990 and 1991	
California	165
All others	185
1992	
FLT and Dyna	
California	160
All others	175
FXR and Softail	
California	160
All others	165
1993 and 1994 FLT*	
Early 1993 California	160
Late 1993 and all 1994 California	165
49 state and International	175
1995 FLT	
US, Swiss	175
International	180
1996-on FLT	
49 state	175
California, International, Swiss	180
1993-on FXR*	
Early 1993 California	160
Late 1993 an all 1994 California	165
49 state and International	165
1993-on Softail and Dyna	
1993 California	160
1993 49 state	175
1993 International	165
1994 (all)	165
1995 US and Swiss	165
1995 International	180
1996-on California	175
1996-on 49 state	170
1996-on International	180

Slow jet sizes *(1984 and later models only)*

1984 through 1997 (all)	50
1988 and 1989	
California	42
All others	52
1990 and 1991	
California	42
All others	45
1992	45

1993 and 1994 FLT*
    Early 1993.. 40
    Late 1993 and all 1994 US 42
    Late 1993 and all 1994 International 40
1995-on FLT
    All except 1995 Swiss 42
    1995 Swiss 40
1993-on FXR*
    Early 1993.. 40
    Late 1993 and all 1994 US 42
    Late 1993 and all 1994 International 40
1993-on Softail and Dyna
    1993 US... 42
    1993 International.. 40
    1994 (all) 42
    1995 (except Swiss) 42
    1995 Swiss 42
    1996-on (all)... 42

*Early 1993 includes production dates prior to March 1993 on California models and January 1993 on 49-state models.

Torque specifications

Tillotson carburetor

Inlet needle valve seat	40 to 45 inch-lbs (4.5 to 5.0 Nm)
Diaphragm cover plug	23 to 28 inch-lbs (2.6 to 3.0 Nm)

Keihin carburetor (1976 through 1983)

Carburetor mounting nuts	10 to 14 ft-lbs (14 to 19 Nm)
Air cleaner bracket-to-rocker arm cover	13 to 20 ft-lbs (18 to 27 Nm)
Air cleaner bracket-to-backplate...	10 to 15 ft-lbs (14 to 20 Nm)
Air cleaner bracket-to-carburetor	75 to 80 inch-lbs (8.5 to 9.0 Nm)

Keihin carburetor (1984-on)

Carburetor-to-intake manifold bolts .... 15 to 17 ft-lbs (20 to 23 Nm)
Rubber compliance fitting
    Mounting bolts .... 40 to 60 inch-lbs (4.5 to 7.0 Nm)
    Hose clamps .... 15 to 20 inch-lbs (1.7 to 2.2 Nm)
Intake manifold mounting bolts/nuts (1990 only) .... 72 to 120 inch-lbs (8 to 14 Nm)
Air cleaner mounting bolts/nuts
    1984 and 1985 (FLT)
        Bracket-to-cylinder heads .... 13 to 17 ft-lbs (18 to 23 Nm)
        Bracket-to-backplate... 10 to 15 ft-lbs (14 to 20 Nm)
        Backplate-to-carburetor .... 75 to 80 inch-lbs (8.5 to 9.0 Nm)
        Cover screws .... 12 to 17 ft-lbs (16 to 23 Nm)
    1984 and 1985 (except FLT)
        Bracket-to-cylinder heads .... 13 to 17 ft-lbs (18 to 23 Nm)
        Backplate-to-bracket and carburetor .... 84 to 120 inch-lbs (9 to 14 Nm)
        Backplate bottom bolt .... 13 to 17 ft-lbs (18 to 23 Nm)
        Cover screws .... 12 to 17 ft-lbs (16 to 23 Nm)
    1986-on (FLT and FXR)
        Backplate
            To cylinder heads and bracket............................... 120 to 144 inch-lbs (14 to 16 Nm)
            To carburetor.. 36 to 60 inch-lbs (4 to 7 Nm)
        Cover screws .... 36 to 60 inch-lbs (4 to 7 Nm)
    1986-on (except FLT and FXR)
        Head bolt and backplate bottom bolt........................... 120 to 144 inch-lbs (14 to 16 Nm)
        Captive carburetor bolt .... 36 to 60 inch-lbs (4 to 7 Nm)
        Cover screw .... 36 to 60 inch-lbs (4 to 7 Nm)

Fuel injection system

Fuel pressure .... 40 to 47 psi (280 to 325 kPa)

Engine temperature

Sensor resistance
    14-degrees F (-10-degrees C)... 16,559 ohms
    68-degrees F (20-degrees C)... 3,747 ohms
    176-degrees F (80-degrees C)... 377 ohms

3

1 Fuel system - general information

The fuel system on carbureted models consists of the fuel tank, the control valve, the fuel line and the carburetor. Gasoline is fed by gravity to the carburetor through the control valve, which contains a built-in filter. The control valve has three positions; On, Off and Reserve. The reserve position provides a small amount of fuel after the main supply has run out, so the engine will still run for a short time.

Three different makes of carburetors were installed on the motorcycles covered by this manual. Tillotson carburetors were used on 1970 and 1971 models, Bendix carburetors were used on 1972 through 1976 models and Keihin carburetors were used on 1977 and later models. Beginning in 1990, a constant velocity (CV) version of the Keihin carburetor was standard equipment.

All carburetors have a butterfly throttle (CV carburetors also have a slide, but it's vacuum operated and responds to throttle butterfly movement) and incorporate an accelerator pump. The Bendix and Keihin carburetors have an integral float chamber. Each carburetor has a manual choke to facilitate easy starting in low outside temperatures.

The fuel system on fuel injected models consists of the fuel tank with in-tank fuel pump and filter, induction module, electronic control module (ECM), sensors, hoses, wiring harnesses and control cables. The sensors indicate supply the ECM with information on crankshaft position, manifold absolute pressure, intake air temperature, engine temperature, throttle position and vehicle speed. The induction module contains two fuel injectors and an idle air control motor.

A large capacity air cleaner is attached to the carburetor or induction module on all

2.3 Loosen or remove the hose clamp (arrow) and detach the crossover hose from one side of the tank

models. Refer to Chapter 1 for filter maintenance instructions.

All 1985 and later California models are equipped with an evaporative emission control system to reduce air pollution that stems from evaporation of gasoline in the fuel tank when the motorcycle is parked.

Several fuel system routine maintenance procedures are included in Chapter 1.

 Warning: On fuel injected models, the fuel lines contain fuel under high pressure, even with the engine off. Relieve fuel system pressure as described in Section 13 before doing any work that includes disconnecting fuel lines.

2 Fuel tank - removal and installation

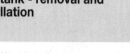

 Warning: Gasoline is extremely flammable, so take extra precautions when you work on any part of the fuel system. Don't smoke or allow open flames or bare light bulbs near the work area, and don't work in a garage where a natural gas-type appliance (such as a water heater or clothes dryer) is present. Since gasoline is carcinogenic, wear fuel-resistant gloves when there's a possibility of being exposed to fuel, and, if you spill any fuel on your skin, rinse it off immediately with soap and water. Mop up any spills immediately and do not store fuel-soaked rags where they could ignite. When you perform any kind of work on the fuel system, wear safety glasses and have a fire extinguisher suitable for a Class B type fire (flammable liquids) on hand.

Removal - all models

1   On carbureted models, turn the fuel control valve to the Off position and disconnect the fuel line from the carburetor. On fuel injected models, relieve the fuel system pressure (see Section 13). Some hose clamps installed at the factory must be cut or pried off and can't be reused.

2   Insert the end of the fuel line into a clean gasoline container and turn the fuel valve to the On position to drain the tank. Use a funnel to direct the gasoline into the container.

3   On two-piece fuel tanks and some one-piece tanks, the crossover hose, that connects the two tanks or the lower portions of the one-piece tank, must be disconnected from one of the fittings. Release the clamp and slide it down the hose **(see illustration)**. Some clamps have to be cut off with wire cutters and can't be reused - install a worm-drive clamp when the hose is reinstalled.

Removal - one-piece fuel tanks

1970 through 1979

4   The front of the tank is secured by a single bolt running through the frame at the head stock and passing through the two flanges welded to the front of the fuel tank.

5   The rear of the tank is secured by a coil spring which hooks onto tabs attached to the tank. After removal of the bolt and the spring, the tank can be lifted off.

1980-on

6   Remove the seat (see Chapter 7).

FLT models (1980 through 1988)

7   Remove the seat bracket and plastic frame cover (if equipped). Unplug the fuel gauge wire harness connector (you may have to cut one or more plastic wire ties as well, if they're used to secure the harness to the frame).

8   Remove the screws at the rear of the tank and the mounting bolt at the front to detach the tank. If the tank is being replaced, remove the trim and sending unit for installation on the new one.

FLT models (1989 and later)

9   Follow the instructions in Step 7 above.

10   Remove the three console mounting screws (one at the rear and two at the front, under the locked cover).

11   Remove the gas cap and gently lift up on the console to separate it from the tank. Mark the hoses and fittings if necessary, then disconnect the rubber overflow and emissions hoses from the console.

12   Follow the instructions in Step 8 above.

Caution: DO NOT remove the nut attaching the yellow wire to the sending unit. The float will drop into the tank if you do.

FXR models (except FXLR/FXRS - 1988 and later)

13   Remove the three tank center panel screws and the gas cap.

14   Carefully lift up on the center panel and detach all wires. On some models, the speedometer cable will have to be disconnected as well.

15   Detach the fuel gauge ground wire clipped to the underside of the tank. Remove the front tank mounting bolt and detach the center panel.

16   Remove the rear mounting bolts and carefully lift up on the tank to remove it. Don't damage the wire harness between tank and frame.

17   Transfer the sending unit to the new tank if the old one is being replaced.

FXLR models

18   Follow the procedure for FXR models (Steps 13 through 17), but ignore any references to the center panel and fuel gauge.

FXRS models

19   Remove the two instrument panel screws, then carefully lift it up and disconnect the speedometer cable and wires.

20   Remove the front tank mounting bolt.

21   Follow the instructions in Steps 16 and 17 above.

Dyna models

22   Remove the instrument panel from the tank (two screws or single domed nut, according to model) and disconnect the drive cable(s) and wiring.

23   Disconnect the crossover hose and emission/vent hose from the tank.

24   Remove the single front and rear mounting bolts and lift the tank free.

25   The fuel gauge is situated in the false left-hand gas cap. If the tank is being replaced, remove the gauge and transfer it and the sending unit to the new tank. Pry the gauge, gently from the tank and disconnect its wiring. The sending unit is secured by five screws.

Removal - two-piece fuel tanks

26   If a choke control knob is attached to the instrument panel, unscrew the knob and the locknut (see the Instruments section of Chapter 8 if necessary).

27   Remove the instrument panel from the top of the tank (see Chapter 8).

28   The tanks are held independently at the rear by two bolts. On early models the front mountings consist of two long bolts which pass through frame brackets and into nuts on the other side. Later models use shorter bolts which screw into the frame brackets, and thus allow one tank to be removed independently from the other.

29   Remove the pin securing the front of the seat to the seat post. Hinge the seat all the way up and support it in this position.

30   Remove the two front bolts/nuts first, then remove the rear bolt/nut holding each tank half. **Note:** *Spacers and washers are used at all mounting bolt locations. Keep track of them and be sure to install them in the same locations during reassembly.*

31   Disconnect the crossover hose from one of the tanks and disconnect any emission hoses (where fitted).

32   Lift the tanks off the frame.

33   After the fuel tank is removed from the vehicle, it should not be placed in an area where sparks or open flames could ignite the fumes coming out of the tank. Be especially careful inside garages where a natural gas-type appliance is located, because the pilot light or electronic ignition could cause an explosion.

Cleaning and repair

34   All repairs to the fuel tank should be carried out by a professional who has experience in this critical and potentially dangerous work. Even after cleaning and flushing of the

3.4 Remove the screws (arrows) to disassemble the fuel control valve

fuel system, explosive fumes can remain and ignite during repair of the tank.

Installation (all models)

35   When replacing the fuel tank(s), reverse the above procedure. Be sure to install any spacers or washers in their original locations. Replace cracked or deteriorated hoses and clamps with new ones.

36   If a new tank is installed on 1985 and later FLT and FXR models equipped with a California EVAP system, you'll have to drill or punch a 0.03 to 0.06-inch (0.762 to 1.524 mm) hole in the fitting on the new tank's filler neck. Use a sharp awl and a hammer or a 1/16 inch drill bit to make the hole. If a drill is used, be sure to clean any metal chips produced out of the tank before installing it.

---

3   Fuel control valve (carbureted models) - removal and installation

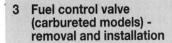

⚠ **Warning: Gasoline is extremely flammable, so take extra precautions when you work on any part of the fuel system.** *Don't smoke or allow open flames or bare light bulbs near the work area, and don't work in a garage where a natural gas-type appliance (such as a water heater or clothes dryer) is present. Since gasoline is carcinogenic, wear fuel-resistant gloves when there's a possibility of being exposed to fuel, and, if you spill any fuel on your skin, rinse it off immediately with soap and water. Mop up any spills immediately and do not store fuel-soaked rags where they could ignite. When you perform any kind of work on the fuel system, wear safety glasses and have a fire extinguisher suitable for a Class B type fire (flammable liquids) on hand.*

1   If the control valve is leaking or the filter must be cleaned, the valve must be detached from the bottom of the tank. Drain the fuel into a clean gasoline container first

3.5a Remove the lever, spring nut . . .

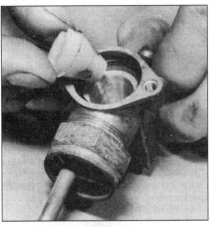

3.5b . . . and nylon valve assembly

(see Section 2), then detach the fuel line from the valve. Most hose clamps installed at the factory must be pried or cut off and can't be reused.

2   Unscrew the large nut and detach the valve from the bottom of the fuel tank.

3   Refer to Chapter 1 for instructions on cleaning and replacing the fuel filter.

4   If the valve leaks badly or doesn't work correctly, it must be replaced with a new one. Pre-1975 models have a sealed fuel valve which can't be repaired. The control valve on 1975 and later models can be disassembled by removing the two screws from each side of the lever **(see illustration)**.

5   The lever, spring and nylon valve can be removed after the screws are removed **(see illustrations)**.

6   Before installing the valve in the fuel tank, apply Teflon tape or sealant that's resistant to gasoline to the tank threads. On 1975 and later models, the valve has a left-hand thread and the fitting on the bottom of the fuel tank has a right-hand thread. As the large nut is tightened, the fuel valve and the tank are drawn together.

7   When the fuel valve is securely fastened to the tank, connect the fuel line to it. Install a new hose clamp if necessary.

3

4.2a Turn the fuel control valve to the Off position . . .

4.2b . . . and detach the clamp securing the fuel line to the carburetor fitting (original equipment clamps must be cut off and discarded)

4.4 Loosen the setscrew (arrow) securing the choke lever to the carburetor

4 Carburetor- removal and installation

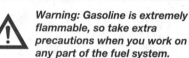

Warning: Gasoline is extremely flammable, so take extra precautions when you work on any part of the fuel system. *Don't smoke or allow open flames or bare light bulbs near the work area, and don't work in a garage where a natural gas-type appliance (such as a water heater or clothes dryer) is present. Since gasoline is carcinogenic, wear fuel-resistant gloves when there's a possibility of being exposed to fuel, and, if you spill any fuel on your skin, rinse it off immediately with soap and water. Mop up any spills immediately and do not store fuel-soaked rags where they could ignite. When you perform any kind of work on the fuel system, wear safety glasses and have a fire extinguisher suitable for a Class B type fire (flammable liquids) on hand.*

Note: *Although it isn't absolutely necessary, you probably will find it easier to remove the carburetor if the fuel tank is removed first* (see Section 2).

1   Refer to Section 8 and remove the air cleaner assembly.

2   Turn the fuel control valve to the Off position and disconnect the fuel line from the carburetor **(see illustrations)**. Most hose clamps installed at the factory must be pried or cut off and can't be reused.

3   Disconnect the throttle cable(s) from the carburetor. Tillotson and Bendix carburetors use setscrews to secure the throttle cable. To disconnect the cable(s) from a Keihin carburetor, turn the throttle valve open by hand and pull the cable ferrule out of the hole in the throttle lever. On 1981 and later models, there are two cables attached to the throttle lever.

4   Disconnect the choke cable from the carburetor - it's attached with a setscrew on all carburetors **(see illustration). Note:** *The CV carburetor used on 1988 and later mod-*

els doesn't have a choke. It has an enrichener valve that's cable-operated just like the choke. To detach it, unscrew the fitting and pull the valve out of the left (rear) side of the carburetor. Be careful not to damage the end of the valve while it's exposed.

5   Disconnect the vacuum and EVAP (emission) system hose(s) from the carburetor (some later California models only).

6   On 1990 and later FLTC and FLHTC Ultra models, detach the cruise-control servo cable from the carburetor bracket and throttle lever. It's held in place with C-clips and a washer.

7   On 1989 and earlier models, remove the nuts and bolts that secure the carburetor to the intake manifold. **Note:** *On 1983 and later models, remove the nut and washer and detach the VOES bracket from the carburetor mounting stud. Remove the stud and lower bolt. Carefully separate the carburetor from the intake manifold. On 1977 and 1978 Keihin carburetors, an O-ring seal is installed between the carburetor and intake manifold. All other models have a gasket.*

8   On 1990 and later models, simply

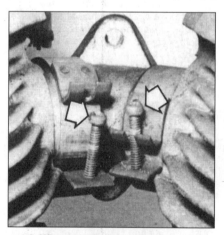

4.9 Where applicable, loosen the two clamp screws and pull the intake manifold out of the heads

loosen the hose clamp and pull the carburetor out of the intake manifold.

9   If necessary, remove the intake manifold from the cylinder heads. On early models, loosen the clamp screws and pull the manifold out of the heads **(see illustration)**. On later models, remove the Allen bolts that secure the manifold flanges to the heads.

10   Installation is the reverse of the removal procedure. If the manifold was removed, install new O-rings (early models) or sealing rings (later models). Install a new gasket or O-ring between the intake manifold and carburetor.

11   Replace the gasket between the air cleaner baseplate and the carburetor with a new one.

5 Carburetor overhaul - general information

1   Poor engine performance, hesitation and little or no engine response to idle fuel/air mixture adjustments are all signs that major carburetor maintenance is required.

2   Keep in mind that many so-called carburetor problems are really not carburetor problems at all, but mechanical problems in the engine or ignition system faults. Establish for certain that the carburetor needs maintenance before assuming an overhaul is necessary.

3   For example, fuel starvation is often mistaken for a carburetor problem. Make sure the fuel filter, the fuel line and the gas tank cap vent hole are not plugged before blaming the carburetor for this relatively common malfunction.

4   Most carburetor problems are caused by dirt particles, varnish and other deposits which build up in and block the fuel and air passages. Also, in time, gaskets and O-rings shrink and cause fuel and air leaks which lead to poor performance.

5   When the carburetor is overhauled, it's generally disassembled completely and the

metal components are soaked in carburetor cleaner (which dissolves gasoline deposits, varnish, dirt and sludge).

Caution: Don't soak any rubber parts (especially the vacuum piston diaphragm on the CV carburetor) in carburetor cleaning solvents. They will be damaged if you do.

The parts are then rinsed thoroughly with solvent and dried with compressed air. The fuel and air passages are also blown out with compressed air to force out any dirt that may have been loosened but not removed by the carburetor cleaner. Once the cleaning process is complete, the carburetor is reassembled using new gaskets, O-rings, diaphragms and, generally, a new inlet needle and seat.

6   Before taking the carburetor apart, make sure you have all of the necessary O-rings and other parts, some carburetor cleaner, solvent, a supply of rags, some means of blowing out the carburetor passages and a clean place to work.

7   Some of the carburetor settings, such as the sizes of the jets and the internal passageways, are predetermined by the manufacturer after extensive tests. Under normal circumstances, they won't have to be changed or modified. If a change appears necessary, it can often be attributed to a developing engine problem.

---

6   Carburetor - disassembly, inspection and reassembly

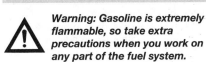

⚠ **Warning: Gasoline is extremely flammable, so take extra precautions when you work on any part of the fuel system.**
Don't smoke or allow open flames or bare light bulbs near the work area, and don't work in a garage where a natural gas-type appliance (such as a water heater or clothes dryer) is present. Since gasoline is carcinogenic, wear fuel-resistant gloves when there's a possibility of being exposed to fuel, and, if you spill any fuel on your skin, rinse it off immediately with soap and water. Mop up any spills immediately and do not store fuel-soaked rags where they could ignite. When you perform any kind of work on the fuel system, wear safety glasses and have a fire extinguisher suitable for a Class B type fire (flammable liquids) on hand.

1   Before disassembling the carburetor, clean the outside with solvent and lay it on a clean sheet of paper or a shop towel.

2   After it's been completely disassembled, submerge the metal components in carburetor cleaner and allow them to soak for approximately 30 minutes. Do not place any plastic or rubber parts in it - they'll be damaged or dissolved. Also, don't allow carburetor cleaner to get on your skin.

3   After the carburetor has soaked long enough for the cleaner to loosen and dissolve the varnish and other deposits, rinse it thoroughly with solvent and blow it dry with compressed air. Also, blow out all the fuel and air passages in the carburetor body.

Caution: Never clean the jets or passages with a piece of wire or drill bit - they could be enlarged, causing the fuel and air metering rates to be upset.

Tillotson carburetor

4   Carefully turn the idle mixture adjustment screw in until it bottoms, while counting the number of turns, then remove it, along with the spring. Record the number of turns - you'll need to refer to it later. Remove the intermediate mixture adjusting screw in the same manner. By counting the number of turns until they bottom, the adjustment screws can be returned to their original positions and adjustments will be kept to a minimum.

5   Note the position of the throttle valve before removing it to ensure it's reinstalled in the same position. Remove the two screws securing the throttle valve to the shaft and detach the valve.

6   Remove the screw securing the throttle shaft and accelerator pump. Pull the throttle shaft out of the carburetor body along with the throttle shaft spring and washers, then remove the dust seals from both sides of the carburetor body.

7   Invert the carburetor and remove the screws securing the diaphragm cover. Carefully lift off the cover, then remove the diaphragm and gasket. Separate the diaphragm from the gasket by peeling them apart.

8   Take out the screw that secures the accelerator pump plunger, then withdraw the plunger.

9   Remove the plug screw from the diaphragm cover.

10   Remove the inlet control lever screw. This will permit the control lever pin, the control lever and the inlet needle to be removed. These parts are very small and easily lost if you aren't careful. Remove the control lever tension spring from below the assembly.

11   Remove the inlet needle valve seat and gasket with a thin-wall 3/8-inch socket. Note the position of the seat insert with the smooth side toward the inside of the cage. The gasket can be lifted out with a scribe.

12   Unscrew the main jet plug, then remove the main jet and gasket.

13   Drill a 1/8-inch hole in the center of the main nozzle welch plug. Be careful not to drill beyond the welch plug, since damage to the main nozzle can result. Insert a small punch through the hole and carefully pry the plug out of the casting.

14   Remove the idle port welch plug as described in the previous Step.

15   Using a small punch, remove the welch plug over the economizer check ball and let the check ball roll out.

16   Remove the screws securing the choke

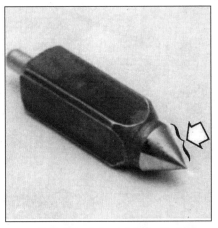

6.19 Check the inlet needle valve for a groove or ridge in the tapered area (arrow)

valve and lift out the bottom part of the valve.

17   Slide the choke shaft assembly out of the carburetor (when this is done, the upper part of the choke valve will be released and can be removed). Remove the choke spring and the choke shaft friction ball and spring. Pry the choke shaft dust seal out of the carburetor body.

18   Clean and inspect the parts as described in Steps 2 and 3 of this Section. Inspect the carburetor body for cracks and make sure the throttle shaft turns freely without excessive play. If it's sloppy, a new carburetor will be needed (although sometimes the throttle shaft bores can be reamed out and bushings installed - check with a dealer service department).

19   Make sure the inlet control lever rotates freely on the pin and the forked end of the lever engages with the slot in the inlet needle valve. Check the end of the control lever for wear and burrs. Check the spring to be sure it isn't stretched or distorted. Check the inlet needle valve and seat for nicks and a pronounced groove or ridge on the tapered end of the valve (**see illustration**). If there is one, a new needle and seat should be used when the carburetor is reassembled.

20   Examine the rest of the parts for wear and damage.

21   Reassemble the carburetor by reversing the disassembly sequence. Use a new diaphragm as well as new gaskets and seals and don't overtighten any of the small fasteners or they may break off.

22   Seat the new welch plugs by striking them with a punch slightly smaller than the plug itself. When the plug is seated, it should be flat, not concave. This will ensure a tight fit around the edge of the casting opening.

23   The inlet control lever tension spring should be installed in the carburetor body. Be sure it attaches to the protrusion on the inlet control lever. Bend the diaphragm end of the control lever so when the lever is installed, it's flush with the floor of the metering chamber.

3

6.25 Disconnect the lever and remove the accelerator pump (Bendix carburetor)

6.27 Unscrew and withdraw the idle tube (Bendix carburetor)

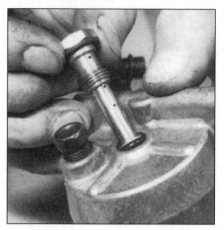

6.28 Unscrew the main jet and tube assembly from the float bowl (Bendix carburetor)

24   Be sure to tighten the inlet needle valve seat and the diaphragm cover plug to the torques listed in this Chapter's Specifications.

Bendix carburetor

25   Remove the screw securing the accelerator pump lever to the throttle shaft. Disconnect the accelerator pump boot from the float bowl. Remove the accelerator pump and lever **(see illustration)**.

26   Compress the spring on the accelerator pump shaft, rotate the pump lever 1/4-turn and disengage the pin at the top of the shaft from the lever.

27   On 1972 through 1974 models, unscrew the idle tube from the top of the carburetor body and detach the gasket at the same time **(see illustration)**.

28   Unscrew the main jet and tube assembly from the bottom of the float bowl **(see illustration)**. This will release the float bowl. Remove the O-ring and fiber washer from the main jet assembly.

29   Note how the float spring is positioned **(see illustration)**, then push the float pivot pin out of the throttle body. You may have to use a small punch to push the pin out. Remove the float assembly along with the inlet needle valve and the float spring **(see illustration)**. Remove the float bowl gasket.

30   Carefully screw the idle mixture adjusting screw in until it bottoms, while counting the number of turns, then remove it along with the spring. Remove the throttle stop screw and spring in the same manner. Counting and recording the number of turns required to bottom the screws will enable you to return them to their original positions and minimize the amount of adjustment required after reassembly.

31   Close the choke and remove the screws securing the choke valve to the shaft. Pull the choke shaft and lever out, releasing the spring and the plunger.

32   Pry the choke shaft seal and retainer out of the carburetor body. Remove the choke shaft cup plug only if it's damaged and must be replaced.

33   Close the throttle valve and remove the two screws securing it to the shaft. Remove the valve, then slide the shaft out of the carburetor body. Release the spring from the throttle shaft.

34   Pry the throttle shaft retainers and seals out of both sides of the carburetor body.

35   Clean and inspect the parts as described in Steps 2 and 3 of this Section. Make sure the throttle shaft turns freely without excessive play. If it's sloppy, a new carburetor will be needed (although sometimes the throttle shaft bores can be reamed out and bushings installed - check with a dealer service department). Check the inlet needle valve and seat for nicks and a pronounced groove or ridge on the tapered end of the valve **(see illustration 6.19)**. If there is one, a new needle and seat should be used when the carburetor is reassembled. Check float pivot pin and its bores for wear - If the pin is a sloppy fit in the bores, excessive amounts of fuel will enter the float bowl and flooding will occur. Shake the float to see if there's gasoline in it. If there is, install a new one.

36   Reassembly is the reverse of disassembly. Use new gaskets and seals. Whenever

an O-ring or seal is installed, lubricate it with grease or oil. Don't overtighten any of the small fasteners or they may break off.

37   Position the throttle shaft so the flat section is facing out and install the throttle valve (leave the screws slightly loose). Open and close the throttle a few times to center the valve on the shaft. Hold the valve firmly in place while tightening the screws.

38   Insert the choke shaft seal and seal retainer into the choke shaft hole and stake the retainer in place with a small punch.

39. Connect the choke valve to the choke shaft in the same manner as the throttle valve.

40   When the inlet needle valve assembly is installed, be sure the clip is attached to the float tab **(see illustration)**. Check and adjust the float level as described in Section 7.

41   Turn the idle mixture adjusting screw and the throttle stop screw in until they bottom and back each one out the number of turns required to restore them to their original positions.

42   Invert the carburetor and rotate the long end of the float spring up, against the float. Position the float bowl carefully over the

6.29a Note the position of the float spring before removing the pivot pin (Bendix carburetor)

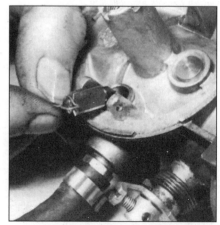

6.29b Lift out the inlet needle valve with the retaining clip attached (Bendix carburetor)

6.40 Be sure the inlet needle valve is correctly seated during reassembly - the retainer clip fits over the tab on the float (arrow) (Bendix carburetor)

6.42 The long end of the float spring (arrow) must be positioned as shown (Bendix carburetor)

6.44 Remove the screws securing the float bowl (Keihin non-CV carburetor)

throttle body, releasing the float spring so the long end of the spring is pressed against the side of the float bowl **(see illustration)**.

43   Install the main jet and tube assembly through the bottom of the float bowl and into the throttle body. Tighten it securely.

Keihin carburetor (except CV type)

44   Remove the screws securing the float bowl to the bottom of the throttle body and detach the float bowl **(see illustration)**.

45   Loosen the float retaining screw and slide the pivot pin out **(see illustration)**, then carefully separate the float assembly from the carburetor.

46   Remove the inlet needle valve and retaining clip from the float assembly.

47   Separate the rubber boot from the float bowl, then disengage the accelerator pump rod from the rocker arm **(see illustration)**.

48   Remove the plug from the bottom of the throttle body to gain access to the low speed jet **(see illustration)**. On some models, the low speed jet is accessible only after removing the main jet and main nozzle as

6.45 Loosen the retaining screw to release the float pin (Keihin non-CV carburetor)

described below.

49   Unscrew the main jet **(see illustration)**. On 1976 through 1978 models, tip the throttle body to remove the main nozzle, then unscrew the low speed jet.

50   Unscrew the nut securing the throttle

6.47 Disconnect the accelerator pump rod from the rocker arm (Keihin non-CV carburetor)

cable pulley or the fast idle cam assembly in place **(see illustration)**. Remove the throttle cable pulley and the return spring from the throttle shaft **(see illustration)**.

51   Remove the screws and detach the choke and throttle cable brackets **(see illustration)**.

6.48 Remove the low speed jet plug (Keihin non-CV carburetor)

6.49 Remove the main jet (Keihin non-CV carburetor)

6.50a Remove the throttle cable pulley mounting nut (Keihin non-CV carburetor)

3

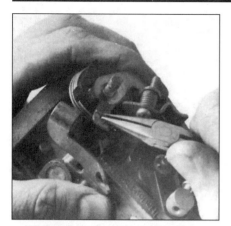

6.50b Disconnect the throttle return spring from the throttle shaft (Keihin non-CV carburetor)

6.51 Locations of the throttle cable (1) and choke cable (2) brackets (Keihin non-CV carburetor)

6.52 Remove the throttle stop screw (Keihin non-CV carburetor)

6.59a Remove the cover screws (Keihin CV carburetor) . . .

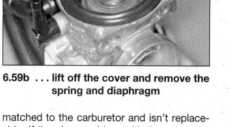

6.59b . . . lift off the cover and remove the spring and diaphragm

6.60 Lift out the vacuum piston and jet needle (Keihin CV carburetor)

52   Remove the low speed mixture adjusting screw (1975 through 1979 models only) and the throttle stop screw as described in Step 30 (see illustration). Note: *Late 1977 through 1979 models have a limiter cap on the low speed mixture screw that must be pried off to remove the screw. Models built after 1979 don't have a low speed mixture screw - the idle mixture is preset and can't be changed.*
53   Don't disassemble the throttle valve - it's

matched to the carburetor and isn't replaceable. If there's a problem with the valve, the carburetor must be replaced with a new one.
54   Clean and inspect the parts as described in Step 35.
55   Check the accelerator pump boot for cracks, the rod for distortion and the diaphragm for holes, cracks and other defects. If any wear or damage is evident, replace the pump components with new ones.

56   Reassembly is the reverse of disassembly. Use new gaskets and seals. Whenever an O-ring or seal is installed, lubricate it with grease or oil. Don't overtighten any of the small fasteners or they may break off. Check the float level (Section 7) before installing the float bowl.
57   Turn the low speed mixture adjusting screw (if used) and the throttle stop screw in until they bottom and back each one out the number of turns required to restore them to their original positions.

Keihin CV carburetor

58   Remove the carburetor from the machine as described in Section 4. Set the assembly on a clean working surface.
59   Remove the four screws securing the top cover to the carburetor body (see illustration). Lift the cover off and remove the piston spring (see illustration).
60   Peel the diaphragm away from its groove in the carburetor body, being careful not to tear it. Lift out the diaphragm/piston assembly (see illustration).
61   Remove the piston spring seat and separate the needle from the piston (see illustrations).
62   Refer to the accompanying illustration and note the following (see illustration):

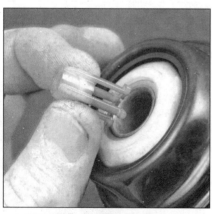

6.61a Remove the vacuum piston spring seat from the piston (Keihin CV carburetor)

6.61b Remove the needle from the piston (Keihin CV carburetor)

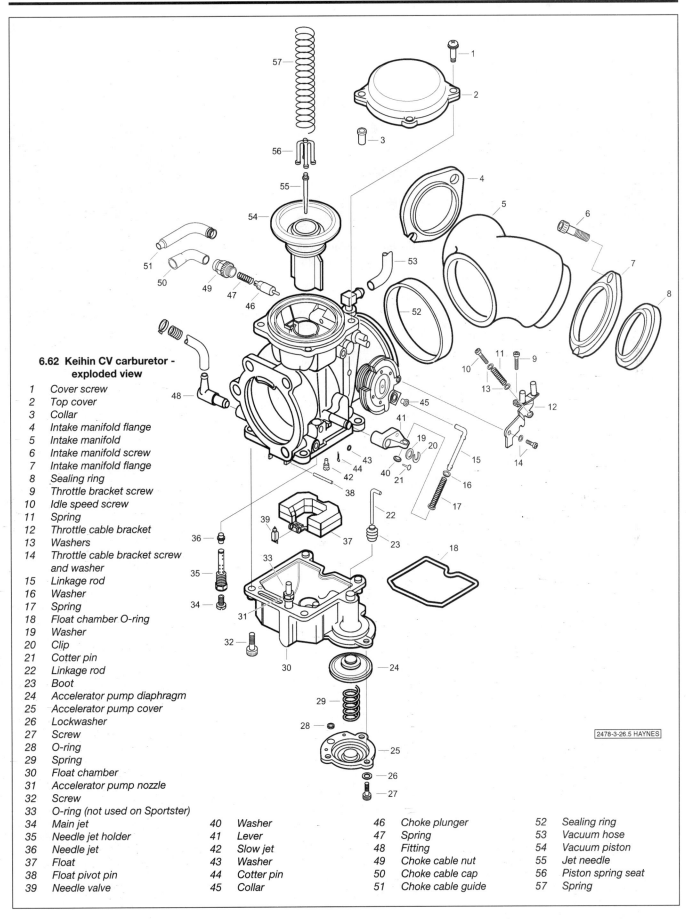

**6.62 Keihin CV carburetor -
exploded view**

1   Cover screw
2   Top cover
3   Collar
4   Intake manifold flange
5   Intake manifold
6   Intake manifold screw
7   Intake manifold flange
8   Sealing ring
9   Throttle bracket screw
10 Idle speed screw
11 Spring
12 Throttle cable bracket
13 Washers
14 Throttle cable bracket screw
    and washer
15 Linkage rod
16 Washer
17 Spring
18 Float chamber O-ring
19 Washer
20 Clip
21 Cotter pin
22 Linkage rod
23 Boot
24 Accelerator pump diaphragm
25 Accelerator pump cover
26 Lockwasher
27 Screw
28 O-ring
29 Spring
30 Float chamber
31 Accelerator pump nozzle
32 Screw
33 O-ring (not used on Sportster)

34 Main jet	40 Washer	46 Choke plunger	52 Sealing ring
35 Needle jet holder	41 Lever	47 Spring	53 Vacuum hose
36 Needle jet	42 Slow jet	48 Fitting	54 Vacuum piston
37 Float	43 Washer	49 Choke cable nut	55 Jet needle
38 Float pivot pin	44 Cotter pin	50 Choke cable cap	56 Piston spring seat
39 Needle valve	45 Collar	51 Choke cable guide	57 Spring

2478-3-26.5 HAYNES

3

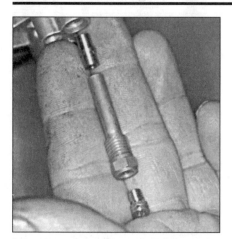

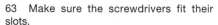

6.64 Here's how the needle jet, needle jet holder and main jet are arranged (Keihin CV carburetor)

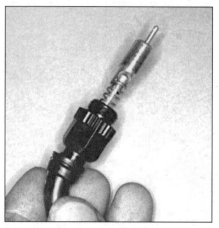

6.67a Unscrew the starter valve from the carburetor and compress the spring . . .

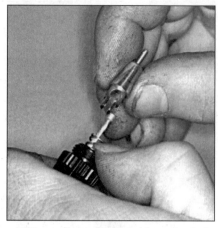

6.67b . . . then slip the cable end out of the plunger to separate the plunger from the cable (Keihin CV carburetor)

63   Make sure the screwdrivers fit their slots.

64   Remove the float chamber cover and O-ring for access to the jets and floats. Hold the needle jet holder with a wrench while you unscrew the main jet. Note which way the needle jet goes in the bore **(see illustration)**.

65   Push out the float pin to remove the floats.

66   When removing the diaphragm covers, do not lose the small O-ring in the passage next to the diaphragm.

67   The choke plunger is part of the choke cable **(see illustration)**. To remove it, unscrew it from the carburetor, then compress the spring and slip the cable end out of the plunger **(see illustration)**.

68   Remove the accelerator pump diaphragm screws **(see illustration 6.62)**. Take out the pump cover, noting the location of the O-ring. Take out the spring and diaphragm.

69   Check the operation of the choke plunger. If it doesn't move smoothly, replace it, along with the return spring. Check the tapered end of plunger for wear and replace if it's worn **(see illustration)**.

70   Check the carburetor body, float bowl and top cover for cracks, distorted sealing surfaces and other damage. If any defects are found, replace the faulty component, although replacement of the entire carburetor will probably be necessary (check with your parts supplier for the availability of separate components).

71   Check the diaphragms for splits, holes and general deterioration. Holding them up to a light will help to reveal problems of this nature.

72   Insert the vacuum piston in the carburetor body and see that it moves up-and-down smoothly. Check the surface of the piston for wear. If it's worn excessively or doesn't move smoothly in the bore, replace the carburetor.

73   Check the jet needle for straightness by rolling it on a flat surface (such as a piece of glass). Replace it if it's bent or if the tip is worn.

74   Check the tip of the fuel inlet valve needle. If it has grooves or scratches in it, it must be replaced. Push in on the rod in the other end of the needle, then release it - if it doesn't spring back, replace the valve needle.

75   Check the O-rings. Replace them if they're damaged.

76   Operate the throttle shaft to make sure the throttle butterfly valve opens and closes smoothly. If it doesn't, replace the carburetor.

77   Check the floats for damage. This will usually be apparent by the presence of fuel inside one of the floats. If the floats are damaged, they must be replaced.

78   Assembly is the reverse of disassembly, with the following additions.

79   Be sure the jet needle's spring doesn't cover the hole at the bottom of the vacuum piston - reposition it if necessary **(see illustration)**.

80   When installing the diaphragm, make sure the bead is seated in the groove and the diaphragm isn't distorted or kinked **(see illustration 6.59b)**. If the diaphragm doesn't want to seat in the groove, place the top cover over the diaphragm, insert your finger into the throat of the carburetor and push up

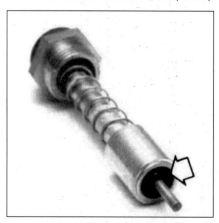

6.69 Check the plunger tip and seal (arrow) for wear (Keihin CV carburetor)

on the vacuum piston. Push down gently on the top cover - it should drop into place, indicating that the diaphragm has seated in its groove. Install the top cover, tightening the screws to the torque listed in this Chapter's Specifications.

7   Carburetor - adjustments

Tillotson carburetor

1   Carburetor adjustments should be made with the engine at normal operating temperature. Also, be sure the air filter element is clean and the air cleaner assembly is installed securely. Adjustments cannot be done accurately unless the air cleaner assembly is in place.

2   Make sure the twist grip closes the throttle lever on the carburetor completely. Turn the idle mixture screw in until it seats lightly, then back it out 7/8 turn. Adjust the intermediate mixture screw in a similar fashion.

6.79 Don't let the jet needle retainer block the vacuum hole (arrow) (Keihin CV carburetor)

7.6 Locations of the throttle stop screw (1) and the idle mixture adjusting screw (2) (Bendix carburetor)

3   Start the engine and adjust the throttle stop screw until the engine is running at approximately 2000 rpm. Turn the intermediate mixture screw in both directions until the highest engine speed is obtained without any misfiring or surging. Turn the screw an additional 1/8-turn counterclockwise.

4   Turn the throttle stop screw to adjust the idle to the recommended speed.

Bendix carburetor

5   The float level must be adjusted before anything else is done to the carburetor. The carburetor must be removed and the float bowl detached to adjust the float level. Refer to Section 4 for carburetor removal and Section 6 for removal of the float bowl. Invert the carburetor and measure the distance between the lower edge of the float, opposite the pivot pin, and the gasket mating surface. The distance should be 3/16-inch (insert a 3/16-inch drill bit between the gasket surface and the float as a gauge). If adjustment is necessary, bend the tab that contacts the inlet needle valve with needle-nose pliers. Reassemble and install the carburetor.

6   Run the engine until it reaches normal

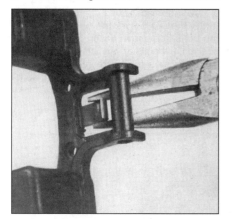

7.11b Bend the tab to adjust the float level (Keihin non-CV carburetor)

7.11a Measure the float level with the carburetor held vertically (1979 through 1989 Keihin carburetor)

operating temperature, then shut it off. Carefully turn the idle mixture adjusting screw in until it seats lightly (see illustration). Back it out 1-1/2 turns. Adjust the engine speed by turning the throttle stop screw until it runs at 700 to 900 rpm with the twist grip closed.

7   Adjust the idle mixture screw until the engine will run smoothly at idle speed and accelerate crisply. If necessary, adjust the throttle stop screw until the engine idles at 700 to 900 rpm.

8   Remember, all adjustments must be made with the engine at normal operating temperature and the air cleaner securely in place.

Keihin carburetor (except CV type)

Float level (1976 through 1978 models)

9   These models must have the float level measured in both the open and closed positions. Hold the carburetor upside-down and measure the distance between the gasket surface and the upper edge of the float. The distance should be 35/64 to 5/8-inch (14 to 16 mm).

7.21 Fast idle adjusting screw (arrow) (1981 through 1987 Keihin carburetor, 1980 similar)

10   Hold the carburetor right side up and measure the distance between the gasket surface and the lower edge of the float while it's suspended. The distance should be 1-3/32 to 1-3/16-inches (28 to 30 mm). Bend the tabs on the float, as necessary, to obtain the proper float levels.

Float level (1979 through 1989 models)

11   Hold the carburetor vertically with the float pivot pin at the top. Measure the distance between the outside edge of the float and the gasket surface (see illustration). The distance should be 0.630 to 0.670-inch (16 to 17 mm). If necessary, bend the tab on the float until the desired float level is attained (see illustration).

Low speed mixture adjustment (1977 and 1978 models)

12   Adjustments should be made with the engine at normal operating temperature and the air cleaner securely mounted.

13   Turn the low speed mixture adjusting screw in (clockwise) carefully until it seats lightly, then back it out 7/8-turn.

14   Adjust the throttle stop screw until the engine runs at 700 to 900 rpm. Turn the low speed mixture screw until the engine runs smoothly or until it reaches its highest rpm. Readjust the throttle stop screw, if necessary, to obtain the specified idle speed.

Low speed mixture adjustment (1979 models)

15   There's a limiter cap installed over the low speed mixture adjusting screw on these models. Normally the limiter cap shouldn't be removed. The low speed mixture screw should be turned only within the limits of the cap. If necessary, the limiter cap can be removed and the mixture can be altered.

16   Turn the mixture screw in until it seats lightly, then back it out 1-1/4 turns. Reinstall the limiter cap in the center position on the adjusting screw.

17   Adjust the idle speed with the throttle stop screw to 900 rpm. Turn the limiter cap to the leanest setting that still permits the engine to run smoothly. **Note:** *Turn the limiter cap counterclockwise for a richer mixture and clockwise for a leaner mixture.*

18   Readjust the idle speed, if necessary, to the specified setting.

Low speed mixture adjustment (1980 and later models)

19   The low speed mixture for 1980 and later models is set at the factory and sealed - it's not possible to adjust it.

20   Adjust the idle speed with the choke completely open. Turn the throttle stop screw until the engine is idling at the speed listed in this Chapter's Specifications.

21   Pull the choke out to the second position and turn the fast idle adjusting screw (see illustration) until the engine is idling at the specified speed.

3

8.3 Remove the screws and nuts holding the baseplate to the carburetor (arrows)

8.4 Remove the flexible connectors to reveal hollow breather passage bolts on 1983 and later models

Keihin CV carburetor

Float level (1990 through early 1991 models)

22   The carburetor must be removed and the float bowl detached when checking the float level. Make sure the floats are aligned with each other - bend them carefully to realign them if necessary.

23   Invert the carburetor and measure the distance from the float bowl mounting surface to the very bottom (curved) side of the float(s) with a dial or vernier caliper. Don't push down on the float(s) as this is done. It should be 0.725 to 0.730 inch (18.4 to 18.5 mm).

24   If the level is incorrect, carefully bend the tab on the float that contacts the inlet needle valve until it is.

25   Reinstall the float bowl and the carburetor.

Float level (late 1991 and later models)

26   Remove the carburetor and detach the float bowl. Place the carburetor body face down on a flat surface, on its engine manifold side.

27   Tilt the body at an angle of 15 to 20 degrees until the float tang is seen to just contact the needle valve tip, but not compress it. Do not tilt any more or less than the specified angle or the reading will be inaccurate.

28   Measure the distance from the top of the float to the bowl mounting surface; it should be within 0.413 to 0.453 inches (10.5 to 11.5 mm) (1991) and 0.413 to 0.453 inches (10.5 to 11.5 mm) (1992-on).

29   If the level requires adjustment carefully bend the tab on the float that contacts the inlet needle valve, then recheck the setting.

30   Reinstall the float bowl and carburetor.

Enrichener valve cable

31   The enrichener valve control knob should open, remain open and close without binding. The knurled plastic nut behind the knob controls the amount of resistance the cable offers.

32   If adjustment is required, loosen the locknut at the back of the cable bracket, then detach the cable from the bracket.

33   Grip the flats on the cable housing with an adjustable wrench, then turn the knurled plastic nut until the enrichener operates as described in Step 31.

34   Reattach the cable to the bracket and tighten the locknut. Do not lubricate the cable or housing - it must have a certain amount of resistance to work properly.

35   When the knob is closed, make sure the valve at the carburetor is closed completely.

Slow idle

36   With the engine at normal operating temperature and the enrichener valve fully closed, turn the throttle stop screw until the idle speed is correct (see this Chapter's Specifications). If the motorcycle doesn't have a tachometer, a hand-held instrument will be needed to measure the engine rpm.

8   Air cleaner - removal and installation

Note: *Although the air cleaners used on the models and years covered by this manual differ slightly in some details, they are all basically the same. They consist of a backplate, fastened to the carburetor with screws and a gasket. mounting bracket(s), a filter element and a cover. The following procedure is typical of what must be done to completely remove the air cleaner assembly - take notes, label parts and make a simple sketch of the mounting bracket(s) if the air cleaner on the machine you have appears different from the one described in the text. Make sure the gasket between the backplate and carburetor is in place and in good condition and hook up all hoses during installation. Use thread locking compound on the backplate mounting screws/bolts to prevent the screws from backing out during engine operation.*

1   Remove the screws or bolts securing the outer cover to the air cleaner assembly. Pull the cover off.

2   Remove the baffle plate (unless riveted in place) and filter element (see Chapter 1). If hoses are attached to the air cleaner assem-

bly, detach them from their fittings.

3   Flatten the tabs on the lockplate (if used), then remove the screws/bolts securing the baseplate to the carburetor **(see illustration)**. Some models also have nuts/bolts attaching the baseplate to brackets or directly to the cylinder head. The mounting bolts may be safety-wired together to prevent them from loosening.

4   Most later models have a vent hose attached to the rear of the baseplate, which must be disconnected to remove the plate. Many later models also have a crankcase breather hose, attached to the bottom of the baseplate, that must be removed. From 1993 the baseplate-to-cylinder head bolts are hollow; they allow crankcase vapor, routed up through the pushrod tubes and through an umbrella valve in the middle rocker cover, to pass into the intake system. Short flexible connectors fit in the hollow bolt heads and the rear of the filter element **(see illustration)**.

5   Installation is the reverse of removal. Be sure to install a new gasket between the baseplate and carburetor. On models with safety-wired bolts, the bolts must be rewired or have a thread locking compound applied to the threads before they're reinstalled. If the bolts somehow loosen and fall out of position, the bolts or washers could possibly be drawn through the carburetor and into the engine, causing serious internal damage. **Note:** *Do not overtighten the hollow bleed bolts on 1993 and later models; the recommended torque is 10 to 12 ft-lbs (14 to 16 Nm).*

9   Evaporative emission control system - general information

1   This system, installed on all 1985 and later California models, is virtually maintenance-free and shouldn't be tampered with

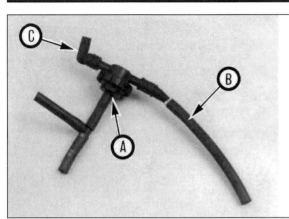

9.4 Vacuum operated valve port locations (1988 through 1991 California models) - see text

10.3 Connect the throttle cable(s) (single cable shown)

unless a new canister, hoses or valves are required because of leaks or deterioration.

2   An occasional check to make sure the hoses are routed properly, secured to the fittings and not kinked or blocked should be sufficient. Make sure the hoses don't come too close to or touch the exhaust system components. Also, check all canister and valve mounting fasteners to see if they're tight. On 1988 through 1991 models, check the reed valves in the air cleaner assembly backplate to make sure they aren't cracked or broken off.

3   The system is designed to prevent fuel vapor from escaping from the tank into the atmosphere when the engine is off. The vapor is directed from the tank through a hose and valve to a charcoal-filled canister (mounted on a frame front tube, under the seat or behind the gearbox (depending on the model), where it's absorbed by the charcoal. When the engine is started, the vapor is drawn from the canister into the carburetor and then into the engine, where it's burned in the cylinders. A large diameter hose also purges the canister with fresh air from the air cleaner during engine operation. The vapor valve prevents raw fuel from entering the vent hose when the motorcycle is at extreme angles.

4   1988 through 1991 models also have a Vacuum Operated Electric Switch (VOES) and a vacuum operated valve. The VOES directs vacuum to the vacuum operated valve, which seals off the carburetor float bowl vent when the engine's off (it also vents it to the atmosphere when the engine's running). If the diaphragm in the vacuum valve starts to leak, the fuel/air mixture would be upset (leaned out) at high speeds. To check the valve, apply a small vacuum (1 to 2 in/Hg only) to port A **(see illustration)**. The vacuum should remain steady and the valve should be open (you should be able to blow through port B or C - air should pass through). Release the vacuum and make sure the valve is closed (no air should pass through when blowing into port B or C). If the valve doesn't function as described, install a new one.

5   1992 and later models retain the VOES described above, but venting of the carburetor vent hose is controlled electrically by a solenoid-operated butterfly valve, clamped

to the rear of the air cleaner baseplate. The butterfly valve itself resides in a housing at the bottom of the air cleaner and if functioning correctly, should remain closed when the engine is stopped, yet open when the starter circuit operates and stay open until the engine is stopped. If failure is suspected, check first the mechanical linkage from the valve pivot to the solenoid plunger. If this is in order, check the solenoid operation as described in Chapter 8.

10 Throttle cable and grip - removal, installation and adjustment

Removal

1   On early models with a spiral-type throttle grip, remove the handlebar end screw, screw spring and grip sleeve. Remove the roller pin and the rollers from the throttle cable plunger. Disconnect the throttle cable from the carburetor, then pull the plunger from the end of the handlebar with the cable still attached to it. Loosen the setscrew that secures the cable end to the control coil plunger and detach the cable.

2   On later models with a drum-type throttle, remove the screws that hold the bottom and top halves of the throttle assembly together. Separate the housing halves and detach the end of each cable from the pulley.

3   Detach the cable from the carburetor. If the bike has a single throttle cable, loosen the setscrew and disconnect the cable from the throttle lever **(see illustration)**. If the bike has dual cables, label them (pull cable and idle cable). Lift each cable out of its pulley groove, rotate the cable to align with the slot and slip the cable end out of the pulley.

Installation

4   Route the cable(s) into place. Make sure they don't interfere with any other components and aren't kinked or bent sharply.

5   If you're working on a dual-cable model, lubricate the end of the pull cable with multi-purpose grease and connect into the throttle pulley at the carburetor. Pass the inner cable through the slot in the bracket,

then seat the cable housing in the bracket. Repeat the procedure to install the other cable.

6   Lubricate the throttle grip friction area on the handlebar with graphite grease. If you're working on a drum-type throttle grip (dual or single cable) lubricate the inner surfaces of the upper and lower throttle housing halves where they contact the throttle grip.

7   Reverse the disassembly procedure to reassemble the throttle grip on the handlebar.

Adjustment

8   Adjust cable freeplay as described in Chapter 1.

9   Turn the handlebars back and forth to make sure the cable(s) don't cause the steering to bind.

10   Operate the throttle and check the cable action. The cable(s) should move freely and the throttle pulley or lever at the carburetor should move back and forth in response to both acceleration and deceleration. If this isn't the case, find and fix the problem before you operate the motorcycle.

⚠ *Warning: Do not over-tighten the throttle grip friction screw. Riding with the friction screw too tight is not recommended because of the danger involved when the engine won't return to idle automatically in an emergency.*

11   Start the engine. With the engine idling, turn the handlebars all the way to left and right while listening for changes in idle speed. If idle speed increases as the handlebars turn, the cables are improperly routed. This is dangerous. Find the problem and fix it before riding the bike.

11 Choke knob and cable - removal and installation

1   On all except Keihin CV carburetors, loosen the setscrew that secures the choke cable to the carburetor **(see illustration)**.

3

2 On Keihin CV carburetors, unscrew the starter plunger and remove it from the carburetor **(see illustration 6.64)**.

3 Unscrew the nut that secures the choke knob to the bracket and remove the knob together with the cable.

4 Installation is the reverse of the removal steps.

 12 Exhaust system - removal and installation

1 Loosen the clamps and remove the heat shields. **Note:** *Later models use Torca clamps, which must be replaced with new ones once they're removed.*

2 On early models, remove the clamps at the cylinder head. On later models, unscrew the exhaust pipe-to-cylinder head nuts.

3 Unbolt the mufflers.

4 Remove the exhaust system as a unit, then disassemble it as needed.

5 Installation is the reverse of the removal steps. Tighten all of the fasteners securely, but don't overtighten them and strip the threads.

 13 Relieving fuel injection system pressure

1 Remove the seat and fuse block cover (see Chapters 7 and 8).

2 Locate the fuel pump fuse and remove it from the wiring harness (see Chapter 8).

3 Start the engine and let it idle until it stalls. Once it stalls, crank the engine with the starter for three seconds to relieve any residual fuel pressure, then turn the key off.

 14 Fuel injection system pressure test

1 Relieve fuel system pressure (see Section 13). Reinstall the fuel pump fuse.

2 Disconnect the fuel supply line fitting and attach a fuel pressure test fitting (Schrader valve) to the disconnected end of the line. Be sure to use two adapters to avoid twisting the line. Tug on the connections to make sure they're secure.

3 Start the engine and let it idle long enough to re-pressurize the fuel system, then bleed the gauge line of air, following the gauge manufacturer's instructions.

4 Rev the engine and note the fuel pressure reading. It should stabilize at a steady reading within the limits listed in this Chapter's Specifications.

5 Relieve fuel system pressure and remove the gauge. Reconnect the fuel supply line.

6 If the fuel pressure reading wasn't within the specified range, check the fuel fil-

11.1 On all except Keihin CV carburetors, attach the choke cable and secure it with the setscrew

ter and the pump inlet screen for clogging and replace it as necessary.

7 If the pump inlet screen and filter are clear, check for an internal leak in the fuel tank. The easiest way to do this is to turn the key to On with a low fuel level in the tank. During the first two seconds of fuel pump operation, fuel from an internal leak may be heard spraying against the sides of the tank.

8 If the pump, inlet screen and fuel filter are good and there's no internal leak, the pressure regulator may be at fault. Have it tested by a dealer service department or other qualified shop, or substitute a regulator known to be good.

 15 Fuel injection system relay test

1 Remove the seat and locate the fuel system relay on the fuse block (see Chapter 8 if necessary). Remove the relay.

2 Connect an ohmmeter between terminals 87 and 30 on the relay (if the terminal numbers aren't stamped on the relay, refer to the wiring diagrams at the end of this manual). The ohmmeter should indicate infinite resistance (no continuity).

3 Connect a 12-volt battery to terminals 85 and 86 on the relay (the motorcycle's battery will work if it's fully charged). There should now be continuity (little or no resistance) between terminals 87 and 30.

4 If the relay doesn't perform as described, replace it.

 16 Fuel injection system pump and filter - removal and installation

Fuel filter replacement

1 Relieve fuel system pressure (see Section 2).

2 Drain the fuel tank (see Section 3).

3 Remove the instrument panel or console from the top of the fuel tank (see Chapter 7 or 8). Remove the fuel tank top plate and gasket.

⚠️ **Warning: Don't cut yourself on the edges of the fuel tank opening while reaching inside.**

4 Reach inside the right side of the tank and cut the clamp on the short hose connected to the fuel filter.

5 Remove the filter mounting nut, lockwasher, washer and bolt.

6 Detach the filter mounting bracket from the inside of the tank and lift it up for access to the remaining fuel line clamp. Cut the clamp and take the filter out.

7 Installation is the reverse of the removal steps. Use new hose clamps and crimp them securely. The hose that runs to the fuel pump (long hose) goes on the filter fitting farthest from the mounting bracket.

Fuel pump removal and installation

8 Reach inside the left side of the fuel tank and lift the pump off its mounting posts.

9 At the top of the fuel pump, cut the hose clamp and disconnect the hose from the pump. Disconnect the pump electrical connectors.

10 Connect the wires and fuel hose to the fuel pump. The black wire goes on the same side of the pump as the fuel inlet screen. Use a new clamp on the hose and crimp it securely.

11 The remainder of installation is the reverse of the removal steps.

 17 Diagnostic trouble codes

1 These models have self-diagnostic capabilities. When the engine is running, the ECM monitors the system component circuits. If a malfunction occurs in one of these circuits, the module stores a diagnostic code and turns on the Check Engine lamp.

2 When the ignition key is turned to On (after it's been turned to Off for 10 or more seconds), and the engine kill switch is in the Run position, the Check Engine lamp lights for about 4 seconds, then goes out.

3 If the Check Engine Lamp does not come on when the ignition key is turned to ON, or if it fails to go out after four seconds, there is a malfunction in one or more of the monitored circuits in the ignition system.

4 There are three ways to output any diagnostic trouble code(s) stored in the ignition module. Harley-Davidson dealers use "Scanalyzer" or "Digital Technician" diagnostic equipment which interfaces directly with the ignition module through the Data Link Connector. This method is beyond the

scope of the home mechanic. The other method, which can be done at home, requires no fancy tools. This method is simply a matter of determining the two-digit trouble code(s) by counting the number of flashes of the Check Engine lamp.

5   Fabricate a two-inch jumper wire from 18-gauge wire with the correct terminal (Harley part no. 72191-94) on each end.

6   Remove the seat (see Chapter 7) and locate the Data Link Connector. The Data Link Connector has four wires (light green/red, black, violet/red, white/black) on one side of the connector, and none on the other side. Bridge terminals 1 and 2 (light green/red and black wires) with the jumper wire. Turn the ignition switch key to IGNITION and wait about eight seconds for the Check Engine Lamp to begin flashing.

7   Each stored code is preceded by a series of rapid flashes (about three per second), followed by a two-second pause (lamp is off), followed by the code. (If the lamp continues to flash at the faster rate, no codes are stored.)

8   The lamp indicates the first digit of the trouble code by flashing one or more times. Each flash is about one second in duration, followed by a one-second pause (lamp off). To determine the first digit, simply count the number of times the lamp flashes (it could be one, two, three, four or five flashes). Write down this number.

9   After the lamp has flashed the first digit of the code, there is another two-second pause (lamp off). The lamp then flashes one or more times to indicate the second digit of the code (two, four, five or six flashes).

10   After the lamp has flashed the second digit of the code, there is another two-second pause. Then, if there are no other codes stored, the lamp will repeat this trouble code again. If there is more than one code stored, the lamp will flash out the second stored code, in the same manner as the first. Again, jot down the code. This will be followed by another two-second pause, then the lamp will either repeat the first two codes again or, if there's a third code, it will display that code.

11   After the lamp has completed its output of all stored codes, it repeats, starting with the first code again. Once you note that the lamp is repeating itself, there is no need for further observation. (You may wish to record them a second time just to be sure that you counted the correct number of flashes for each digit of each code the first time.)

12   Compare the displayed trouble codes to the following list. You now know which circuit(s) has/have a problem. **Note:** *Some of the following components are used on fuel injected models and are covered in this Chapter. Others are part of the ignition system and are used on carbureted and fuel injected models. These are covered in Chapter 4.*

   11   Throttle position sensor
   12   Barometric pressure or MAP sensor

   14   Engine temperature sensor
   15   Intake air temperature sensor
   16   Battery voltage (high or low)
   23   Front fuel injector
   24   Front ignition coil
   25   Rear ignition coil
   32   Rear fuel injector
   33   Fuel pump relay
   35   Tachometer
   41   Crankshaft position sensor
   42   Camshaft position sensor
   44   Bank angle sensor
   52   ECM RAM error
   53   ECM ROM error
   54   EEPROM error
   55   Microprocessor malfunction
   56   Crankshaft or camshaft position sensor signal error

13   The first things to check in any circuit with an apparent problem are the connectors and the wires. Make sure that all connectors are clean, dry, corrosion-free and tight. Inspect each wire in the circuit and make sure that it's not grounded, open or shorted. If all the connectors and wires are in good shape, take the bike to a dealer service department or other qualified shop. No further diagnosis is possible at home.

14   To take the ignition module out of diagnostic mode, remove the jumper wire from the Data Link Connector and turn the ignition switch to OFF. Once any problems have been corrected, the trouble codes can be cleared in one of two ways. The convenient method requires the Scanalyzer. The other method is not convenient, but can be done at home if necessary. It requires 50 "start-and-run" cycles (each start-and-run cycle consists of starting the engine, allowing it to run for at least 30 seconds, then turning it off).

18 Fuel injection system - check

1   Check the ground wire connections for tightness, referring to the wiring diagrams at the end of this manual. Check all wiring and electrical connectors that are related to the system. Loose electrical connectors and poor grounds can cause many problems that resemble more serious malfunctions. A quick way to check for loose connections is to gently shake the wiring harness with fingers and note whether the symptom changes.

2   Check to see that the battery is fully charged, as the control unit and sensors depend on an accurate supply voltage in order to properly meter the fuel.

3   Check the air cleaner element - a dirt or partially blocked filter will severely reduce performance and economy (see Chapter 1).

4   If a blown fuse is found, replace it and see if it blows again. If it does, search for a grounded wire in the harness related to the system.

5   Check the intake manifold and induc-

tion module for leaks, which will result in an excessively lean mixture. Also check the condition of the vacuum hoses connected to the intake manifold. **Note:** *An easy way to check for vacuum leaks is to spray water on the induction module and vacuum hoses with the engine idling. If the engine runs better, there's a leak which is being temporarily sealed by the water.*

6   Remove the air cleaner housing and check the intake area of the induction unit for carbon and residue build-up. If it's dirty, clean it with aerosol carburetor cleaner and a toothbrush.

7   If the engine runs, start it and let it idle. Check the operation of each injector using a stethoscope or sounding rod; each injector will make a steady clicking noise if it's working (similar to a noisy valve lifter). If either injector is quiet, either the injector or its wiring harness is defective.

8   If the engine doesn't run, disconnect the electrical connector from each injector. Connect a fuel injector test lamp, sometimes called a "noid" light, to each connector in turn. Crank the engine with the starter and watch the test lamp. It should flash steadily if the injector is receiving current. If it doesn't flash, the wiring is probably at fault; if it does, the injector may be the problem, especially if there's a trouble code indicating a problem with the injector circuits.

9   If the injectors aren't sealing properly, they can leak fuel into the engine, which may cause erratic running and hard starting. To check for this problem, remove the air cleaner housing (see Section 22). While holding the throttle wide open, turn the key to On for two seconds, then turn it to Off for two seconds. Do this on-off sequence a total of five times, then check for liquid gasoline in the intake tract (use a flashlight if necessary). If there is any, one or both injectors are leaking and should be replaced.

10   The remainder of the system checks should be left to a dealer service department or other qualified shop, as there is a chance the control unit may be damaged if the checks are not performed properly.

19 Induction module - removal and installation

1   The induction module on these models consists of the throttle body, intake manifold, fuel injection system sensors, idle air control motor, fuel pressure regulator and fuel injectors. The throttle body and intake manifold are a single unit.

2   Remove the fuel tank partway and prop it up (see Section 3).

3   Remove the air cleaner housing (see Section 22).

4   Disconnect the electrical connectors for the throttle position sensor, intake air temperature sensor, idle air control motor and fuel injectors. **Note:** *To disconnect the fuel*

3

injector connectors, pull back the wire bail and rock the connector back-and-forth while pulling it free.

5   Disconnect the throttle cables (see Section 21). If you're working on a bike equipped with cruise control, disconnect the cruise control cable as well.

6   If you're working on a California model, disconnect the evaporative emission hose from the throttle body.

7   Disconnect the vacuum hose from the fuel pressure regulator on the underside of the induction module.

8   Remove two bolts on each side of the intake manifold to detach the manifold flanges from the cylinder heads (hex-head bolts on the left side, Allen-head bolts on the right side). Take the assembly off the engine and remove the sealing rings from the intake passages.

9   If you're planning to replace the fuel lines, remove the external retaining rings and slip the lines off the fittings. Use new O-rings and retaining rings when you reinstall the lines.

10   Install new manifold seals in the passages with their tapered sides facing toward the manifold. Position the flanges (they're marked R and L for right and left sides of the engine) and manifold on the engine, then tighten the screws evenly until they're just snug.

11   Connect the cables, wires and hoses, then install the air cleaner housing (see Section 8).

12   Tighten the manifold screws to the torque listed in this Chapter's Specifications.

13   The remainder of installation is the reverse of the removal steps. Check the throttle cable adjustment (see Chapter 1).

20 Fuel injectors - replacement

1   Remove the fuel tank partway and prop it up for access to the induction module (see Section 3).

2   Disconnect the fuel injector electrical connectors. **Note:** *To disconnect the fuel injector connectors, pull back the wire bail and rock the connector back-and-forth while pulling it free.*

3   Remove the Torx screw and retaining plate that secure the injectors to the induction module.

4   Free the injectors from the induction module. The ideal way to do this is with Harley tool HD-41320 or equivalent. This is a prying tool shaped to fit around the injectors. If you don't have the tool, work the injectors back-and-forth to free them from the module, taking care not to crack the plastic.

5   Check the injector filter screens for clogging or damage. Clean the screens or replace the injectors as necessary.

6   Installation is the reverse of the removal steps, with the following additions:

a)   *Wipe the injector O-rings with clean engine oil.*

b)   *Set the injectors in their bores so they line up with the retaining plate. Place the retaining plate over the injectors to verify the alignment, then push the injectors into their bores until they seat.*

c)   *Tighten the retaining plate Torx screw to the torque listed in this Chapter's Specifications.*

21 Engine temperature sensor - check, removal and installation

Check

1   If you're working on a Softail, relieve fuel system pressure (see Section 13). Disconnect the fuel line from under the fuel tank (this is part of the fuel tank removal procedure; see Section 2).

2   If you're working on a Touring model, remove the seat (see Chapter 7).

3   Locate the engine temperature sensor on the back of the front cylinder and disconnect its electrical connector.

4   Connect an ohmmeter between the terminals of the sensor. At low engine temperatures, sensor resistance should be very high, and at high temperatures it should be much lower. An approximate reading is listed in this Chapter's Specifications.

5   If sensor readings are not within approximately the specified range (a variation of +/-20% is acceptable), replace the sensor.

Replacement

6   If you haven't already done so, disconnect the electrical connector from the sensor.

7   Unscrew the sensor with a socket and take it off the cylinder head.

8   Installation is the reverse of the removal steps. Thread the sensor into the engine two or three turns, then tighten it to the torque listed in this Chapter's Specifications.

22 Throttle position sensor (fuel injected models) - check and replacement

The throttle position sensor on these models requires a voltmeter that can read to three decimal places to check and adjust it, as well as a breakout box to connect test equipment into the wiring harness. Checking, adjustment and replacement should be done by a dealer service department or other qualified shop.

23 Idle air control motor (fuel injected models) - check, removal and installation

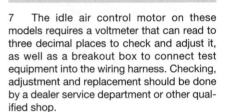

7   The idle air control motor on these models requires a voltmeter that can read to three decimal places to check and adjust it, as well as a breakout box to connect test equipment into the wiring harness. Checking, adjustment and replacement should be done by a dealer service department or other qualified shop.

24 Barometric pressure sensor (fuel injected models) - check and replacement

Check

1   Remove the right side cover (see Chapter 7).

2   Locate the sensor on the electrical panel. Backprobe terminals B and C of the sensor with a voltmeter (for terminal identification, refer to the wiring diagrams at the end of this manual).

3   Remove the rubber seal from the pressure port and connect a vacuum pump to the port.

4   Turn the key to On but don't start the engine. The BARO sensor should indicate a high voltage (about 4.0 to 4.8 volts), which should drop (to about 3 volts) as vacuum is applied to the port.

5   If the sensor doesn't perform as described, it's probably defective. Refer further service to a dealer service department or other qualified shop.

Replacement

6   Disconnect the electrical connector from the sensor.

7   Work the sensor free of its rubber seal. The seal can be re-used if it's in good condition.

8   Install the new sensor in the seal and connect the connector.

9   Install the side cover.

25 Fuel pressure regulator (fuel injected models) - removal and installation

1   The fuel pressure regulator on these models is mounted on the underside of the induction module, between the "V" of the intake manifold runners.

2   Remove the fuel tank (see Section 3).

3   From the upper side of the induction module, remove the Torx screw that secures the fuel injector retaining plate.

4   Reach under the induction module and work the fuel pressure regulator free (it's held

in place by an O-ring).

5   Installation is the reverse of the removal steps. Use a new O-ring, coated with a thin layer of clean engine oil. Position the vacuum port directly under the bracket bolt on the underside of the induction module.

26 Intake air temperature sensor (fuel injected models)

Check

1   Locate the intake air temperature sensor on the induction module and disconnect its electrical connector.

2   Connect an ohmmeter between the terminals of the sensor. At low engine temperatures, sensor resistance should be very high, and at high temperatures it should be much lower. An approximate reading is listed in this Chapter's Specifications.

3   If sensor readings are not within approximately the specified range (a variation of +/-20% is acceptable), replace the sensor.

Replacement

4   If you haven't already done so, disconnect the electrical connector from the sensor.

5   Remove the sensor mounting screws, then take the sensor and gasket off the throttle body.

6   Installation is the reverse of the removal steps. Use a new gasket.

3

Notes

Chapter 4
Ignition system

Contents

Degrees of difficulty

Easy, suitable for novice with little experience	**Fairly easy,** suitable for beginner with some experience	**Fairly difficult,** suitable for competent DIY mechanic	**Difficult,** suitable for experienced DIY mechanic	**Very difficult,** suitable for expert DIY or professional

Specifications

Ignition system type
1970 through early 1978 .... Mechanical contact breaker point
late 1978 and later .... Breakerless inductive discharge (electronic)

Air gap
1979 only .... 0.004 to 0.006 inch (0.102 to 0.152 mm)

Ignition coil resistance
1970 through early 1978
    Primary .... 4.7 to 5.7 ohms
    Secondary .... 16,000 to 20,000 ohms
Late 1978 and 1979
    Primary .... 4.7 to 5.7 ohms
    Secondary .... 16,500 to 20,000 ohms
1980 through 1983
    Primary .... 3.3 to 3.7 ohms
    Secondary .... 16,500 to 19,500 ohms
1984 and later
    Primary .... 2.5 to 3.1 ohms
    Secondary
        Except 1993-on FLT, FXR, Dyna .... 11,250 to 13,750 ohms
        1993-on FLT, FXR, Dyna .... 10,000 to 12,500 ohms

1 General information

In order for the engine to run correctly, an electrical spark must ignite the fuel/air mixture in the combustion chambers at exactly the right moment in relation to engine speed and load. The ignition system operation is based on feeding low tension (primary) voltage from the battery to the coil where it's converted to high tension (secondary) voltage by a process known as induction. The secondary voltage is powerful enough to jump the spark plug gap in the cylinders many times a second under high compression pressures, provided the system is in good condition and all adjustments are correct.

The ignition system installed on 1970 through early 1978 models as standard equipment is a mechanical contact breaker point type. The points are contained in a cone-shaped housing on the right side of the engine.

The system installed on late 1978 and later models is a breakerless inductive discharge system (electronic ignition).

Both systems are divided into two circuits: the primary (low tension) circuit and the secondary (high tension) circuit. The primary circuit consists of the battery, the contact breaker points (early models), the ignition timer (late 1978 and 1979) or the computerized ignition timer (1980-on), the primary coil, the ignition switch and the wires connecting the components.

The secondary circuit consists of the secondary coil, the spark plugs and the wires. All models use one spark plug per cylinder.

Mechanical flyweights are incorporated in the ignition systems on pre-1980 models to advance the ignition timing mechanically. On 1980 and later models, the computer (control module) advances the timing electronically. On 1983 and later carbureted models, a Vacuum Operated Electric Switch

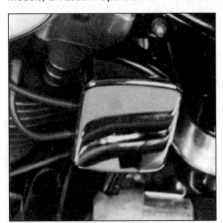

2.3 The ignition coil on early models is located under a chrome cover on the left side of the engine

(VOES) senses vacuum in the intake manifold and sends a signal to the computer, which advances or retards the ignition timing as needed.

2 Ignition coil - check, removal and installation

1 Detach the wires from the coil and connect an ohmmeter to the coil primary wire terminals. The primary resistance should be as listed in this Chapter's Specifications - if it isn't, the coil is probably defective. If an ohmmeter isn't available, take the coil to a dealer service department to have it checked or temporarily install a known good coil.

Caution: Be sure to connect the wires to the correct terminals to avoid damaging other ignition components. If the ignition system trouble is eliminated by the temporary installation of the new coil, install it permanently.

2 Models with contact breaker point ignitions should be checked to make sure the condenser is good before replacing the coil. A bad condenser can act just like a defective coil, but the condenser is much more likely to fail. **Note:** *The easiest way to check for a defective condenser is to substitute a known good component. If the ignition system problem goes away when the new condenser is installed, the original condenser is defective.*

3 On early models, the coil is mounted on the frame downtube, to the left of the rear cylinder, and is protected by a chrome cover **(see illustration)**. On later models, it's mounted under the front of the fuel tank.

4 Label the primary (small) wires and coil terminals, then disconnect the wires. Detach each spark plug wire from the coil by pulling the boot back, grasping the wire as close to the coil as possible and pulling the wire out of the coil.

5 Remove the bolts/nuts and detach the coil.

6 If a new coil is being installed, make sure it's the right one.

Caution: 1980 and later models must have a coil marked "Electronic Advance." Installing the wrong type of coil could result in failure of the electronic components.

7 Installation of the coil is the reverse of removal. Be sure the spark plug wire boots are seated on the coil towers to keep dirt and moisture away from the terminals. Install new boots if the originals are cracked or torn.

3 Condenser - removal and installation

1 A condenser is included in the primary circuit of 1970 through early 1978 models to prevent arcing across the contact breaker

points as they open. If it fails, the ignition system will malfunction.

2 If the engine is difficult to start, or if misfiring occurs, it's possible the condenser is defective. To check it, separate the contact breaker points by hand when the ignition switch is on. If a spark occurs across the points and they appear to be discolored and burned, the condenser is defective.

3 It isn't possible to check the condenser without special test equipment. Since the cost is minimal, install a new condenser to see the effect on engine performance.

4 Because the condenser and contact breaker points supply a spark to both cylinders, it's virtually impossible for a faulty condenser to cause a misfire on one cylinder only.

5 The condenser is attached to the contact breaker baseplate by a clamp and screw. If the wire is disconnected and the screw removed, the condenser can be detached from the baseplate.

6 When installing the new condenser, be sure the clip around the body (which forms the ground connection) makes good contact with the baseplate. Tighten the mounting screw securely.

4 Air gap (1978 and early 1979 models) - check and adjustment
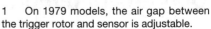

1 On 1979 models, the air gap between the trigger rotor and sensor is adjustable.

2 Remove the gearcase cover from the right side of the engine (see Chapter 2).

3 Remove the spark plugs and rotate the crankshaft until the wide lobe on the trigger rotor is centered in the sensor.

4 Insert a feeler gauge of the specified thickness between the lobe of the rotor and the sensor. If the air gap isn't correct, loosen the screws securing the sensor and move it until the specified gap is obtained. Rotate the crankshaft 180-degrees until the other lobe of the rotor is centered in the sensor and measure the gap to be sure it's the same.

5 Electronic ignition system - check

All models

1 Check the condition of the spark plugs and the spark plug wires as described in Chapter 1. One way to check the ability of the ignition system to produce a strong enough spark is to construct a simple homemade test tool **(see illustration)** and hook it up to the plug wires, one at a time (with the alligator clip grounded on the engine), to see if the spark will jump the gap. Another way, though less conclusive, is to attach a spark plug that's known to be good to the spark

5.1 A simple spark test tool can be made from a block of wood, a large alligator clip, two nails, a screw and a piece of wire

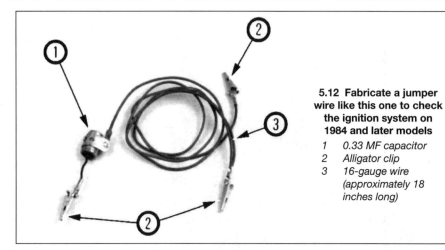

5.12 Fabricate a jumper wire like this one to check the ignition system on 1984 and later models

1   *0.33 MF capacitor*
2   *Alligator clip*
3   *16-gauge wire (approximately 18 inches long)*

plug wires and ground the plug against the engine. Crank the engine over and check for spark. If there is a spark, the coil and ignition system are working properly. Check the choke and the carburetor and replace the spark plugs with new ones if the engine doesn't run right.

2   If no spark is obtained, attach a voltmeter to the battery (black lead to the negative terminal, red lead to positive) and turn the ignition switch and the engine stop switch to the On position. The reading on the voltmeter should be at least 11.5 volts.

3   Measure the air gap (late 1978 and 1979 models only) between the sensor and both trigger rotor lobes (refer to Section 4). If the gap between both rotor lobes can't be adjusted within the range given, replace the trigger rotor and/or the timer mechanism.

4   Make sure the ground cable from the battery is secure and making good contact.

5   Check the ground for the module at the timer plate on the engine (late 1978 and 1979 models) or at the frame (1980 and later models). It should be clean and tight to ensure a good connection.

6   Attach a voltmeter between the positive terminal of the coil and ground (red lead to the coil, black lead to ground). Rotate the crankshaft until the lobes of the trigger rotor (late 1978 and 1979 models) or the slots in the rotor (1980 and later models) are equal distances from the center of the sensor. Turn the ignition switch and the engine kill switch to the On position and read the voltage on the meter. It should be within 1/2-volt of the battery voltage. If not, the trouble is somewhere between the battery and the coil. Check the connections at the ignition switch, the engine kill switch and the circuit breaker.

7   Disconnect the blue wire (pink wire 1991-on) from the negative terminal of the ignition coil and attach a voltmeter between the terminal and ground. With the ignition and kill switches on, the voltage should be the same as the battery. If the voltage is different, the coil should be replaced with a

new one (after checking the resistance as described in Section 3).

Late 1978 and 1979 models

8   Reconnect the blue wire to the negative terminal of the coil, then connect the voltmeter between ground and the negative terminal of the coil. The voltmeter should read 1.0 to 2.0 volts. Place the blade of a screwdriver against the face of the sensor and read the voltmeter. The reading should be between 11.5 and 13.0 volts. By removing the screwdriver, the voltage should drop to 1.0 to 2.0 volts. If not, the ignition module is defective and must be replaced with a new one.

9   Attach a known good spark plug to the plug wire and ground the plug against the engine. Check for spark each time the screwdriver is placed against the face of the sensor. If there is no spark, the ignition coil should be replaced with a new one.

1980 through 1983 models

10   Unplug the connector between the module and the sensor plate. Connect a voltmeter between the red and black wires in the connector on the module side (positive voltmeter lead to the red wire, negative lead to black). Turn the ignition and the engine kill switches on and read the voltmeter. It should indicate 4.5 to 5.5 volts. If not, the ignition module is defective and should be replaced with a new unit.

11   A special jumper cable test adapter is needed to do the following test. It's available from a Harley-Davidson dealer (part number HD 94465-81). Attach the test adapter to the connector halves between the module and sensor. Be careful not to let the exposed wire touch a grounded component or each other or damage to the module will result. Recheck the voltage between the red and black wires. Connect the voltmeter between the green and black wires to test the sensor output (voltmeter positive lead to the green wire, negative lead to the black wire). The voltmeter should read 4.5 to 5.5 volts with the rotor slots away from the sensor, and zero to 1.0 volt with the slot aligned with the sensor.

If either of these voltage readings is not attained, the sensor plate must be replaced with a new unit.

1984 and later models

12   Assemble a jumper wire from 16-gauge wire, a 0.33 microfarad capacitor and three alligator clips **(see illustration)**. A known good condenser from a breaker point ignition system can be used if a capacitor isn't available.

13   Attach a known good spark plug (or the home-made test tool) to one of the plug wires and ground the plug or tool on the engine.

14   Connect the jumper wire with the capacitor in it to the negative coil primary terminal (the blue wire [pink wire 1991-on] was disconnected from the terminal in Step 7). Attach the jumper wire common alligator clip to a good ground.

15   Momentarily touch the remaining jumper wire alligator clip to the negative terminal on the ignition coil - when you do, a spark should occur at the plug or test tool.

16   If not, replace the ignition coil - it's defective. If a spark occurred, proceed to Step 17.

17   Follow the instructions in Step 10 above. If the voltage readings are not as specified, check the ignition module power and ground wires for loose and dirty connections. On 1991-on models note that the black wire described is black/white, and that the expected result is 12V+/-0.5V.

18   If the wires and connections are okay, turn the ignition and kill switches on and momentarily connect the black (black/white 1991-on) and green wire connector pins in the module wire connector with a jumper wire or a screwdriver. If a spark occurs at the plug or test tool when the screwdriver or jumper wire is disconnected, the sensor is probably defective (check the sensor resistance as described below before buying a new one).

19   If no spark occurred during the test in Step 18, check the module resistance (as described below) and install a new one if the resistance isn't as specified.

4

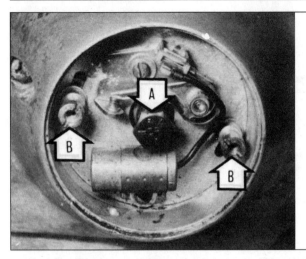

6.2 Remove the bolt (A) and the two screws (B), the lift out the contact breaker baseplate

6.4 Remove the contact breaker point cam and the centrifugal advance unit by pulling them out

Intermittent ignition problem check

20 Check the battery terminals and the module ground connection to make sure they're clean and tight.

21 Disconnect the white wire from the ignition coil primary terminal (not the white wire that goes to the module from the same terminal).

22 Connect a 16-gauge jumper wire with alligator clips to the positive battery post and the terminal on the coil the white wire was disconnected from.

23 Start the engine and see if the problem is eliminated. If it is, the problem is possibly in the starter safety switch connections (they're probably loose).

Caution: The engine won't stop running until the jumper wire is removed.

24 If the intermittent problem still exists, remove the ignition component covers to gain access to the ignition sensor.

25 Start the engine and spray canned compressed air (available from electronics or computer supply stores) on the sensor - be sure to wear safety glasses or a face shield as this is done! **Note:** *Turn the can upside down for the maximum effect.*

 Warning: Avoid skin contact and don't breathe the vapors.

26 If the engine dies, the sensor is temperature sensitive (to cold) and should be replaced with a new one.

27 If the engine keeps running, allow it to reach normal operating temperature, then use a blow dryer to apply heat to the sensor. If the engine stops, the sensor is temperature sensitive (to excess heat) and should be replaced with a new one.

28 If the engine doesn't stop, apply heat to the ignition module. If the engine stops. the module is defective and should be replaced.

Sensor resistance check

Note: *The following resistance test applies to 1984 through 1990 models - no resistance test details are available for 1991-on models.*

29 Position the ohmmeter selector switch on the Rx1 scale. Unplug the sensor wire harness connector and attach the positive (red) lead from the ohmmeter to each of the sensor harness terminals in the connector, one at a time, with the negative (black) ohmmeter lead connected to a good ground (use the sensor plate). If each terminal reading indicates infinite resistance, the sensor is good. If any of the terminal connections produce a resistance reading, the sensor is bad.

30 Connect the positive ohmmeter lead to the green sensor wire and the negative lead to the black sensor wire. If the ohmmeter indicates infinite resistance, the sensor is good. If a resistance reading is produced, the sensor is bad.

31 Reverse the ohmmeter leads. If the ohmmeter reads 300-to-750 K-ohms, the sensor is good. If it indicates infinite resistance, the sensor is defective.

Ignition module resistance check

32 Position the ohmmeter selector switch on the Rx1 scale. Unplug the ignition sensor-to-module wire harness connector and on 1984 through 1990 models, attach the positive (red) lead from the ohmmeter to the black wire terminal in the module side of the connector - the negative (black) ohmmeter lead should be connected to the black module ground wire. On 1991-on models attach the positive meter lead to the black/white wire terminal and the negative lead to ground on the frame. If the ohmmeter indicates 0-to-1 ohm, the module is good. If it indicates more than 1 ohm, check for a faulty ground circuit and make any needed repairs. If the ground circuit is good, replace the module.

33 The following resistance tests apply to 1986 through 1990 models only. No similar data is available for 1991-on models; if a fault is suspected with the module and all other ignition components checked out, including the wiring, then replacement of the module is the only solution.

34 Connect the positive ohmmeter lead to the white module wire at the ignition coil (disconnect it from the coil first) and check the meter reading again. If it's 800-to-1300 K-ohms, the module is good. If it indicates infi-

nite resistance, the module is defective.

35 Reverse the ohmmeter leads (red lead to ground, black lead to the white module wire at the coil). If the ohmmeter indicates infinite resistance, the module is good. If it indicates any resistance, the module is bad.

36 Attach the positive ohmmeter lead to the blue module wire at the coil (disconnect it from the coil first) and attach the negative lead to the black module ground wire. If the meter indicates infinite resistance, the module is good. If it indicates any resistance, the module is bad.

37 Reverse the ohmmeter leads. If the ohmmeter indicates 400-to-800 K-ohms, the module is good. If infinite resistance is indicated, the module is defective.

38 If the module fails any of the tests, replace it with a new one.

6 Ignition components - removal and installation

Removal

1970 through early 1978 models

1 Remove the screws securing the breaker point cover to the gearcase cover. Detach the point cover and the gasket.

2 Scribe a line across the baseplate and gearcase. The scribed line will ensure the ignition timing is close to the required setting after reassembly. Remove the center bolt that retains the contact breaker point cam and the two screws that secure the contact breaker baseplate assembly **(see illustration)**.

3 Lift off the baseplate.

4 Pull off the contact breaker point cam and the centrifugal advance unit **(see illustration)**.

Late 1978 and 1979 models

5 Remove the outer cover from the gearcase cover by removing the two screws or drilling the heads off the two rivets.

6.10 On later models with electronic ignition, drill out the rivet heads and remove the outer cover . . .

6.11 . . . then remove the screws (arrows) and detach the inner cover and gasket to get at the sensor plate

6.13 Mark the sensor plate (carbureted models only), then remove the screws (arrows) . . .

6.14 . . . and pull out the sensor plate, then remove the bolt (arrow) and rotor

6   Lift the ignition module out of the timing case - be careful, the wires are still attached - and set it aside.

7   Remove the screws securing the timer plate, then remove the bolt from the center of the trigger rotor.

8   Remove the small screws and detach the sensor from the timer plate and the electrical lead from the module to the timer plate.

9   Lift the timer plate out of position and pull the trigger rotor off the advance assembly. The advance assembly can now be removed from the gearcase cover.

1980 and later models

10   Remove the outer cover from the gearcase cover by drilling the heads off the two rivets **(see illustration)**.

11   Remove the two screws securing the inner cover, then detach the cover and gasket **(see illustration)**.

12   Unplug the wire harness connector (follow the wires to the connector).

13   Mark the sensor plate and gearcase (timing) cover with a scribe or permanent felt-tip marker to ensure the ignition timing can be returned to its original setting, then remove the screws and detach the sensor plate **(see illustration)**. The sensor plate can stay with the gearcase cover if you don't want to try to pull the wires through the hole and thread them back in again later. Just be very careful not to damage the sensor as the gearcase cover is handled (wrap a clean shop rag around it and secure it with tape to protect it).

14   Remove the rotor bolt and detach the rotor **(see illustration)**.

Installation

1970 through early 1978 models

15   Installation of the ignition components and the advance unit is the reverse of the removal procedure.

16   The centrifugal advance on all but early 1978 models will locate on the protruding end of the camshaft.

17   Install the contact breaker point baseplate, aligning the scribed marks made during disassembly so the timing is approximately correct.

Late 1978 and 1979 models

18   Be sure to seat the advance assembly for the late 1978 and 1979 ignition system squarely on the end of the camshaft. Install the trigger rotor with its flat side next to the cam stop roll pin on the advance assembly base. It must also engage both flyweights on the advance unit.

1980 and later models

19   When installing the rotor bolt, the threads should be coated with thread locking compound. If the sensor plate was completely removed on these models, it may be necessary to install new sockets, wire pins and body receptacle.

20   On carbureted models, adjust the timing as described in Chapter 1. The timing on fuel injected models is controlled by the electronic control unit and can't be adjusted.

21   When installing the outer cover, special rivets must be used. These rivets are designed so the end doesn't fall off in the timing compartment. The use of regular rivets could damage the ignition components. The recommended rivets are Harley-Davidson part no. 8699.

---

7   Vacuum Operated Electric Switch (VOES) - check and replacement

1   The Vacuum Operated Electric Switch is controlled by intake manifold vacuum, sensed through an opening in the carburetor body. Under low vacuum conditions, such as hard acceleration, the switch is open, which causes the ignition module to retard the timing, reducing detonation. When high vacuum is present in the intake manifold, the ignition module switches to the advanced timing

mode for better fuel economy and performance.

Check

2   Set the ignition timing with a timing light (see Chapter 1).

3   With the engine idling, detach the VOES vacuum hose from the carburetor and plug the carburetor fitting. The ignition module will select the retard mode and engine rpm should drop.

4   Reconnect the vacuum hose. Engine speed should increase and the timing mark should reappear in the timing plug hole.

5   If the engine speed doesn't change when the hose is disconnected and reconnected, check the wire between the VOES and the ignition module and the VOES ground wire.

Replacement

6   Detach the air cleaner cover and backplate, then remove the rear fuel tank mounting bolt and raise the rear of the tank to get at the VOES (see Chapter 3).

7   Disconnect the wire from the VOES to the ignition module.

4

8   Disconnect the VOES ground wire (to the engine).

9   Detach the vacuum hose from the VOES (and the carburetor or T-fitting, if necessary).

10   Remove the nut, bolt and washer and detach the VOES from the bracket.

11   Installation is the reverse of removal. Make sure the ground wire is securely attached to the engine bracket with the VOES mounting bolt. Position the high-temperature conduit sleeve over the wire connectors and secure them to the frame with the nylon strap. The VOES and wires must not come in contact with the engine rocker arm covers - heat and vibration from the engine could damage them.

8   Vehicle attitude sensor (fuel injected models) - check and replacement

1   The vehicle attitude sensor is mounted on the ignition rotor plate. It consists of a magnet in a fluid-filled channel. If the bike's lean angle exceeds 80 degrees, the magnet moves from its normal position, causing an open in the ignition module circuit. When the module detects this open, it shuts off the ignition system.

Check

2   Remove the ignition timer cover (see Section 6).

3   Start the engine.

4   Locate the vehicle attitude on the sensor plate. Put a magnet on top of the vehicle attitude. If the sensor is operating correctly, the magnet inside the sensor will move, cause an open circuit, shut off the ignition system and stop the engine. Remove the magnet and turn the ignition switch to OFF. This resets the vehicle attitude sensor (unless it was defective).

Replacement

5   If the vehicle attitude sensor fails to operate as described, replace it as a unit with the camshaft position sensor (see Section 6).

Chapter 5
Steering, suspension and final drive

Contents

Degrees of difficulty

Easy, suitable for novice with little experience	**Fairly easy,** suitable for beginner with some experience	**Fairly difficult,** suitable for competent DIY mechanic	**Difficult,** suitable for experienced DIY mechanic	**Very difficult,** suitable for expert DIY or professional

Specifications

Front suspension
Fork oil capacity and type .... See Chapter 1

Suspension torque specifications
Axle nuts .... See Chapter 6

1970 through early 1978
Pinch bolts .... 22 to 26 ft-lbs (30 to 35 Nm)

Late 1978 through 1983 (four-speed)
FL models
   Lower pinch bolts .... 30 to 35 ft-lbs (41 to 47 Nm)
   Upper pinch bolts .... 22 to 28 ft-lbs (41 to 47 Nm)
FX models - pinch bolts
   FXWG only .... 30 to 35 ft-lbs (41 to 47 Nm)
   All other FX models .... 20 to 25 ft-lbs (27 to 34 Nm)

1980 through 1983 (five-speed)
FLT models
   Fork stem nuts .... 45 ft-lbs (61 Nm)
   Slider cap nuts (bottom of fork leg) .... 132 inch-lbs (15 Nm)
   Final drive chain housing rubber boot clamps .... 36 to 48 inch-lbs (4.0 to 5.4 Nm)
   Swingarm pivot shaft nuts .... 45 ft-lbs (61 Nm)
FXR models
   Slider cap nuts (bottom of fork leg) .... 132 inch-lbs (15 Nm)
   Swingarm pivot shaft nuts .... 45 ft-lbs (61 Nm)
   Swingarm pivot shaft mounting bracket bolts .... 34 to 42 ft-lbs (446 to 57 Nm)

5

1984 and later

FLT models
Steering stem nut .... 35 to 45 ft-lbs (47 to 61 Nm)
Slider cap nuts (bottom of fork leg)..................................... 108 to 156 inch-lbs (12 to 18 Nm)
Final drive chain rubber boot fasteners (1984 only) .... 36 to 48 inch-lbs (4.0 to 5.4 Nm)
Rear shock absorber mounting bolts
Upper
1984 through early 1988... 35 to 40 ft-lbs (47 to 54 Nm)
Late 1988-on .... 33 to 35 ft-lbs (45 to 47 Nm)
Lower .... 35 to 40 ft-lbs (47 to 54 Nm)
Swingarm pivot shaft nut/bolt
Late 1986 through 1988 (12-point bolt head) .... 85 ft-lbs (115 Nm)
All others .... 45 ft-lbs (61 Nm)
FXR models
Slider cap nuts
FXLR (all) and 1987 FXRSE.. 84 to 108 inch-lbs (9.4 to 12 Nm)
All others .... 16 to 20 ft-lbs (12 to 18 Nm)
Swingarm pivot shaft nut/bolt
Late 1986 through 1988 (12-point bolt head) .... 85 ft-lbs (115 Nm)
All others .... 45 ft-lbs (61 Nm)
Swingarm pivot shaft mounting bracket bolts .... 34 to 42 ft-lbs (446 to 57 Nm)
FX/Softail models
Slider cap nuts (bottom of fork leg)..................................... 108 to 156 inch-lbs (12 to 18 Nm)
Springer forks
Steering stem bearing retainer .... 72 inch-lbs (8 Nm)
Rigid fork leg studs
Through 1994 .... 60 to 65 ft-lbs (81 to 88 Nm)
1995 and later .... 45 to 50 ft-lbs (61 to 68 Nm)
Upper triple clamp pinch bolt
Through 1992 .... 45 to 50 ft-lbs (61 to 68 Nm)
1993 and later .... 20 to 25 ft-lbs (27 to 34 Nm)
Steering stem acorn nut.. 20 to 25 ft-lbs (27 to 34 Nm)
Shock absorber acorn nuts.. 45 to 50 ft-lbs (61 to 68 Nm)
Handlebar riser locknuts .... 25 to 35 ft-lbs (25 to 35 Nm)
FXD Dyna models
Fork pinch bolts
FXD, FXDB, FXDC, FXDL, FXDS-CONV .... 25 to 30 ft-lbs (34 to 41 Nm)
FXDWG .... 30 to 35 ft-lbs (41 to 47 Nm)
Upper triple clamp-to-steering stem pinch bolt............................... 21 to 27 ft-lbs (28 to 37 Nm)
Rear shock absorber mountings.. 25 to 40 ft-lbs (34 to 54 Nm)

Rear sprocket tightening torques

Through 1983
Rear sprocket to wheel hub
FLT.. 65 to 75 ft-lbs (88 to 102 Nm)
All others .... 35 to 50 ft-lbs (47 to 68 Nm)
1984 through 1990
FLT with enclosed chain .... 65 to 75 ft-lbs (88 to 102 Nm)
FLT/FXR with open chain.. 50 to 55 ft-lbs (68 to 75 Nm)
FLT with belt drive and all FX/Softails
Grade 5 bolts .... 45 to 50 ft-lbs (61 to 68 Nm)
Grade 8 bolts .... 65 to 70 ft-lbs (85 to 95 Nm)
1991 and later
FLT (1991)
Spoked wheel .... 45 to 50 ft-lbs (61 to 68 Nm)
Cast wheel
Grade 5 bolts... 45 to 50 ft-lbs (61 to 68 Nm)
Grade 8 bolts... 65 to 70 ft-lbs (85 to 95 Nm)
FLT (1992)
Spoked wheel .... 45 to 50 ft-lbs (61 to 68 Nm)
Cast wheel .... 45 to 55 ft-lbs (61 to 75 Nm)
FLT/FXR (1993-on)
Spoked wheel .... 45 to 55 ft-lbs (61 to 75 Nm)
Cast wheel .... 55 to 65 ft-lbs (75 to 88 Nm)
FXR (1991 and 1992) .... 45 to 55 ft-lbs (61 to 75 Nm)

FX/Softail
  1991 with disc wheel
    Grade 5 bolts .... 45 to 50 ft-lbs (61 to 68 Nm)
    Grade 8 bolts .... 65 to 70 ft-lbs (85 to 95 Nm)
    1991-1992 spoked and 1992 disc wheel .... 45 to 55 ft-lbs (61 to 75 Nm)
  1993-on .... 55 to 65 ft-lbs (75 to 88 Nm)
FXD Dyna
  1991 .... 50 to 55 ft-lbs (68 to 75 Nm)
  1992 .... 65 to 70 ft-lbs (85 to 95 Nm)
  1993-on
    Spoked wheel .... 45 to 55 ft-lbs (61 to 75 Nm)
    Cast wheel .... 55 to 65 ft-lbs (75 to 88 Nm)

1 General information

The front forks on all except Softail Springer models are of the conventional coil spring, hydraulically-damped telescopic type.

Some 1984 through 1987 models (FLT, FXRD and FXRT) include air forks with an anti-dive feature. The anti-dive operation is controlled by a solenoid activated by either brake switch (front or rear). The FXRD and FXRT have an air accumulator attached to the lower triple clamp. On FLT models, the engine guard serves as an air reservoir as well. Some 1988 and later models (FLT, FXRT, FXRS-SP and FXRS-CONV, also have air forks and anti-dive. The system is very similar to the earlier one, but the handlebar serves as an air reservoir on all models and the FXRT doesn't have an accumulator.

Softail Springer models (1989 and later FXSTS) have a unique, retro-look front suspension, consisting of a pair of front forks, a lever linkage, exposed springs and a single shock absorber. One fork (the fixed fork) is fixed to the frame through the steering head. The other fork (the spring fork) is free to move separately from the fixed fork, with its motion controlled by the springs and shock absorber. At the bottom, both forks are connected to the front axle through the lever linkage. As the wheel moves up and down, the levers pivot on the bottom of the fixed fork, pushing and pulling the spring fork through its vertical travel. The movements of the spring fork are cushioned by the springs and damped by the shock absorber.

The steering head on all models uses tapered roller bearings.

The rear suspension on all except Softail models consists of two coil spring/shock absorbers and a swingarm. Some 1985 and later models include an air pressure adjustment mechanism in the rear suspension.

The rear suspension on 1985 and later Softail models is a simulated rigid frame, consisting of a rocker-type swingarm with dual shock absorbers. On 1988 and earlier Softail models, separate fluid reservoirs, with hoses connected to the forward shock mounts, are used to store excess fluid and prevent fluid cavitation due to the horizontal shock position.

The final drive on all models consists of a chain (early models) or cogged rubber belt (later models) and sprockets at the transmission and rear wheel.

2 Handlebars - removal and installation

1   These motorcycles use a one-piece handlebar, clamped in risers that extend upward from the fork legs.

2   Before removing the handlebars, look for a punch mark indicating the position of the handlebar in the brackets (see illustration). Make your own mark if you can't see one.

3   If the handlebars must be removed for access to other components, such as the forks or the steering head, simply remove the clamp bolts and lift the handlebar off (see illustration). It's not usually necessary to

2.2 Mark the clamp position on the handlebar (arrow) and remove the clamp bolts (arrows) . . .

2.3a . . . some models use a one-piece clamp with four bolts or screws (arrows)

5

2.3b Be sure to label all wires and terminals if they must be disconnected

2.5a The handlebar clamp/risers are secured by bolts (arrow) on early models . . .

2.5b . . . on later models, separate risers are secured by bolts (arrows)

3.12 Slide the fork legs down through the triple clamps to remove them

disconnect the cables, wires or hoses **(see illustration)**, but it is a good idea to support the assembly with a piece of wire or rope, to avoid unnecessary strain on the cables, wires and (on the right side) the brake hose.

4   Check the handlebar for cracks and distortion and replace it if any undesirable conditions are found.

5   If the handlebar risers need to be removed, unscrew their bolts from the underside of the upper triple clamp **(see illustrations)**. Pull the riser out and immediately reinstall its hardware in the correct order so you don't forget how it goes.

6   Installation is the reverse of the removal steps. Tighten the clamp bolts to the torque listed in this Chapter's Specifications, but don't overtighten them or the brackets may break. This will leave a gap between the riser(s) and clamp on some models.

Caution: Don't overtighten the bolts trying to close the gap or they will strip out or break.

3 Forks - removal and installation

Removal

Note: *Detach the negative battery cable from the battery before beginning this procedure. On models with air-assisted forks, bleed the air out of the system and remove the banjo bolts from the fork caps. Loosen or remove the air tubes.*

1   The forks can be removed very simply by separating the fork tubes from the triple clamps. Do not disassemble the steering head components unless the bearings require attention (see Section 8).

2   Raise the front of the machine until the front wheel is off the ground. Support it securely on blocks. This will require a little thought and planning because the lower frame tubes are close together and the machine won't be very stable unless it has

some side support.

3   Remove the front wheel as described in Chapter 6.

4   Remove the front fender (see Chapter 7). On most 1984 and later models, the front fender and headlight bracket must be removed. Let the headlight hang by the wire harness.

5   On models with front disc brakes, remove the clamp securing the hydraulic lines to the fork legs or fender. Disconnect the caliper(s) from the fork leg(s) and tie the caliper(s) to the frame, out of the way.

FL models

6   Remove the fairing, instrument panel and light bar (1986 and later FLHTC models) from the forks (see Chapters 7 and 8). The mounting method will depend on the type of fairing installed.

7   Remove the headlight bulb (see Chapter 8).

8   Remove the headlight housing and spotlight switches (see Chapter 8).

9   Remove the handlebars (see Section 2).

10   Loosen the pinch bolts securing the fork legs to the upper and lower triple clamps.

11   Remove the caps from the top of the fork legs.

12   Carefully remove each fork leg from the triple clamps **(see illustration)**. You may have to twist the fork leg to break it loose from the clamps. Be careful (if the forks have not been drained) or the fluid will be ejected out of them. If the fork legs are stuck in the triple clamps, screw the caps back onto the fork legs and strike the caps sharply with a soft-faced hammer. Do not use excessive force or the internal threads may be damaged. On 1984 and later FLT models, remove the rubber fork stop from each fork leg.

FX models

13   Remove the handlebars (see Section 2).

14   Remove the instruments and mounts from the top of each fork leg (see Chapter 8).

15   Remove the screws and lift the cover up

to expose the upper triple clamp. Do the same for the lower triple clamp cover (if equipped). Unscrew the cap at the top of each fork leg, but don't remove them at this point unless they retain the fork leg in the upper triple clamp.

16   Loosen the pinch bolts in the triple clamps, under the plated covers (some models only have pinch bolts in the lower triple clamp). Remove the two bolts that secure the mounting bracket between the upper and lower triple clamps and detach the bracket (not used on all models).

17   On some models, the upper ends of the fork tubes are tapered and mate with a matching taper in the upper triple clamp. To break the taper, give the loosened fork caps a sharp tap with a hammer and block of wood - do not use excessive force or the internal threads of the fork tube may be damaged. If the fork legs are tight, try tapping on the upper triple clamp at the same time. On models which have parallel-sided fork tube ends take note of the tube's installed height in the triple clamp before removing; some are fitted flush with the triple clamp surface, whereas others project 0.42 to 0.50 inches (11 to 13 mm) measured from top of cap bolt to clamp surface.

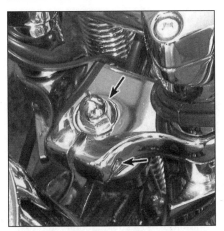

3.29 On Springer models, loosen the clamp bolt (lower arrow) and remove the acorn nut and rubber washer (upper (arrow)

4.3 Unscrew the cap from the top of the fork tube . . .

4.4 . . . and remove the fork spring (all models) and guide (if equipped) from the fork tube

18   After the forks are free, remove the caps from the top of each fork leg.

19   Remove the fork legs from the lower triple clamp by pulling only on the fork tubes.

Caution: Do not compress the fork tube and slider or oil may spurt out the open end of the tube. Keep the fork leg upright until the caps are installed (also, store them in an upright position).

All models

20   Install the fork legs in the triple clamps by reversing the removal procedure. Be sure to push only on the fork tubes as the fork legs are slipped into place and do not compress the fork tube and slider until the caps are in place.

21   Tighten the lower pinch bolts temporarily, then add the specified amount of fork oil to each fork leg (see Chapter 1).

22   Install the fork caps, tighten them securely, then tighten the lower pinch bolts to the specified torque.

23   Install the anti-dive air control system (where fitted).

24   Install the instruments and handlebars, then attach the fender to the forks. Refer to Chapter 6 and install the front wheel and related components.

Springer forks

Note 1: *Do not attempt to disassemble the Springer forks. If problems are encountered with the springs, fork legs or rocker assemblies, take the machine or the forks to a Harley-Davidson dealer.*

Note 2: *Springer forks are removed together with the steering stem.*

25   Detach the front brake caliper and remove the wheel (see Chapter 6).

26   On models through 1992 the front fender can be released from the forks after removing its four retaining nuts and bolts. On 1993 and later models the fender is not fixed rigidly to the forks, but floats with wheel movement via a mounting on the brake reaction link and short link rods to the forks.

Note: *The fender-to-reaction link pivot can be dismantled, while taking note of the exact fitted position of the washers and spacers, but the fender-to-fork links require the use of a Harley-Davidson service tool to hold the links in position while the fender is removed.*

27   Remove the headlight and mounting bracket. Let the headlight hang by the wire harness.

28   Remove the acorn nuts and washers, then pull out the bolts and detach the shock absorber (see Section 6 if necessary).

29   Remove the fork (steering) stem acorn nut and washer, then loosen the upper triple clamp pinch bolt **(see illustration)**.

30   Remove the handlebars and detach the risers (see Section 2).

31   Remove the studs from the upper ends of the rigid fork legs, then lift off the upper triple clamp.

32   Remove the hex-shaped bearing retainer and dust shield from the top of the fork stem.

33   Withdraw the fork stem from the bottom and detach the forks from the steering head on the frame.

34   Installation is the reverse of the removal procedure. When installing the hex-shaped

4.5a Remove the damper retaining nut (shown) or bolt from the bottom of the fork slider

bearing retainer, tighten it to 6 ft-lbs (8 Nm). When installing the rigid fork leg studs, start both of them, then tighten them evenly to the specified torque. Use anti-seize compound on the upper triple clamp pinch bolt threads. Use thread locking compound on the shock absorber mounting bolt/nut threads. Use new locknuts when installing the handle-bar risers. Center the bosses in the washer cutouts as the riser locknuts are tightened.

4   Forks (1970 through 1983 models) - disassembly, inspection and reassembly

1   Remove the fork legs as described in Section 7.

2   Always disassemble one fork leg at a time to avoid mixing up parts.

Disassembly

All models

3   Remove the cap, turn the fork leg upside-down and drain the oil into a container **(see illustration)**. Keep in mind when the fork is inverted the spring will slide out - don't let it fall. Compress the fork tube and slider a few times to ensure it drains completely.

4   When most of the oil has drained, slide out the spring and wipe off as much oil as possible **(see illustration)**.

5   Secure the slider in a vise equipped with soft jaws. Clamp it very lightly - just enough to prevent it from rotating while the Allen-head bolt is removed from the end of the slider. On some models a locknut is used in place of the bolt **(see illustration)**. If the nut or bolt won't loosen because the damper rod turns, try to lock the rod by installing and applying pressure to the fork spring with the cap. On most models, the top of the damper rod has a slotted or milled head. If rotation can't be prevented by compressing the fork spring, an improvised tool or a long screwdriver can be used to hold the rod stationary **(see illustrations)**.

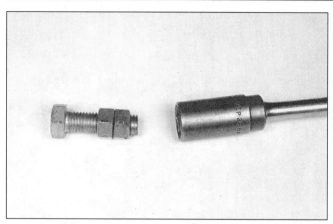

4.5b To make a damper rod holder, thread two nuts onto a bolt with a head that will wedge inside the damper rod and tighten the nuts against each other . . .

4.5c . . . then install the nut-end into a socket (connected to a long extension) and tape it into place

6   Pull the dust boot off the slider (if used) and remove the circlip/retaining ring **(see illustrations)**, washer(s) and felt dust seal (if used). Note the installed order of the washers so they can be reinstalled in the same locations during reassembly.

7   Pull the fork tube out of the slider. Many models have a bushing on the fork tube and in the top of the slider. Due to the fork tube bushing being slightly wider in OD than the slider bushing ID, when the fork tube and slider are pulled apart in a 'slide-hammer' action the fork tube bushing will displace the slider bushing.

1970 through early 1977

8   Remove the internal circlip/retaining ring from the fork tube **(see illustration)**.

9   The damper unit can now be removed **(see illustration)**. It can be disassembled if parts require replacement. There are a variety of dampers used in the forks on these models. To keep the parts in the correct order, disassemble one damper at a time, using the damper from the other fork leg as a guide. The pistons and bushings are the parts most likely to wear, which will be greatly accelerated if the forks are run without enough oil or with contaminated oil.

Late 1977 through 1983

10   Remove the spring (if still in place) and damper tube from the fork tube.

11   Detach the wear rings from the slots in the damper tube.

12   Remove the sleeve or the damper rod seat from the slider.

All models

13   The oil seal in the top of the fork slider can be pried out after the circlip (not used on early models) has been removed **(see illustration)**. This seal should not be disturbed unless it's worn or if the bushings (early models only) in the slider are worn and must be replaced with new ones.

Inspection

14   The parts most likely to wear over an extended period of time are the fork bushing(s) and oil seals. Worn bushings cause a shudder when the front brake is applied, and with the forks compressed and the front brake held on it will be possible to detect an amount of play between the slider and fork tube (but don't confuse this with head bearing play).

15   Replacing bushings may prove difficult due to the need to ream them to size after installation, a task that is best left to a Harley-Davidson dealer.

16   The oil seal in each slider can be pried

4.6a Pry the circlip (if equipped) out of the slider groove . . .

4.6b . . . then remove the serrated washer and felt dust seal

4.8 Remove the circlip . . .

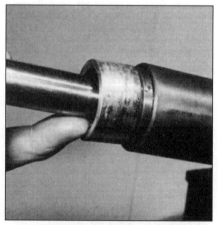

4.9 . . . to allow the damper rod to be pulled out (1970 through early 1977 models)

4.13 The oil seal (arrow) can be removed after the circlip

out after the circlip has been removed. New oil seals should be installed with great care and located correctly before the circlip is installed. Be very careful when the fork tube is being reinstalled during reassembly of the forks - the seal lip is easily damaged. Coat

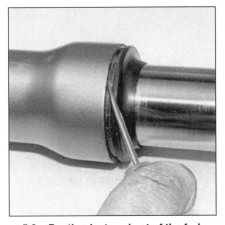

5.6a Pry the dust seal out of the fork slider with a small screwdriver

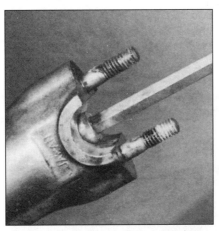

5.5 Remove the damper rod Allen bolt from the bottom of the fork slider

the seal lip with grease first.

17   If the fork damping is inadequate, the damper pistons (pre-1978 models) of the damper assembly should be replaced (these are the parts most likely to wear).

18   Before reassembling the forks, check the sliding surfaces of the fork tubes. If they're pitted, scuffed, scored or badly worn, they should be replaced, along with the fork bushings (if equipped).

19   It isn't possible to straighten forks bent in an accident, even if a repair service is available. There is no way of knowing whether the parts have been overstressed and will be subject to sudden fatigue failure. The tubes should be checked for straightness by rolling them on a flat surface.

20   The triple clamps are also prone to twist or distort in an accident. They also should be replaced, not repaired, especially since they're more difficult to align correctly.

Reassembly

21   Reassembly is the reverse of the dismantling procedure. Always fit a new oil seal and install with the lettered side facing

upwards; coat the seal lips with fork oil to prevent damage as the fork tube is installed.

22   Be sure to tighten the slider Allen-head bolt or the locknut securely. Use thread locking compound on the threads.

23   Refer to Section 7 and reinstall the forks (don't forget to add oil).

---

5   Forks (1984 and later models) - disassembly, inspection and reassembly

1   Remove the fork legs from the steering head yokes as described in Section 3.

2   Always disassemble one fork leg at a time to avoid mixing up parts.

Disassembly

3   Turn the fork leg upside-down and drain the oil into a container. Keep in mind that when the fork is inverted the spring will slide out - don't let it fall. Compress the fork tube and slider a few times to ensure that it drains completely.

4   When most of the oil has drained, slide out the spring (and spring guide if equipped) and wipe off as much of the oil as possible **(see illustration 4.4)**.

5   Secure the slider in a vise equipped with soft jaws. Clamp it very lightly - just enough to prevent it from rotating while the Allen-head screw is removed from the end of the slider **(see illustration)**. You may find that once loosened, the damper tube turns inside the fork tube, preventing removal of the Allen screw. Try installing the fork spring and cap and compressing the fork to apply pressure to the damper rod head to hold it still. If this fails, obtain either the Harley-Davidson service tool, or make your own **(see illustrations 4.5b and 4.5c)**. With the exposed section of the tool held tightly, unscrew the Allen screw.

6   Refer to the accompanying illustrations to disassemble the fork **(see illustrations)**.

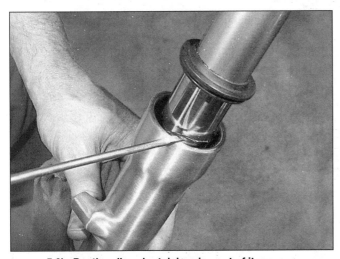

5.6b Pry the oil seal retaining ring out of its groove

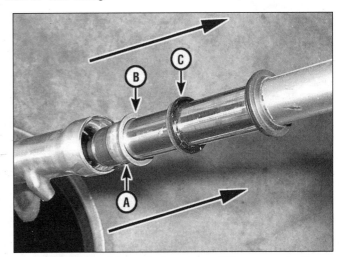

5.6c Yank the slider and tube apart until they separate; the slider bushing (A), back-up ring (B) and oil seal (C) will pop out of the slider

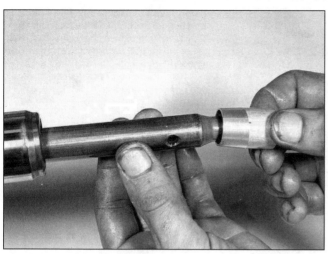

5.6d Remove the damper rod base from the damper rod (if it's not there, it's probably in the bottom of the slider) . . .

5.6e . . . remove the damper rod and rebound spring from the other (upper) end of the fork tube; don't remove the Teflon rings unless you plan to replace them

Inspection

7   Check the fork bushings for wear. Wear can be felt as shuddering when the front brake is applied and the increased amount of play can be detected by pulling and pushing on the handlebars when the front brake is applied hard (do not confuse this with steering head play though).

8   The slider bushing is displaced during disassembly and a new one installed relatively easily. Only remove the fork tube bushing if it requires replacement - pry it apart at its split sufficiently to ease it off the end of the fork tube, followed by the slider bushing **(see illustrations)**. Install the new slider bushing, then ease the new fork tube bushing over the end of the fork tube **(see illustration)**.

9   New oil seals must be fitted in the slider every time the fork is dismantled. A wire retaining clip secures each seal in the top of the slider. Take note of any washers present and install them in their original position. Apply fork oil to the oil seal lips to prevent damage during fork reassembly.

10   If fork damping action decreases, replace the damper tube wear rings and check that all holes in the damper tube are clear. Don't remove the wear rings from the damper unless you plan to replace them with new ones.

11   Before reassembling the forks, check the sliding surfaces of the fork tubes. If they're scuffed, scored or badly worn, they should be replaced, together with the fork bushings.

12   It's not possible to straighten forks that have been bent in an accident, even if a repair service is available. There's no way of knowing whether the parts concerned have been overstressed. The tubes should always be checked for straightness by rolling them on a flat surface.

13   The triple clamps are also liable to twist

or distort in an accident. As in the case of the fork tubes, they should be replaced and not repaired, especially since they are far more difficult to align correctly.

Reassembly

14   Refer to the accompanying illustrations to reassemble the fork **(see illustrations)**.

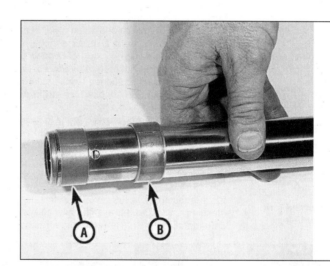

5.8a The fork tube bushing (A) and slider bushing (B) are on the bottom of the fork tube

5.8b Pry the fork tube bushing apart at the slit just enough to slide it off . . .

5.8c . . . the slider bushing can now be slid off the fork tube

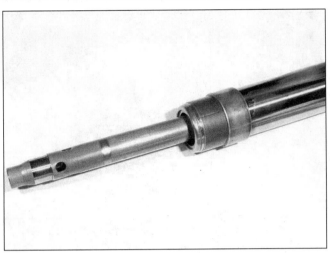

5.14a Put the rebound spring on the damper rod, then (all models) place the damper rod in the fork tube so it protrudes from the lower end like this

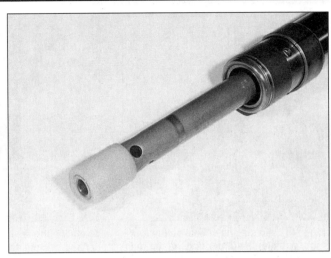

5.14b Install the damper rod base on the damper rod

5.14c The damper rod, base and damper rod bolt fit together like this in the lower end of the fork slider (slider removed for clarity)

5.14d Install the slider bushing (1984 and later) and back-up ring on the fork tube

5.14e Using a seal driver or equivalent tool . . .

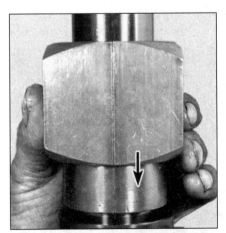

5.14f . . . tap down gently and repeatedly to seat the slider bushing firmly against the shoulder inside the slider

5.14g If you don't have a bushing driver, you can use a section of pipe (be sure to tape the ends of the pipe so it doesn't scratch the fork tube)

5.14h Coat the inner lip and the outer circumference of the new seal with fork oil . . .

5

5.14i . . . and install the seal on the fork tube; don't let the upper edge of the fork tube damage the seal lip

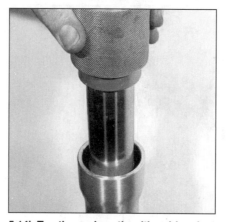

5.14j Tap the seal gently with a driver just until it's fully seated

5.14k This is the JIMS seal driver

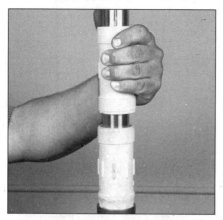

5.14l You can make a driver with plastic plumbing fittings; place one fitting on the seal and strike it with the other piece

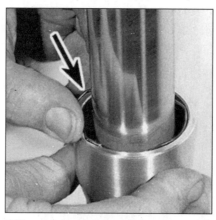

5.14m Compress the retaining ring and fit it securely into its groove in the fork slider

5.14n Use any of the tools previously shown to drive the dust seal (1984 and later) into place

6 Front shock absorber (Softail Springer models) - removal and installation

1   Support the bike securely upright.
2   Remove the acorn nuts from the shock absorber bolts, then remove the bolts and take the shock off the motorcycle (see illustrations).
3   Installation is the reverse of the removal Steps. Use non-permanent thread locking agent on the bolt threads and tighten them to the torque listed in this Chapter's Specifications.

7 Steering head bearings - adjustment

Adjustment

1   Adjustment of the steering head bear-

6.2a Remove the acorn nut (arrow) from the bottom of the shock absorber . . .

6.2b . . . then remove the nut and bolt from the top (arrow)

7.3a If the steering head bearings are adjusted with a bolt (not a nut), loosen the steering head pinch bolt (arrow) . . .

ings is critical. They should be tightened sufficiently to eliminate all play, but they must not be over-tightened. Note that it is possible to place a load of several tons on the bearings by over-tightening and yet still be able to turn the handlebars. When the adjustment is correct, there should be no play in the bearings and, when the front wheel is raised off the ground, a light tap on the end of the handlebar should cause the forks to swing to the full lock position.

2   Over-tightened bearings in the steering head will cause the machine to roll at slow speeds, while loose bearings will cause front fork shudder when the front brake is applied.

3   Adjustment is accomplished by turning the adjusting nut or bolt at the top of the steering head, immediately above the upper triple clamp **(see illustrations)**. In some cases, it will be necessary to remove the handlebars and upper triple clamp for access. In others, the bolt can be reached from above, or the adjusting nut can be turned once the locknut has been loosened.

4   Before making the adjustment, remove any aftermarket accessories, such as a nonstock windshield. Check to make sure the

clutch and throttle cables don't cause pull or drag. If they do, reroute or disconnect the cables to correct the problem. It won't be possible to measure steering head adjustment accurately if a cable is affecting the adjustment.

5   Loosen the fork lower pinch bolts. This allows the necessary vertical movement of the steering stem in relation to the fork tubes. Also loosen the steering stem pinch bolt, or bend back the lockwasher and loosen the nut.

6   The manufacturer provides specifications for measuring front wheel fall-away swing. These measurements will tell you if the steering head bearings are adjusted accurately.

7   Before you start, remove any aftermarket accessories, such as a non-stock windshield. If you have to remove stock fairing or headlight components for access to the steering head bolt, reinstall them during the measurement. Check to make sure the clutch and throttle cables don't cause pull or drag. If thy do, reroute or disconnect the cables to correct the problem (on FLT models, detach the clutch cable from the fairing or handlebar). It won't be possible to measure steering head adjustment accurately if a cable is affecting the adjustment.

8   Checking the adjustment requires that the front wheel be raised off the ground. Jack up the bike and support it securely so it can't be knocked over during this procedure. Keep in mind that the procedure involves swinging the front wheel, which could knock the bike over if it isn't securely supported.

All except Springer and FLT models

9   You'll need a way to measure the side-to-side movement of the front wheel accurately. There are two ways to do this. One is to place a strip of masking tape across the leading edge of the front fender, and set up a pointer on the floor with its tip centered on the tape (you can make the pointer out of wood). Another is to hang a plumb bob from

the rear edge of the fender and lay a ruler beneath it.

10   Center the pointer on the tape and center the wheel in the straight-ahead position. Slowly push the wheel to one side until it begins to move on its own. Note where the pointer is when the wheel starts to move and either mark it on the tape or write the measurement down.

11   Center the wheel again, then slowly push it in the other direction. Once again, note where the pointer is when the wheel starts to move on its own.

12   Measure the distance between the two marked points and compare it to the value listed in this Chapter's Specifications. If the measured distance is greater than specified, loosen the adjustment as described below. If it's less than specified, tighten the adjustment.

13   If adjustment is necessary, loosen the steering stem pinch bolt, or bend back the lockwasher and loosen the steering stem nut.

14   On models equipped with a steering head bolt, tighten or loosen the bolt to change the bearing adjustment. Turn the bolt only a little at a time, then recheck the adjustment.

15   On models equipped with a steering stem nut (above the upper triple clamp), make the adjustment with the adjusting nut below the upper triple clamp. Turn the adjusting nut by tapping it with a hammer and punch. Turn the nut a little at a time; even one notch can make a noticeable difference. Retighten the steering stem nut to the torque values listed in this Chapter's Specifications and secure it with the lockwasher.

16   Recheck the steering head bearings for play as described above. If necessary, repeat the adjustment procedure. Reinstall all parts previously removed.

Softail Springer models

17   To adjust the bearings, you'll either need to make a special tool or remove the handlebars, risers, rigid fork leg studs and

7.3b . . . and turn the adjusting bolt (arrow) to adjust the bearings . . .

7.3c . . . on some models, the bolt is under a decorative cover (arrow)

5

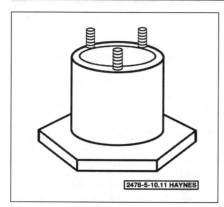

7.18 If you make a tool like this from an extra bearing retainer, you won't need to remove the handlebars and upper triple clamp (Softail Springer models)

7.23 The Springer bearing retainer (arrow) is beneath the upper triple clamp

8.7a Lower the steering stem and bearing out of the steering head

upper triple clamp so you can use a socket. If you use the special tool, it will only be necessary to remove the upper triple clamp acorn nut and washer.

18   Make the tool from an extra bearing retainer (Harley part no. 48306-88) and three roll pins (Harley part no. 614). Secure a pin in each of the three holes in the retainer with thread locking agent, then cut the pins so they extend 1/2-inch from the retainer **(see illustration)**.

19   If you're using the special tool, remove the acorn nut and rubber washer from the upper triple clamp.

20   Turn the front wheel all the way to the left.

21   Set up a plumb bob and ruler as described in Step 8 above, but start the measurement with the front wheel turned all the way to the left, rather than centered.

22   Slowly turn the wheel to the right until it begins to move by itself. Note the distance the plumb bob travels along the ruler and compare it with the value listed in this Chapter's Specifications.

23   If the measured distance is greater than specified, loosen the bearing retainer **(see illustration)**. If it's less, tighten the bearing retainer. If you don't have the special tool, use a socket.

24   Recheck the steering head bearings for play as described above. If necessary, repeat the adjustment procedure. Reinstall all parts previously removed and tighten the fasteners to the torques listed in the Chapter 5 Specifications.

FLT models

25   Remove fairing and headlight components as necessary for access to the steering stem nut, then reinstall them during the adjustment.

26   Bend back the tab on the lockwasher, then check the torque of the steering stem nut. It should be within the range listed in this Chapter's Specifications. The tightness of the nut affects the measurement.

27   Check the steering head bearings for play. To do this, turn the handlebar all the

way to the left, hold it there, then let it go. The handlebar should swing - by itself - to the right, back to the left, then to the right a second time (three swings total). It should stop by itself after three swings. The swings don't have to be all the way, and the handlebar doesn't have to stop at the straight-ahead position. But if it swings twice or less, the steering head is too tight. If it swings more than three times, the steering head is too loose.

27   Adjust the bearings by tapping the tabs on the adjusting nut with a hammer and punch. Adjust only a little at a time; even one notch can make a noticeable difference in how tight or loose the bearings are.

28   Recheck the bearings for play as described in Step 26. If necessary, repeat the adjustment procedure. Tighten the steering stem nut (above the triple clamp) to the torque listed in this Chapter's Specifications. Bend the lockwasher against the steering stem nut.

29   Reinstall all parts previously removed.

8   Steering head bearings - removal, inspection and installation

Removal

All except Softail Springer models

1   If the steering head bearing check (see Chapter 1) reveals excessive play in the steering head bearings, the entire front end must be disassembled and the bearings and races replaced with new ones.

2   Refer to Chapter 6 and remove the front wheel.

3   Remove the forks from the triple clamps as described in Section 3.

4   Remove the fork stem retaining nut or bolt. Some models use a tab washer to lock the nut in position. On these models, bend the ears of the tab washer down before loosening the nut. On models with a fork stem bolt, loosen the pinch bolt in the upper

triple clamp.

5   Remove the upper triple clamp. Depending on model, you'll need to remove the handlebars (see Section 2) and fairing components (see Chapter 7).

6   Remove the upper bearing dust shield, followed by the upper bearing. The bearing may be easier to remove if the lower triple clamp is partially removed from the bottom of the steering head.

7   Remove the lower triple clamp from the steering head and lift the bearing and dust shield off the stem **(see illustrations)**. Do not mix the upper and lower bearings up. They should be reinstalled in their original locations.

Softail Springer models

8   Remove the fork assembly (see Section 6).

9   Lift the dust shield off the upper bearing and lift the upper bearing out of the steering head.

Inspection

10   Clean all the parts with solvent and dry them thoroughly, using compressed air, if available. If you do use compressed air, don't let the bearings spin as they're dried -

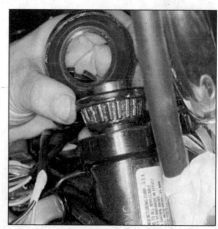

8.7b Lift off the bearing cover and upper bearing

it could ruin them. Wipe the old grease out of the frame steering head and bearing races.

11   Examine the races in the steering head for cracks, dents, and pits. If even the slightest amount of wear or damage is evident, the races should be replaced with new ones.

12   To remove the races, drive them out of the steering head with a bearing driver. A slide hammer with the proper internal-jaw puller will also work. Since the races are an interference fit in the frame, installation will be easier if the new races are left overnight in a refrigerator. This will cause them to contract and slip into place in the frame with very little effort. Before installing the races, coat the outsides of the races with clean engine oil. Tap them gently into place with a hammer and bearing driver or a large socket. Do not strike the bearing surface or the race will be damaged.

13   Check the bearings for wear. Look for cracks, dents, and pits in the races and flat spots on the bearings. Replace any defective parts with new ones. If a new bearing is required, replace both of them as a set.

14   To remove the lower bearing from the steering stem on all except Softail Springer models, cut the roller retainer with a chisel. While holding the steering stem upside down, heat the inner race until the bearing expands and falls off the steering stem. Don't remove this bearing unless it, or the grease seal underneath, must be replaced.

15   To remove the lower bearing from the steering stem on Softail Springer models, pry it loose, using the notches in the steering stem. Don't remove this bearing unless it, or the grease seal underneath, must be replaced.

16   Check the grease seal under the lower bearing and replace it with a new one if necessary.

17   Inspect the steering stem/lower triple clamp for cracks and other damage. Do not attempt to repair any steering components. Replace them with new parts if defects are found.

18   Check the bearing cover - if it's worn or deteriorated, replace it.

Installation

All except Softail Springer models

19   Pack the bearings with high-quality grease (preferably a moly-based grease) **(see illustration)**. Harley-Davidson recommends Harley-Davidson Special Purpose Grease, part no. 99857-97. Coat the outer races with grease also.

20   Install the grease seal and lower bearing onto the steering stem. Drive the lower bearing onto the steering stem using a section of pipe with a diameter the same as the inner race of the bearing **(see illustration)**.

Caution: Don't use a piece of pipe bigger than the inner race, or the bearing cage will be damaged.

Drive the bearing on until it is fully seated.

21   Insert the steering stem/lower triple clamp into the frame head. Install the upper

8.19 Work the grease completely into the rollers

bearing and the race cover.

22   If the bike is equipped with a bearing adjusting nut, install it. Tighten it just enough so there's no looseness (shake) in the bearings. The steering stem must pivot freely from side to side.

Caution: Don't overtighten the adjusting nut or the bearings will be damaged.

23   Install the upper triple clamp. If the bike has an upper triple clamp retaining nut, install it, using a new lockwasher.

24   If the bike is equipped with a steering stem adjusting bolt, install the bolt and tighten it just enough so there's no looseness (shake) in the bearings. The steering stem must pivot freely from side to side.

Caution: Don't overtighten the stem bolt or the bearings will be damaged.

25   The remainder of installation is the reverse of the removal steps, with the following additions:

   a) *Fill the steering head with the same grease used to lubricate the bearings, using the grease nipple on the steering head.*

   b) *Adjust the steering head bearings (see Section 7).*

   c) *Use Loctite on the threads of the steering stem pinch bolt (if equipped) and tighten it to the torque listed in this Chapter's Specifications.*

26   The remainder of installation is the reverse of the removal steps. Check the steering head bearing play and adjust it if necessary (see Section 7).

Softail Springer models

27   This procedure is part of fork installation, described in Section 6.

9   Rear shock absorbers - removal and installation

1   Raise the rear of the motorcycle and support it securely on blocks. If blocks aren't

8.20 Drive the grease seal and bearing lower race on with a hollow driver (or equivalent piece of pipe) and a hammer

available, remove one shock absorber at a time.

2   Remove the saddlebags, if necessary, to gain access to the shock absorbers.

3   On some models the mufflers must be turned out of the way of the bottom shock absorber mounting bolts (loosen the clamps first). On others (FLT, FXR, FXRS Sport and FXRT), the mufflers must be completely removed.

4   On models with air shocks, the air line must be detached from the shock absorber fitting.

5   On Softail models (with horizontal shock absorbers), remove the reservoir clamp bolt (it holds both reservoirs in place) and detach the reservoirs (models through 1988).

⚠️ *Warning: Do not detach the hoses from the reservoirs or the shock absorbers for any reason!*

The left shock absorber hose on 1985 and earlier models is attached to the bottom of the transmission mounting plate with a clamp that must be removed as well.

6   Remove the mounting nuts securing the shock absorbers to the swingarm and frame **(see illustration)** (later models use bolts and

9.6 Remove the upper and lower mounting bolts (lower bolt shown) to detach the shock absorber

5

11.8 Tab washers are used on some models to secure the swingarm pivot bolt - bend down the tabs before removing the bolt

11.12 Withdraw the swingarm from the frame towards the rear

nuts and some models have bolts with internal threads that mate with a frame stud at the upper mount). Carefully separate the shock absorber from the frame and swingarm. When the shock absorber is removed, the rear wheel and swingarm will drop to the ground if not supported **(see illustration)**. **Note:** *Softail models require adapter no. SRES24 or SRES28 (as applicable), available from Snap-On Tools Corporation, to remove and refit the shock absorber mounting bolts.*

7   Clean and inspect all of the components for wear and damage (especially the rubber parts). Replace any defective components with new parts. The shock absorber can be disassembled in some cases for replacement of individual parts, but the job should be done by a dealer service department or other qualified shop. Air-assisted shock can't be dismantled.

8   Have an assistant lift the rear wheel and swingarm to the correct level to install the shock absorber. With one shock absorber in place, the swingarm should be in the correct position to install the other shock.

9   Tighten the nuts (and bolts) to the torque listed in this Chapter's Specifications and lower the motorcycle off the support blocks.

10 Swingarm bearings - check

1   The swingarm pivots on bearings, which rarely wear out.

2   Raise the rear of the motorcycle off the ground and support it securely on blocks. Grab the swingarm in front of the axle and move it from side-to-side. If there's any discernible movement, the bearings may be worn out.

3   The swingarm should be removed and inspected as described in the following Section.

11 Swingarm - removal, inspection and installation

Removal

1   With the motorcycle on a level surface, raise the rear wheel. Support it securely on blocks under the frame where the engine rests.

2   Disconnect the final drive from the rear wheel sprocket. On chain drive models, remove the master link from the chain and separate it from the rear sprocket (see Chapter 1, if necessary). On models with fully enclosed chains, you'll have to remove the rubber boots from the rear sprocket housing before the master link can be disconnected. On belt drive models, the rear wheel must be removed in order to disconnect the belt from the rear wheel sprocket.

3   Remove the rear wheel as described in Chapter 6.

4   On early models with rear drum brakes, remove the brake components from the swingarm, as described in Chapter 6, and tie them up securely, out of the way.

Caution: Do not let the brake components hang by the hydraulic brake line or the line may be damaged.

5   Separate the disc brake caliper and hose from the swingarm, on models so equipped, and securely tie the caliper to the frame (see Chapter 6 if necessary).

Caution: Do not allow the caliper to hang by the hydraulic brake line or the line may be damaged.

6   On some models the exhaust system must be disconnected from the swingarm. Usually the brackets can be unbolted, but on some models the exhaust pipe and muffler or even the entire exhaust system must come off.

7   Support the swingarm and remove the lower shock absorber mounting bolts (rear bolts on Softail models). Remove the shock reservoir clamp bolt on 1988 and earlier Softail models.

8   Flatten the tab washer ears (if equipped)

securing the swingarm pivot shaft **(see illustration)**.

9   On models other than those described in Steps 10 and 11, unscrew and withdraw the pivot shaft from the swingarm.

10   On Softail models, remove the bolt threaded into each side of the swingarm axis tube and detach the lock washer (right side), spacer (left side) and axis tube (inside the swingarm). The swingarm can now be pulled out of the frame mounts.

11   On five-speed transmission models, proceed as follows:

   a)   *On models through early 1986 - Remove the nut and spacer from the right end of the pivot shaft.*

   b)   *On late 1986 through 1988 models - Remove the right pivot bolt while holding the left pivot bolt.*

   c)   *On 1989 and later models - Hold the right side nut(11/16-inch six point head) and remove the left side locknut (3/4-inch six-point head) and cup washer.*

   d)   *On all five-speed models - Remove the passenger footrest brackets (FLT) and the pivot shaft mounting brackets (FXR).*

   e)   *On all models through 1988 - Tap the pivot shaft out of position from the right side (on models through early 1986, it isn't necessary to remove the nut and washer from the left side of the shaft).*

   f)   *On 1989 and later models - Tap the pivot shaft out from the left side.*

12   Pull the swingarm out of the frame mounts **(see illustration)**.

Inspection

Four-speed models

Note: *The inspection procedure applies only to 1970 through early 1978 models equipped with tapered roller swingarm bearings. Late 1978 through 1984 models have spherical bearings that are lifetime lubricated and require no service other than cleaning.*

13   Mount the swingarm securely in a vise and pull the seal collars off each end. The inner bearing races are obscured under the seals. The inner bearing races can be driven out with a drift punch and hammer inserted through the swingarm crossmember from

11.17a Pack the swingarm bearing and race with grease (early models only)

11.17b Install a new seal after the bearing is in place (early models only)

11.17c Install the seal collar (early models only)

the opposite side. This will also drive the seals out of position.

14   Clean and examine the tapered roller bearings for signs of wear and damage, which should be self-evident. If there is any doubt about the condition of the bearings, replace them both as a precaution. Most bearings fail as a result of pitting, which occurs on the inner and outer races.

15   It's also a good idea to replace the seals with new ones every time they're tampered with.

Five-speed models

16   Clean and inspect the swingarm around the pivot shaft. Check the pivot shaft bushings for signs of wear and deterioration. If the cleveblocs or bushings are worn, the swingarm must be taken to a Harley-Davidson dealer to have the defective components replaced.

Installation

Four-speed models

17   Reassemble and install the swingarm by reversing the above procedures. Be sure the bearings are liberally packed with grease and absolutely clean (see illustration). Even a small amount of grit on a bearing will accelerate wear. Install the seals and collars in each side of the swingarm (see illustrations).

18   After the pivot bolt has been installed, set the preload on the roller bearings. This is done by attaching a spring scale to the extreme end of one of the swingarm legs before the shock absorbers are installed. Take a reading (in pounds) required to make the swingarm turn on the pivot. The pivot bolt must be tightened only slightly so the swingarm will move freely. Now tighten the pivot bolt until the drag is increased by about two pounds, as measured on the spring scale.

19   When the proper preload is attained, bend the ears of the tab washer up to secure the pivot bolt.

Five-speed models

20   Installation of the swingarm is the reverse of the removal procedure. Special tool (no. HD-33805) may be required to spread the swingarm Cleveblocs. You can make a substitute tool from a piece of threaded stock, nuts and washers (see illustration).

21   On early 1986 and earlier models, coat the pivot shaft with anti-seize compound. Insert the shaft through the left side rubber mount (small diameter side of mount facing OUT), then install the left side washer and nut on the shaft. Tighten the nut until it bottoms on the shaft threads. Slide the left side nylon washer onto the shaft (small diameter side of washer facing the swingarm), then insert the pivot shaft through the swingarm and transmission from the left side of the machine. Install the nylon washer on the right side of the shaft (small diameter side facing the swingarm), followed by the rubber mount (small diameter side facing OUT), washer and nut. Position the dowel pin holes in the nylon washers at the top. Tighten the right side nut finger-tight.

22   On late 1986 through 1988 models, thread the left side pivot bolt onto the center stud, then coat the shank of the pivot bolt with anti-seize compound and insert the bolt through the left side rubber mount (small

diameter side of mount facing the bolt head). Slide the left side nylon washer onto the bolt (small diameter side of washer facing the swingarm), then insert the left side pivot bolt and center stud assembly through the swingarm and transmission from the left side of the machine. Coat the right side pivot bolt shank with anti-seize compound, then install the right side rubber mount (small diameter side of mount facing the bolt head) and the right side nylon washer (small diameter side facing the swingarm). Insert the right side bolt into the swingarm and thread it onto the center stud finger-tight.

23   On 1989 and later models, coat the pivot shaft with anti-seize compound. Insert the shaft through the right side rubber mount (small diameter side of mount facing the shaft bolt head), then slide the right side nylon washer onto the shaft (small diameter side of washer facing the swingarm). Insert the pivot shaft through the swingarm and transmission from the right side of the machine. Install the nylon washer on the left side of the shaft (small diameter side facing the swingarm), followed by the rubber mount (small diameter side facing OUT), cup washer and nut. Tighten the nut finger-tight.

24   When installing the footrest or the pivot shaft mounting brackets, be sure the roll pins engage the locating hole in the rubber

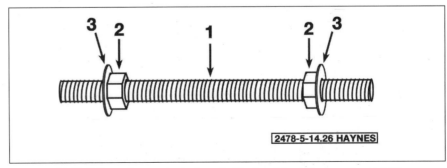

2478-5-14.26 HAYNES

11.20 If the swingarm is equipped with cleveblocs, they can be spread for installation with a tool like this

| 1   Threaded stock | 2   Nuts | 3   Washers |

5

mount. Also be sure the flat on the pivot shaft registers with the flat on the rubber mount on the right.

25   Position the footrests so they will fold up at a 45-degree angle to the rear before tightening them.

26   Tighten the pivot shaft nut/bolt(s) to the specified torque. **Note:** *If the pivot shaft is a three-piece bolt and stud type, hold one bolt while tightening the other to the specified torque. Make sure the clips are installed in the shaft mounting brackets. The flat side of the clip must be at the bottom. On 1989 and later models, hold the right side nut and tighten the left side nut to the specified torque.*

27   On FLT models with an enclosed final drive chain, the **r**ear chain boots and their mating surfaces on the inner primary chaincase and transmission must be coated with RTV-type sealant.

12 Drive chain - removal, cleaning, inspection and installation

Removal

1   Remove the chain guard.

2   Loosen the chain adjusters to create slack in the chain (see Chapter 1).

3   Remove the master link retaining clip with pliers **(see illustration 3.11 in Chapter 1)**. Be careful not to bend or twist it. Slide out the master link and remove the chain from the sprockets.

4   Check the chain guard on the swingarm for wear or damage and replace it as necessary.

Cleaning and inspection

5   Soak the chain in a high flash point solvent for approximately five or six minutes. Use a brush to work the solvent into the spaces between the links and plates.

6   Wipe the chain dry, then check it carefully for worn or damaged links. Replace the chain if wear or damage is found at any point.

7   Stretch the chain taut and measure its length. Then carefully compress all the links together and measure the length again. If the difference between the measurements is more than one inch, the chain is worn enough to need replacement. If the chain needs to be replaced, refer to Section 14 and check the sprockets. If they're worn, replace them also. If a new chain is installed on worn sprockets, it will wear out quickly.

8   Lubricate the chain as described in Chapter 1.

Installation

9   Installation is the reverse of the removal steps. Position the master link clip with its open end facing rearward (away from the direction of chain travel) **(see illustration 3.15 in Chapter 1)**. Refer to Chapter 1 and adjust the chain.

13 Drive belt - removal, inspection and installation

Note: *This is a time-consuming procedure, due to the necessity of removing the entire primary chaincase assembly. On FLT models, the swingarm pivot bolt must be partially removed as well. It's a good idea to read through the procedure before starting, including the primary chaincase removal procedure in Chapter 2B and, on FLT models, the swingarm removal procedure in this Chapter. You may find it more practical to have the job done by a dealer service department or other qualified shop.*

1   Jack up the rear end of the motorcycle and support it securely.

2   If you're working on an FLT model, remove the left saddlebag and the left side of the exhaust system (see Chapters 7 and 3).

3   Remove the rear wheel (see Chapter 6).

4   Loosen the drive belt (see Chapter 1).

5   Remove the engine sprocket, primary drive chain or belt and clutch as a unit (see Chapter 2B).

6   Remove the primary chaincase (see Chapter 2B).

7   Take the belt off the transmission sprocket.

8   Installation is the reverse of the removal steps. Adjust belt tension (see Chapter 1).

14 Sprockets - check and replacement

1   Support the bike securely so it can't be knocked over during this procedure.

2   Whenever the sprockets are inspected, the chain or belt should be inspected also and replaced if it's worn. Installing a worn chain or belt on new sprockets will cause them to wear quickly.

Check

Chain final drive

3   Check the teeth on the front and rear sprockets for wear. With the chain tension correctly adjusted, try to pull the chain away from the rear sprocket where the chain wraps around the sprocket. If you can make a gap of more than 1/4-inch between the chain and sprocket, the chain and sprockets should be replaced.

Belt final drive

4   Check the sprocket teeth for wear and for chips or other damage (see Chapter 1).

All models

5   If the sprockets are worn, remove the rear wheel (see Chapter 6) and the chain or belt (Section 12 or 13).

Replacement

Rear sprocket (drum brake models)

Note: *Special tools are required to install a new sprocket on drum brake models. Read the procedure before beginning removal - you may decide to have a Harley-Davidson dealer do the job.*

6   The rear wheel sprocket is riveted to the brake drum. If examination indicates some of the teeth are chipped, broken or hooked, the brake drum must be removed from the wheel. It's attached to the wheel by five bolts.

7   Remove the bolts securing the brake drum to the hub.

8   The sprocket is attached to the brake drum with rivets. Using a sharp chisel, cut the heads off the rivets and dowel pins.

9   If the rivet holes aren't worn or elongated, the new rivets can be installed in the same holes. However, if they're worn or elongated, a new set of holes should be drilled midway between the existing holes and the dowel pin holes. A 0.19335-inch (no. 10) drill bit is required to bore the holes.

10   New dowel pin holes should be drilled also (use a 3/16-inch drill bit). The dowel pins must be a tight fit. Use the new sprocket as a template.

11   Drill a rivet hole, then place the sprocket in position on the drum. Insert a rivet through the hole but don't head the rivet. Drill another hole across from the first rivet and insert another rivet. Again, don't head the rivet.

12   Drill the remaining holes, then drill the four dowel pin holes.

14   Remove the sprocket from the brake drum and deburr the newly drilled holes.

15   Position the drum and sprocket on the center support of the riveting jig (special tool no. 95600-33B).

16   The dowel pins are installed first, followed by the rivets. The dowel pins and the rivets must be installed through the brake drum side.

17   Using a hollow driver, seat the dowel pin and rivet simultaneously, driving the sprocket and hub flange together.

18   Using a concave punch, flare the end of the dowel pin. Head the end of the rivet until it extends 3/32-inch above the face of the sprocket.

19   Repeat Steps 16 through 18, seating the rivets and dowel pins on the opposite side of the hub until all of them are in place. This will prevent distortion of the sprocket as the rivets are installed.

20   Install the brake drum on the hub and reinstall the rear wheel as described in Chapter 6.

Rear sprocket (disc brake models)

21   The sprocket is attached to the rear wheel hub with five bolts.

22   On chain drive models, if examination of the sprocket indicates the teeth are chipped, broken or hooked, the sprocket should be

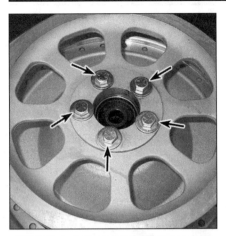

14.24 Unbolt the rear sprocket from the wheel (arrows) (belt drive shown)

14.27a The transmission sprocket nut has left-hand threads

14.27b On 1992 and later models, remove the locking plate bolts, then unscrew the nut and remove the sprocket

replaced with a new one. If the rear wheel sprocket is worn, the final drive sprocket on the transmission is probably worn also. It's a good idea to replace both sprockets at the same time, as well as the chain. This will alleviate rapid wear that results from mixing old and new parts.

23 On belt drive models, examine the sprocket teeth and flange for signs of damage (see Chapter 1). The sprocket will not wear to the same extent as chain drive models, it being more likely that the belt itself will require replacement.

24 Remove the bolts securing the sprocket to the hub **(see illustration)**. Lift the sprocket off and place the new one in position.

25 Install the sprocket mounting bolts and washers (having applied a drop of thread-locking compound to the bolt threads) and tighten the bolts to the torque listed in this Chapter's Specifications.

26 Install the rear wheel as described in Chapter 6.

Front sprocket (all models)

27 Either bend back the lockwasher and unscrew the nut, remove the lock screw, or remove the screws and lock plate depending on the model being worked on **(see illustrations)**. Pull the sprocket off the transmission shaft, using a puller if necessary.

28 The oil seal behind the sprocket is exposed when the sprocket is removed. Pry the seal out (taking care not to scratch the seal bore) and tap in a new seal with a socket the same diameter as the seal.

29 Install the retainer (if applicable), then slip the final drive sprocket over the splined mainshaft.

30 Install the tab washer (early models) behind the nut that secures the sprocket. You'll have to lock the engine to tighten the nut. When the nut is tight, bend the tab washer over the nut to lock it in place. Later models have a lock screw instead of a tab washer.

1985 through 1991 models

31 Install the sprocket on the mainshaft

and secure with its nut. Lock the engine and tighten the nut to 35 to 65 ft-lbs (47 to 88 Nm), check if one of the three holes for the lockscrew aligns with any of the nut flats. In none align, continue tightening (do not exceed maximum of 90 ft-lbs, 122 Nm) until one of the holes aligns. At this point, apply a drop of thread locking compound to the lock screw and tighten it to 50 to 60 in-lbs (6 to 7 Nm).

1992-on models

32 Install the spacer on the mainshaft with its chamfered side inwards, followed by the sprocket.

33 Apply a few drops of Loctite 262 (red) thread locking compound to the nut threads and install the nut on the mainshaft, remembering that it has a left-hand thread. Tighten to 110 to 120 ft-lbs (149 to 163 Nm).

34 On all chain drive models and 1991 belt drive models, align one of the sprocket lock screw holes as described in Step 4, not exceeding the maximum torque of 150 ft-lbs (203 Nm). Apply a drop of Loctite 242 (blue) to the lock screw threads and tighten it to 50 to 60 in-lbs (6 to 7 Nm).

35 On 1992 through 1994 models with belt drive, fit the lock plate over the nut in such a way that it can be secured diagonally by the two lock screws **(see illustration)** - tighten the nut further if necessary as described above. Apply a drop of Loctite 242 (blue) to the lock screw threads and tighten them to 80 to 110 in-lbs (9 to 12 Nm).

36 On 1995 and later models, install the nut as described in Step 5, but tighten it only to 50 ft-lbs (68 Nm). Draw a line across the nut and sprocket with a felt pen. Tighten another 30 to 40-degrees, aligning two of the lock plate holes with the holes in the sprocket. Try repositioning the lock plate if the holes don't line up; the lock plate holes are offset. If the holes can't be lined up within the 40-degree range, tighten further, but not more than a total of 45-degrees (1/8-turn) from the felt pen mark. Don't loosen the nut to line up the holes. Once the holes are aligned, install the lock plate Allen bolts and

14.35 The sprocket lockplate (1992 and later) must be installed so the bolt holes align

tighten to 80 to 110 in-lbs (9 to 12 Nm). The Allen bolts come from the factory with a spot of Loctite on the threads and can be reinstalled three to five times. If you aren't sure how many times they've been installed, use new ones.

37 The remainder of installation is the reverse of the removal steps. Refer to Chapter 1 and adjust the chain or belt.

15 Anti-dive system - check

5

General check

1 Check the system lines and fittings for leaks and make sure everything is tight.

2 Attach a no-loss air gauge to the system air valve on the engine guard, accumulator or handlebar.

3 Make sure the ignition switch is off, then apply the front brake and bounce the front end of the machine.

4 Watch the air gauge - it should fluctuate

as the front end moves up-and-down.

5   Turn the ignition switch on and repeat the check. This time the air pressure must remain constant as the front end moves.

Solenoid check

6   The solenoid is mounted just below the upper fork assembly triple clamp.

7   With the ignition switch on, apply either brake and listen for a faint click from the solenoid. The sound is very faint, so it may help to touch the solenoid as the brake is applied and released. You should feel the solenoid operate.

8   If the solenoid doesn't seem to be working, check the winding resistance by connecting an ohmmeter to the solenoid wires. The meter should indicate 10-to-20 ohms on models through 1992 and 10-to-30 ohms on models from 1993. If it doesn't, replace the solenoid.

9   Attach one ohmmeter lead to one of the wires and the other lead to the solenoid metal case. The ohmmeter must indicate infinite resistance. If it doesn't, replace the solenoid.

10   To remove the solenoid, proceed as follows:

a) *FLT models - On 1984 through 1987 FLT models, unscrew the hose fitting and remove the O-ring from the bottom of the solenoid. On 1988 and later FLT models, remove the banjo bolt, O-rings and hose fitting from the bottom of the solenoid. On all FLT models, remove the nut (if used) and withdraw the case, solenoid, spacer and rubber washer. The plunger body can be unscrewed with a spanner wrench, by locking two thin nuts together on the plunger body threads or with a screwdriver (1985-on). Remove the spring, plunger and O-ring.*

b) *1984 through 1987 FXRT and FXRD models - On 1985 and earlier models, detach the accumulator hose at the solenoid right-angle fitting (the hose clamp will have to be cut or pried off), then unscrew the fitting and remove the O-ring, washer and nut. Unscrew the large nut at the bottom of the solenoid case. Remove the case bolts/nuts and detach the case, solenoid and spacer. On 1986 and later models, remove the banjo bolt, fitting and O-rings from the bottom of the solenoid, then detach the case, solenoid and spacer. The plunger can be removed as described in Paragraph a).*

c) *1988 and later FXRT FXRS-SP and FXRS-CONV models - Remove the banjo bolt or hex hose fitting from the bottom of the solenoid and detach the fitting and O-rings. Pull down on the case and detach the solenoid, the rubber washer, the metal washer and the O-ring from the plunger body. Remove the plunger as described in Paragraph a).*

Chapter 6
Brakes, wheels and tires

Contents

Degrees of difficulty

Easy, suitable for novice with little experience		**Fairly easy,** suitable for beginner with some experience		**Fairly difficult,** suitable for competent DIY mechanic		**Difficult,** suitable for experienced DIY mechanic		**Very difficult,** suitable for expert DIY or professional	

Specifications

Wheel bearing end play
FLT models
1980 and 1981	0.004 to 0.014 inch (0.1 to 0.35 mm)
1982-on	0.002 to 0.006 inch (0.05 to 0.15 mm)

All other models
Through mid-1991	0.004 to 0.008 inch (0.1 to 0.2 mm)
Late 1991 and later	0.002 to 0.006 inch (0.05 to 0.15 mm)

Wheel runout
All wheels (cast and spoke)
Lateral	3/64-inch (0.040 inch, 1.0 mm)
Radial	1/32-inch (0.030 inch, 0.8 mm)

Brakes
Minimum brake lining thickness	See Chapter 1
Disc runout (warpage) limit	3/32 inch (2.38 mm)
Rear pedal height setting	See text
Rear pedal freeplay	See text
Front brake lever freeplay (at end of lever)	1/4-inch (6.35 mm)

Caliper piston retraction (minimum)
Front	0.020 to 0.025 inch (0.5 to 0.6 mm)
Rear	0.033 to 0.038 inch (0.8 to 1.0 mm)

Torque specifications

Axle nuts (front and rear)
1970 through 1983	50 ft-lbs (68 Nm)

1984 and later (front)
FLT models	50 to 55 ft-lbs (68 to 75 Nm)
FXR and Dyna models	50 ft-lbs (68 Nm)
FXSTS models	60 to 65 ft-lbs (81 to 88 Nm)
All others	45 to 50 ft-lbs (61 to 68 Nm)
1984 and later (rear)	60 to 65 ft-lbs (81 to 88 Nm)

6

Brake disc-to-hub

Through 1983
    FLT and FXR .... 34 to 42
    All others
        Spoke wheel (16 and 21-inch) .... 23 to 27 ft-lbs (31 to 37 Nm)
        Spoke wheel (19-inch) .... 16 to ft-lbs (22 to 26 Nm)
        Cast wheel (16-inch) .... 23 to 27 ft-lbs (31 to 37 Nm)
        Cast wheel (19-inch) .... 14 to 16 ft-lbs (19 to 22 Nm)
1984 and later (front)
    FLT/FXR
        1984 through 1990 .... 16 to 18 ft-lbs (22 to 24 Nm)
        1991 and later .... 16 to 24 ft-lbs (22 to 33 Nm)
    FX/Softail and FL/Softail .... 16 to 24 ft-lbs (22 to 33 Nm)
    FXD Dyna
        1991 with spoked wheel .... 16 to 18 ft-lbs (22 to 24 Nm)
        All others .... 16 to 24 ft-lbs (22 to 33 Nm)
1984 and later (rear)
    FLT
        1984 through 1990 .... 24 to 30 ft-lbs (33 to 41 Nm)
        1991 .... 30 to 35 ft-lbs (41 to 47 Nm)
        1992-on .... 30 to 45 ft-lbs (41 to 61 Nm)
    FXR
        1984 through 1991 .... 23 to 27 ft-lbs (31 to 37 Nm)
        1992-on .... 30 to 45 ft-lbs (41 to 61 Nm)
    FX/Softail
        Through 1990 .... 23 to 27 ft-lbs (31 to 37 Nm)
        1991
            Spoked wheel .... 16 to 24 ft-lbs (22 to 33 Nm)
            Disc wheel .... 23 to 27 ft-lbs (31 to 37 Nm)
        1992-on
            Allen screws .... 23 to 27 ft-lbs (31 to 37 Nm)
            Torx screws .... 30 to 45 ft-lbs (41 to 61 Nm)
    FXD Dyna
        1991 and 1992 .... 23 to 27 ft-lbs (31 to 37 Nm)
        1993-on
            Allen screws .... 23 to 27 ft-lbs (31 to 37 Nm)
            Torx screws .... 30 to 45 ft-lbs (41 to 61 Nm)

Brake caliper

1974 through 1977 .... 130 inch-lbs (17 Nm)
1978 through 1983 (except FLT/FXR) .... 120 inch-lbs (14 Nm)
1980 through 1983
    FLT .... 90 inch-lbs (10 Nm)
    FXR .... 12 to 15 ft-lbs (16 to 20 Nm)
1984-on (front)
    FXST/C, FLST/C/F/N, FLT, FXR and FXD Dyna .... 25 to 30 ft-lbs (34 to 41 Nm)
    FXSTS
        Top .... 42 to 46 ft-lbs (57 to 62 Nm)
        Bottom .... 25 to 30 ft-lbs (34 to 41 Nm)
1984-on (rear)
    FLT/FXR .... 15 to 20 ft-lbs (20 to 27 Nm)
    Softail .... 12 to 15 ft-lbs (16 to 20 Nm)
    All others
        1984 through mid-1987 .... 12 to 15 ft-lbs (16 to 20 Nm)
        Late 1987 and later .... 15 to 20 ft-lbs (20 to 27 Nm)

Brake drum

Drum-to-hub bolts (all) .... 335 ft-lbs (47 Nm)

Rear master cylinder

Mounting bolts .... 155 to 190 inch-lbs (17.5 to 21 Nm)
Mounting nut (late 1987 and later FXR) .... 30 to 40 ft-lbs (41 to 54 Nm)

Miscellaneous

Rear brake anchor nut .... 50 ft-lbs (68 Nm)
Rear brake reaction pin nut (FXST/C only) .... 20 ft-lbs (27 Nm)
Brake hose-to-caliper banjo bolts (1985-on)
    With copper washers .... 30 to 35 ft-lbs (41 to 47 Nm)
    With steel and rubber washers .... 17 to 22 ft-lbs (23 to 30 Nm)

1 General information

Depending on the model, either wire spoke wheels or cast alloy wheels are standard equipment. Wire wheels require frequent inspection and maintenance, while cast wheels are virtually maintenance-free.

Brakes are various combinations, depending on model and year; 1970 through 1972 FX models and 1970 and 1971 FL models are equipped with drum brakes on both front and rear wheels. Beginning with 1972 FL models and 1973 FX models, the front and rear wheels are both equipped with disc brakes (dual discs are installed on the front wheels of 1978 models).

Most 1979 and later models are equipped with dual front discs and a single rear disc.

 Warning: Dust created by the brake system may contain asbestos, which is harmful to your health. Never blow it out with compressed air and don't inhale any of it. An approved filtering mask should be worn when working on the brakes. Do not, under any circumstances, use petroleum-based solvents to clean brake parts. Use brake system cleaner or denatured alcohol only.

2 Wheels - inspection and repair

Wire wheels

1 Wire wheels should be inspected frequently to ensure the wheel runs true and to prevent potential damage from loose or broken spokes.

2 Clean the wheels thoroughly to remove mud and dirt, then make a general check of the wheels and spokes as described in Chapter 1.

3 Raise the motorcycle so the front wheel is off the ground and support it securely with blocks. Because the frame is relatively narrow under the engine, be sure to support the motorcycle so it can't fall over sideways. Attach a dial indicator to the fork slider and position the stem against the side of the rim. Spin the wheel slowly and check the side-to-side (axial) runout of the rim. In order to accurately check the radial runout with the dial indicator, the wheel would have to be removed from the machine and the tire removed from the wheel; with the axle clamped in a vise, the wheel can be rotated to check the runout.

4 An easier, though slightly less accurate, method is to attach a stiff wire pointer to the fork slider and position the end a fraction of an inch from the wheel (where the wheel and

tire join). If the wheel is true, the distance from the pointer to the rim will be constant as the wheel is rotated. Repeat the procedure to check the rear wheel.

5 A wheel that wobbles from side-to-side can be trued by loosening the spokes that lead to the hub from the high side of the rim and tightening the spokes that lead to the hub from the low side. This in effect will pull the bulge out of the rim. Always tighten/loosen spokes in small increments to avoid distorting the rim and make sure all the spokes are uniformly tight (see Chapter 1).

6 An out-of-round wheel can be trued by loosening the spokes (both sides of the hub) that lead to the low area, and tightening the spokes that lead to the high or bulged-out area.

7 Generally, the wheels will probably have a combination of side-to-side wobble and out-of-roundness. Keep in mind that tightening and loosening spokes will affect wheel runout in both directions. Wheel truing requires patience and practice to develop any degree of skill, so it's best left to a dealer service department or motorcycle repair shop.

8 If the inspection reveals a bent, cracked, or otherwise damaged rim, the entire wheel will have to be rebuilt using a new rim and spokes. This is a complicated task requiring experience and skills beyond those of the average home mechanic and should be done by a dealer service department or motorcycle repair shop.

Cast wheels

9 The cast alloy wheels should be visually inspected for cracks, flat spots on the rim and other damage. Check the axial and radial runout as described previously for wire wheels.

10 If damage is evident, or if runout in either direction is excessive, the wheel will have to be replaced with a new one. Never attempt to repair a damaged cast wheel.

3 Front wheel - removal and installation

Caution: On disc brake equipped models, do not operate the brake lever while the front wheel is removed - the piston in the caliper might be forced out. If the piston is forced out of the bore, the caliper will have to be completely disassembled and rebuilt.

Note: *After the wheel is reinstalled, the wheel bearing end play must be checked with a dial indicator. If it falls outside the range listed in this Chapter's Specifications, the long spacer in the wheel hub or thin spacer washer (as applicable) will have to be replaced by another of different length - see Section 22.*

1 Raise the front wheel off the ground and support the machine securely on blocks. Be sure the motorcycle is stable from side-to-side. The frame under the engine is very nar-

3.5 Loosen the slider cap nuts before removing the axle (1970 and 1971 FL models)

row, so it may be necessary to support the side of the motorcycle.

1970 and 1971 FL models

2 Straighten the cotter pin at the end of the axle and pull it out.

3 Unscrew the axle nut and remove the washer from the axle.

4 Remove the screws securing the brake drum to the wheel hub.

5 Loosen the nuts securing the caps at the bottom of the fork sliders and pull the axle out **(see illustration)**.

6 Apply the front brake to hold the brake drum in place while the wheel is removed from the forks.

7 Installation of the front wheel is done by reversing the removal procedure. Be sure the mating surfaces of the wheel hub and brake drum are clean to ensure a tight fit.

8 Tighten the screws securing the brake drum to the torque listed in this Chapter's Specifications. Use a criss-cross pattern to avoid warping the drum.

9 Tighten the axle nut to the specified torque, followed by the fork slider cap nuts. Install a new cotter pin in the axle.

1970 through 1972 FX models

10 Disconnect the front brake cable from the front wheel by removing the clevis pin from the brake operating arm. Remove the brake backing plate anchor bolt and the lock washer.

11 Unscrew the nut from the end of the axle.

12 Loosen the pinch bolts (at the bottom of each fork leg) that secure the axle to the forks **(see illustration 3.5)**.

13 Tap the axle out of position and remove the front wheel.

14 Installation is the reverse of the removal procedure. Inject an ounce of multi-purpose grease into the wheel hub before installing the axle. Tighten the axle nut to the torque listed in this Chapter's Specifications, followed by the axle pinch bolts.

6

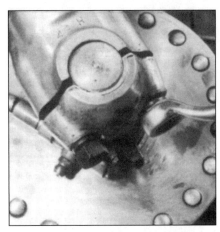

3.16 Loosen the axle cap nuts before removing the axle (1973 FX models)

3.38 On later models, remove the caliper mounting bolts (1), axle nut (2) and slider cap nuts (3) to detach the front wheel

1973 FX models

15   Remove the axle nut and washer from the front axle.
16   Loosen the nuts securing the axle cap to the bottom of the right fork slider **(see illustration)**.
17   Tap the axle **o**ut of position and lower the front wheel. Pull the speedometer drive out of the front hub (see Chapter 8). Leave the speedometer drive unit connected to the cable and tie them up out of the way.
18   Reverse the removal procedure for installation of the front wheel. Align the brake pads on each side of the brake disc while installing the wheel.
19   Engage the speedometer drive gear with the hole in the wheel hub.
20   Tighten the axle nut to the specified torque, followed by the slider cap nuts.

1974 through 1977 FX models

21   Remove the brake caliper mounting bolt, the washers and the locknut.
22   Remove the axle nut from the axle, along with the washer and lockwasher.
23   Loosen the bolts securing the axle caps to the bottom of each fork slider.
24   Tap the end of the axle to loosen it, then pull the axle out of the forks and front hub.
25   Lower the front wheel until the speedometer drive unit can be disengaged from the front hub. Tie the speedometer drive unit and cable out of the way.
26   Remove the front wheel.
27   Installation is the reverse of the removal procedure. Align the brake pads on each side of the brake disc while installing the front wheel.
28   Engage the speedometer drive gear with the hole in the wheel hub. Tighten the axle nut to the specified torque, followed by the slider cap nuts.

1972 through early 1978 FL models

29   Straighten the ends of the cotter pin in the end of the axle and remove it.

30   Remove the axle nut and flat washer from the axle.
31   Loosen the slider cap nuts and remove the axle. You may have to tap the end of the axle with a soft-faced hammer to remove it from the wheel.
32   Remove the front wheel.
33   Installation is the reverse of the removal procedure. Align the brake pads on each side of the brake disc while placing the wheel in position.
34   Tighten the axle nut to the specified torque and install a new cotter pin to secure the nut.
35   Tighten the two slider cap nuts.

1978 and later FX models (except Springer)

36   Detach the front brake calipers from the fork legs and tie them up, out of the way.
37   Remove the nut, lock washer and flat washer from the axle.
38   Loosen the bolts/nuts securing the axle caps to the bottom of the fork slider(s) **(see illustration)**. **Note:** *On 1987 and later FXR models and FXDB/C/L Dyna models, loosen the pinch bolt locknut on the right side fork slider.*
39   Tap the end of the axle to loosen it, then pull it out of the wheel.
40   Lower the wheel from the forks and disconnect the speedometer drive unit from the hub (some models don't have a speedometer drive unit on the front wheel). Remove the front wheel. On FLST models, the hub cap will come off with the wheel.
41   Installation of the front wheel is the reverse of the removal procedure. Align the brake pads on each side of the brake discs while placing the wheel in position.
42   A spacer is installed between the left fork leg and the wheel on some FXWG models; a spacer with a groove also fits between the right fork leg and the wheel on some FXWG models.
43   Engage the speedometer drive gear with the hole in the wheel hub (except FXWG models).
44   Tighten the axle nut to the specified

torque before tightening the slider cap nuts.
45   Securely tighten the caliper mounting hardware.

Late 1978 through 1980 FL models

46   Remove the caps from the ends of the axle (they're held in place with a small setscrew).
47   Remove the axle nut, lock washer and flat washer.
48   Loosen the nuts securing the slider cap and pull out the axle.
49   Remove the front wheel, along with the hub cap and spacer.
50   Reverse the removal procedure to install the front wheel. Align the brake pads on each side of the brake disc.
51   Apply multi-purpose grease to the axle and insert it through the right fork leg, through the wheel, spacer, hub cap and the left fork leg.
52   Tighten the axle nut to the specified torque before tightening the slider cap nuts.
53   Install the caps on the ends of the axle.

1981 and later FL models (except FLT)

54   Remove the caps from the ends of the axle (they're held in place with a small set screw).
55   Remove the axle nut, lock washer and flat washer from the left side of the wheel.
56   Loosen the slider cap nuts and remove the axle.
57   Remove the wheel, along with the spacer, speedometer drive and hub cap.
58   Installation is the reverse of the removal procedure. Be sure to align the brake pads on each side of the brake disc.
59   Coat the axle with multi-purpose grease before installing it.
60   Insert the axle through the right fork leg, through the speedometer drive, hub cap, wheel, spacer and the left fork leg.
61   Tighten the axle nut to the specified torque, followed by the slider cap nuts.
62   Install the caps on the ends of the axle.

1980 and later FLT models

63 Remove the brake caliper mounting nuts and bolts and tie the calipers out of the way.

64 Remove the axle nut and washers from the left side of the axle.

65 Loosen the slider cap nuts on the bottom of the right fork leg. Tap the axle out of the left fork leg with a soft-faced hammer.

66 Lift the wheel and speedometer drive out of position. **Note:** *The speedometer drive on 1987 and later models is mounted on the left side instead of the right side as on previous years. The speedometer drive is also equipped with a rubber washer-type seal between the drive unit and the front wheel.*

67 Reverse the removal procedure to install the front wheel. The valve stem must be on the left side of the machine when the wheel is installed.

68 Install the speedometer drive between the right side of the forks and the wheel (left side on 1987 and later models). The tab on the drive must engage with the slot in the brake disc.

69 Apply multi-purpose grease to the axle and insert the axle through the wheel and forks from the right side. Install the wheel spacer on the correct side, between the fork leg and the wheel.

70 Tighten the axle nut to the specified torque before tightening the slider cap nuts. **Note:** *The calipers on later models are secured with locknuts. When the locknuts are removed, they're destroyed and must be replaced with new ones.*

Springer forks

71 Remove the brake caliper and suspend it out of the way.

72 If necessary, remove the speedometer cable (models through 1995).

73 Remove the axle locknut and flat washer. Discard the nut.

74 Carefully slide the axle out of the hub, then separate the wheel from the fork rockers. The washers and spacers will fall out as the axle and wheel are removed - try to note how they're installed.

75 Position the wheel between the rockers with the brake disc on the right side.

76 Insert the axle from the right side until it's just barely through the rocker. **Note:** *The thrust washers are not the same. The one with the large ID goes inside the brake bracket and the one with the small ID goes outside the bracket. The Teflon coated side of the washers must be against the brake bracket. If the Teflon coating is worn off, install new washers.*

77 Slide the wave washer and the large ID thrust washer onto the spacer, then slide the spacer and washer assembly into the hole in the brake bracket.

78 Position the small ID thrust washer over the axle, then slide the axle through the brake bracket/spacer and into the hub.

79 Continue sliding the axle through the hub while positioning the seal (and speedometer drive assembly on models through 1995) in the left side. Make sure the speedometer drive unit engages the notch in the hub correctly.

80 Install the washer and a NEW locknut. Tighten the locknut to the torque listed in the Chapter 1 Specifications.

4 Front drum brake - inspection and brake shoe replacement

1 Drum brakes don't usually require frequent maintenance, but they should be checked periodically to ensure proper operation. If the linkage is properly adjusted, the brake shoes aren't contaminated or worn out and the return springs and cables are in good condition, the brakes should work fine.

2 Check the cable ends to make sure they aren't frayed and check the lever pivot for binding and excessive play. As a general rule, the cable should be adjusted so the brake shoes don't drag when the lever is released and the lever doesn't touch the handlebar when the brake is applied.

3 If the lever doesn't operate smoothly, lubricate the cable, the cable ends and the pivot (refer to Chapter 1). If the brakes still don't operate smoothly, the problem is in the shoe actuating mechanism.

4 If the brake shoe wear check (refer to Chapter 1) indicates the shoes are near the wear limit, refer to Section 3 and remove the front wheel. Measure the thickness of the brake shoe lining and compare it to the Specifications in Chapter 1. If the shoes have worn beyond the allowable limits, or if they're worn unevenly, they must be replaced with new ones.

5 If the linings are acceptable as far as thickness is concerned, check them for glazing, high spots and hard areas. A light touch-up with a file or emery paper will restore them to usable condition. If the linings are extremely glazed, they have probably been dragging. Be sure to properly adjust the lever free play to prevent further glazing.

6 Occasionally the linings may become contaminated with grease from the wheel bearings or brake cam. If this happens, and it's not too severe, cleaning the shoes with a brake system solvent (available at auto parts stores) may restore them. Better yet, replace the shoes with new ones - the cost is minimal.

7 To remove the shoes from the brake plate on FX models, remove the pivot stud bolt, the operating shaft nut and the operating lever. Tap on the operating shaft and lift out the shaft, the pivot stud, the brake shoes and the springs as an assembly.

8 On FL models, grab both brake shoes simultaneously, fold them upward into a V and release them from the brake backing plate.

9 Remove the cotter pin from the end of the cam lever stud and lift off the cam

lever washer.

10 Loosen the clamp nut on the cable clevis and depress the brake lever. The cable ferrule can now be disconnected from the anchor pin in the hand lever. When the cable is disconnected, the cam lever can be removed from the cam lever stud.

11 On all models, remove the springs from the shoes and check the springs for cracks and distortion. Replace them with new ones if defects are noted.

12 Clean the brake plate with solvent to remove brake dust and dirt. Also clean the operating shaft and the pivot stud. If compressed air is available, use it to dry the parts thoroughly.

13 Check the operating shaft and the hole in the brake plate for excessive wear. Slide the operating shaft back into the hole and make sure it turns smoothly without binding. If excessive side play is evident, the brake plate will have to be replaced with a new one. Check the shoe contact areas of the cam for wear also.

14 Before installing the new shoes, file a taper on their leading edges. Install the springs, then apply a thin coat of high-temperature grease to the shoe contact areas of the cam and pivot stud.

15 Clean the brake drum out with a wet rag. Don't use solvent in the brake drum because the rubber seals in the hub will be damaged by it.

Caution: Don't blow the brake drum out with compressed air - the brake dust may contain asbestos, which can damage your lungs if inhaled.

16 Check the drum for rough spots, rust and evidence of excessive wear. If the outer edge of the drum has a pronounced ridge, excessive wear has occurred. Measure the diameter of the drum at several places to determine if it's worn out-of-round. Excessive wear and out-of-roundness indicate the need for a new hub/drum. Slight rough spots and roughness can be removed with fine emery paper. Use one of the brake shoes as a sanding block so low spots aren't created in the drum.

17 On FX models, slip the brake shoe assembly into position in the brake plate and install the pivot stud bolt and washer and the operating lever and shaft nut.

18 Insert the brake shoe assembly into the brake drum and install the front wheel as described in Section 3.

19 On FL models, assemble the brakes in the reverse order of the disassembly procedure. Connect the brake shoes with the top spring only and set the shoes in position on the pivot stud and cam lever. Be sure the spring hooks are in the shoe spacer notch nearest the side cover.

20 Attach the cable ferrule to the anchor pin of the hand lever with the slot in the anchor pin facing in. On earlier models with slotted end anchor pins, the open end of the pin should face down when the cable is installed.

6

5.4 The minimum brake disc thickness is stamped in the disc

5.7 Remove the screw securing the brake hose to the fender or fork leg

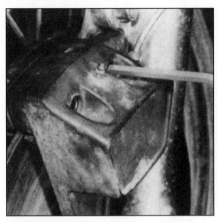

5.11a Remove the Allen bolts . . .

5.11b . . . and separate the caliper sections to get at the brake pads on 1972 through 1983 FL models and 1973 FX models

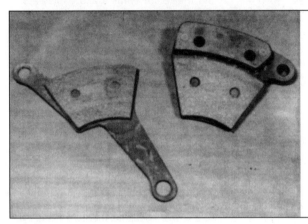

5.12 The amount of lining material remaining on the brake pads can be determined once they're out of the caliper

21   Install the front wheel.

22   Check the adjustment of the brake as described in Step 2 of this Section. If the brake needs adjusting, loosen the locknut on the adjusting sleeve, then turn the adjusting sleeve nut until the lever moves freely for about one-quarter of its full movement before the brakes begin to drag. Tighten the locknut against the adjusting sleeve.

23   If the adjustment is correct, but the brakes drag, the brake shoes must be centered in the brake drum. Loosen the pivot stud bolt and the axle nut, then spin the front wheel. While the wheel is spinning, apply the brake and tighten the pivot stud bolt and the axle nut. Recheck the adjustment.

5   Front disc brake - inspection and brake pad replacement

Inspection

1   Carefully examine the master cylinder, the hoses and the caliper unit for evidence of brake fluid leakage. Pay particular attention to the hoses. If they're cracked, abraded, or otherwise damaged, replace them with new ones. If leaks are evident at the master cylinder or caliper, they should be rebuilt by referring to the appropriate Sections in this Chapter.

2   Check the lever for proper operation. It should feel firm and return to its original position when released. If it feels spongy, or if lever travel is excessive, the system may have air trapped in it. Refer to Chapter 1 and bleed the brakes.

3   Check the brake pads for excessive wear by referring to Chapter 1.

4   Examine the brake disc for cracks and score marks. Measure the thickness of the disc. If it's worn beyond the allowable limit (see illustration), it must be replaced with a new one.

5   If the brake lever pulsates when the brake is applied during operation of the machine, the disc may be warped. Attach a dial indicator set up to the fork slider and check the disc runout. If the runout is greater than specified, replace the disc with a new one. If a dial indicator isn't available; a dealer service department or motorcycle repair shop can make this check for you.

6   If the brake pads are worn out or contaminated with brake fluid or dirt, they must be replaced with new ones. Failure to replace the pads when necessary will result in damage to the disc and severe loss of stopping power.

Pad replacement

Caution: Do not operate the brake lever while the caliper is apart - the piston will be forced out of the caliper. Always replace all pads in the front brake caliper(s); never replace only one pad or the pads in only one caliper on dual disc models.

1972 through 1983 FL models (except FLT) and 1973 FX models

7   Remove the clamp securing the brake hose to the fork leg (see illustration).

8   Unscrew the bolts holding the caliper together, then separate the outer half and the damper spring from the rest of the caliper.

9   Remove the mounting pin and the inner half of the caliper.

10   Disengage the brake pad mounting pins and detach the brake pads. Late 1978 through 1983 models are equipped with a plate and an insulator between the piston and the brake pad.

1974 through 1977 FX models

11   Remove the Allen-head bolts and locknuts holding the caliper together. Separate the two caliper halves (see illustrations).

12   Remove the brake pads and check them for wear (see illustration).

5.13 Front brake caliper details (1978 through 1983 FX and 1980 through 1983 FLT)

1 Bolt (holds caliper sections together)
2 Inner caliper half
3 Outer caliper half
4 Pad guide pin (2)
5 Pad shims
6 Brake pads
7 Piston
8 Boot
9 Seal

5.15a Remove the bolt holding the caliper sections together . . .

5.15b . . . then lift off the inner caliper half and remove the pads and shims

5.17 On all 1984 and later models, loosen the inner pad retainer screw on the back of the caliper (caliper removed for clarity) . . .

1978 through 1983 FX and 1980 through 1983 FLT models

13 Using a socket, universal joint and extension, loosen the bolt securing the two halves of one of the calipers together **(see illustration)**. You have to work from the back side of the caliper to loosen the bolt.

14 Remove the Allen-head bolts and nuts attaching the caliper to the lower fork leg.

15 Detach the caliper from the forks and separate the two halves. Remove the brake pads from the guide pins **(see illustrations)**.

16 Repeat the procedure for the remaining caliper.

1984 and later models (except FXSTS)

17 Loosen the pad retainer screw at the back (inner) side of the caliper **(see illustration)**.

18 Remove the upper mounting bolt and the lower mounting pin **(see illustration)**. Move the caliper to the rear and down

slightly, away from the fork slider, then remove the outer pad, pad holder and spring clip from the caliper as an assembly. Pull out the bushing the upper mounting bolt threads into, then slide the caliper off the brake disc. You may have to cut the plastic tie-wrap

holding the wire to the brake hose to produce enough slack in the hose to remove the caliper.

19 Note how the pad retainer is installed in

5.18 . . . then remove the caliper mounting bolt and pin

1 Caliper mounting bolt
2 Caliper mounting pin
3 Brake hose banjo bolt (12-point head)

6

5.20 Here's what the outer brake pad and spring clip look like when correctly installed in the caliper

5.31 Clean and lubricate the pin/bushing friction surfaces (1984 and later shown)

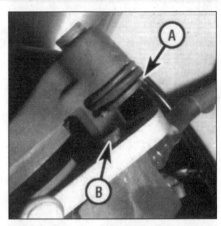

5.32 Caliper upper mounting bolt bushing flanged head (A) and rivet (B)

the caliper, then remove the screw and detach the pad retainer and inner brake pad.
20   Note how the pad and spring clip are positioned in the holder **(see illustration)**. Push the pad out of the clip to remove it from the holder.

FXSTS model

21   Loosen the pad retainer screw at the back (inner) side of the caliper **(see illustration 5.17)**.
22   Remove the caliper upper mounting bolt (with washer) and lower mounting pin and lift the caliper off the disc and away from the brake reaction link bracket. Rocking the caliper gently back and forth will push the piston back into its bore and ease removal.
23   Remove the outer pad, pad holder and spring clip as an assembly. Pull out the upper mounting bolt threaded bushing.
24   Refer to Steps 19 and 20 for the rest of the procedure.

All models

25   While the caliper assembly is apart, check the movement of the piston in the outer caliper half. Mount a dial indicator on the back of the outer caliper, so the plunger rests on the piston face. Apply the handlebar lever gently until the piston is extended and set the indicator to zero. Release the brake lever. If the piston movement isn't restricted it should be as specified.
26   Clean the disc surface with brake system cleaner, lacquer thinner or acetone.

 Warning: Do not use petroleum-based solvents.

27   The piston(s) in the caliper must be pressed into the bore as far as possible when new pads are installed.
28   Don't touch the faces of the brake pads when installing them. Make sure the pads are in the correct position and facing the right direction during reassembly.
29   Reassemble the calipers, with the new pads, in the reverse order of disassembly.

30   On 1974 through 1977 FX models, install new locknuts on the caliper.
31   On 1984 and later models, apply a smear of high-temperature disc brake grease to the friction surfaces of the pad pins **(see illustration)**. Position the spring clip and the pad with the insulator backing material in the pad holder. The pad lining (friction face) and the spring clip loop must face away from the caliper piston **(see illustration 5.20)**.
32   When installing the upper mounting bolt threaded bushing on 1993 and later models, note that its flanged head must locate under the mounting plate rivet so that one of its cutout slots over the rivet body **(see illustration)**.
33   Check the brake fluid level in the master cylinder after the pads are installed (see Chapter 1). The level may be too high, requiring the excess fluid to be siphoned off.

6   Front brake disc - removal and installation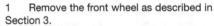

1   Remove the front wheel as described in Section 3.
2   Remove the bolts/nuts and separate the disc from the hub. Later models may have

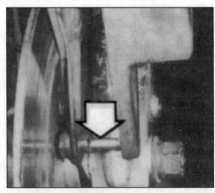

7.4 On 1974 through 1977 FX models, pull the caliper straight out until the pin (arrow) clears the torque arm

Torx-head bolts which require a special tool for removal and installation.
3   Before installing the disc, be sure the threads on the bolts and nuts (or in the hub) are clean and undamaged. Use thread locking compound and be sure to tighten the bolts/nuts in a criss-cross pattern, in several steps, until the specified torque is reached.

7   Front disc brake caliper - removal and installation

Removal

1972 through 1983 FL models (except FLT) and 1973 FX models

1   The caliper is held in place by the four bolts that secure the two caliper halves together.
2   Remove the clamp securing the brake hose to the fork leg, then remove the four caliper bolts.
3   The caliper can be removed by sliding the mounting pins out of the fork slider bushings after separating the outer caliper half from the inner half (see Section 5).

1974 through 1977 FX models

4   Remove the two Allen-head bolts and locknuts holding the caliper halves together, then detach the caliper by pulling out on it until the pin is disengaged from the torque arm **(see illustration)**.

1978 through 1983 FX and 1980 through 1983 FLT models

5   Loosen the bolt securing the two caliper halves together **(see illustration 5.13)**. If both calipers are being removed, loosen the bolt in each caliper.
6   Remove the Allen-head bolts and nuts attaching the caliper(s) to the fork leg(s), then detach the caliper(s).

1984-on (all models)

7   Loosen the brake hose-to-caliper banjo

fitting bolt, but don't unscrew it **(see illustration 5.18)**. A 12-point socket will be required to fit the bolt head.

8   Remove the upper mounting bolt and the lower caliper pin **(see illustration 5.18)**.

9   Detach the caliper. You may have to cut the plastic tie-wraps securing the wire to the brake hose near the caliper to allow enough movement to detach the caliper.

All models

Caution: While the caliper is apart or removed from the brake disc, do not operate the front brake lever - it will force the piston out of the caliper bore.

10   Unscrew the brake line union or banjo fitting bolt at the caliper. Plug the end of the brake line and the opening in the caliper to prevent dirt from entering the hydraulic system.

Installation

11   Installation of the caliper is the reverse of the removal procedure. Apply Teflon tape to the threads of the brake line fitting before attaching the line to the caliper. On later models, discard the original washers used at the brake line banjo fitting and install new ones.

12   On 1974 through 1977 FX models, be sure the locating pin at the bottom of the outer caliper engages the backing plate for the brake pad as well as the torque arm **(see illustration 7.4)**.

13   Coat the caliper pins (that allow the caliper to move back-and-forth) with high-temperature grease and tighten the mounting bolts to the specified torque.

14   After the calipers are installed, the brake system must be bled as described in Chapter 1.

---

8   Front disc brake caliper - overhaul

1   The caliper should not be disassembled unless it leaks fluid around the piston or doesn't operate properly. If the piston travel

8.16 On 1978 through 1983 FX and FLT models, the piston can be carefully pried out of the caliper with two screwdrivers

(Section 5) is not as specified, the piston will have to be removed and inspected. Before disassembling the caliper, read through the entire procedure and make sure you have the correct caliper rebuild kit. Also, you'll need some new, clean brake fluid of the recommended type and some clean rags. **Note:** *Disassembly, overhaul and reassembly of the brake caliper must be done in a spotlessly clean work area to avoid contamination and possible failure of the brake hydraulic system components. If such a work area isn't available, have the caliper rebuilt by a dealer service department or a motorcycle repair shop.*

1972 through 1983 FL models (except FLT) and 1973 FX models

2   Remove the caliper as described in Section 7 but DO NOT disconnect the hydraulic brake line.

3   Remove the brake pads as described in Section 5.

4   Slowly pump the brake lever until the piston doesn't move any further.

5   Disconnect the brake line from the caliper and plug the line and the opening in the caliper.

6   Pull the piston boot away from the groove in the piston, then remove the piston from the bore in the caliper.

7   Remove the snap-ring from the piston (if used), then lift off the backing plate, the wave spring (1974 and earlier models), the friction ring and the O-ring. On late 1978 through 1983 models, remove the O-ring or seal from the piston.

8   Unscrew the bleeder valve from the caliper body.

1974 through 1977 FX models

9   Remove the caliper and the brake pads as described in Sections 5 and 7.

10   Disconnect the brake line from the caliper and plug it.

11   Remove the rubber boot, then, using two screwdrivers, pry the piston out of the caliper bore.

12   Check the friction ring at the end of the piston. If it's damaged, remove it and install a new one.

13   Carefully pry the O-ring out of the caliper bore with a wood or plastic tool.

14   Unscrew the bleeder valve from the caliper.

1978 through 1983 FX and 1980 through 1983 FLT models

15   Remove the caliper and brake pads as described in Sections 5 and 7. Disconnect the brake line from the caliper and plug it.

16   Carefully pry the piston out of the caliper, then remove the boot **(see illustration)**. If the piston cannot be pried out, place the caliper face down on a clean work surface. Position a clean towel under the piston and apply low pressure air to the inlet hole to force the piston out.

17   Carefully remove the seal from the caliper bore **(see illustration 5.13)**. Use a wood or plastic tool to remove the seal (to avoid scratching the caliper bore).

1984 and later models

18   Remove the caliper and brake pads as described in Sections 5 and 7. Disconnect the brake line from the caliper and discard the washers.

19   Pry out the boot retainer by inserting a small screwdriver into the notch at the bottom of the piston bore.

20   Note how it's installed, then remove the rubber piston boot.

21   Place the caliper face down on a clean work surface. Position a clean towel under the piston and apply low pressure air to the inlet hole to force the piston out.

22   Remove the seal from the caliper bore with a wood or plastic tool.

23   Note how they're installed, then remove the threaded bushing from the caliper and pull the pin boot out.

24   Remove the O-rings from the mounting bolt/pin holes.

All models

25   Clean all the brake components (except for the brake pads) with brake system solvent (available at auto parts stores), isopropyl alcohol or clean brake fluid.

Caution: Do not, under any circumstances, use petroleum-based solvents to clean brake parts. If compressed air is available, use it to dry the parts thoroughly.

26   Check the caliper bore and the outside of the piston for scratches, nicks and score marks. If damage is evident, the caliper must be replaced with a new one.

27   Reassembly of the caliper is done in the reverse order of disassembly. Be sure to lubricate all of the components with clean brake fluid during reassembly and install new O-rings.

28   Install the brake pads as described in Section 5 and connect the brake line to the caliper (see Section 7).

29   Attach the caliper assembly to the forks and bleed the system as described in Chapter 1.

---

9   Front disc brake master cylinder - removal and installation

1   If the master cylinder is leaking fluid, or if the lever doesn't feel firm when the brake is applied, and bleeding the brakes doesn't help, master cylinder replacement or overhaul is recommended. Before disassembling the master cylinder, read through the entire procedure and make sure you have the correct rebuild kit. Also, you'll need some new, clean brake fluid of the recommended type, some clean rags and internal snap-ring pliers. **Note:** *Disassembly, overhaul, and*

6

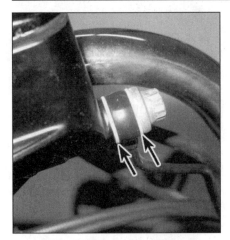

9.6 Unscrew the banjo fitting bolt; use new sealing washers (arrows) on installation

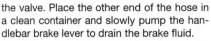

9.11 Place a wedge between the handle and bracket (arrow)

9.12 Remove the mounting bolts (arrows)

reassembly of the brake master cylinder must be done in a spotlessly clean work area to avoid contamination and possible failure of the brake hydraulic system components. If such a work area isn't available, have the master cylinder rebuilt by a dealer service department or motorcycle repair shop.

1972 through 1981 models

2   Turn the handlebars so the brake master cylinder is as level as possible and remove the cover and gasket from the master cylinder. Disconnect the hydraulic brake line from the master cylinder and catch the fluid in a container.
3   Remove the handlebar switch assembly and disconnect the brake light wires (see Chapter 8).
4   Remove the snap-ring and pivot pin so the handlebar brake lever can be removed. It'll pull out with the brake lever pin, plunger, spring, two washers and the dust wiper.

1982 through 1995 models

5   Open the bleeder valve on one of the front calipers and attach a piece of hose to

the valve. Place the other end of the hose in a clean container and slowly pump the handlebar brake lever to drain the brake fluid.
6   Remove the bolt attaching the brake line to the master cylinder (**see illustration**). Throw away the washers on either side of the brake line.
7   Remove the cover and gasket from the master cylinder.
8   Remove the snap-ring securing the pivot pin, then lift out the pivot pin. Separate the brake lever and the reaction pin from the master cylinder.
9   Remove the master cylinder clamp and detach the assembly from the handlebars.

1996 and later models

10   Perform Steps 7 and 8 to drain the brake fluid from the master cylinder.
11   Make a wedge of cardboard 5/32-inch thick (wood or plastic will also work). Pull the brake lever and slip the wedge between the end of the lever and its bracket on the front side of the master cylinder (this protects the brake light switch plunger and boot) (**see illustration**).
12   Remove the two Torx screws and

washers that secure the master cylinder clamp to the cylinder (**see illustration**). Separate the clamp from the cylinder body and remove the master cylinder from the handlebar.
13   Wear eye protection and remove the lever snap-ring from the underside of the master cylinder (**see illustration**). Withdraw the pivot pin, bushing and brake lever.

All models

14   On 1973 through 1981 models, attach the brake light wires and assemble the handlebar switch.
15   On later models, clamp the master cylinder to the handlebars, aligning the notch in the bracket with the tab on the throttle housing (**see illustration**).
16   Make sure the relief port in the master cylinder is uncovered when the brake lever is released.
17   Connect the brake line to the master cylinder (using new washers on 1982 and later models).
18   Fill the master cylinder with the recommended brake fluid and bleed the system as described in Chapter 1.

9.13 Secure the pivot pin with the snap-ring (arrow)

9.15 Align the notch in the bracket with the tab on the throttle housing (arrow)

10 Disc brakes - bleeding

1   Bleeding the brake is simply the process of removing all the air bubbles from the brake fluid reservoir, the hose and the brake caliper. Bleeding is necessary whenever a brake system hydraulic connection is loosened, when a component or hose is replaced, or when the master cylinder or caliper is overhauled. Leaks in the system may also allow air to enter, but leaking brake fluid will reveal their presence and warn you of the need for repair.

2   To bleed the brake, you will need some new, clean brake fluid of the recommended type (see Chapter 1), a length of clear vinyl or plastic tubing, a small container partially filled with clean brake fluid, some rags and a wrench to fit the brake caliper bleed valve.

3   Cover the fuel tank and other painted components to prevent damage in the event that brake fluid is spilled.

4   Remove the reservoir cap and slowly pump the brake lever a few times, until no air bubbles can be seen floating up from the holes at the bottom of the reservoir. Doing this bleeds the air from the master cylinder end of the line. Reinstall the reservoir cap.

5   Attach one end of the clear vinyl or plastic tubing to the brake caliper bleeder valve and submerge the other end in the brake fluid in the container (see illustration).

6   Remove the reservoir cap and check the fluid level. Do not allow the fluid level to drop below the lower mark during the bleeding process.

7   Carefully pump the brake lever three or four times and hold it while opening the caliper bleeder valve. When the valve is opened, brake fluid will flow out of the caliper into the clear tubing and the lever will move toward the handlebar.

8   Retighten the bleeder valve, then release the brake lever gradually. Repeat the process until no air bubbles are visible in the

brake fluid leaving the caliper and the lever is firm when applied. Remember to add fluid to the reservoir as the level drops. Use only new, clean brake fluid of the recommended type. Never reuse the fluid lost during bleeding.

9   Replace the reservoir cap, wipe up any spilled brake fluid and check the entire system for leaks. **Note:** *If bleeding is difficult, it may be necessary to let the brake fluid in the system stabilize for a few hours (it may be aerated). Repeat the bleeding procedure when the tiny bubbles in the system have settled out.*

10   If you're working on a four-piston rear caliper, repeat the procedure for the other bleed valve.

 If it's not possible to produce a firm feel to the lever or pedal, the fluid may be aerated. Let the brake fluid in the system stabilize for a few hours, then repeat the procedure when the tiny bubbles in the system have settled out. Also check to make sure that there are no "high spots" in the brake hose where air bubbles can become trapped - this will occur most often in an incorrectly mounted hose union, but also can be caused by bleeding the brakes while some of the brake system components are at such an angle to encourage this. Reversing the angle or moving the affected component around will normally dislodge any trapped air.

11 Rear wheel - removal and installation

Caution: On disc brake equipped models, do not operate the brake lever while the front wheel is removed - the piston in the caliper might be forced out. If the piston is forced out of the bore, the caliper will have to be completely disassembled and rebuilt. Also, after the wheel is reinstalled,

the wheel bearing end play must be checked with a dial indicator. If it falls outside the range listed in this Chapter's Specifications, the long spacer in the wheel hub or thin spacer washer (as applicable) will have to be replaced by another of different length - see Section 21.

Removal

1   Raise the rear of the motorcycle and support is securely on blocks so the tire is at least four inches off the ground (it must be stable from side-to-side so it won't tip over).

1970 through 1972 models

2   Remove the two screws from the rear fender support and lift the end of the fender so the wheel will clear it.

3   Five socket head (Allen) screws secure the brake drum to the rear wheel hub. Remove the screws one at a time (they can only be removed at the rear of the axle). Remove the nut and lock washer from the end of the axle, then tap the axle out from the drum side.

4   Remove the spacer between the wheel hub and the axle clip on the right side.

5   Apply pressure to the rear brake pedal and remove the rear wheel.

1973 through early 1978 models

6   Rotate the wheel until the master link on the drive chain is positioned on the rear wheel sprocket. Detach the master link and disengage the chain from the sprocket. Don't separate the chain from the front sprocket.

7   Remove the cotter pin securing the brake anchor nut and remove the nut.

8   Unscrew the axle nut and remove the washers from the axle.

9   Note the position of the spacer between the sprocket and the swingarm before removing the axle. Tap the axle out with a soft-face hammer from the right side (see illustration).

10   With the axle removed, the wheel is free to come out the rear (see illustrations).

10.5 Here's the bleed valve on a typical single-piston front caliper

11.9 On 1973 through early 1978 models, withdraw and axle from the right side of the rear wheel

11.10a A spacer (arrow) is used between the sprocket and swingarm on 1973 through early 1978 models

11.10b Let the wheel drop down, then roll it out to separate it from the swingarm

Late 1978 and later models (except FLT with enclosed chain)

11 Remove the saddlebags, if applicable. On some later models the belt/chain guard must be removed as well.

12 Remove the cotter pin (if used) and discard it, then unscrew the axle nut and remove the washer(s). **Note:** *On 1990 FLSTF models and all other models from 1991 on, the axle nut is installed on the left side for proper clearance during operation of the motorcycle. When reinstalling the axle, make sure the nut is on the left side.*

13 Pull the axle out from the left side and allow the wheel to drop down. You may have to tap the axle out with a soft-face hammer.

14 Note the position of the spacer (debris deflector on some models) between !he swingarm and the sprocket, then remove the spacer.

15 Detach the belt or chain from the sprocket on the rear wheel.

16 Separate the wheel from the swingarm.

Late 1978 and later FLT models with enclosed chain

17 Remove the mufflers to gain access to the rear wheel mounting components.

18 Remove both saddlebags.

19 Remove the rubber plug from the housing to get at the rear sprocket mounting screws. Insert a 3/8-inch Allen wrench through the plug opening and remove the sprocket mounting screws. Turn the wheel after each screw is removed until the next screw is accessible.

20 Support the swingarm and remove the lower shock absorber mounting bolts. Lower the rear wheel to the ground.

21 Remove the bolts from the caliper mounting bracket and anchor.

22 Unscrew the axle nut and remove the washers from the axle.

23 Tap the axle out with a soft-face hammer far enough to clear the wheel but still support the sprocket and chain housing. Slide the brake caliper up and swing it away from the wheel.

24 Support the swingarm, then separate

the wheel from the sprocket and chain housing and roll it out of the swingarm.

Installation

1970 through 1972 models

25 Reverse the removal procedure to install the rear wheel. Be sure the mating surfaces of the brake drum and wheel hub are clean, then install the mounting screws. Tighten the screws to the torque listed in this Chapter's Specifications, following a criss-cross pattern.

26 Tighten the axle nut to the specified torque.

1973 through early 1978 models

27 Install the rear wheel by reversing the removal procedure. Tighten the axle nut and the brake anchor nut to the specified torque.

28 Adjust the chain as described in Chapter 1.

Late 1978 and later models (except FLT)

29 Set the rear wheel in position in the swingarm. Connect the belt or chain to the sprocket on the rear wheel.

30 Lift the wheel until the axle hole is aligned with the holes in the swingarm. Place the spacer in position on the left side of the swingarm.

31 Apply a coat of multi-purpose grease to the axle and insert it through the swingarm, spacer and rear wheel hub.

32 Install the washer and a new lock washer on the axle and thread the nut on.

33 Adjust the tension of the belt or drive chain, as described in Chapter 1, and tighten the axle nut to the specified torque. Install a new cotter pin.

34 Check the end play of the rear wheel bearings and compare it to the Specifications. If the end play is incorrect, different size spacers can be installed to change it.

Late 1978 and later FLT models

35 Position the rear wheel in the swingarm and engage it in the chain housing and sprocket. Reposition the brake caliper.

36 Apply a thin coat of multi-purpose grease to the axle, then insert it through the swingarm and wheel from the left side (right side from 1991 and later). You may have to tap it into position with a soft-face hammer.

37 Install the washer, a new lock washer and the nut on the end of the axle. Tighten the axle nut to the specified torque.

38 Install the two brake caliper mounting bolts and the anchor bolt. If it was disconnected, reattach the brake line to the front mounting bolt.

39 Raise the swingarm and reinstall the lower shock absorber mounting bolts.

40 Apply clean engine oil to the sprocket mounting screws and carefully install them. When all of the sprocket mounting screws are in place, tighten them to the specified torque in a criss-cross pattern.

41 Check the rear wheel bearing end play and compare it to the value listed in this Chapter's Specifications. If the end play doesn't fall within the specified limits, the bearing assembly will have to be replaced (refer to Section 22).

42 Adjust the final drive chain/belt as described in Chapter 1.

43 Install the mufflers and saddlebags (see Chapters 3 and 7) .

12 Rear drum brake - inspection and brake shoe replacement

Warning: The dust created as the brake shoes wear may contain asbestos, which is harmful to your health. Never blow it out with compressed air and don't inhale any of if. An approved filtering mask should be worn when working on the brakes. Do not, under any circumstances, use petroleum-based solvents to clean brake parts. Use brake cleaner or denatured alcohol only!

1 Drum brakes don't normally require frequent maintenance, but they should be checked periodically to ensure proper operation. If the hydraulic system is free of air, if the brake shoes aren't contaminated or worn out and if the return springs are in good condition, the brakes should work fine.

2 If the brake shoe wear check (Chapter 1) indicates the shoes are near the wear limit, refer to Section 11 and remove the rear wheel. Measure the thickness of the brake shoe lining and compare it to the Specifications. If the shoes have worn beyond the allowable limits, or if they're worn unevenly, they must be replaced with new ones.

3 If the linings are acceptable as far as thickness is concerned, check them for glazing, high spots and hard areas. A light touch-up with a file or emery paper will restore them to usable condition. If the linings are extremely glazed, they have probably been dragging. Be sure to properly adjust the pedal free play to prevent further glazing.

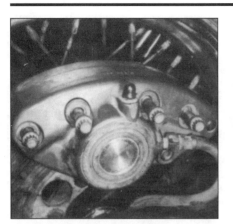

13.8a 1972 through 1980 rear calipers (except FLT and FXR) are held together with four 12-point bolts

13.8b Remove the bolts, then detach the outer caliper half from the bracket . . .

13.9 . . . the inner caliper section can then be removed

4   Occasionally the linings may become contaminated with grease from the wheel bearing or brake cam. If this happens, and it's not too severe, cleaning the shoes with brake system solvent (available at auto parts stores) may restore them. However, the best approach is to replace the shoes with new ones.

5   Disconnect the upper brake shoe return spring and lift the brake shoes and lower return spring off the backing plate.

6   If you have to detach the wheel cylinder, remove the two mounting screws located on the outside of the backing plate.

7   Remove the lower spring from the brake shoes and check them for cracks and distortion. Replace the springs with new ones if defects are noted.

8   Clean the backing plate to remove brake dust and dirt. Also, clean the operating shaft and the pivot stud. If compressed air is available, use it to dry the parts thoroughly.

9   Examine the backing plate and the wheel cylinder for signs of leaking fluid. If leaks are evident, determine if the wheel cylinder or the brake line-to-wheel cylinder connection is leaking.

10   Clean the brake drum out with a wet rag.

11   Check the drums for rough spots, rust and excessive wear (if the outer edge of the drum has a pronounced ridge, excessive wear has occurred). Measure the diameter of the drum at several places to determine if it's worn out-of-round. Excessive wear and out-of-roundness indicate the need for a new hub/drum. Slight rough spots can be removed with fine emery paper. Use one of the brake shoes as a sanding block so low spots aren't created in the drum.

12   If the wheel cylinder is leaking or sticking, a repair kit or new wheel cylinder should be installed. Remove the wheel cylinder and mount it in a vise with soft jaws (use blocks of wood if necessary).

13   Remove the outer boots from the wheel cylinder.

14   Remove the piston, cups and piston return spring from the wheel cylinder.

15   Inspect the bore for score marks, corrosion and other damage. Small marks and corrosion can be removed with a brake cylinder hone. However, if the bore condition is questionable, replace the wheel cylinder with a new one.

16   Clean the wheel cylinder with brake solvent.

17   Coat all of the parts in the repair kit with brake assembly lubricant or clean brake fluid.

18   Install the return spring between the two cups. Make sure the cups are installed wide-side in. Insert a piston into each end of the bore with the concave side facing out. Install a boot over each end of the wheel cylinder.

19   Install the wheel cylinder on the backing plate. Carefully attach the hydraulic brake line.

20   Assemble the brake shoes and springs in the backing plate in the reverse order of disassembly. Apply a light coat of grease to the backing plate, where the shoes make contact, and to the hold-down springs. The short hook on the spring must be inserted into the elongated hole in the front brake shoe.

21   Install the rear wheel. If the wheel cylinder was disconnected, bleed the brakes as described in Section 10.

13 Rear disc brake - inspection and brake pad replacement

Inspection

1   Carefully examine the master cylinder, the hoses and the caliper for evidence of brake fluid leakage. Pay particular attention to the hoses. If they're cracked, abraded, or otherwise damaged, replace them with new ones. If leaks are evident at the master cylinder or caliper, they should be rebuilt or replaced, referring to the appropriate Sections in this Chapter.

2   Check the pedal for proper operation. It should feel firm and return to its original position when released. If it feels spongy, or if pedal travel is excessive, the system may have air trapped in it. Refer to Section 10 and bleed the brakes.

3   Check the brake pads for excessive wear (see Chapter 1).

4   Examine the brake disc for cracks and score marks. Measure the thickness of the disc. If it has worn beyond the limit stamped on the side of the disc, it must be replaced with a new one.

5   If the brake pedal pulsates when the brake is applied during operation of the machine, the disc may be warped. Attach a dial indicator to the swingarm and check the disc runout. If the runout is greater than specified, replace the disc with a new one. If a dial indicator isn't available, a dealer service department or motorcycle repair shop can make this check for you.

6   If the brake pads are worn out or contaminated with brake fluid or dirt, they must be replaced with new ones. Failure to replace the pads when necessary will result in damage to the disc and severe loss of stopping power.

Pad removal

1972 through 1980 models (except FLT and FXR)

7   Remove the clamp securing the brake line to the swingarm.

8   **Note:** *Don't operate the brake pedal while the caliper is apart - the piston will be forced out of the caliper.* Unscrew the bolts holding the caliper together, then separate the outer half and the damper spring from the rest of the assembly **(see illustrations)**.

9   Remove the mounting pin and the inner half of the caliper **(see illustration)**.

10   Disengage the brake pad mounting pins and remove the brake pads. Late 1978 through 1980 models are equipped with a plate and insulator between the piston and the brake pad.

6

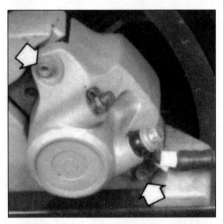

13.21 On 1986 and later FLT models and all 1987 and later models, the rear caliper slides on two mounting pins (arrows)

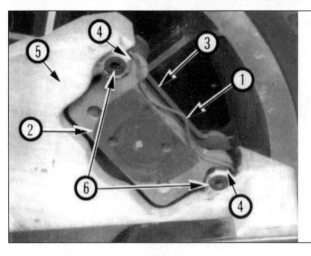

13.22 Brake pads and related components (1986-on FLT, all 1987-on models)

1 Wire retainer clip
2 Outer brake pad
3 Inner brake pad
4 Pad shim (2)
5 Bracket
6 Rubber bushing (2)

1980 through 1985 FLT and 1981 through 1984 FL models (except 1983 and 1984 FLHS)

11 Unscrew the bolts from the pins, then remove the pins, washers, spring (wave) washers, seals and bolts. **Note:** *Don't operate the brake pedal while the caliper is apart - the piston will be forced out of the caliper.*
12 Detach the caliper and remove the brake pads, plates and springs (springs are used only on FLT models).

1980 through early 1987 FXR, 1983 through early 1987 FX (except FXE) and 1983 through early 1987 FLHS models

13 **Note:** *Don't operate the brake pedal while the caliper is apart - the piston will be forced out of the caliper.* Remove the screws securing the caliper to the mounting bracket.
14 Detach the caliper and remove the brake pads.
15 Remove the upper and lower pins from the bracket, along with the boots, and detach the pad spring from the body of the caliper.

1981 and 1982 FX and 1983 FXE models

16 **Note:** *Don't operate the brake pedal while the caliper is apart - the piston will be forced out of the caliper.* Remove the bolts holding the caliper halves together.
17 Separate the caliper halves from the mounting bracket and remove the damper and sleeve from the outer half of the caliper.
18 Remove the brake pads, guide pins, plates, insulator and pad retaining spring clip. Note the arrangement of the components to simplify reassembly.

1986 and later FLT, late 1987 and later (all other models)

19 On FLT models, detach the right saddlebag and side cover, then on all except 1993 and later models remove the battery and its carrier.

20 On FX/Softail models, remove the muffler to make room for brake pad removal.
21 Remove the caliper mounting (pin) bolts **(see illustration)**, then carefully lift the caliper up and off the brake disc and pads. **Note:** *The caliper piston may catch on the rear face of the pad and prevent removal; rock the caliper to push the piston back in its bore slightly.*
22 Carefully note how it's installed, then remove the wire retainer clip from the back side of the bracket **(see illustration)**. Slide the outer brake pad off the bracket.
23 Slide the inner pad off toward the wheel.
24 Detach the pad shims from the bracket.

All models

25 While the caliper assembly is apart, check the movement of the piston(s) in the caliper. Mount a dial indicator on the back of the outer caliper, so the plunger rests on the piston face. Gently apply the brake pedal until the piston is extended, then zero the indicator. Release the brake pedal. If the piston movement isn't restricted it should retract from 0.033 to 0.038-inch.

Pad installation

26 Clean the disc surface with brake system cleaner, lacquer thinner or acetone. Do not use petroleum-based solvents.
27 The piston(s) must be pressed into the caliper bore(s) as far as possible when new pads are installed.
28 Don't touch the faces of the brake pads when installing them. Make sure the pads are in the correct position and facing the right direction during reassembly.
29 Reassemble the calipers, with the new pads, in the reverse order of disassembly.
30 On late 1978 through 1980 models (except FLT and FXR), install the plate between the outer brake pad and the piston so the wheel will rotate into the notch.
31 Coat the screws with multi-purpose grease and secure the caliper halves to the mounting bracket. Tighten the screws to the specified torque.

1981 and 1982 FX and 1983 FXE models

32 Set the insulator in position, then attach the brake pad pins to the outer half of the caliper. Assemble the plate and brake pads in the outer half of the caliper.
33 Attach the spring, with the are towards the top and the prongs facing the right side of the caliper, on top of the brake pads.
34 Place the damper and sleeve on the mounting bracket, then set the left caliper half in position on the mounting bracket.
35 Apply a coat of multi-purpose grease to the screws that connect the caliper halves and tighten them to the specified torque.

1980 through early 1987 FXR, 1983 through early 1987 FX (except FXE) and 1983 through early 1987 FLHS models

36 Attach the pad spring to the top of the caliper with the long tab above the piston. The short tab must be hooked above the ridge on the caliper casting, opposite the piston, to hold the spring in place.
37 Position the pads on the bracket and place the caliper on the bracket without turning the pins. The flat sides of the pin heads should be parallel with the opening in the bracket.
38 Install the caliper mounting bolts and tighten them to the torque listed in this Chapter's Specifications.

1980 through 1985 FLT and 1981 through 1984 FL models (except 1983 and 1984 FLHS)

39 Position the caliper, plates and brake pads on the mounting bracket.
40 Install the O-ring seals, followed by the pins, spring (wave) washers, washers and mounting bolts. Coat the pins with multi-purpose grease before installing them.

1986 and later FLT, late 1987 and later (all other models)

Caution: Ensure that only the correct parts are fitted when replacing pads, discs or shims. Modifications to the pad

13.41 Position the pad shims (arrow) with looped ends outward (mid-1991 and later)

and disc material from 1992 and later and redesign of the shims and pad shape from mid-1991 prevent the mixing of early and late components.

41 On all models through mid-1991 position the pad shims on the mounting bracket with the tabs seated in the holes. From mid-1991 fit the shims so that their looped ends are positioned outwards (towards the piston) and hold them in place while the pads and wire retainer are fitted **(see illustration)**.

42 Slide the inner pad onto the shims from the wheel side. Slide the outer pad on from the outside.

43 Insert the wire retainer clip ends into the mounting bracket holes and position the clip over the outer brake pad **(see illustration 13.22)**.

Caution: Make sure the pads are still riding on the shims after the retainer clip is installed.

44 Make sure the mounting (pin) bolts are clean so the caliper can move freely. Carefully lower the caliper over the pads and disc and align the holes, then install the mounting bolts.

45 Tighten the mounting bolts to the torque listed in this Chapter's Specifications.

All models

46 Check the brake fluid in the master cylinder after the pads are installed. The level may be too high, requiring the excess fluid to be siphoned off.

14 Rear disc brake caliper - removal, overhaul and installation

1 If the caliper is leaking fluid around the piston, it should be removed and overhauled to restore braking performance. Before disassembling the caliper, read through the entire procedure and make sure you have the correct caliper rebuild kit. Also, you'll need some new, clean brake fluid of the recommended type and some clean rags. **Note:** *Disassembly, overhaul and reassembly of the*

brake caliper must be done in a spotlessly clean work area to avoid contamination and possible failure of the brake hydraulic system components. If such a work area isn't available, have the caliper rebuilt by a dealer service department or motorcycle repair shop.

2 Remove the caliper as described in Section 13.

1972 through 1980 models (except FLT and FXR)

3 Remove the brake pads.

4 Slowly pump the brake lever until the piston doesn't move any further.

5 Disconnect the brake line from the caliper and plug the line and the fitting in the caliper.

6 Pull the piston boot away from the groove in the piston, then remove the piston from the bore in the caliper.

7 On 1972 through early 1978 models, remove the snap-ring (if used) from the piston, then lift off the backing plate, the wave spring (1972 through 1974 models), the adjusting ring and the O-ring. On late 1978 through 1980 models, remove the O-ring or seal from the piston with a wood or plastic tool.

8 Unscrew the bleeder valve from the caliper body.

1980 through 1985 FLT and 1981 through 1984 FL models (except 1983 and 1984 FLHS)

9 Remove the brake pads as described in Section 13.

10 Slowly pump the brake pedal until the pistons don't move any further. Disconnect the brake line and plug the line and the fitting in the caliper. Don't lose the brake hose seat.

11 Remove the pistons, dust boots and seals from the caliper. You may have to apply low pressure air to the caliper inlet to dislodge the pistons. If so, position the caliper so the pistons are facing down and place a clean towel under them. Be careful because the pistons may come out with considerable force. Use a wood or plastic tool to remove the seals.

1980 through early 1987 FX, FXR and FXE and 1983 through early 1987 FLHS models

12 Remove the brake pads from the caliper.

13 Detach the retaining wire and remove the rubber boot from the caliper.

14 Slowly pump the brake pedal until the piston doesn't move any further.

15 Disconnect the brake line from the caliper and plug the line and the fitting in the caliper.

16 Remove the piston and seal from the caliper. You may have to force the piston out of the caliper with air pressure. Place the caliper on a clean workbench with the piston facing down. Place a clean towel under the piston and apply low pressure air to the caliper inlet. Be careful - the piston may

come out with considerable force. Use a wood or plastic tool to remove the seal.

1986 and later FLT, late 1987 and later (all other models)

17 Detach the retaining wire and remove the rubber boot from the caliper.

18 Slowly pump the brake pedal until the piston doesn't move any further.

19 Disconnect the brake line from the caliper and plug the line and the opening in the caliper.

20 Remove the piston and seal from the caliper. You may have to force the piston out of the caliper with air pressure. Place the caliper on a clean workbench with the piston facing down. Place a clean towel under the piston and apply low pressure air to the caliper inlet. Be careful - the piston may come out with considerable force. Use a wood or plastic tool to remove the seal.

21 Remove the rubber bushings from the mounting bracket bores. If they're worn or damaged, install new ones.

All models

22 Clean all of the brake components (except for the brake pads) with brake system solvent (available at auto parts stores), isopropyl alcohol or clean brake fluid.

 Warning: Do not, under any circumstances, use petroleum-based solvents to clean brake parts.

If compressed air is available, use it to dry the parts.

23 Check the caliper bore and the outside of the piston for scratches, nicks and score marks. If damage is evident, the caliper must be replaced with a new one.

 Warning: Don't attempt to rebore or hone the caliper.

24 Before reassembling the caliper, soak the new rubber parts in clean brake fluid for 10 or 15 minutes. Lubricate the caliper bore with brake fluid, then install the seal.

 Warning: Always install a new seal - do not reuse the old one if it was removed from the bore.

25 Carefully insert the piston as far as possible into the bore. Install the boot and retaining wire (if used).

26 Reattach the brake hose and complete reassembly as described in Section 13. **Note:** *If the brake hose is attached to the caliper with a banjo fitting and bolt, use new washers when installing the bolt. The replacement washers must be the same type as the originals (some are zinc-plated copper while others are steel with a rubber O-ring). Be sure to tighten the banjo fitting bolt to the correct torque - it's different, depending on the type of washers used.*

27 Fill the master cylinder with the recommended brake fluid and bleed the system as described in Section 10.

6

15.5 On most models, the master cylinder is attached to the frame bracket with two bolts

15 Rear brake master cylinder - removal and installation

1   If the master cylinder is leaking fluid, or if the pedal doesn't feel firm when the brake is applied - and bleeding the brakes doesn't help - master cylinder overhaul **or** replacement is recommended. **Note:** *Disassembly, overhaul and reassembly of the master cylinder should be done by a dealer service department or motorcycle repair shop.*
2   Disconnect the master cylinder-to-caliper brake line from the master cylinder and plug the end. Use a flare-nut wrench on early models to avoid rounding off the fitting (later models have a banjo fitting and bolt, so a flare-nut wrench isn't necessary).

Caution: If DOT 3 brake fluid (used on early models) is spilled on a painted surface, remove it immediately or the paint will be damaged.

1970 through 1979 models

3   Disconnect the master cylinder plunger from the brake pedal by removing the cotter pin from the clevis pin. Remove the washer from the clevis pin, then pull the clevis pin out.
4   Pull the plunger out of the master cylinder.
5   Remove the mounting bolts and detach the master cylinder from the bracket **(see illustration)**.

1980 through early 1987 FXR and 1983 through 1991 FLT models

6   Remove the cover from the master cylinder fluid reservoir.
7   Disconnect the brake reservoir hose from the master cylinder fitting and drain the brake fluid into a container.
8   Disconnect the wire from the brake light switch.
9   Remove the mounting bolts and detach the master cylinder from the pushrod.

1985 through early 1987 FLST models

10   Remove the two bolts that attach the master cylinder to the bracket, then pull the master cylinder off the pushrod.

1983 through early 1987 models (except those listed above)

11   Remove the cover from the master cylinder fluid reservoir.
12   Disconnect the brake reservoir hose from the master cylinder fitting and drain the brake fluid into a container.
13   Remove the mounting bolts and detach the master cylinder.

Late 1987 and later FXR, FXST/C, FXSTS, all FXD, and 1992 and later FLT models

14   Where necessary, remove the exhaust pipe/muffler for access to the master cylinder connections. Disconnect the clevis pin from the brake pedal (it's held in place by a cotter pin). Remove the banjo fitting bolt and detach the brake line from the fitting on the master cylinder. Discard the washers - new ones must be used on installation.
15   On all except FXD models, carefully remove the hose clamp and detach the reservoir hose from its fitting on the master cylinder. The fitting is easily damaged, so don't use excessive force.
16   Drain the fluid from the reservoir while taking care not to spill any on the surrounding parts.
17   Release the lockplate tabs, then remove the large nut that attaches the master cylinder to the mounting bracket.
18   Loosen the jam nut on the pedal pushrod, then raise the pedal so the master cylinder can be moved forward and out of the bracket.
19   Turn the master cylinder to unscrew the pushrod from the pedal rod. There are flats on the pushrod so a wrench can be used if necessary.
20   Clean the exterior of the master cylinder, then thread the banjo bolt into the cartridge body.

Late 1987 and later FLST/C/F/N models

21   Remove the exhaust pipe/muffler to gain access to the master cylinder. Also remove the chromed cover over the reservoir.
22   Remove the master cylinder mounting bolts and detach the clevis pin from the brake pedal (it's held in place by a cotter pin).
23   Remove the banjo fitting bolt and detach the brake line from the master cylinder. Discard the washers.
24   Remove the large nut that attaches the master cylinder to the mounting bracket.

All models

25   Install the master cylinder by reversing the removal procedures. Note the following:
a) *Make sure the drain hole in the rubber boot is facing down.*
b) *On FXR, FXST/C, FXSTS, FXD Dynas and 1992 and later FLT models, the square on the reservoir adapter must engage in the square hole in the mounting bracket with the reservoir hose fitting on top. The lockplate lip should fit over the bracket. Tighten the large mounting nut to 30 to 40 ft-lbs, then bend the tab on the lockplate over one of the nut flats.*
c) *On FLST/C/F/N models, don't tighten the large mounting nut until after the brake hose banjo fitting bolt is tightened. Bend the tab on the lockplate over one of the nut flats.*
26   Carefully attach the hose/line to the master cylinder. If a banjo fitting is used, be sure to install new washers of the correct type (DO NOT interchange zinc-plated copper washers with steel/rubber washers) and tighten the bolt to the torque listed in this Chapter's Specifications - the torque is different, depending on the type of washers used. Fill the reservoir with the recommended brake fluid.
27   Connect the wire to the brake light switch, if so equipped.
28   Bleed the brakes as described in Chapter 1.
29   Check the brake pedal height setting and master cylinder pushrod free play as described in Section 16.

16 Brake pedal - check and adjustment

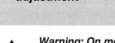

⚠️ *Warning: On models with hydraulic disc brakes, rear brake pedal adjustment is very important. Insufficient pedal clearance may result in interference with brake operation - inadequate master cylinder pushrod free play could result in dragging brakes.*

FLT models

1980 through 1982

1   The rear brake master cylinder pushrod must have 3/32-to-1/8 inch of freeplay between the stop bolt and brake pedal. To adjust it, loosen the locknut and turn the stop bolt. Once the free play is correct, hold the stop bolt and tighten the locknut securely.

1983-on

2   The rear brake pedal must have a minimum of 2-1/4 inches of clearance above the footboard (measured from the upper surface of the footboard to the lower corner of the pedal pad). Check the clearance whenever the footboard, the brake pedal height or

master cylinder pushrod free play is adjusted.

 Warning: Insufficient rear brake pedal clearance will cause the pedal to contact the footboard and interfere with rear brake operation.

3   To change the pedal height, remove the screw from the clevis assembly, remove the clevis assembly from the brake pedal shaft and turn the pedal to the desired position.

4   Install the clevis assembly on the shaft. Install the screw and tighten it to 30-to-35 ft-lbs. Adjust the footboard to obtain the correct clearance.

5   On 1992 and later models fine pedal height adjustment can be made by loosening the pushrod jam nut, disconnecting the clevis pin from the pedal and turning the push rod to adjust (the linkage should not be adjusted to the point where more than 1/2 inch (13 mm) of thread is exposed otherwise there is danger of the pushrod being detached from the piston).

6   On 1983 through 1991 models check the pushrod free play adjustment, measured between the stop bolt and clevis assembly; it should be 3/32-to-1/8 inch (2.4 to 3.1 mm). To adjust, loosen the locknut and turn the pedal stop bolt in or out as required. Tighten the locknut while holding the stop bolt to keep it from turning. Pushrod free play is preset from 1992 onwards.

FXR models (except FXRD)

1984 through early 1987

7   There are two important adjustments relating to proper FXR rear brake operation: brake pedal height and pushrod free play, which should be adjusted together.

8   The top of the rear brake pedal should be 4-1/8 to 4-3/8 inches above the center of the pivot shaft with the machine upright. Measure from the floor to the center of the pivot shaft, then measure from the floor to the top of the brake pedal - the difference should be 4-1/8 to 4-3/8 inches.

9   To adjust the pedal, proceed as follows:

a) *Make sure the pedal doesn't contact the footpeg bracket. The center of the foot-peg rubber should be 7/8 to 1-3/16 inch ABOVE the center of the pivot shaft. Adjust the footpeg if necessary.*

b) *Loosen the locknut and turn the brake pedal stop bolt in or out to obtain the specified pedal height (Step 7).*

c) *Tighten the locknut while holding the brake pedal stop bolt to keep it from turning.*

d) *The pushrod must have 1/16-inch of free play before actuating the master cylinder piston. Measure the free play between the brake pedal and stop bolt.*

e) *Loosen the locknut and turn the pushrod to obtain the specified freeplay.*

f) *Tighten the locknut while holding the pushrod.*

Late 1987 and later

10   The top of the rear brake pedal should be 4-1/8 to 4-3/8 inches above the center of the pivot shaft with the machine upright. Measure from the floor to the center of the pivot shaft, then measure from the floor to the top of the brake pedal. The difference should be 4-1/8 to 4-3/8 inches. Adjust it by loosening the jam nut and turning the pushrod (use a wrench on the pushrod flats).

 Warning: Don't lengthen the pushrod excessively or insufficient thread engagement between the pushrod and brake rod could cause brake failure and possible personal injury!

11   Make sure the pedal doesn't contact the footpeg bracket. The center of the foot-peg rubber should be 7/8 to 1-3/16 inch ABOVE the center of the pivot shaft. Adjust the footpeg if necessary.

12   Pedal freeplay is built into the master cylinder and no adjustment is required. When the pedal is pushed down by hand, a small amount of freeplay must be felt.

FXRD models

13   Brake pedal height and pushrod free play are two important adjustments for proper rear brake operation. Because one adjustment affects the other, the brake pedal adjustment is followed immediately by pushrod adjustment.

 Warning: When adjusting the brake pedal, it should never be positioned to provide less than 1/16-inch of pushrod free play. It's also important that the pedal is positioned where full leverage can be applied with good foot-to-pedal contact. The pedal must have full travel to bottom the master cylinder without interference by the footboard. An improperly adjusted brake pushrod could cause the brakes to drag.

14   The brake pedal can be positioned to suit the leg reach of individual riders. The rider should sit on the machine and apply the brake at different pedal positions to establish which position is most comfortable and effective.

15   Loosen the locknut and turn the brake pedal stop bolt in or out to obtain the desired pedal position.

16   Tighten the locknut while holding the stop bolt to keep it from turning.

17   The pushrod must have 1/18-inch of freeplay before actuating the master cylinder piston. Measure the freeplay between the brake pedal and stop bolt. Loosen the locknut and turn the pushrod to obtain the specified freeplay.

18   Tighten the locknut while holding the pushrod.

All other models

Late 1978 through 1984 FL models

19   The rear brake master cylinder pushrod

must have 1/16-inch of freeplay. Work the brake pedal up-and-down by hand to check the freeplay (slight movement before the pushrod contacts the master cylinder piston).

20   On late 1978 and early 1979 models, loosen the master cylinder rear bolt and the brake pedal stop plate bolt. Move the front end of the stop plate down to decrease free play or up to increase free play.

21   On late 1979 through 1984 models, loosen the locknut and turn the stop bolt (clockwise to decrease free play, counterclockwise to increase it). Tighten the locknut to 10 ft-lbs.

Late 1978 through 1984 FX models

22   The rear brake master cylinder pushrod should have 1/16-inch of freeplay.

23   On FXWG models through 1983, loosen the locknut and turn the stop bolt (clockwise to decrease free play, counterclockwise to increase it). Hold the stop bolt to keep it from turning and tighten the locknut to 10 ft-lbs.

24   On FX models (except FXDG and 1984 FXST/FXWG), loosen the locknut and turn the pushrod on the clevis threads (forward to increase free play, to the rear to decrease free play). Adjustment should be made with the linkage loose, then turn the pushrod to the rear until the correct free play is obtained.

25   On FXDG and 1984 FXST/FXWG models, loosen the jam nut and adjust the pedal stop bolt to obtain the desired pedal-to-foot-peg relationship. Loosen the locknut and turn the master cylinder pushrod on the clevis threads (forward to increase free play, to the rear to decrease free play).

1985 and later FXEF and FXSB

26   Loosen the locknut and turn the pushrod on the clevis (forward to increase free play, to the rear to decrease free play). Adjustment should be done with the linkage very loose, then turn the pushrod to the rear until 1/16-inch of free play is obtained.

1985 and later FXST/C, FXSTS and FXWG

27   Measure the pedal-to-footpeg clearance; it should be within 1/4-to-1/2 inch (6.4 to 13 mm). On early models adjustment is made via the stop bolt and locknut which bears on the clevis assembly, whereas on later models it will be necessary to loosen the pushrod jam nut, disconnect the clevis pin and turn the pushrod to make adjustment.

28   On models through early 1987 pushrod free play should be 1/16 inch (1.8 mm). On later models freeplay is preset.

1985 and later FXDB/C/L Dyna

29   Pedal height should be 1-to-1.2 inches (25 to 30 mm), measured from the front tip of the pedal foot to the top of the footrest rubber. To adjust, first loosen the pushrod jam nut, then disconnect the clevis pin at the pedal. Turn the pushrod to make adjustment.

6

Warning: Do not lengthen the rod to the extent that it is in danger of becoming detached from the master cylinder piston.

30 Pushrod freeplay is preset on these models.

1985 and later FLST/C/F/N and FXDWG Dyna

Note: *The rear brake pedal position is non-adjustable. On models through early 1987, adjust the stop bolt until there's 1/16-inch of freeplay between the stop bolt and brake pedal. On late 1987 and later models, DO NOT MAKE ANY ADJUSTMENTS! The freeplay is built into the master cylinder assembly.*

17 Rear brake disc - removal and installation

1 Remove the rear wheel as described in Section 11.
2 The brake disc is attached to the rear hub with five bolts. Remove the bolts and detach the brake disc from the hub.
3 Before installing the disc, be sure the threads on the bolts and in the hub are clean and undamaged. Use thread locking compound on the bolts and tighten them in small increments, in a criss-cross pattern, until the specified torque is reached.

18 Tubeless tires - general information

1 Tubeless tires are generally safer than tube-type tires but if problems do occur they require special repair techniques.
2 The force required to break the seal between the rim and the bead of the tire is substantial, and is usually beyond the capabilities of an individual working with normal tire irons.
3 Also, repair of the punctured tire and replacement on the wheel rim requires special tools, skills and experience that the average do-it-yourselfer lacks.
4 For these reasons, if a puncture or flat occurs with a tubeless tire, the wheel should be removed from the motorcycle and taken to a dealer service department or a motorcycle repair shop for repair or replacement of the tire.

19 Tube tires - removal and installation

1 To properly remove and install tires, you will need at least two motorcycle tire irons, some water and a tire pressure gauge.
2 Begin by removing the wheel from the

motorcycle. If the tire is going to be re-used, mark it next to the valve stem, wheel balance weight or rim lock.
3 Deflate the tire by removing the valve stem core. When it is fully deflated, push the bead of the tire away from the rim on both sides. In some extreme cases, this can only be accomplished with a bead breaking tool, but most often it can be carried out with tire irons. Riding on a deflated tire to break the bead is not recommended, as damage to the rim and tire will occur.
4 Dismounting a tire is easier when the tire is warm, so an indoor tire change is recommended in cold climates. The rubber gets very stiff and is difficult to manipulate when cold.
5 Place the wheel on a thick pad or old blanket. This will help keep the wheel and tire from slipping around.
6 Once the bead is completely free of the rim, lubricate the inside edge of the rim and the tire bead with soap and water or rubber lubricant (do not use any type of petroleum-based lubricant, as it will cause the tire to deteriorate). Remove the locknut and push the tire valve through the rim.
7 Insert one of the tire irons under the bead of the tire at the valve stem and lift the bead up over the rim. This should be fairly easy. Take care not to pinch the tube as this is done. If it is difficult to pry the bead up, make sure that the rest of the bead opposite the valve stem is in the dropped center section of the rim.
8 Hold the tire iron down with the bead over the rim, then move about 1 or 2 inches to either side and insert the second tire iron. Be careful not to cut or slice the bead or the tire may split when inflated. Also, take care not to catch or pinch the inner tube as the second tire iron is levered over. For this reason, tire irons are recommended over screwdrivers or other implements.
9 With a small section of the bead up over the rim, one of the levers can be removed and reinserted 1 or 2 inches farther around the rim until about 1/4 of the tire bead is above the rim edge. Make sure that the rest of the bead is in the dropped center of the rim. At this point, the bead can usually be pulled up over the rim by hand.
10 Once all of the first bead is over the rim, the inner tube can be withdrawn from the tire and rim. Push in on the valve stem, lift up on the tire next to the stem, reach inside the tire and carefully pull out the tube. It is usually not necessary to completely remove the tire from the rim to repair the inner tube. It is sometimes recommended though, because checking for foreign objects in the tire is difficult while it is still mounted on the rim.
11 To remove the tire completely, make sure the bead is broken all the way around on the remaining edge, then stand the tire and wheel up on the tread and grab the wheel with one hand. Push the tire down over the same edge of the rim while pulling the rim away from the tire. If the bead is cor-

rectly positioned in the dropped center of the rim, the tire should roll off and separate from the rim very easily. If tire irons are used to work this last bead over the rim, the outer edge of the rim may be marred. If a tire iron is necessary, be sure to pad the rim as described earlier.
12 Refer to Section 20 for inner tube repair procedures.
13 Mounting a tire is basically the reverse of removal. Some tires have a balance mark and/or directional arrows molded into the tire sidewall. Look for these marks so that the tire can be installed properly. The dot should be aligned with the valve stem.
14 If the tire was not removed completely to repair or replace the inner tube, the tube should be inflated just enough to make it round. Sprinkle it with talcum powder, which acts as a dry lubricant, then carefully lift up the tire edge and install the tube with the valve stem next to the hole in the rim. Once the tube is in place, push the valve stem through the rim and start the locknut on the stem.
15 Lubricate the tire bead, then push it over the rim edge and into the dropped center section opposite the inner tube valve stem. Work around each side of the rim, carefully pushing the bead over the rim. The last section may have to be levered on with tire irons. If so, take care not to pinch the inner tube as this is done.
16 Once the bead is over the rim edge, check to see that the inner tube valve stem is pointing to the center of the hub. If it's angled slightly in either direction, rotate the tire on the rim to straighten it out. Run the locknut the rest of the way onto the stem but don't tighten it completely.
17 Inflate the tube to approximately 1-1/2 times the pressure listed in the Chapter 1 Specifications and check to make sure the guidelines on the tire sidewalls are the same distance from the rim around the circumference of the tire.

Warning: Do not over inflate the tube or the tire may burst, causing serious injury.

18 After the tire bead is correctly seated on the rim, allow the tire to deflate. Replace the valve core and inflate the tube to the recommended pressure, then tighten the valve stem locknut securely and tighten the cap.

20 Tubes - repair

1 Tire tube repair requires a patching kit that's usually available from motorcycle dealers, accessory stores or auto parts stores. Be sure to follow the directions supplied with the kit to ensure a safe repair. Patching should be done only when a new tube is unavailable. Replace the tube as soon as possible. Sudden deflation can

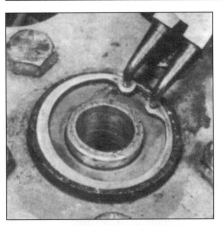

21.22 Remove the snap-ring securing the bearing to the hub . . .

21.23 . . . then lift out the washer

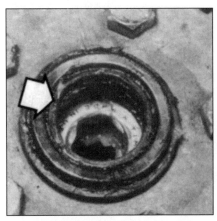

21.24 The oil seal (arrow) can now be pried out of the hub

cause loss of control and an accident.

2   To repair a tube, remove it from the tire, inflate and immerse it in a sink or tub full of water to pinpoint the leak. Mark the position of the leak, then deflate the tube. Dry it off and thoroughly clean the area around the puncture.

3   Most tire patching kits have a buffer to rough up the area around the hole for proper adhesion of the patch. Roughen an area slightly larger than the patch, then apply a thin coat of the patching cement to the roughened area. Allow the cement to dry until tacky, then apply the patch.

4   It may be necessary to remove a protective covering from the top surface of the patch after it has been attached to the tube. Keep in mind that tubes made from synthetic rubber may require a special patch and adhesive if a satisfactory bond is to be achieved.

5   Before replacing the tube, check the inside of the tire to make sure the object that caused the puncture is not still inside. Also check the outside of the tire, particularly the tread area, to make sure nothing is projecting through the tire that may cause another puncture. Check the rim for sharp edges or damage. Make sure the rubber trim band is in good condition and properly installed before inserting the tube.

21 Wheel bearings - inspection and maintenance

Note: *The following procedures are based an the assumption the wheel has been removed from the motorcycle. Because of detail changes made from model year-to-model year, the procedures and illustrations included here may not match the motorcycle you're working on exactly. To avoid possible problems, lay the parts out in the correct order and orientation as they're removed from the hub or make a simple sketch of the parts detailing how they fit in the hub.*

Pre-1973 models (16-inch wheel)

1   Pre-1973 front and rear wheels are equipped with permanently sealed and lubricated bearings. The bearings on these models don't require attention at any set intervals.

2   To remove the bearings, the brake drum or brake disc flange must first be removed from the wheel hub.

3   Slide the bearing spacer out of the hub.

4   Using a piece of pipe as a drift, press the bearing components out of the brake drum from the hub side.

5   Remove the bearing locknut retainer from the hub on late 1970 through 1972 models.

6   Unscrew the ball bearing locknut from the hub. The locknut has a slotted head and should be removed with a special tool. It also has left-hand threads, requiring the nut to be turned *clockwise* to loosen it.

7   Carefully pry the seal out of the hub with screwdrivers and lift out the spacer.

8   The remaining bearing can now be pressed out of the drum side of the hub.

9   Inspect the bearings for wear and damage. Turn each bearing by hand to see if there's any roughness or excessive looseness between the inner and outer races. Check the lip of the seal for wear and damage.

10   Replace any defective parts with new ones.

11   Assemble the bearings and related components in the hub in the reverse order of disassembly. Fill the space on both sides of the bearing on the wheel side and the inside of the bearing on the drum side with multi-purpose grease.

12   Tighten the bearing locknut securely by striking the handle of the special tool with a hammer. When the nut is tight, stake the threads with a center punch to prevent it from loosening. On later models with a locknut retainer, simply drive the retainer into the slotted head with a chisel to hold the locknut in position.

Pre-1973 models (19-inch wheel)

13   Carefully pry the seal out of the hub with a screwdriver.

14   Remove the snap-ring from the other side of the hub using snap-ring pliers.

15   Tap the ball bearing, on the grease seal side of the hub, in until it's against the seat in the hub. This will cause the bearing on the other side of the hub to be driven out enough so the spacer between the two bearings can be moved away from the bearing on the snap-ring side.

16   Insert a drift punch through the hub from the grease seal side and drive out the bearing on the snap-ring side of the hub.

17   Remove the spacer from the center of the hub and drive the remaining bearing out of the hub.

18   Clean the bearings and related components and inspect them for wear and damage. If any of the bearings are pitted, chipped or scored, they should be replaced with new ones. Pack the bearings with fresh multi-purpose grease.

19   Position the bearing on the snap-ring side in the hub with the shielded side facing out. Press the bearing in until it's against the shoulder in the hub.

20   Secure the bearing with the snap-ring. Be sure the flat side of the snap-ring is facing the bearing.

21   Insert the spacer into the center of the hub and press the other bearing into the hub. When the bearing is seated against the shoulder of the hub, tap a new grease seal into position. The lip of the seal should be lubricated with grease or oil before installation.

1973 through 1978 models (16 inch wheel)

22   Remove the snap-rings from both sides of the hub with snap-ring pliers **(see illustration)**.

23   Lift the washers out of the hub **(see illustration)**.

24   Using a screwdriver, carefully pry the seals out of the hub **(see illustration)**.

6

21.30 Coat the ends of the center bearing spacer with grease before installing it in the hub

21.31 Pack the bearings with grease before placing them in the hub

25 Remove the spacers - note how they're installed in the hub. This will help during reassembly.

26 Remove the bearings and clean all of the components. Don't mix the parts up. Bearings and spacers must be reinstalled in the same location they're removed from.

27 The bearing outer races (bearing cups) in the hub don't have to be removed unless the bearings must be replaced with new ones. A standard bearing puller must be used to remove the races. If this tool isn't available, most motorcycle repair shops can remove the races and install the new ones. It's also possible to drive the races out of the hub with a drift punch and hammer. Working from the back side of the race, carefully tap it out of position. Be sure to move the punch around the race to drive it out straight.

28 Inspect the bearings for defects. Look for chips, pits and flat spots. Check the bearing races also. If any damage is visible, the bearing and race must be replaced as a matched set.

29 Pack the bearings with multi-purpose grease and coat the seal lips with oil or grease.

30 If new races are being installed, place them in position, then press them in until they're seated in the hub. A large socket of the correct size and a hammer can be used to drive the race into position. Apply grease to the bearing spacer and slide it into the hub **(see illustration)**.

31 Insert the bearing, packed with grease, into the hub **(see illustration)**.

32 Install the spacers in the hub (make sure they're facing the correct direction).

33 Press the seal into the hub until it's 1/4 to 3/16-inch below the outside edge of the hub. Set a washer in each side of the hub and secure them with the snap-rings.

1979 through 1983 models (19 inch wheel) except FLT, FXR and FXWG models

34 Carefully pry the seals out of the hub with a screwdriver.

35 Remove the spacer from the hub. Pay attention to the side of the hub the spacer is removed from and the direction it's facing when installed.

36 Lift the bearings out of the hub. Don't allow the bearings to get mixed up. They must be installed in the same location they were removed from. Remove the spacer from the center of the hub.

37 Refer to Steps 27 through 31 for bearing inspection and replacement procedures. Be sure to insert the spacer into the center of the hub.

38 Install the spacer in the hub, followed by the seals. Lubricate the seal lips before installation. The seals should be pressed flush with the outer surface of the hub.

1978 through 1983 models (21-inch wheel and all rear hubs) except FLT and FXR models

39 Remove the snap-rings from both sides of the hub with snap-ring pliers.

40 Lift out the washers and spacers. Note which way the spacers are installed in the hub.

41 Pry the seals out of the hub and lift out the bearings and the inner spacer.

42 Refer to Steps 27 through 31 for bearing inspection and replacement procedures. Be sure to install the spacer in the center of the hub.

43 Lubricate the lips of the seals and tap them into position, 3/64 to 7/32-inch below the edge of the hub.

44 Install the spacers and washers and secure them with the snap-rings.

1980 and 1981 FLT (front hub)

45 Remove the screws securing the discs to the front hub.

46 Detach the disc and bearing assembly from the right side of the hub, followed by the spacer from the center of the hub.

47 Pry the seal out of the left side of the hub, then slide the bearing inner race out of

the hub.

48 Special tool no. HD-95760-69 must be used to pull the bearing from the hub.

49 Clean the bearings and associated components and inspect them for wear and damage. If any component is defective, it must be replaced with a new one. If a new bearing must be pressed into the hub, be sure to press only on the side of the bearing the numbers or letters are stamped on. Special tool no. HD-94440-81 must be used to install both the bearing and the seal.

50 Insert the inner race and the center spacer. Use moderate pressure to install the spacer. This will drive the inner race slightly out of the hub and seal. Be sure to install the spacer with the flat edge against the inner bearing race.

51 Place the right side bearing assembly on the hub, aligning the bolt holes. Set the right disc on top of the bearing assembly and secure it to the hub with the longer set of mounting screws. Coat the threads of the mounting screws with thread locking compound before installation and tighten them to the specified torque (see Chapter 6).

1982 and later FLT (front hub)

52 On 1982 models, remove the snap-rings from both sides of the hub with snap-ring pliers, then lift the washers out of each side.

53 Pay attention to the order the following parts are installed in the hub while you remove them. Keep the components from the left side separate from the components from the right side of the hub.

54 Remove the spacers from both sides and pry the seals out of the hub. Lift the bearings out of position.

55 Remove the spacer washer and spacer from the left side of the hub and the large spacer and sleeve from the right side of the hub.

56 Refer to Steps 27 through 31 for bearing inspection and replacement procedures.

57 Install the large spacer, sleeve, spacer washer and small spacer in the center of the hub.

58 Insert the bearings into position and press a new seal into each side of the hub. The lip of each seal should be lubricated with grease or oil before installation. Press the seal in 13/64 to 7/32-inch below the edge of the hub.

59 Install the spacers in the hub.

60 On 1982 models, place a washer in position on each side of the hub and secure the assembly with the two snap-rings.

1980 and later FXR (front hub)

61 Pry the seals out of both sides of the hub and remove the spacer from the left side of the hub.

62 Lift the bearings out of the hub, then slide the center spacer out. On later models there will be a spacer washer and thin spacer behind the right side bearing (shoulder on spacer washer should face the bearing).

63   Refer to Steps 27 through 31 for bearing inspection and replacement procedures.

64   Insert the long spacer into the hub and, where fitted, install the thin spacer and spacer washer (shoulder facing the bearing). Install the bearings.

65   Place the spacer in the left side of the hub and press the seals in. Be sure to lubricate the lips of the seals before installation. The seals should be flush with the edge of the hub when they're seated.

1980 and 1981 FLT and 1980 through 1983 FXR (rear hub)

66   Remove the spacer from the left side of the hub.

67   Pry the seal out of the right side of the hub, then remove the inner bearing race.

68   If the bearing must be removed, special tool no. HD-95760-69 must be used.

69   Clean the bearing and associated components and inspect them for wear and damage. If any component is defective, it must be replaced with a new one. If the bearing was removed from the hub, it must be pressed back into the hub using special tool no. HD-94440-81. When pressing the bearing into the hub, be sure to press only on the side of the bearing with the numbers or letters stamped on it.

70   Using the same special tool, press the seal into the hub. Be sure to lubricate the seal lip with oil before installation.

71   Remove the special tool from the hub but leave the inner bearing race inside the bearing and seal.

72   Install the spacer in the hub from the left side. The flat end of the spacer should go against the inner bearing race. Push the spacer into the hub as far as possible, using moderate thumb pressure. This should cause the inner bearing race to project slightly from the seal on the right side of the hub.

1982-on FLT and 1984-on FXR (rear hub)

73   Remove the spacers from the hub sides and pry out the oil seals. Lift the bearings out of the hub and withdraw the center long spacer. A thin spacer and spacer washer are fitted to later models; take note of which side of the hub these are fitted to when removing.

74   Refer to Steps 27 through 31 for bearing race replacement.

75   Install all components in the reverse of the removal procedure, noting that the thin spacer and spacer washer must be positioned in the correct hub side, as noted on removal (the flanged face of the spacer washer must face the bearing).

76   Early models with an enclosed drive chain will have the left side bearing race installed in the sprocket boss.

1985-on FX/Softail and all FXD Dyna models

Front hub

77   Where fitted, remove its retaining ring and lift off the chromed hub cover. Remove the spacer from the hub and pry out the oil seals on both sides. Lift out the bearings. On later models there will be a spacer washer and thin spacer on one hub side; take note of which side it is fitted. Remove the long center spacer.

78   Follow the procedure in Steps 27 through 31 to replace the bearing races. Refit all components in a reverse of the removal procedure, noting that the spacer washer on later models must be installed with its flanged shoulder facing the bearing.

Rear hub

79   These models have a spacer, seal, bearing and bearing race on each side of the hub, plus a long spacer in the hub center. Later models also have a spacer washer and thin spacer on one side of the hub (take note of which side before removing); the spacer washer must be installed with its shoulder facing the bearing.

80   Follow the procedure in Steps 27 through 31 for bearing race replacement.

6

Notes

TIRE CHANGING SEQUENCE - TUBED TIRES

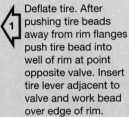 **1** Deflate tire. After pushing tire beads away from rim flanges push tire bead into well of rim at point opposite valve. Insert tire lever adjacent to valve and work bead over edge of rim.

2 Use two levers to work bead over edge of rim. Note use of rim protectors.

3 Remove inner tube from tire.

4 When first bead is clear, remove tire as shown.

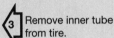 **5** When fitting, partially inflate inner tube and insert in tire.

6 Work first bead over rim and feed valve through hole in rim. Partially screw on retaining nut to hold valve in place.

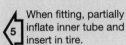 **7** Check that inner tube is positioned correctly and work second bead over rim using tire levers. Start at a point opposite valve.

8 Work final area of bead over rim while pushing valve inwards to ensure that inner tube is not trapped.

Notes

Chapter 7
Frame and bodywork

Contents

Degrees of difficulty

Easy, suitable for novice with little experience	Fairly easy, suitable for beginner with some experience	Fairly difficult, suitable for competent DIY mechanic	Difficult, suitable for experienced DIY mechanic	Very difficult, suitable for expert DIY or professional

Specifications

Windshield bolts (FLHS)
    Shouldered bolts ....   96 to 120 inch-lbs (11 to 14 Nm)
    Adjustable window screws...   3 to 5 inch-lbs (0.3 to 0.6 Nm)
Windshield screws (FLTR) ....   6 to 13 inch-lbs (0.7 to 1.5 Nm)
Inner fairing stud nuts (FLTR) ....   40 to 50 inch-lbs (4.5 to 5.7 Nm)
Inner fairing screws (FLTR)
    Short screws ....   6 to 12 inch-lbs (0.7 to 1.4 Nm)
    Long screws...   12 to 15 inch-lbs (1.4 to 1.7 Nm)
Radio bracket locknuts (FLTR) ....   96 to 144 inch-lbs (10.8 to 16.3 Nm)

7

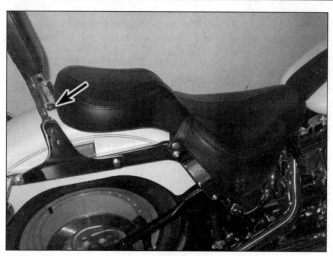

3.19a Remove the thumbscrew at the rear of the seat (arrow) . . .

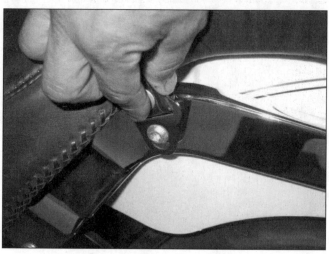

3.19b . . . disengage the seat strap . . .

1 General information

The machines covered by this manual use a backbone frame made of steel tubing. This Chapter covers the procedures necessary to remove and install the saddlebags, windshield, fairing, side covers and other body parts. Since many service and repair operations on these motorcycles require removal of the side covers and/or other body parts, the procedures are grouped here and referred to from other Chapters.

2 Frame - inspection and repair

1   The frame should not require attention unless accident damage has occurred. In most cases, frame replacement is the only satisfactory remedy for such damage. A few frame specialists have the jigs and other equipment necessary for straightening the frame to the required standard of accuracy, but even then there is no simple way of assessing to what extent the frame may have been over stressed.
2   After the machine has accumulated a lot of miles, the frame should be examined closely for signs of cracking or splitting at the welded joints. Rust can also cause weakness at these joints. Loose engine mount bolts can cause ovaling or fracturing of the mounting tabs. Minor damage can often be repaired by welding, depending on the extent and nature of the damage.
3   Remember that a frame which is out of alignment will cause handling problems. If misalignment is suspected as the result of an accident, it will be necessary to strip the machine completely so the frame can be thoroughly checked.

3 Seat - removal and installation

1970 through 1984 FL/FX models

Solo seat

1   Remove the clip and clevis pin that secure the seat to the top of the post. Pivot the seat forward.
2   Remove the nut, lockwasher and pivot bolt. Remove the seat from the motorcycle.
3   Installation is the reverse of the removal Steps.

Comfort Flex seat (1977-on)

4   Pull out the pin that secure the front of the seat to the post.
5   Remove the two clamps that secure the seat to frame, then remove the seat from the motorcycle.
6   Installation is the reverse of the removal Steps.

1984 through 1990 FLT models

7   At the rear of the seat, remove the two bolts (with nuts and lockwashers) to detach the seat from the handrail.
8   Pull the seat back and lift it up to disengage the tabs at the front of the seat from the mounting point in the frame.
9   Installation is the reverse of the removal Steps.

1991 and later FLT models

All except FLHR

10   If the motorcycle has a rear luggage compartment, open the lid and move the rear seatback for access. If the luggage compartment is installed in the forward position, you'll need to move it to the rear.
11   Remove the screw at the rear of the seat. Cover the rear seat bracket with your hand to protect the luggage compartment and, while pushing the seat to the front, lift the rear of the seat up until it clears the luggage compartment.
12   Pull the seat rearward to disengage the tang at the front end of the seat from the slot in the frame and lift the seat off.
13   Installation is the reverse of the removal Steps.

FLHR models

14   Remove the screw (with lockwasher and nylon washer) at the rear of the passenger seat and pull the seat rearward off of the studs.
15   Unscrew the studs to free the rear edge of the front seat, disengage the tang at the front end of the seat from the slot in the frame and lift the seat off.
16   Installation is the reverse of the removal steps.

FX/Softail models

17   These models are equipped with one-piece or two-piece seats.
18   If the bike has a one-piece seat, unbolt the mounting bracket from beneath the fender. Pull the seat up and back to disengage it from the front mounting point, then lift it off.
19   If the bike has a two-piece seat, remove the screw at the rear of the passenger seat **(see illustration)**. Disengage the seat strap (if equipped) **(see illustration)**. Remove the screw from each side of the front seat **(see illustration)**. If necessary for access, lift the saddle flap **(see illustration)**. Disengage the tang at the front end of the seat from the slot in the frame and lift the seat off.
20   Installation is the reverse of the removal steps. Install the rear screw first, then the two side screws.

Dyna models

21   Remove the screw at the rear of the seat. Note the nylon washer or retaining clip

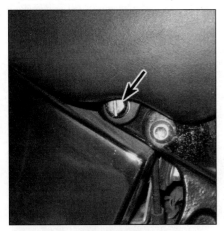

3.19c ... and remove the screw on each side of the front seat

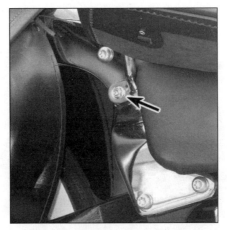

3.19d On some models, you'll need to lift the seat flaps for access to the side screws

Dyna models

15 Hold the saddlebag by the handle and push the pin on the lower end of the saddlebag release.

16 Pull the lower edge of the saddlebag clear of the frame, then slide the saddlebag frame forward off the mounting pins. Lift the saddlebag off the motorcycle.

17 To install, position the saddlebag over the mounting pins, then slide it down and to the rear until the retaining pin locks into position. Tug on the saddlebag to make sure it's securely attached.

---

5 Rear luggage compartment - removal and installation

Early FL models

1 Turn the luggage compartment key slightly counterclockwise, then all the way clockwise.

2 Detach the luggage compartment from the rack by pushing it down and forward.

3 To install, engage the rear hooks with the luggage rack and push the luggage compartment forward until it snaps into place.

Late FL models

4 Open the luggage compartment and remove the rubber mat.

5 Flip up the wire bails on the quick-release fasteners and use them to twist the quick-release retainers 1/4-turn counterclockwise while pressing down on the fasteners. Lift the luggage compartment out.

6 Installation is the reverse of the removal steps. If quick-release fasteners are used, start them with their slots vertical, then twist them 1/4-turn clockwise, while pressing down, until they snap into place.

FLT models

7 Open the luggage compartment. Remove the rubber mat (except Ultra) or map pocket (Ultra).

8 Disconnect the radio antenna cable and electrical connectors. Push the antenna

---

between the seat bracket and the fender. This must be reinstalled or the paint will be scratched (don't substitute any other hardware for it).

22 If the bike is equipped with a seat strap, lift the seat, reach under it and unscrew the nut that secures the seat strap to the fender.

23 Pull the seat rearward to disengage the tang at the front end of the seat from the welded bracket on the frame.

24 Installation is the reverse of the removal steps. Be sure to reinstall the nylon washer or clip in the rear screw hole, between the fender and the seat bracket.

---

4 Saddlebags - removal and installation

FL models

1 Remove the cover from the saddlebag. Disengage the locking hooks and lift the saddlebag off the motorcycle.

2 Installation is the reverse of the removal Steps.

FLT models

3 The saddlebags are retained by two bolts or quick-release fasteners. Open the saddlebag and determine which type of fasteners is used.

4 If the fasteners are conventional bolts, unscrew them.

5 If the quick-release retainers have wire bails, flip them out and use them to twist the quick-release retainers 1/4-turn counterclockwise. If the retainers are not equipped with wire bails, use a screwdriver. Remove the retainers and washers and pull the saddlebag off the mounting studs.

6 Installation is the reverse of the removal steps. If quick-release fasteners are used, start them with their slots vertical, then twist them 1/4-turn clockwise until they snap into place.

7 Make sure the bottom of the saddlebag

---

rests firmly on the support rail. If not, adjust the brackets so it does.

FXRS-CONV models

8 Work the saddlebag handle free of the fender brace so you can hold on to the handle, supporting the saddlebag as it's removed.

9 Turn the knobs on the three retaining screws (one at the rear, two at the front) until the screws disengage. Pull the saddlebag off.

10 Install the chrome plugs in the well nuts from which the retaining screws were removed.

11 Installation is the reverse of the removal Steps. Don't forget to remove the chrome plugs from the well nuts before installing the saddlebag.

Softail models

12 Remove the acorn nut from the lower saddlebag support bracket (forward of or behind the saddlebag, depending on model).

13 Open the saddlebag and unscrew the mounting nuts or bolts **(see illustration)**. Slip the saddlebag off the studs and remove it from the motorcycle.

14 Installation is the reverse of the removal steps.

4.13 Saddlebags on FLSTS models are secured by a nut at the front and two nuts inside (arrows)

7

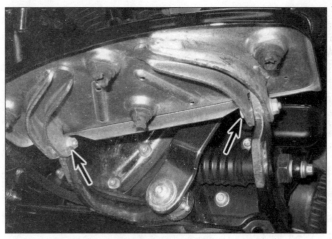

6.1a Typical floorboard mounting pivots (arrows)

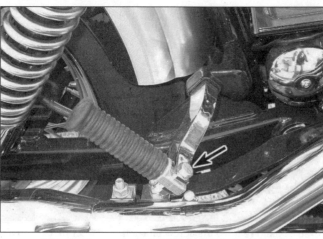

6.1b Footpegs are secured by pivot bolts (arrow)

cable grommet into the compartment and remove it from the cable, then slip the wires out of the compartment through the grommet hole.

9   Hold the mounting nuts from underneath the compartment and unscrew the mounting bolts from within it. Be careful not to drop the compartment as the last bolt is removed. Once the compartment is unbolted, lift it off the rack and locate the bolt spacers.

10   Installation is the reverse of the removal steps. Position the concave end of the spacers to align with the rails of the luggage rack.

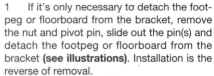

6   Footpegs, floorboards and brackets - removal and installation

1   If it's only necessary to detach the footpeg or floorboard from the bracket, remove the nut and pivot pin, slide out the pin(s) and detach the footpeg or floorboard from the bracket (see illustrations). Installation is the reverse of removal.

2   If it's necessary to remove the entire bracket from the frame, remove the bolts that secure the bracket to the frame.

3   Installation is the reverse of removal.

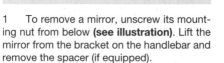

7   Jiffy stand (sidestand) - maintenance, removal and installation

Maintenance

1   The sidestand pivots in a bracket bolted to the frame. An extension spring ensures that the stand is held in the retracted position.

2   Make sure the pivot bolt is securely fastened and the extension spring is in good condition and not overly stretched (see illustration). An accident is almost certain to occur if the stand extends while the machine is in motion.

Removal

3   Securely support the motorcycle upright so it won't tip over when the sidestand is removed.

All except FXR models

4   On FLT models, unbolt the footboard bracket and move it out of the way.

5   Unhook the spring and remove the pivot nut or bolt. Slide the stand down out of the bracket.

FXR models

6   Place the stand in the retracted position if it's not already there.

7   Place a jack beneath the engine. Loosen the front engine mount fasteners (but don't remove them) and raise the engine slightly for access to the spring adjusting screw.

8   Loosen the adjusting screw (you'll need a 3/16-inch ball hex driver for this).

9   Unhook the end of the upper spring from the spring anchor above the stand.

10   Unscrew the nut from the upper end of the pivot pin (you'll need a 7/16-inch combination wrench for this).

11   Remove the spring bracket and upper spring from the pivot pin.

12   Pull out the pivot pin, then remove the stand and lower spring from the frame.

All models

13   If necessary, detach the bracket from the frame.

Installation

14   Installation is the reverse of the removal steps, with the following additions:

a)   If you removed the bracket bolts, apply non-permanent thread locking agent (Loctite Threadlocker 243 (blue) or equivalent) to the threads of the bolts.

b)   Be sure the side of the stop labeled DOWN goes downward.

8   Rear view mirrors - removal and installation

1   To remove a mirror, unscrew its mounting nut from below (see illustration). Lift the mirror from the bracket on the handlebar and remove the spacer (if equipped).

2   Installation is the reverse of removal. Position the mirror.

7.2 Make sure the sidestand spring is securely hooked

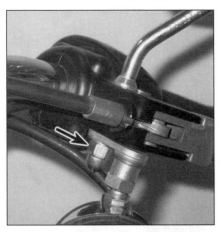

8.1 Remove the mounting nut (arrow) and take the mirror off

9 Side covers - removal and installation

1   The side covers used on FXR and FLT models are secured by screws. To remove a cover, remove the screws and gently pull the cover off.
2   Installation is the reverse of the removal steps.

10 Front fender - removal and installation

All except Softail Springer models

1   If you're working on a 1997 or later FLT, remove the outer fairing (see Section 15).
2   If you're working on an FLHR, remove the headlamp assembly (see Chapter 8).
3   Disconnect the electrical connector for the fender tip lamp (if equipped). Free the wiring harness and pass it between the fender and fork bracket.
4   Remove the front wheel (see Chapter 6).
5   If the fender bolts are secured by tab lockwashers, bend back the tabs. Remove the nuts or bolts that attach the fender to the fork legs and take it off **(see illustration)**.
6   Installation is the reverse of the removal steps. Tighten the fender mounting bolts securely, but don't overtighten them and strip the threads.

Softail Springer

FLSTS models

7   Remove the brake caliper and front wheel (see Chapter 6).
8   Remove the instrument console (see Chapter 8).
9   Unbolt the front end of the fuel tank and move the left side of it for access to the wiring harness. Follow the wiring harness from the fender lamp to the main harness under the fuel tank and unplug the lamp connector.
10   Pull the clip out of the Allen bolt and unscrew the nut **(see illustration)**.
11   Slip the axle into the fender to use as a handle. Hold the fender up with the axle and remove the Allen bolt and washer. Hold the fender at the rear to support it, then pull the axle out.
12   Working on the right side of the bike, lower the fender between the fork legs until its mounting bracket is slightly forward of the rigid fork leg on the left side of the bike. Turn the top of the fender away from you, keeping it between the fork legs. This will cause the fender struts to rotate toward you, so the bottom of the right fork leg is between the fender and the struts. At this point, lower the fender straight down untie it clears the fork legs, then remove it.
13   Inspect the front fender bearings. If they're worn or damaged, have them pressed out and new ones pressed in by a dealer service department or other qualified shop.

14   Installation is the reverse of the removal steps, with the following addition: Use a new nut on the bracket bolt, tighten it to the torque listed in this Chapter's Specifications and secure it with the clip.

FXSTS models

15   Remove the cotter pin from the Allen bolt that attaches the brake reaction link to the caliper mounting bracket. Unscrew the locknut and shaft nut from the bolt, then remove the washer and remove the bolt from the reaction link and caliper bracket.
16   Repeat Step 12 on the other side of the bike.
17   Place a spacer (Harley part no. HD-39754 or equivalent) between the fender pivot links to keep the correct spacing between them while the fender is removed.
18   Working inside the fender, unscrew the pivot link nut on each side. Remove the pivot link shoulder bolts. **Note:** *The bolt bushings are loose in the fender. Locate them if they fall out.*
19   Carefully lift the fender out from between the fork legs.
20   If necessary, remove the spacer tool from between the pivot links, then remove the pivot links, washers and rubber spacers from their shafts. The shafts are secured with, so don't remove them unless necessary.
21   Installation is the reverse of the removal steps. If the pivot link shafts were removed, apply thread locking agent (Loctite Threadlocker 262 (red) or equivalent) to the threads and tighten the shafts to the torque listed in this Chapter's Specifications.
22   Bend the lockwasher tabs away from the fender mounting bolts. Unscrew the bolts and lift the fender out from between the fork legs.
23   Installation is the reverse of the removal steps. Tighten the fender mounting bolts to the torque listed in this Chapter's Specifications and bend the lockwasher tabs against the flats to secure the bolts.

10.5 On some models, the fender bolts are exposed on the outside of the fork legs (arrows); on others, they're accessible from inside the fender

10.10 On Softail FLSTS models, remove the clip (left arrow) and nut, then unscrew the Allen bolt (right arrow) to separate the caliper bracket from the fender

11 Rear fender - removal and installation

1   Remove the seat (see Section 3). Remove the saddlebags and luggage rack (if equipped) (see Section 4).
2   Disconnect the negative cable from the battery. Disconnect the electrical connectors for the brake/taillight and rear turn signals.
3   If you're working on an FLT or FXR, detach the upper ends of the rear shock absorbers (see Chapter 5).
4   Remove the fender mounting bolts and nuts and lift the fender out. On some models, the saddlebag studs also serve as fender mounting bolts.
5   Installation is the reverse of the removal steps.

12 Windshield - removal and installation

Note: *Windshields on models not covered in this section are removed together with the fairing, as described in other Sections of this Chapter.*

FXRS-CONV

1   Cover the headlight and front turn signals with a thick towel or blanket to protect them from scratches.
2   Loosen the Torx bolts that secure the windshield toggles. A Torx wrench for this purpose is included in the bike's tool kit.
3   Have an assistant support the windshield. Open the toggles and free the hinges from the front fork sliders. Lift the windshield off.
4   Installation is the reverse of the removal Steps, with the following additions:
  a) *Make sure the windshield's lower edge is behind the turn signals.*
  b) *Take care not to damage the brake line.*
  c) *Make sure there's nothing between the hinges and the fork tubes before you try to close them.*
  d) *Make sure the windshield doesn't contact the motorcycle at any point.*
  e) *Tighten the toggle bolts just until they are snug. Overtightening will cause them to work loose.*

FLHS

Removal

5   Have an assistant support the windshield.
6   Unscrew the shouldered Allen bolts, then remove the Belleville (cupped) washers and flat washers. Lift the windshield off.

Caution: Don't substitute any other hardware for the shouldered bolts and Belleville washers.

12.19 Lift the spring latches (upper arrow), pull the upper hooks off of the grommets (center arrow) and pull the lower hooks off the grommets (lower arrow)

Installation

7   Loosen the fasteners on the windshield's adjustable window and slide it all the way up.
8   Place a Belleville washer and flat washer on each shouldered bolt. The cupped side of the Belleville washers faces away from the bolt head (toward the windshield).
9   Position the right adjusting bracket on the outer side of the right mounting bracket. Slip the bolts through the brackets, install the Belleville washer on the other side with its cupped side toward the bracket, then loosely thread the bolt into the nut. Make sure the shoulders of the bolts haven't caught on the washers or brackets.
10 Repeat Step 8 on the left side of the motorcycle.
11 Adjust the windshield so the rider can just see over the top of it when sitting upright, then tighten the shouldered bolts on both sides of the motorcycle to the torque listed in this Chapter's Specifications.
12 Lower the adjustable window, but don't let it touch the headlight housing. Tighten the window screws to the torque listed in this Chapter's Specifications.

Softail FLSTC

13 Have an assistant support the windshield.
14 Unscrew the acorn nuts and remove the mounting screws. Lift the windshield off the motorcycle.
15 Installation is the reverse of the removal Steps.

FXDS-CONV

16 Have an assistant support the windshield.
17 Loosen the mounting clamps and remove the windshield from the motorcycle.
18 Installation is the reverse of the removal Steps.

FLHR

19 Unhook the wire spring latch on each side of the windshield (see illustration).

20 Stand in front of the motorcycle and straddle the front wheel. Pull up on the top of the windshield to disengage the upper hooks form their grommets.
21 Shift your grip on the windshield as necessary and pull the lower hooks out of the mounting grommets. Lift the windshield off the motorcycle.
22 Installation is the reverse of the removal steps. Make sure the spring latches hook over the grommets. If they don't, loosen the mounting bolts, rotate them until they do and tighten the mounting bolts.

13 Windshield and fairing (1970 through 1984 FL models) - removal and installation

1   Have an assistant support the windshield.
2   Working inside the fairing, remove the mounting nuts and bolts. Lift the fairing off the motorcycle.
3   Installation is the reverse of the removal Steps.

14 Windshield and fairing (FLTR) - removal and installation

Windshield
Removal

Note: *If you're planning to remove the outer fairing, remove the windshield and outer fairing together as described below.*

1   Loosen the five Phillips screws align the lower edge of the windshield, starting with the center screw and working outward. Once the screws are all loose, lift the windshield off the fairing.
2   Remove the nuts from the holes, taking care not to push them into the fairing. If the nuts are damaged or deteriorated, replace them.

Installation

Caution: If you're installing a new windshield, poke screw holes through the decal from the inside. Poking holes from the outside will push the decal out of place.

3   Insert the screws and washers in the holes, start them into the nuts, then position the nuts in the holes.
4   Tighten the center screw first, then tighten the remaining screws in a criss-cross pattern to the torque listed in this Chapter's Specifications.

Outer fairing

4   Pad the top of the fender so it won't be scratched when you remove the fairing. You'll need to set the fairing on top of the fender while it's being removed.
5   Sitting on the seat, locate the outer fairing Torx screws. There are three on each side of the fairing, one at the bottom, one just outboard of the speaker and one just outboard of the upper gauge (voltmeter and fuel gauge).
6   Unscrew the bottom left screw, then the center left screw. Loosen the two upper screws (don't remove them), then remove the center right and bottom right screws.
7   Above each turn signal lamp, remove the acorn nuts and plate washer from the studs on the turn signal lamp bracket. Push the studs out of the fairing and remove the stud plate.
8   **Note:** *The next steps will be easier with an assistant.* Remove the two top screws loosened earlier. Lift the fairing and lower it to the pad on the front fender.
9   Disconnect the electrical connector for the headlight wiring harness and take the fairing off the motorcycle.
10   Installation is the reverse of the removal steps. Install the stud plates with their shorter studs toward the front of the motorcycle. Tighten the four upper fairing screws evenly to the torque listed in this Chapter's Specifications, then tighten the two lower screws. Note that the two long screws go below the glove compartment and had flat washers on early models.

Inner fairing

11   Remove the instrument bezel (see Chapter 8).
12   Unscrew the odometer reset switch's rubber boot to detach the switch from the instrument nacelle, then pull the switch out of its hole.
13   Remove the outer fairing as described above.
14   Pull the wiring harnesses, including the speedometer and tachometer harness, forward and straighten them out.
15   Disconnect the jumper harness and main harness connectors from the interconnect harness connectors (refer to wiring dia-

grams at the end of the book if necessary). Disconnect the ignition switch harness from the main harness.
16   Disconnect the handlebar switch electrical connectors.
17   Free the wiring harnesses from any retainers, then pull all of the harnesses to the front of the motorcycle and straighten them out. Wrap the harnesses with towels or a blanket to protect the fender, then lay them on the fender.
18   Remove the radio bracket nuts to detach the radio bracket and inner fairing from the fairing bracket. Lift the inner fairing and radio bracket off the fairing bracket.
19   Installation is the reverse of the removal steps. Tighten the radio bracket locknuts to the torque listed in this Chapter's Specifications.

15 Windshield and outer fairing (FLHT, FLHTC, FLHTU) - removal and installation

1984 and 1985 models

1   Have an assistant support the windshield.
2   Unscrew the two bolts that secure the windshield to the fairing, then remove the bolts, nuts and lockwashers. Lift the windshield off.
3   If necessary, remove the four nuts and washers that secure the fairing to the bracket and lift the fairing off.
4   Installation is the reverse of the removal Steps.

1986 through 1995 models

Outer fairing

5   Remove the headlight assembly (see Chapter 8).
6   Unbolt the outer fairing from the inner fairing and windshield, but don't try to remove it yet.
7   Place padding on the fender to protect it from scratches.
8   Loosen, but don't remove, all four of the bolts that secure the passing light bracket and outer fairing to the front fork. Remove the two lower bolts and lower the passing light bracket onto the padding.
9   Reach through the headlight opening and loosen the locknuts on the four fairing studs. Pull the fairing straight toward the front of the motorcycle, sliding the bracket slots off of the studs.
10   Installation is the reverse of the removal Steps.

Windshield

11   Remove the outer fairing as described above.
12   Remove the acorn nuts, screws and

washers that secure the windshield to the bracket and take it off.
13   Installation is the reverse of the removal Steps.

1996 and later models

14   Remove the seat (see Section 3). Disconnect the negative cable from the battery.
15   From the front side of the fairing, remove the three Torx screws from the fairing below the windshield.
16   From the rear side of the fairing, remove the two outer screws, one on each side outboard and below the radio speakers.
17   Reach under the fairing cap and remove the two remaining screws (you'll need to turn the handlebars back-and-forth to reach the screws).
18   **Note:** *This step will be easier with an assistant.* Tilt the top of the fairing forward and disconnect the headlight electrical connectors. Lift the fairing off the motorcycle.
19   Installation is the reverse of the removal steps.

16 Fairing cap (1996 and later FLHT, FLHTC, FLHTU) - removal and installation

1   Remove the ignition switch knob (see Chapter 8).
2   Remove the Torx screw from each end of the fairing cap.
3   Lift the fairing cap slightly and free the trim plate tabs from the fairing cap slots.
4   Turn the handlebars all the way to the left and disconnect the electrical connector for the fairing cap switches.
5   Lift the fairing cap off. Disconnect the cruise control wire (if equipped).
6   Installation is the reverse of the removal steps.

17 Windshield and fairing (FLT, FLTC, FLTCU) - removal and installation

Note: *This procedure applies to 1984 through 1994 models.*

1   Have an assistant support the windshield. Remove the windshield screws and lift it off.
2   Unplug the fairing electrical connectors.
3   Remove the screws from the fairing clamps (one on each side, below the turn signals).
4   Remove the headlight assembly (see Chapter 8).
5   Working through the headlight opening, remove two fairing mounting bolts. Lift the fairing off.
6   Installation is the reverse of the removal Steps.

7

Notes

Chapter 8
Electrical system

Contents

Degrees of difficulty

| **Easy,** suitable for novice with little experience | | **Fairly easy,** suitable for beginner with some experience | | **Fairly difficult,** suitable for competent DIY mechanic | | **Difficult,** suitable for experienced DIY mechanic | | **Very difficult,** suitable for expert DIY or professional | |

Specifications

Battery

Voltage	12-volts
Capacity	
FL models	
rough 1983	22 amp/hours
1984-on	20 amp/hours at 10-hour rate; 22 amp/hours at 20-hour rate
All others	32 amp/hours
FX models	
1970 through early 1978	7 amp/hours
Late 1978 through 1983	7.5 amp/hours
1984-on (FX/Softail)	19 amp/hours
FXE, HXS, FXR, FXEF, FXB, FXSB and FXWB models	19 amp/hours
FDX Dyna models	19 amp/hours
Electrolyte specific gravity (at 80-degrees-F)*	
100 per cent charge	1.250 to 1.270
75 per cent charge	1.220 to 1.240
50 per cent charge	1.190 to 1.210
25 per cent charge	1.160 to 1.180
Ground connection	Negative

Applies to fillable batteries only

8

Alternator

Type...	Permanent magnet rotor
Regulated output	
1985-on FX/Softail models and all FXD Dyna models	13.8 to 15-volts
All others	14-volts

Fuses and circuit breakers

Note: *For circuit breakers not listed here, consult a Harley-Davidson dealer.*

Circuit breakers

FX/Softail and Dyna

1985 through 1995	
Main	30 amps
Lights, ignition, accessory, constant	15 amps
1996 through 1999	
Main	30 amps
Lights, ignition, accessory, constant	15 amps
Instruments	15 amps
1993 FLT, 1993 and 1994 FXR	
Main	30 amps
Lights, ignition, accessory, constant..	15 amps
Secondary accessory (FLHS only)	10 amps
Cruise control (if equipped)	15 amps
1994 through 1996 FLT	
Main	50 amps
Lights, ignition, accessory, constant..	15 amps
1997 and 1998 FLT	
Main	50 amps

Fuses

1993 through 1996 FLT	
Radio	10 amps
Radio memory (1994)	1 amp
Pod power	5 amps
CB power	3 amps
CB memory	1 amp
Fender tip (1994-on FLHTC/U)...	1 amp
Fuel pump (fuel injection)	15 amps
Electronic control module (fuel injection)	5 amps
1997 FLT	
Lights, ignition, accessory, instruments (4 fuses)	15 amps
Power and accessory..	15 amps
Radio	10 amps
Radio memory	1 amp
Pod power	5 amps
CB power	3 amps
CB memory	1 amp
Fuel pump (fuel injection)	15 amps
Electronic control module (fuel injection)	5 amps
1998 FLT	
Lights, ignition, accessory, instruments (4 fuses)	15 amps
Secondary accessory..	10 amps
Brakes/cruise control	15 amps
Radio	10 amps
Radio memory	15 amps
Pod power	5 amps
Fuel pump (fuel injection)	15 amps
Electronic control module (fuel injection)	5 amps

Bulbs (1970 through 1983)*

Headlight	
1970 through early 1978	35/45 or 50/60 watts
Late 1978 through 1983	
1980 and 1981 FLT...	30/30 watts
All others	35/45 or 50/60 watts

Brake/taillight	
1970 through early 1978	32/4 cp
Late 1978 through 1983	32/3 cp
FLHT passing lights	30 watts
Instrument lights	1 or 2 cp
Spotlights	30 watts
Turn signal lights	32 cp

For 1984 and later bulb specifications, consult a Harley-Davidson dealer.

Torque specifications

All models

Battery cable-to-starter motor terminal nut	65 to 80 inch-lbs (7 to 9 Nm)

1970 through 1983

Rear bracket-to-engine	144 inch-lbs (16 Nm)
Rear bracket-to-starter motor or battery carrier	72 inch-lbs (8 Nm)
Starter-to-primary chaincase (FLT and FXR models)	120 to 144 inch-lbs (14 to 16 Nm)
Starter through-bolts	
Late 1978 through 1982 FL models	60 to 80 inch-lbs (6.8 to 9 Nm)
All others	20 to 25 inch-lbs (2.2 to 2.8 Nm)

1989-on

Starter mounting bolts	13 to 20 ft-lbs (18 to 27 Nm)
Starter through-bolts	
1989 and 1990	20 to 25 inch-lbs (2.2 to 2.8 Nm)
1991-on	39 to 65 inch-lbs (4.4 to 7 Nm)
Jackshaft bolt	84 to 108 inch-lbs (9 to 12 Nm)

1 General information

All models covered in this manual are equipped with a 12-volt electrical system. The system includes an alternator, mounted on the left end of the crankshaft, a voltage regulator and a battery. Since the output of the alternator is alternating current, the regulator is combined with a rectifier to convert the alternating current (AC) to direct current (DC), which is needed to charge the battery and operate the electrical components on the motorcycle.

A large capacity battery is used for starting the engine, to provide additional current, when necessary over the amount being generated and to operate accessories when the engine isn't running.

On models equipped with an electric starter, a solenoid relay provides power to the starter motor directly from the battery. The solenoid is controlled by a switch on the handlebars.

Keep in mind that electrical parts, once purchased, can't normally be returned. To avoid unnecessary expense, make very sure the defective component has been positively identified before buying a replacement part.

Caution: When working on the electrical system, the battery should be disconnected to avoid accidentally causing a short circuit in the system. Always disconnect the negative cable first, followed by the positive cable.

2 Electrical troubleshooting - general information

A typical electrical circuit consists of an electrical component, any switches, relays, motors, fuses or circuit breakers related to that component and the wiring and connectors that link the component to both the battery and the frame. To help pinpoint electrical circuit problems, wiring diagrams are included at the end of the manual.

Before tackling any troublesome electrical circuit, first study the appropriate wiring diagram to get a complete understanding of what makes up the circuit. Trouble spots, for instance, can often be narrowed down by noting if other components related to the circuit are operating properly. If several components or circuits fail at one time, chances are the problem is in a fuse or ground connection, because several circuits are often routed through the same ones.

Electrical problems usually stem from simple causes, such as loose or corroded connections, a blown fuse or a bad relay. Visually check the condition of all fuses, wires and connections in a problem circuit before troubleshooting it.

If test instruments are going to be utilized, use the diagram to plan ahead of time where to make the connections in order to accurately pinpoint the trouble spot.

The basic items needed for electrical troubleshooting include a battery and bulb test circuit or a continuity tester, a test light and a jumper wire. A multimeter capable of reading volts, ohms and amps is a very useful alternative and performs the functions of all of the above, and is necessary for performing more extensive tests and checks where specific voltage, current or resistance values are needed.

 Refer to Troubleshooting Equipment in the Reference section for details of how to use electrical test equipment.

8

3 Charging system check - general information

1   If the battery loses its charge even thought the bike is being ridden, the charging system should be checked first, followed by testing the individual components (the generator/regulator or alternator/regulator/ rectifier). Before beginning the checks, make sure the battery is fully charged and all system connections are clean and tight (particularly the battery cables).

2   Checking the output of the charging system and the operation of the components in the system requires special electrical test equipment. A voltmeter and ammeter or a multimeter are the absolute minimum tools required. In addition, an ohmmeter is generally required for checking the remainder of the electrical system.

3   When making the checks, follow the procedures carefully to prevent incorrect connections and short circuits - irreparable damage to electrical system components may result if a short circuit occurs. Because of the special tools and expertise required, checking the charging system normally should be left to a dealer service department or a reputable motorcycle repair shop.

4 Battery - check and maintenance

Check and maintenance

1   The battery on models through 1996 has removable filler caps that allow the addition of water to the electrolyte. Later models are equipped with a sealed, maintenance-free battery. Never remove the cap strip or attempt to add water to a sealed battery.

2   Most battery damage is caused by heat, vibration and/or low electrolyte level. Keep the battery securely mounted and make sure the charging system is functioning correctly. On models through 1996, check the electrolyte level frequently. Refer to Chapter 1 for the electrolyte level checking procedure.

3   On maintenance free batteries, condition is indicated by the battery's open circuit voltage. To check this, disconnect the battery negative cable, then the positive cable. Connect the positive terminal of a voltmeter to the battery positive terminal and the voltmeter's negative terminal to the negative terminal of the battery. Readings are as follows:

a) 13 volts - 100 percent charged
b) 12.8 volts - 75 percent charged
c) 12.5 volts - 50 percent charged
d) 12.2 volts - 25 percent charged

4   On models through 1996, check around the base of the battery for sediment, which is the result of sulfation caused by low electrolyte levels. These deposits will cause internal short circuits, which can quickly discharge the battery. On all models, look for cracks in the case. Replace the battery if either of these conditions is found.

5   Check the battery terminals and the cable ends for tightness and corrosion. If corrosion is evident, remove the cables from the battery and clean the terminals and cable ends with a wire brush or a knife and emery cloth. Reconnect the cables and apply a thin coat of petroleum jelly to the connections to slow further corrosion.

6   The battery case should be kept clean to prevent current leakage, which can discharge the battery over a period of time (especially when it sits unused). Wash the outside of the case with a solution of baking soda and water.

Caution: Do not get any baking soda solution in the battery cells. Rinse the battery thoroughly, then dry it.

7   If acid has been spilled on the frame or battery box, neutralize it with the baking soda and water solution, dry it thoroughly, then touch up any damaged paint. Make sure the battery vent tube is directed away from the frame and the final drive chain or belt and isn't kinked or pinched.

8   If the motorcycle sits unused for long periods of time, charge the battery approximately once every month as described below.

5 Battery - charging

1   If the machine sits idle for extended periods of time or if the charging system malfunctions, the battery can be charged from an external source.

2   To charge the battery properly, you will need a charger of the correct rating. If you're working on a fillable battery, you'll also need a hydrometer, a clean rag and a syringe for adding distilled water to the battery cells.

3   The maximum charging rate for any battery is 1/10 of the rated amp/hour capacity. For example, the maximum charging rate for a 32 amp/hour battery would be **3**.2 amps; the maximum rate for a battery rated at 19 amp/hours is 1.9 amps. If the battery is charged at a higher rate, it could be damaged.

4   Don't allow the battery to be subjected to a so-called quick charge (high rate of charge over a short period of time) unless you're prepared to buy a new battery. The heat this generates can warp the plates inside the battery. If they touch each other, the resulting short will ruin the battery.

5   When charging the battery, always remove it from the machine before hooking it to the charger. If you're working on a fillable battery, be sure to check the electrolyte level and add distilled water to any cells that are low before you start charging the battery.

6   If you're working on a fillable battery, loosen the cell caps and cover the top of the battery with a clean rag. Hook up the battery charger leads (positive to battery positive and negative to battery negative). Then - and only then - plug in the battery charger.

 Warning: Remember, the hydrogen gas escaping from a battery cell is explosive, so keep open flames and sparks well away from the area. Also, the electrolyte is extremely corrosive and will damage anything it comes in contact with.

7   If you're working on a fillable battery, allow the battery to charge until the specific gravity is as specified. The charger must be unplugged and disconnected from the battery when making specific gravity checks.

8   If you're working on a maintenance free battery, charge at a constant 1.8 amps for the following periods of time, depending on the open circuit voltage obtained in Section 4:

a) 12.8 volts - three to five hours
b) 12.5 volts - four to seven hours
c) 12.2 volts - ten hours

9   If the battery gets warm to the touch or gases excessively, the charging rate is too high. Either disconnect the charger and let the battery cool down or lower the charging rate to prevent damage to the battery.

10   If one or more of the cells do not show an increase in specific gravity after a long slow charge (fillable batteries only) or if the battery as a whole doesn't seem to want to take a charge, it's time for a new battery.

11   When the battery is fully charged, unplug the charger first, then disconnect the charger leads from the battery. Install the cell caps (fillable batteries only) and wipe any electrolyte off the outside of the battery case.

6 Battery - removal and installation

 Warning: Be extremely careful when handling or working around the battery. The electrolyte is very caustic and an explosive gas is given off when the battery is being charged.

All models except FLT and FXR

1   Loosen the nuts securing the battery retaining strap and release the strap from the bottom of the battery box **(see illustration)**.

2   On models so equipped, remove the decorative cover from the top of the battery.

3   Disconnect the cable from the negative terminal of the battery first, followed by the positive cable **(see illustration)**.

6.1 The battery retaining strap can be disconnected after loosening the nut (arrow)

6.3 Always disconnect the negative battery cable first and hook it up last

4   Lift the battery out of the box. Note how the vent hose is routed.

FLT models

5   On all models through 1992, remove the saddlebag from the right side of the motorcycle.

6   On 1993 and later models, remove the seat to gain access to the battery (retaining screw accessed from inside the rear luggage compartment).

7   On all models disconnect the negative cable from the battery, followed by the positive cable.

8   Disconnect the battery hold-down strap and lift the battery out.

6.14 Check the condition of the battery carrier

FXR models

9   Release the seat latch and tilt the seat up.

10   Disconnect the battery cables from the battery terminals (be sure to detach the negative cable first).

11   Remove the cable securing the seat to the battery hold-down bracket. Loosen the locknut, then remove the screw so the cable can be released.

12   Push the battery hold-down bracket toward the left rear side of the motorcycle. The bracket can then be separated from the slots in the frame.

13   Lift the battery out of the carrier after disconnecting the vent hose located near the negative terminal.

7.2 On fillable batteries, check the specific gravity with a hydrometer

All models

14   Check the condition of the battery carrier (see illustration). If it's corroded, or if it needs to be removed for access to other components, remove it. The carrier is attached by two rubber mounted studs and two or three bolts.

15   Install the battery by reversing the removal procedure. Be very careful not to pinch or otherwise restrict the battery vent tube, as the battery may build up enough internal pressure during normal charging system operation to explode.

HAYNES HiNT *Battery corrosion can be kept to a minimum by applying a layer of petroleum jelly or battery terminal (dielectric) grease to the terminals after the cables have been connected.*

7   Battery specific gravity (through 1996) - check

Note: *It may be necessary to remove the battery from the motorcycle to perform this check (see Section 6).*

1   Check the electrolyte level in each cell of the battery. If any of the cells are low, fill them to the proper level with distilled water. Do not use tap water (except in an emergency) and do not overfill the battery. The cell holes are quite small, so it might help to use a plastic squeeze bottle with a small spout to add the water.

2   Next, check the specific gravity of the electrolyte in each cell with a small hydrometer made especially for motorcycle batteries (see illustration). They are available at most dealer parts departments and motorcycle accessory shops.

3   Remove the caps, draw some electrolyte from the first cell into the hydrometer and note the specific gravity. Compare the reading to the Specifications. Return the electrolyte to the appropriate cell and repeat the check for the remaining cells. When the check is complete, rinse the hydrometer thoroughly with clean water.

4   If the specific gravity of the electrolyte in each cell is as specified, the battery is in good condition and is apparently being charged by the machine's charging system.

5   If the specific gravity is low, the battery is not fully charged. This may be due to corroded battery terminals, a dirty battery case, a malfunctioning charging system, or loose or corroded wiring connections. On the other hand, it may be that the battery is worn out, especially if it is old, or infrequent use of the motorcycle prevents normal charging from taking place. If the specific gravity of any two cells varies by more than 50 points, replace the battery with a new one.

6   Be sure to correct any problems and charge the battery if necessary before rein-

8

9.1 The chrome headlight trim ring is secured by a single screw

stalling it in the machine. Refer to Sections 4 and 5 for additional battery maintenance and charging procedures.

8 Fuses and circuit breakers - check and replacement

1   All models use one or more circuit breakers. These open in response to an electrical overload, then reset themselves as they cool down. If the condition that caused the overload still exists, the circuit breaker will open again.

2   A main circuit breaker is used on the following models: 1970 through 1972 (all), and 1978 and later (all).

3   A main fusible link is used in the wiring from the battery positive terminal on 1974 through 1977 models. On electric start models, the fusible link may be located between the positive terminal and the starter relay, or between the relay and the solenoid.

4   Separate circuit breakers for the ignition, lighting and accessory circuits are used on all 1973 and later models.

5   An additional circuit breaker, called a constant circuit breaker, is used in the circuit between the ignition switch and the main cir-

cuit breaker on 1986 through 1994 models.

4   Circuit breakers and fuses are located under the seat, behind the left side cover or in the fairing, depending on model and application.

5   To replace a circuit breaker, disconnect the negative cable from the battery. Disconnect the cables or wires from the circuit breaker, then remove it from the vehicle, install a new one and connect the cables or wires.

6   Blown fuses can be identified by a break in the metal element inside the fuse. To replace a cylindrical glass fuse, pry it out of its clips and push in a new one. To replace a mini-fuse (plug-in type), pull it out of its terminals and push in a new one.

⚠ **Warning: Never bridge fuse terminals with wire or any other metal, and never replace a fuse with one of a higher-than-rated amperage. This will allow overheating, which could cause melted wires, ruined components or a fire.**

9 Headlight bulb - replacement

Note: Either a sealed beam or quartz bulb headlight is fitted, depending on the model. The sealed beam unit comprises the reflector, glass and bulb as a single unit, whereas the quartz bulb can be replaced separately from the reflector unit.

Caution: Replaceable quartz headlight bulbs must be handled very carefully. Never touch the glass with your fingers - the oil from your skin will etch the glass and cause the bulb to fail. Wrap the bulb with paper or a clean, dry cloth when handling it.

⚠ **Warning: Let the bulb cool before removing it. Also, wear safety glasses or a face shield - the bulb contains halogen gas under pressure and could cause injury if it breaks.**

1970 through 1980 FL models

1   Remove the screw that retains the chrome plated rim surrounding the headlight **(see illustration)**. Detach the rim.

2   Remove the three screws securing the headlight retaining ring. Do not turn the adjuster screws.

3   Pull the headlight out of the housing until the wire harness can be unplugged from the rear **(see illustration)**.

4   Attach the wire harness plug to the new headlight and position the new headlight in the housing. The headlight is usually marked in some way to indicate the top. Be sure the mark is at the top when the headlight is positioned in the housing.

5   Secure the headlight in the housing by attaching the retaining ring with the three screws.

6   Install the decorative chrome rim around the headlight. Adjustment shouldn't be necessary if the adjusting screws weren't turned.

All FX/Softail/Dyna models

7   Remove the screw from the chrome plated clamp that surrounds the headlight **(see illustration)**. Take off the clamp.

8   Pry the sealed beam out of the rubber mount.

9   Pull the sealed beam out of the housing until the wire connector at the rear of the unit can be unplugged. **Note:** On models with a quartz bulb, the bulb can be removed from the reflector after the retainer clip (where fitted) is released (see **Caution** above).

10   To install the sealed beam unit, attach the wire connector to the rear of the reflector and position it in the rubber mount. Where a quartz bulb is fitted, install the bulb without touching its glass envelope and secure with the retainer clip (where fitted), then attach the wire connector and rubber boot.

11   Install the clamp ring around the headlight and tighten the screw securely.

1980 and later FLT models

12   Remove the three screws and detach the cover plate.

13   Both sealed beams are secured with a retaining ring. Loosen the three screws securing the retaining ring that must be removed (the screws don't have to be removed). As soon as they're loose, the retaining ring can be turned and lifted out.

14   Withdraw the sealed beam until the wire harness plug can be disconnected from the rear of the defective headlight.

15   Connect the wire harness plug to the rear of the new sealed beam and position the headlight in the housing.

16   Rotate the retaining ring into position and tighten the screws securely.

17   Install the cover plate with the three screws.

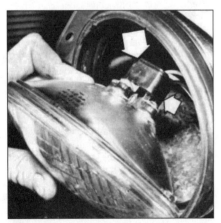

9.3 Unplug the wire harness connector (arrow) from the rear of the sealed beam

9.7 Remove the clamping screw to detach the headlight

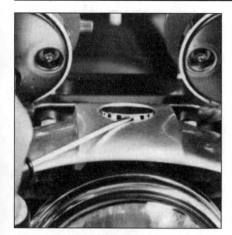

10.10a Pry the decorative plug out of the headlight housing . . .

10.10b . . . and loosen the mounting nut (FX models)

11.1a The taillight lens and . . .

1981 and later FL models (except FLT)

18 Remove the headlight from the fairing as described in Steps 1 through 3 above. On 1985 and earlier models, you may have to loosen and tip the fairing to remove the chrome rim.

19 Remove the rubber boot from the rear of the headlight.

20 Press the wire clip together and pull the bulb out of the reflector.

21 Install the new bulb in the reflector and secure it with the wire clip (see **Caution** above).

22 Attach the rubber boot over the rear of the bulb.

23 Connect the wire harness to the bulb and position the headlight in the fairing.

24 Secure the headlight in the fairing by attaching the retaining ring with the three screws.

25 Install the decorative chrome rim around the headlight.

FXRT and FXRD models

26 Working from the rear side of the fairing, unplug the wire harness connector from the rear of the bulb.

27 Follow the instructions in Steps 19 through 23 above.

All models

28 Adjustment should not have been altered while changing the headlight. If necessary, refer to Chapter 1 for the headlight adjustment procedure.

10 Headlight aim - check and adjustment

1 An improperly adjusted headlight may cause problems for oncoming traffic or provide poor, unsafe illumination of the road ahead. Before adjusting the headlight, be

sure to consult local traffic laws and regulations.

2 To set up the headlight, the machine should be placed on level ground at least 25-feet from a wall in its normal position (off the stand and with a rider - also a passenger if that's usually the case). On high beam, the height of the beam on the wall should be the same as the ground-to-headlight distance. This will ensure that oncoming drivers/riders won't be blinded.

All FL models, FXRT and FXRD

3 The headlight can be adjusted vertically by turning the screw at the top of the light. It may be necessary to remove the trim ring from the headlight assembly to gain access to the adjustment screws. The horizontal adjustment is made similarly, except the adjusting screw is at the side of the headlight.

FXDWG, FXDG, FXLR, FXSTS and FLSTC/F/N

4 Loosen the headlight assembly mounting bolt located below the lower triple clamp to adjust the beam horizontally.

5 Loosen the headlight assembly mounting bolt located above the lower triple clamp to adjust the beam vertically.

6 Tighten the two mounting bolts and recheck beam alignment.

FXSTS model

7 The horizontal and vertical adjusters are located at the rear of the headlight shell, and are accessed from above. Loosen the through-bolt and nut which pass through the side of the mounting block to make vertical adjustment; note that the head lamp should be positioned as far forward as possible in its block so that it does not contact the fork springs.

8 Horizontal adjustment is made by loosening the Allen-head bolt which passes

11.1b . . . the turn signal lenses are secured with two screws

down through the top of the mounting block.

9 Tighten all adjustment bolts when complete and recheck the beam settings.

FXD and all other FXR and FX models

10 Pry the decorative plug out of the top of the headlight housing and loosen the mounting nut. Twist the headlight in the desired direction until the beam is aimed properly **(see illustrations)**.

11 Tighten the mounting nut and recheck the aim.

12 Snap the decorative plug into the top of the housing.

11 Taillight and turn signal bulbs - replacement

1 Remove the screws securing the plastic lens cover to the taillight or the turn signal and detach the cover **(see illustrations)**.

2 Push in on the bulb and simultaneously turn it counterclockwise **(see illustration)**.

8

11.2 The two-filament taillight bulb has offset pins so it can only be installed one way in the socket

12.3 The spotlight sealed beam is retained by a clamp ring

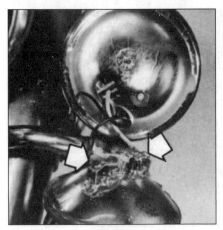

12.4 The wires are attached to the spotlight sealed beam unit with small screws

3   Replace the bulb with a new one of the same type by pushing it into the socket and turning it clockwise. **Note:** *The taillight bulb is a two filament bulb. The pins at the base of the bulb are offset so the bulb can only be inserted into the socket one way. If the bulb will not go into the socket, pull it out and rotate it 180-degrees, then reinsert it into the socket.*

4   Place the lens in position over the housing. Be sure the rubber seal is in good condition and makes contact all around the perimeter of the lens. Secure the lens with the two mounting screws.

12 Spotlight - bulb replacement

1   Many FL models are equipped with two spotlights. These lights are attached to a common mounting bar, one on each side of the headlight. As with the headlight, the bulb is a sealed beam and must be replaced as a complete unit.

2   Disconnect the negative cable from

13.8 Unplug the regulator/rectifier connector at the rubber plug on the crankcase

the battery.

3   Loosen the screw located at the base of the clamp ring and remove the ring **(see illustration).**

4   Withdraw the bulb from the housing and disconnect the wire harness from the rear of the sealed beam **(see illustration).**

5   Attach the wire harness to the new sealed beam and place the light in position in the housing.

6   Attach the clamp ring and tighten the retaining screw securely.

7   Connect the negative cable to the battery.

13 Alternator - check

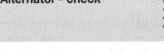

1   Checking the output of the alternator and other charging system components requires various electrical test devices which include a 0-50 amp ammeter, a 0-20 volt voltmeter, a variable resistor (rheostat) of 250 watt, 15 ohm resistance and an accurate ohmmeter. Unless the owner has the necessary equipment and experience required for the following procedures, the check should be done by a Harley-Davidson dealer service department or other qualified shop.

2   If the tests are done, note the following:

a) *Do not run the engine with the battery disconnected and do not reverse the battery cables.*

b) *Do not disconnect or reconnect the alternator-to-rectifier/regulator module wires while the engine is running.*

3   Machines from 1976-on have a similar but modified electrical system compared to the one used on earlier models (particularly in the construction of the rectifier/regulator module). The test procedures and the results differ from one to the other - don't mix them up!

4   Connect the ammeter, voltmeter and variable resistor to the circuit as described in

the following Steps.

5   1975 and earlier models:

a) *Variable resistor between battery terminals*

b) *Ammeter negative: two wires, one to battery positive and one to voltmeter positive*

c) *Ammeter positive to alternator black wire*

d) *Voltmeter positive to ammeter negative (as described above)*

e) *Voltmeter negative to battery negative*

6   1976 and later models:

a) *Variable resistor between battery terminals*

b) *Ammeter negative to battery positive*

c) *Ammeter positive to alternator red wire and voltmeter positive terminal*

d) *Voltmeter positive to alternator red wire (as described above)*

e) *Voltmeter negative to battery negative*

7   Start and run the engine at 3600 rpm and adjust the variable resistor until the output is 3.5 amperes. If the air temperature measured at the rectifier/regulator module is 75-degrees F, the voltage reading should be between 13.8 and 1 5.0 volts. If this test is positive, reduce the engine speed to the rpm noted below and adjust the variable resistor until a constant 13.0 volts is obtained:

a) *On 1975 and earlier models, the current (amperage) reading should be 10.5 amps minimum at 2000 rpm.*

b) *On 1976 through 1983 models, it should be 14 amps minimum at 2000 rpm.*

c) *On 1984 through 1988 models, it should be 19 to 23 amps at 2000 rpm.*

d) *On 1989 through 1992 models, it should be 29 to 33 amps at 2000 rpm.*

e) *On 1993 and later models, it should be 26 to 32 amps at 3000 rpm.*

8   If the above test results are obtained, the alternator and rectifier/regulator module are in good condition. If not, the following test will determine whether the alternator or rectifier/regulator unit is bad. Disconnect the alternator at the socket **(see illustration).**

15.1 Use a pry bar to pry the drive sprocket shaft extension (if equipped) off the end of the crankshaft

15.2 A puller must be used to remove the alternator rotor from the shaft (some later models don't require a puller to remove the rotor)

15.3 Remove the alternator stator screws; early models (shown) use hex screws and lockplates; later models use Torx screws, which must be replaced with new ones

9   On 1970 through 1975 models, run the engine at 2000 rpm. Connect a 0-150 volt AC voltmeter across the two white wire pins; the reading should be 50 to 100 volts AC. Make a similar connection across the blue and red wire pins; the reading should be 75 to 125 volts AC.

10   On 1976 and later models, connect the voltmeter across the two black (stator wire) pins. The reading should be:

a) *On 1976 through 1988 models, 19 to 28 volts AC for every 1000 rpm.*
b) *On 1989 and later models, 16 to 20 volts AC for every 1000 rpm.*

11   On all models, a satisfactory test result indicates the alternator is in good condition. The rectifier/regulator module should be checked as described in the next Section.

14 Rectifier/regulator module - check and replacement

1   The tests carried out in Steps 4 through 7 in the preceding Section will reveal whether the alternator or rectifier/regulator module is malfunctioning.

2   On 1970 through 1975 models, check the module resistance values as shown in the following table. Make one test with positive polarity and the second test with the polarity reversed. The module must be replaced with a new one if the values are not within the specified range.

a) *Probe connection from white wire-to-module base: Positive polarity, infinity; negative polarity, 3 to 15 ohms.*
b) *Probe connection from blue wire-to-black wire: Positive polarity, 3 to 15 ohms; negative polarity, infinity.*
c) *Probe connection from red wire-to-module base: Positive polarity, infinity; negative polarity, infinity.*

3   On 1976 and later models, no test pro-

cedures are possible. If you suspect the rectifier/regulator is malfunctioning, replace it with a new one. It may be a good idea to have your test results confirmed by a dealer service department before buying a new part.

15 Alternator - removal and installation

Removal

Note: *If the alternator is in the frame, disconnect the negative battery cable from the battery, then remove the primary drive components to gain access to the alternator rotor (see Chapter 2B). On 1989 and later FX/Softail models, you don't have to remove the inner primary chaincase to detach the alternator.*

1   If the engine has been removed from the frame, support it on blocks so the alternator is facing up, away from the workbench. Pry the splined shaft extension (if equipped) off the end of the crankshaft **(see illustration)**.

2   The alternator rotor on most models has an internally splined boss and is pressed onto the crankshaft. The rotor must be removed from the crankshaft with a puller. A Harley-Davidson special tool can be used, or a puller with three bolts that will screw into the threaded holes in the alternator rotor boss. Place the plate over the end of the crankshaft and screw the bolts into the rotor boss. Tighten the bolts evenly to draw the rotor off the crankshaft **(see illustration)**.
Note: *The rotors on some Evolution engines (late 1985 through 1987 models) are a slip-fit on the crankshaft and have large spacers on each side. After the compensating sprocket and primary drive components are removed, the spacers and rotor will slip off the shaft. Later engines with splined rotor hubs also*

have large spacer washers on each side - note how they're installed and be sure to return them to their original locations.

3   Bend back the tabs of the lockplates (if equipped) that secure the four stator mounting screws, then remove the screws **(see illustration)**. Later model Evolution engines don't have lockplates and the screws have Torx heads. Discard the Torx screws after they're removed and use new ones during assembly.

4   Remove the two countersunk screws securing the bridge piece that holds the alternator wires in place **(see illustration)**. Remove the bridge piece.

5   The rubber plug in the end of the alternator wiring harness is a tight fit in the crankcase. Use a blunt tool to push the plug in, toward the alternator. Don't use any sharp instruments - they may pierce the plug and damage the wires or plug pins.

6   Lift the alternator stator out.

Installation

7   Place the stator over the left end of the crankshaft so it rests in approximately the correct position.

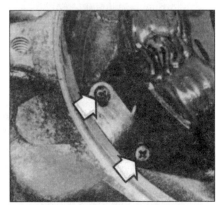

15.4 Remove the screws securing the wiring harness bridge piece

8

16.4 Detach the cable and remove the nut, then pull the clutch arm off the shaft

16.5a On 1970 through 1983 models, remove the two nuts (arrows) . . .

16.5b . . . and detach the drive end of the starter motor from the primary chaincase

8   Insert the wiring plug into the recess in the crankcase and push it carefully into position until the ridge molded in the plug is seated against the inside edge of the case. Place the bridge piece over the wiring and secure it with the two screws.

9   Align the alternator stator so the four retaining screws can be inserted. Lay the lockplates (if equipped) in position and install the screws. **Note:** *If the screws have Torx heads, be sure to use new ones.* Tighten the screws evenly (but don't overtighten them and strip the threads). If lockplates are used, bend the tabs over to secure the screws.

10   Install the alternator rotor on the crankshaft and spacer washer on the crankshaft, in their original order. On 1986 and later Evolution engines, the small-diameter spacer goes on the crankshaft first, followed by the rotor and larger-diameter spacer washer. Carefully tap the rotor into place.

Caution: Don't strike the rotor forcefully, or it may be demagnetized, rendering it useless.

11   Install the primary drive components (see Chapter 2B).

---

16 Starter motor - removal, overhaul and installation

1   Three different types of starter motors are used on these machines, although their operation is similar. One is made by Prestolite (USA) and is used on machines through 1983, while another is made by Hitachi (Japan) and is used on machines from late 1978 through 1988. A third starter, with an integral solenoid and drive/overrunning clutch assembly is used on 1989 and later models. Generally speaking, the starter motor requires very little attention during the normal service life of the machine, although periodic examination of the brushes and commutator is recommended.

2   If the starter motor refuses to function, first eliminate other possible components that may give the impression the starter motor needs attention. Check the wires for good connections and make sure the battery is fully charged. The handlebar switch must make good contact and the starter solenoid should engage with an audible click. Finally, the engine itself may be stiff if it has been recently rebored and had new bearings installed, if it's very cold, or if excessively high viscosity oil has been used.

Removal

1970 through 1988

3   To remove the starter motor from the machine, first remove the battery cover and disconnect the battery cables (negative first, then positive). On some models, the battery and carrier must be removed in order to gain access to the motor (see Section 6).

4   On 1983 and earlier models, disconnect the clutch cable at the operating arm, then remove the arm from the shaft projecting from the end cover of the transmission. The arm is retained by a single nut **(see illustration)**.

5   Disconnect the wires from the starter motor, then remove the outer support bracket, which is attached to the transmission end cover. The starter motor is secured to the rear of the primary chaincase by two nuts on studs **(see illustration)**. Remove the nuts (from the right side) and pull the starter motor out, leaving the driveshaft in position in the case **(see illustration)**. Pull the starter motor driven reduction gear out of the housing.

6   On 1984 and later models, disconnect the solenoid cable from the starter terminal (except FLT and FXR models).

a)   On FXEF, FXSB and FXWG models - Remove the nuts that fasten the master cylinder reservoir bracket to the transmission. Remove the nut and detach the starter bracket. Remove the chrome end cover and detach the starter bracket from the through-bolt stud. Remove the through-bolts and hold the starter by both end covers to keep it from coming apart as you remove it.

b)   On FXST/C and FLST/C models - Remove the nuts that hold the starter bracket to the transmission. Detach the chrome end cover and bracket, then remove the relay-to-starter ground wire. Remove the through-bolts and hold the starter by both end covers to keep it from coming apart as you remove it.

c)   On FLT and FXR models - Remove the bolt that fastens the starter to the transmission side door. Remove the upper bolts (and the battery cable), then detach the starter and solenoid/drive gear as an assembly. Detach the solenoid cable from the starter motor terminal, then remove the through-bolts to separate the motor from the starter shaft housing.

1989-on

Note: *On FX/Softail models, remove the rear exhaust pipe. You may also have to loosen the oil tank mounts to provide room for starter removal.*

7   Remove the primary chaincase cover (see Chapter 2), then hold the starter drive pinion gear and remove the jackshaft bolt and lockplate (flatten the lockplate ear before removing the bolt).

8   Remove the two acorn nuts and detach the chrome end cover from the right side of the motor **(see illustration)**.

9   Remove the two Allen-head starter mounting bolts and pull the starter out, then detach the wires from the starter terminals and remove it from the right side. **Note:** *The jackshaft-to-starter coupling may come off with the starter or it may stay on the jackshaft. If it comes off with the starter, put it back on the jackshaft. On 1990 models, the coupling end with the counterbore must be on the jackshaft.*

Overhaul

10   Remove the two nuts/screws that retain the starter motor end cover, then remove the two long through-bolts (they were already removed on 1984 and later models). Detach the reduction gear housing (not all models).

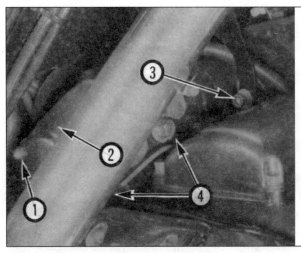

16.8 Starter motor mounting details (1989 and later models)

1   *Acorn nut (one hidden)*
2   *Chrome starter motor end cover*
3   *Mounting bolts (one hidden)*
4   *Wires (remove the nut to detach the large wire)*

16.11a Check and clean the commutator and brushes . . .

16.11b . . . and measure the brush length after removing them from the holders

With the end cover removed, it will be possible to see the brushes, which must be replaced with new ones as a set if they have worn beyond the specified limits.

11   Make sure the brushes can move freely in the holders **(see illustration)**. If not, remove them so the holders can be cleaned with solvent to remove built-up carbon dust **(see illustration)**. Clean the commutator at the same time, using solvent - NOT a harsh abrasive such as emery cloth. If the starter motor has been in service a long time, the mica insulation between the individual copper segments of the commutator must be undercut by 1/32-inch (a task requiring dealer attention). When brushes are replaced with new ones, the original leads will have to be cut off close to the field coil connection (Prestolite) or unsoldered from the brush holder (Hitachi). Do not use too much heat or solder, otherwise the leads will become clogged with solder and lose their flexibility.

12   Before reassembly, make sure none of the leads contact the body of the motor or otherwise short out.

13   Other defects will require dealer attention or the installation of a new starter motor.

Installation

14   Installation is the reverse of removal. On 1989 and later models, make sure the starter jackshaft bolt lockplate tab fits into the keyway in the sleeve.

17 Starter solenoid - check

1   Disconnect the negative cable from the battery to avoid an accidental short circuit.

2   Pry the rubber cap off the rear of the starter solenoid, exposing the wire terminals **(see illustration)**.

3   Label the wires and terminals, then disconnect the wires by removing the nuts.

4   Using jumper wires, connect a 12-volt battery to the terminals on the solenoid. One wire should go to the small terminal and the

other wire should go to the shorter of the large terminals.

5   The solenoid should make a clicking sound. If a click or heavy spark at the terminal does not occur, the solenoid is defective and must be replaced with a new one.

18 Starter drive - disassembly, inspection and reassembly

1   The starter motor utilizes a reduction gear to drive the gear mounted on the clutch outer drum. On all models through 1988, the reduction driven gear turns a shaft on which a free-sliding pinion gear is mounted. When the starter button is operated, the starter solenoid moves the pinion gear into mesh with the clutch outer drum gear a moment before power is provided to the starter motor. The starter solenoid operates a pivot arm, which operates the pinion gear. On 1989 and later models, the pinion shaft is replaced by a jackshaft. A gear on the left end of the jackshaft is always engaged with the gear on the clutch outer drum and the starter drive connects and disconnects the motor from the jackshaft.

1970 through 1988

All except FLT, FXR, FXB, FXSB, FXWG, FXSTIC and FLST/C (belt-drive) models

2   Remove the primary chaincase cover as described in Chapter 2 to gain access to the engagement mechanism. Any broken or worn parts should be obvious immediately.

17.2 On all models through 1988, the solenoid is attached to the primary chaincase - pull back the rubber cap to expose the terminals and wires

18.3 Slide the bronze thrust washer (arrow) off the pinion shaft

18.4 Remove the pin (arrow) to disengage the solenoid plunger from the pivot arm

18.5 Remove the pivot arm screw (arrow) from the top of the chaincase

3   To disassemble the components, pull the bronze thrust washer off the shaft **(see illustration)** and remove the oil seal carrier plate from the opposite end.

4   Push the coil spring on the solenoid plunger back so the retaining pin can be removed **(see illustration)**.

5   The pivot arm rides on a large diameter countersunk screw which threads directly into the inner primary chaincase from above **(see illustration)**. The screw is usually very tight - be very careful to avoid damaging the head when removing it.

6   Manipulate the pivot arm so it leaves the solenoid plunger, then pull the complete shaft assembly out. The components on the shaft can be taken off after removing the end nut (left-hand threads) and pinion shaft collar.

7   The engagement components and pinion shaft can be installed by reversing the removal procedure.

8   Before installation, check the starter drive and reduction (driven) gears for wear and damage **(see illustrations)**. Make sure the splines in the reduction driven gear center hole that mate with the pinion shaft are in good condition (check the fit of the gear and shaft).

9   If either of the pinion shaft needle roller bearings are worn, they must be replaced with new ones. The bearing in the starter motor reduction gear housing is particularly prone to wear, since no means of lubrication is provided **(see illustration)**.

10   Make sure the O-ring in the oil seal carrier plate is in good condition. Replace it with a new one if it's cracked or otherwise deteriorated or damaged **(see illustration)**.

11   During reassembly, remember to install the bronze thrust washer on the left end of the pinion shaft. It's a loose fit and easily misplaced.

18.8a Check the starter gear . . .

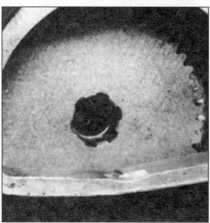

18.8b . . . and the gear teeth and splined hole of the reduction driven gear for wear and damage

18.9 The needle roller bearing in the starter reduction gear housing should turn freely - grease it before installation

18.10 Check the O-ring in oil seal carrier plate - a new one should be installed each time the pinion shaft is removed

FXB, FXSB, FXWG, FXST/C and FLST/C (belt-drive) models

12 Remove the starter motor as described in Section 16, then remove the primary chaincase cover as described in Chapter 2.

13 Unscrew the three bolts securing the outer reduction driven gear housing and remove the housing and gasket.

14 Remove the reduction driven gear, then unscrew the two bolts securing the inner housing. Detach the inner housing and gasket.

15 Disengage the fingers of the shifter lever (pivot arm) from the shifter collar to remove the pinion shaft assembly and pinion gear from the clutch side.

16 Unscrew the solenoid mounting bolts and remove the solenoid, along with the spacer, felt gasket and spring.

17 Remove the screw securing the starter drive engagement lever and detach the lever. It may be necessary to remove the oil tank mounting hardware, the battery and the battery carrier to gain access to the lever retaining screw.

18 Check the gears and bearings for signs of wear and damage. If the reduction driven gear is worn, be sure to check the condition of the starter gear. Replace any defective components with new parts.

19 If the seal in the inner reduction driven gear housing requires replacement, carefully pry it out and press a new seal into the housing with the lip side facing the gear.

20 Use new gaskets during reassembly.

21 Reassembly is the reverse of disassembly. Lubricate the bearing in the outer housing, the starter drive engagement lever, the screw and bearing and the parts on the pinion shaft assembly, with high-temperature grease.

22 Align the groove in the shifter collar with the fingers of the starter drive engagement lever.

23 Lubricate the outer thrust washer and install it on the pinion shaft collar just before installing the primary chain cover.

FLT and FXR models

24 Remove the starter motor as described in Section 16, then remove the primary chaincase cover as described in Chapter 2.

25 Remove the thrust washer from the left end of the pinion shaft, then pull out the shaft.

26 Unscrew the solenoid mounting bolts and detach the solenoid, spring and felt gasket.

27 Remove the solenoid plunger from inside the primary chaincase. Pull the pin out, which will release the collar and the spring from the plunger. The plunger can then be withdrawn from the right side of the chaincase.

28 Unscrew the plug from the top of the chaincase, then remove the shaft securing the pivot arm from the opening in the chaincase.

29 Lift the pivot arm out.

30 Check the components as described in Steps 8 and 9 above.

31 Reassembly can be done by reversing the disassembly procedure. Be sure the lip on the pinion shaft collar fits against the pinion gear during reassembly.

32 Slide the shifter collar onto the pinion gear and secure it with the snap-ring. Install the assembly on the pinion shaft with the snap-ring facing the spacer.

1989 and later

33 Remove the primary chaincase cover and the clutch (see Chapter 2B).

34 Flatten the lockplate ear. Hold the starter drive pinion gear and loosen the jackshaft bolt. Pull out the bolt, lockplate, thrust washer (1990 and later) and O-ring (1989 through 1992).

35 Pull the jackshaft assembly out of the inner chaincase as an assembly.

36 On 1989 models, remove the sleeve from the shaft. The Woodruff key may come out with it.

37 Pull off the pinion gear. Remove the coupling and spring (the spring and a retaining ring are inside the coupling).

38 If the starter coupling didn't come off with the jackshaft assembly, remove it from the starter shaft. Make sure the retaining ring is in place in the groove in the coupling.

39 On FLT and FXR models:

a) Check the bushing, seal and scraper in the back side of the primary chaincase. If the bushing is worn or damaged, remove it and install a new one - it must be flush to 0.010-inch (0.25 mm) below the face of the case.

b) If the seal is leaking, drive the seal and scraper out and discard them. Install a new seal and make sure the inner side is 0.110 to 0.120-inch (2.79 to 3.0 mm) from the end of the case bore. The scraper is no longer needed.

c) Check the bushing in the chaincase cover. If it's worn or damaged, remove it and install a new one - it must be flush to 0.030-inch (0.76 mm) below the case boss.

d) During reassembly make sure the large coupling is installed with the retaining ring end facing the starter. If it's reversed it will contact the inner chaincase and the pinion gear won't engage the clutch ring gear.

40 Install the large coupling on the jackshaft and place the spring inside the coupling.

41 Install the pinion gear, sleeve (1989 only) and Woodruff key.

42 Slide the lockplate, thrust washer (1990 and later) and O-ring (1989 through 1992) onto the bolt, then install the bolt in the jackshaft. Make sure the lockplate tab is in the pinion gear or sleeve cutaway (on 1990 and later models, it must also pass through the thrust washer slot).

43 Place the starter shaft coupling on the inner end of the jackshaft, then slide the jackshaft into the chaincase. **Note:** On 1990 and later models, make sure the end of the starter coupling with the counterbore faces away from the starter shaft.

44 Thread the jackshaft bolt into the end of the starter shaft and tighten it to 7 to 9 ft-lbs (9 to 12 Nm). Bend up the lockplate ear against the bolt head. On 1990 and later models, make sure it doesn't extend past the outside diameter of the pinion gear journal. The jackshaft will jam and the chaincase cover bushing will be damaged if the lockplate ear touches it when the starter drive is engaged.

45 Install the clutch and primary chaincase cover.

19 Handlebar switches - removal and installation

1 Generally speaking, the handlebar switches are trouble-free, but, if necessary, they can be detached by removing the screws and separating the halves, which form a split clamp around the handlebar.

2 To prevent the possibility of a short circuit, disconnect the battery before removing the switches.

3 Most problems are caused by dirty contacts, which can be cleaned with an aerosol contact cleaner specially formulated for this purpose.

4 Switch repair is generally impractical. If a switch breaks or wears out, replace it with a new one.

20 Ignition and light switch - removal and installation

Caution: Disconnect the battery negative cable before working on the ignition switch.

1 The main switch that controls both the ignition system and the lights is mounted in one of four places: in the control console on the fuel tank, in the base of the instrument panel, on a bracket on the left side of the motorcycle just below the fuel tank, or just below the seat on the left side of the motorcycle. Later FLT models also incorporate a fork lock in the switch.

2 If the switch malfunctions, replace it with a new one - repair is not possible. If the switch is replaced, the ignition key will have to be replaced also.

3 The switch doesn't normally require attention and it should never be oiled. If the switch is oiled, there is a risk of oil reaching the electrical contacts and acting as an insulator.

Tank console-mounted switch

4 The switch must be in the OFF position and the key removed. Detach the instrument

8

console from the tank as described in Section 25. Label all wires at the bottom of the switch, then disconnect them **(see illustration)**.

5   Remove the four screws retaining the switch and detach it from the console bracket or console underside (as applicable).

6   Install the switch in the reverse order of removal.

Instrument panel-mounted switch

7   Access to the switch necessitates a considerable amount of dismantling and the use of a service tool to set up the fork lock mechanism on reassembly; it is recommended that this operation is carried out by an authorized Harley-Davidson dealer.

Frame-mounted switch

8   The switch is attached to the mounting plate with a threaded decorative ring around the exterior. When the ring is unscrewed from the switch, it can be removed from the rear of the mounting plate.

9   Unplug the wires from the rear of the switch.

10   Install the new switch by reversing the removal procedure.

20.4 The ignition switch on FL models (arrow) is retained by four screws

21 Horn - adjustment

1   The horn is equipped with an adjusting screw on the back of the horn body so the volume can be varied.

2   To adjust the tone or volume, turn the screw 1/2-turn in either direction and test the sound. If the sound is weaker or lost altogether, turn the screw in the opposite direction. Continue adjusting until the desired tone and volume is achieved.

3   If the horn malfunctions completely and cannot be restored by adjustment, install a new one. Repair of the horn isn't possible, because the assembly is riveted together.

22 Evaporative emission - solenoid test (1992 and later California models)

1   The solenoid is clamped to the rear of the air cleaner baseplate and operates a butterfly valve located in the bottom of the air cleaner housing, a mechanical linkage connects the two components. If operating normally it will shut the valve when the engine is stopped (ignition switch in OFF position), open it when the starter circuit is operated via the pull-in winding, and keep it open while the engine is running via its hold-in winding.

2   To test the two windings trace its wiring up to the 4-pin connector and separate it at

this point. Making the tests on the solenoid side of the connector, use an ohmmeter to measure the resistance between the black/red and gray/black wires (pull-in winding) - a reading of 4 to 6 ohms should be obtained. Take another reading between the white and black wires of the connector (hold-in winding) - a figure of 21 to 27 ohms should be obtained.

3   If either resistance reading is widely different from that specified, the solenoid is confirmed faulty and must be renewed.

4   If the windings prove sound, yet the butterfly valve still fails to operate normally, make continuity checks along the supply and ground circuits to isolate the fault - it will most likely be due to a corroded connector or broken wire.

23 Radio (1997 and later FLHTC) - removal and installation

1   Remove the seat (see Chapter 7).

2   Disconnect the negative cable from the battery.

3   Remove the outer fairing (see Chapter 7).

4   Disconnect the radio electrical connector (two connectors on Ultra models). Disconnect the antenna cable (and CB cable on Ultra models).

5   Locate the main harness to interconnect harness connectors (one gray, one black). The gray connector is at the T-stud forward of the right fairing bracket. The black connector is at the T-stud for the right radio support bracket.

6   Remove two Allen screws on each side of the radio. The screws are accessible through holes in the fairing brackets. To reach them, you'll need an Allen bolt bit (ideally, a ball-end bit) on a long extension.

7   Work the radio out of its bracket, rocking it if necessary to free it from the nose seal.

8   Place the radio in its brackets, aligning the top of the nose seal with the top of the brackets. If this is difficult, lubricate the nose

seal with alcohol, glass cleaner or electrical contact cleaner.

9   Lift the back end of the radio at a 45-degree angle and line up the bolt holes. Install the bolts, rear bolts first, and tighten them to the torque listed in this Chapter's Specifications.

10   The remainder of installation is the reverse of the removal steps.

24 Cruise control (1997 and later FLHTC) - description and check

1   The cruise control system maintains vehicle speed with a stepper motor located in the cruise control module under the left side cover, which is connected to the throttle linkage by a cable. The system consists of the stepper motor, brake switches, control switch, idle cable roll-off switch, module and fuse. Some features of the system require special testers and diagnostic procedures that are beyond the scope the home mechanic. Listed below are some general procedures that may be used to locate common problems.

2   Check the fuse (see Section 8).

3   The brake light switches deactivate the cruise control system. With the key On, operate the front and rear brakes and check brake light operation.

4   If the brake light does not operate properly, correct the problem and retest the cruise control.

5   Check the control cable between the module and carburetor or induction module for wear or damage and have it replaced by a dealer service department or other qualified shop if necessary.

6   The cruise control module reads the speed signal from the speedometer and uses this to control the stepper motor.

7   The module senses the engine speed signal from the tachometer and uses this to shut off the cruise control system if the engine over-revs (for example, if the clutch is disengaged without letting off the throttle). It also uses the tachometer signal to detect

25.24 Remove the choke knob (A), locknut (B) and odometer knob and screw to detach the instrument panel (two-piece fuel tank)

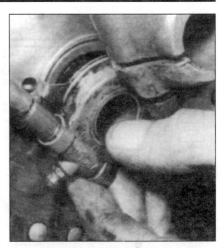

25.28 Lower the front wheel and disengage the speedometer drive unit from the wheel hub (mechanical speedometer)

that the engine stop switch has been activated, and shuts off the cruise control system.

8   The idle cable roll-off switch causes the system to disengage whenever the throttle is closed.

9   The system will also shut off if speed drops below 30 mph (48 kph) while the Set switch is being held on.

---

25 Instruments and bulbs - removal and installation

1970 through 1983 models

Handlebar-mounted instruments

1   Before either of the instruments can be removed, you must disconnect the drive cable (if equipped). Unscrew the coupling nut from the underside of each instrument and pull the cables off. Some later models have an electronic tachometer or speedometer so there will be no cable to remove - instead, the wire will have to be disconnected.

2   The light bulbs will pull away from the underside of each instrument head, along with the bulb holders. The detachable base plate must be removed first, as it acts as a retainer.

3   Apart from defects in either the drive or the drive cable, a speedometer or tachometer that malfunctions is difficult to repair. Install a new or used one.

Fuel tank-mounted instruments

4   Remove the screws securing the instrument panel.

5   Pull the odometer trip knob off (if so equipped).

6   On models where the choke control is in the instrument panel, unscrew the choke knob and the retaining locknut.

7   Lift the panel off the fuel tank and unscrew the mounting hardware.

8   Label the wires at the instrument cluster and disconnect them.

9   Unscrew the speedometer and, if equipped, the tachometer cable.

10   If the instruments are defective, they must be replaced with new ones.

11   Installation is the reverse of the removal procedure. Be sure to connect the wires and cables.

1984 and later models

Note: *The instruments are not repairable, but before replacing a defective component, make sure the electrical connections are clean and tight. Lubricate the speedometer cables with graphite grease every 5,000 miles.*

Caution: Do not turn the instruments upside-down after they are removed - the damping oil used in the fuel gauge will leak out and stain the gauge face.

FLT/C (1984-on) and FLHT/C (1984 and 1985)

12   To replace the bulbs, remove the two screws from the instrument panel. Remove the Phillips screw and pull the odometer trip knob out, then lift up on the panel to expose the bulbs.

13   To remove the instrument panel, disconnect the wire harness and detach the speedometer cable.

14   Remove the fasteners¬ and detach the bracket.

15   Mark all wires, then unplug them and replace the malfunctioning instrument.

16   Installation is the reverse of removal.

FLHT/C (1986-on) and FLHS (1987-on)

17   To replace the bulbs, remove the light bar and outer fairing. The instrument bulbs and all gauges are now accessible from the front of the inner fairing.

18   Unplug all wire connectors from the instrument housing. Remove the four Allen-head screws holding the panel to the fairing.

19   Remove the round knob attaching the trip odometer knob to the fairing.

20   Disconnect the speedometer cable and detach the instrument panel.

21   Remove the fasteners and detach the mounting bracket.

22   Mark all wires, then unplug them and replace the malfunctioning instrument.

23   Installation is the reverse of removal.

Models with fuel tank-mounted instruments

24   On most models, access to the instruments and bulbs is gained by removing the odometer knob (loosen the set screw first), unscrewing the choke knob and removing the choke cable housing locknut or the acorn nut holding the instrument panel to the gas tank **(see illustration)**.

25   On some models the instrument panel is attached to the fuel tank with three Allen-head screws.

26   Disconnect any wires and remove the speedometer cable (if equipped) before replacing the instruments.

Speedometer cable and drive unit

27   Disconnect the upper end of the cable from the speedometer.

28   Remove the front wheel and disengage the speedometer drive unit from the wheel hub **(see illustration)**. Free the cable from any retainers along its length, then remove it from the motorcycle.

29   Installation is the reverse of the removal Steps.

---

26 Wiring diagrams - general information

Prior to troubleshooting a circuit, check the fuse and circuit breaker (if equipped) to make sure they're in good condition. Make sure the battery is fully charged and check the cable connections (Sections 4, 5 and 6). When checking a circuit, make sure all connectors are clean, with no broken or loose terminals or wires. When unplugging a connector, do not pull on the wires. Pull only on the connector housings themselves.

8

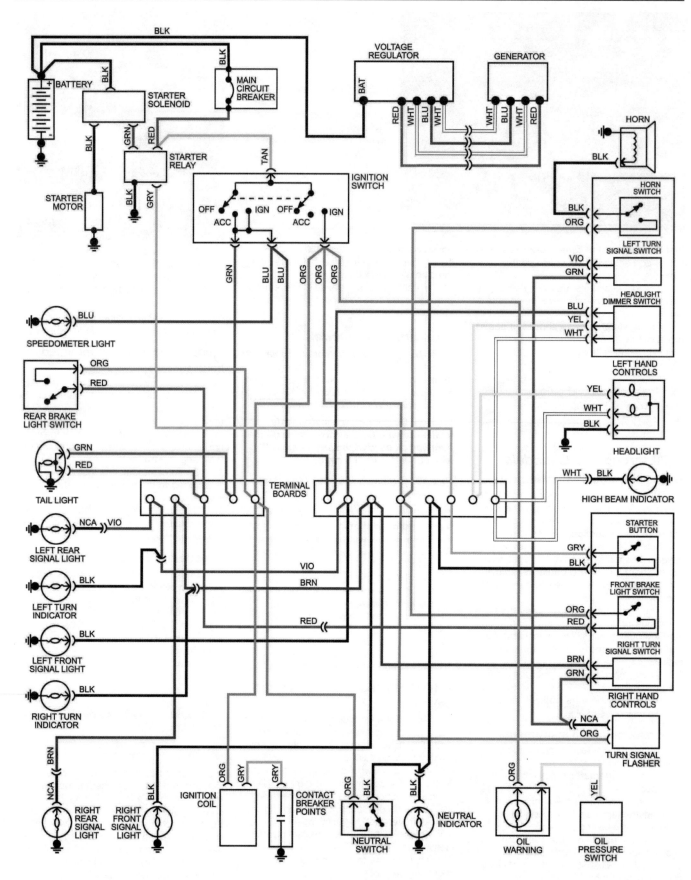

1970 through 1972 FL - typical

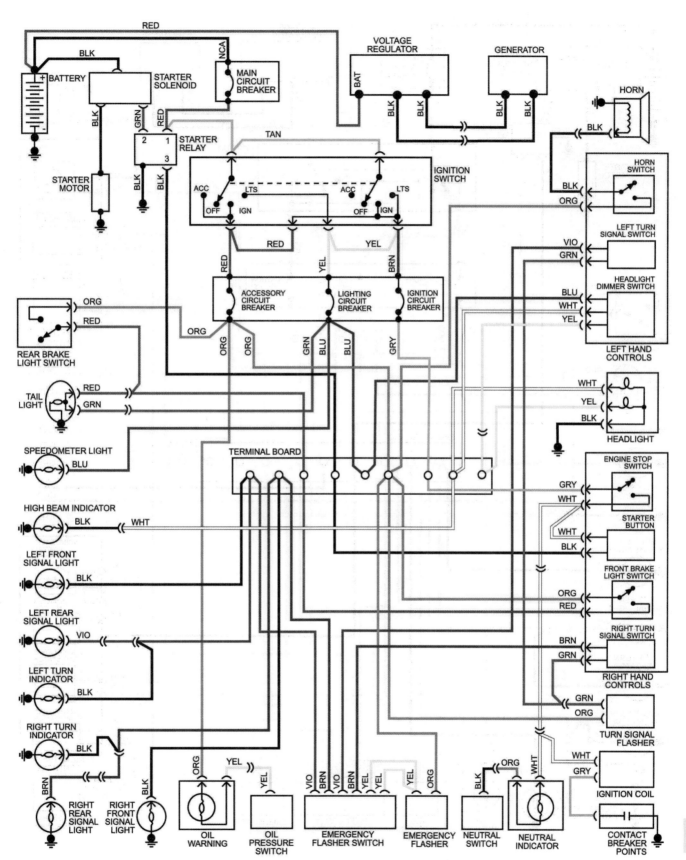

1973 through early 1978 FL models - typical

8

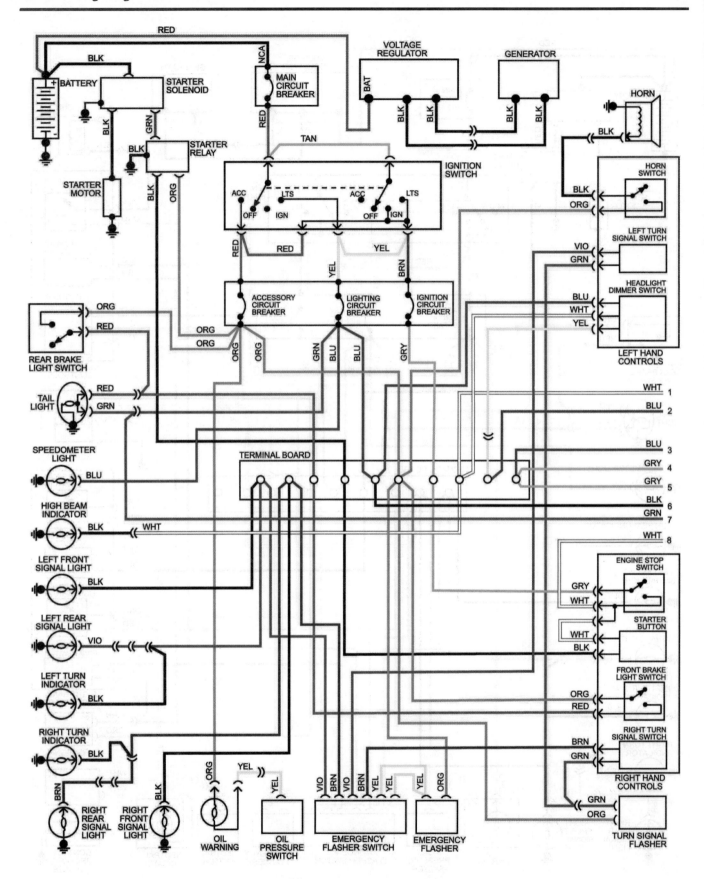

Late 1978 through 1983 FL models - typical (page 1 of 2)

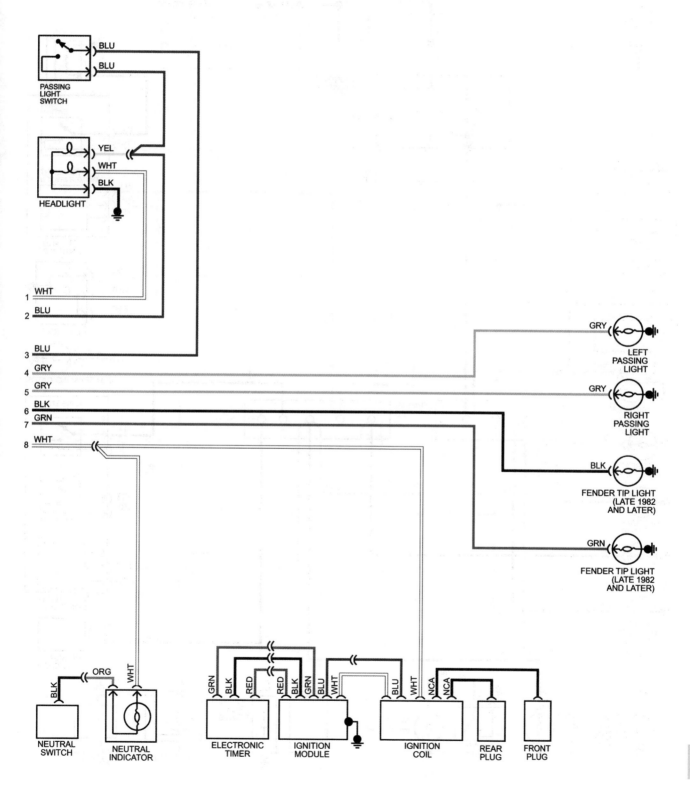

Late 1978 through 1983 FL models - typical (page 2 of 2)

8

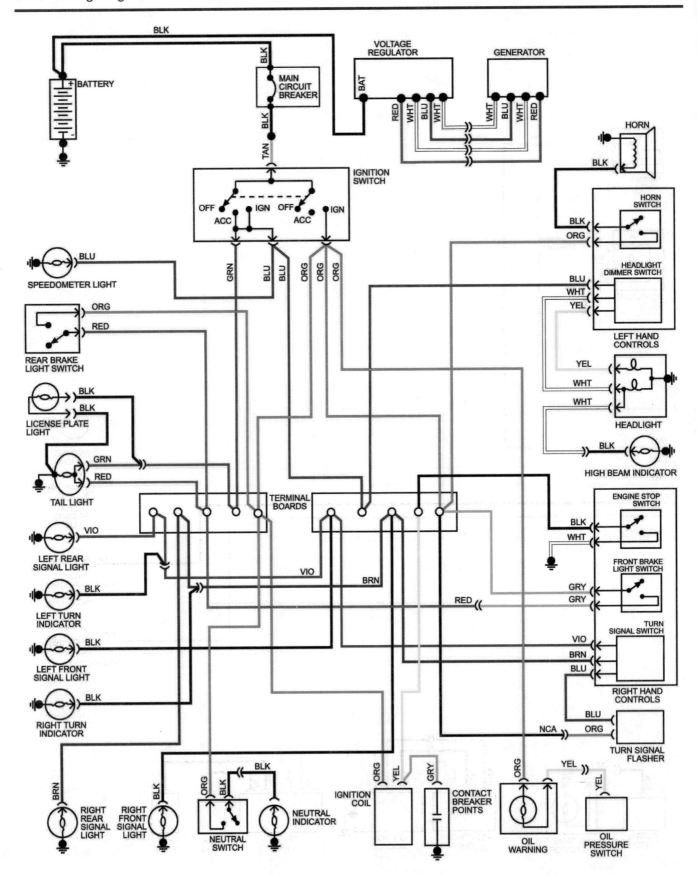

1970 through 1972 FX models - typical

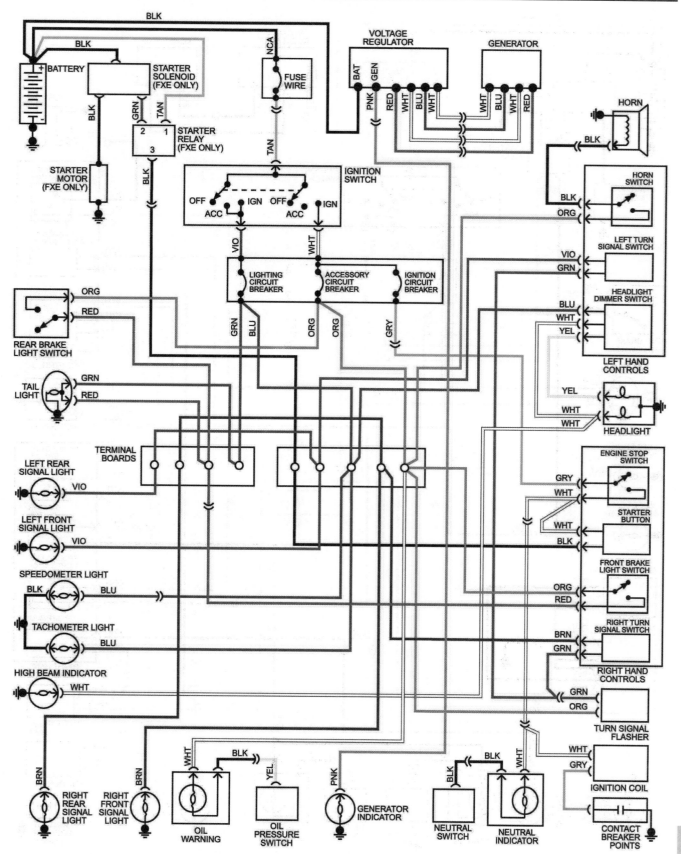

1973 and 1974 FX models - typical

8

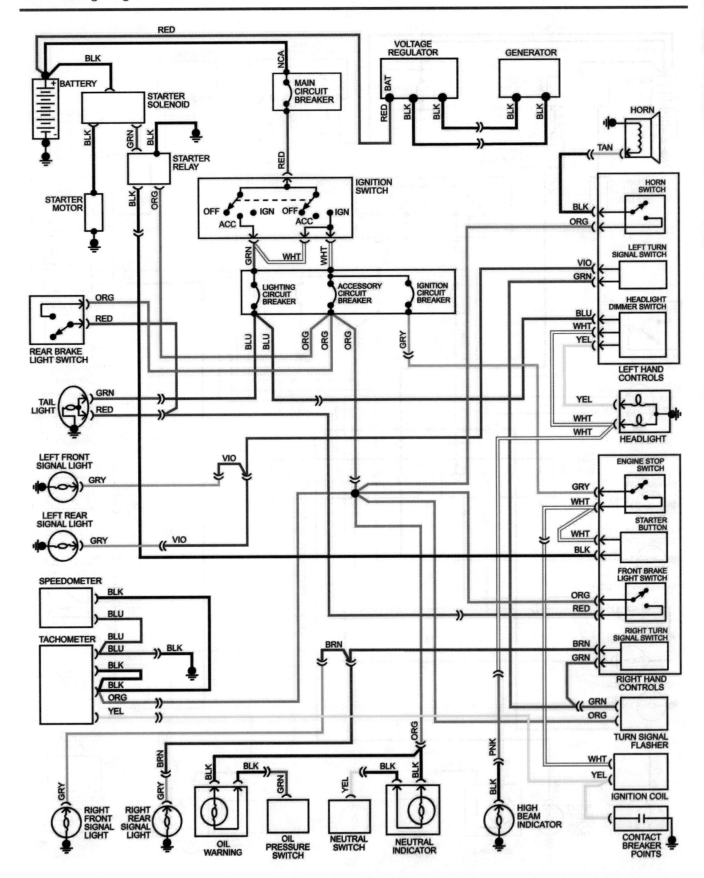

1975 through early 1978 FX models - typical

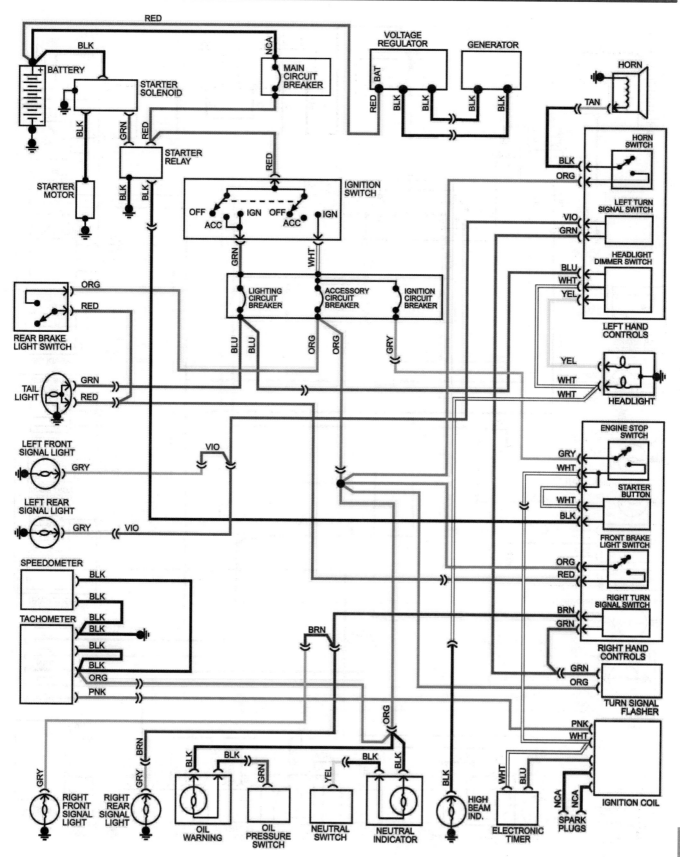

Late 1978 through 1979 FX models - typical

8

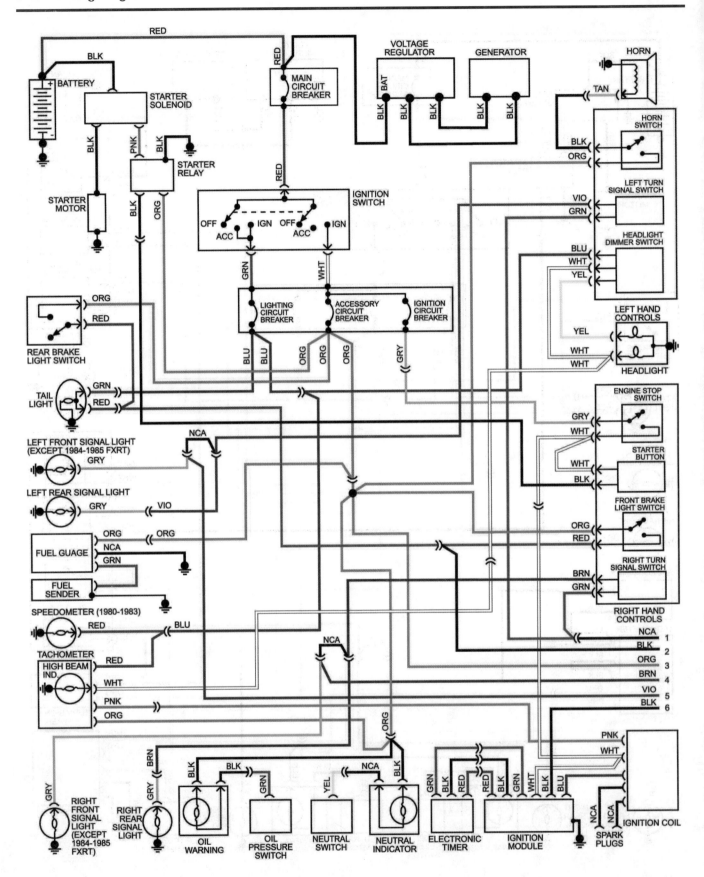

1980 through 1985 FXR models - typical (page 1 of 2)

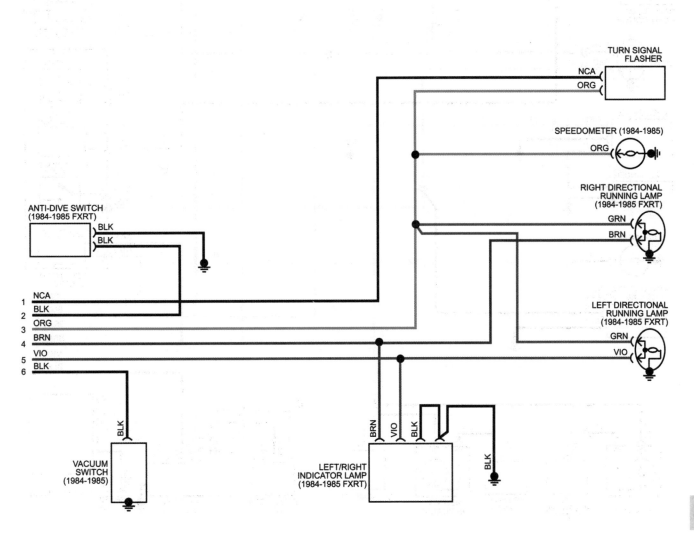

1980 through 1985 FXR models - typical (page 2 of 2)

8

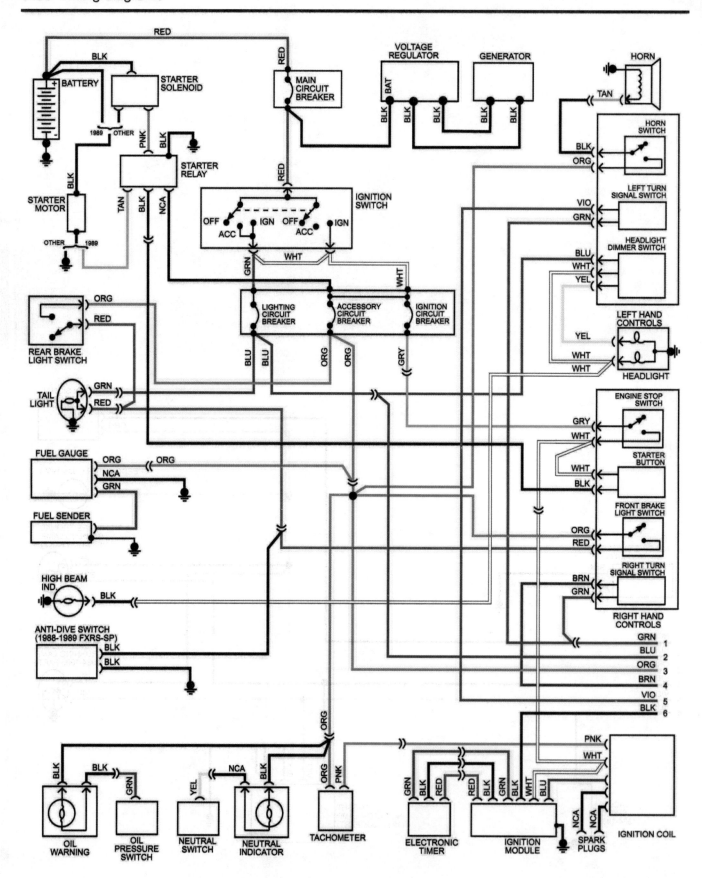

1986 through 1989 FXR models - typical (page 1 of 2)

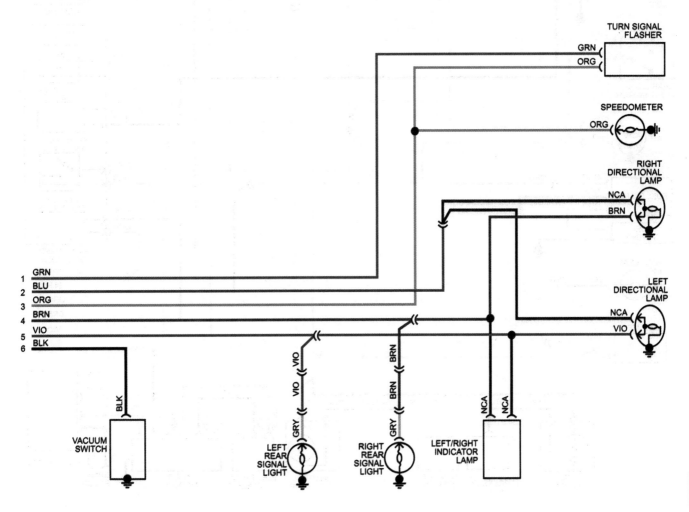

1986 through 1989 FXR models - typical (page 2 of 2)

8

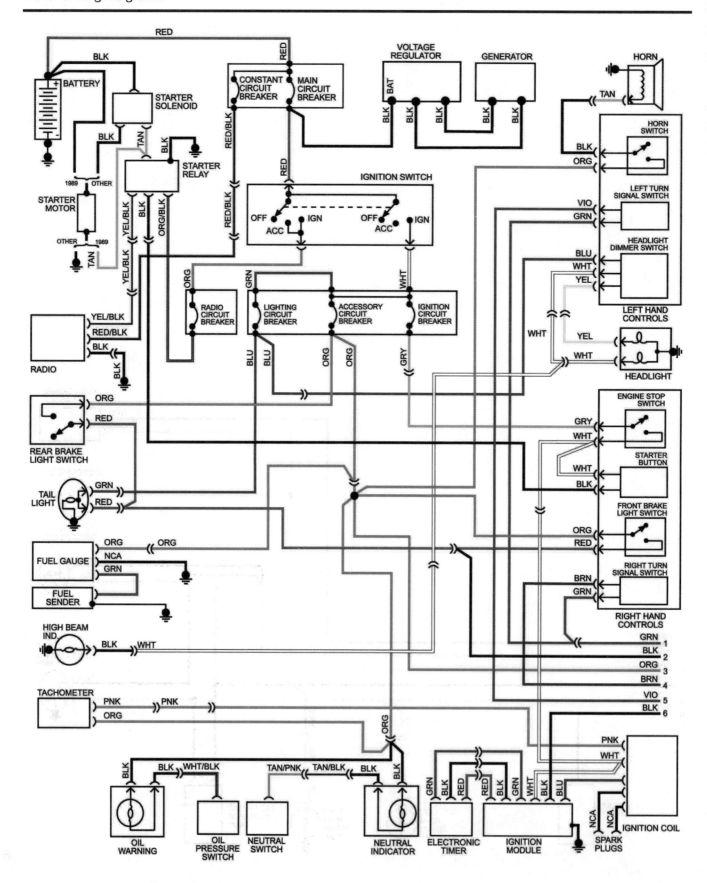

1986 through 1989 FXRT, 1986 FXRD - typical (page 1 of 2)

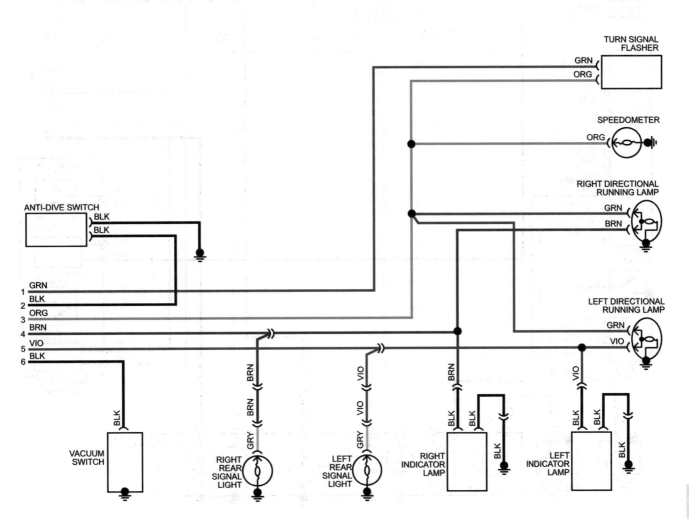

1986 through 1989 FXRT, 1986 FXRD - typical (page 2 of 2)

8

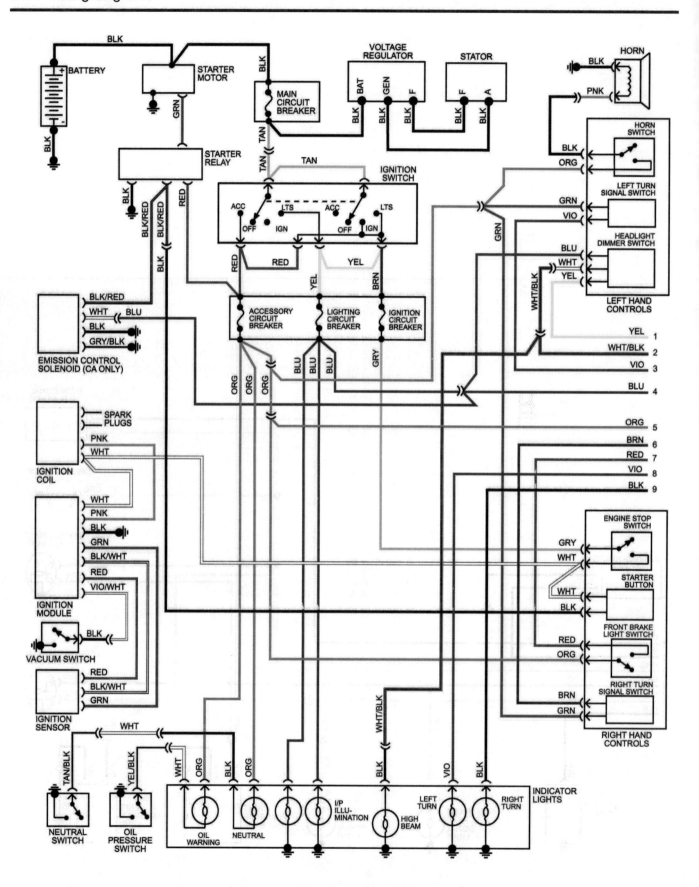

1990 through 1994 Softail - typical (page 1 of 2)

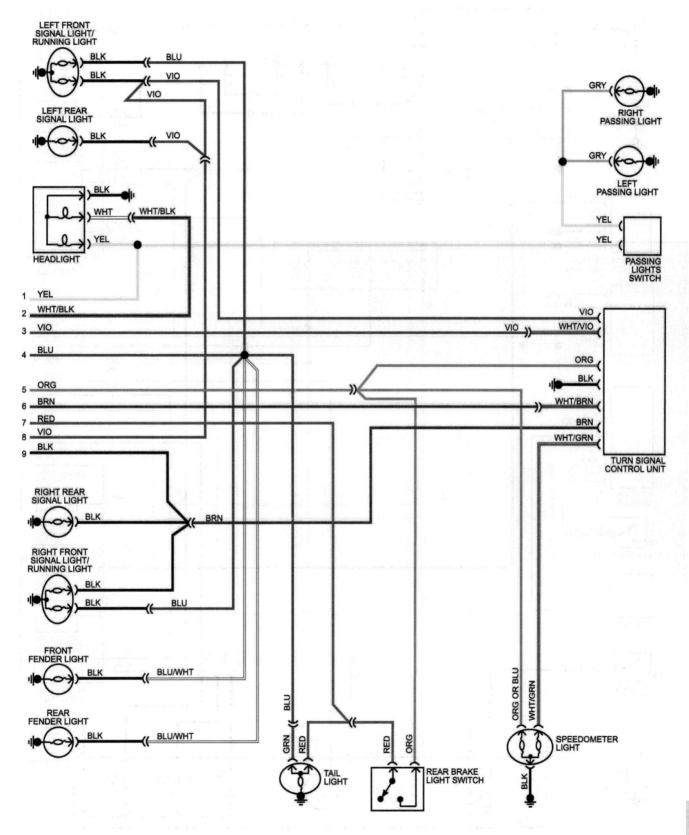

1990 through 1994 Softail - typical (page 2 of 2)

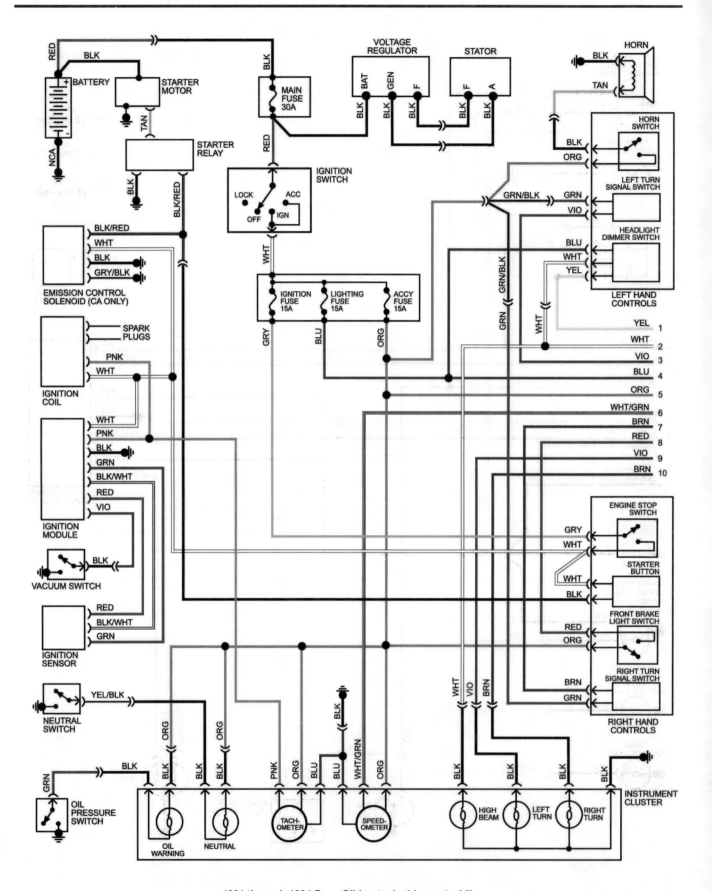

1991 through 1994 Dyna Glide - typical (page 1 of 2)

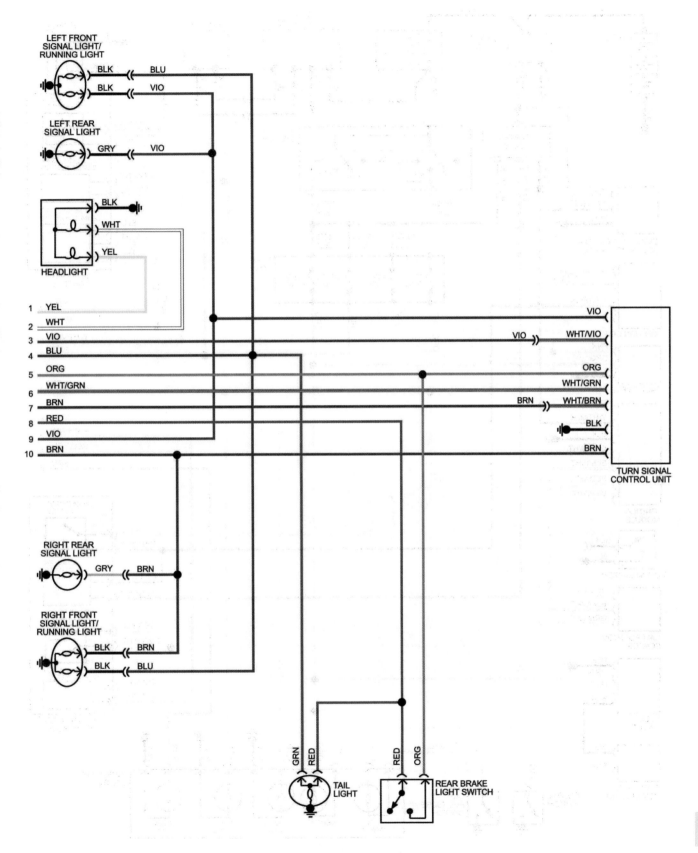

1991 through 1994 Dyna Glide - typical (page 2 of 2)

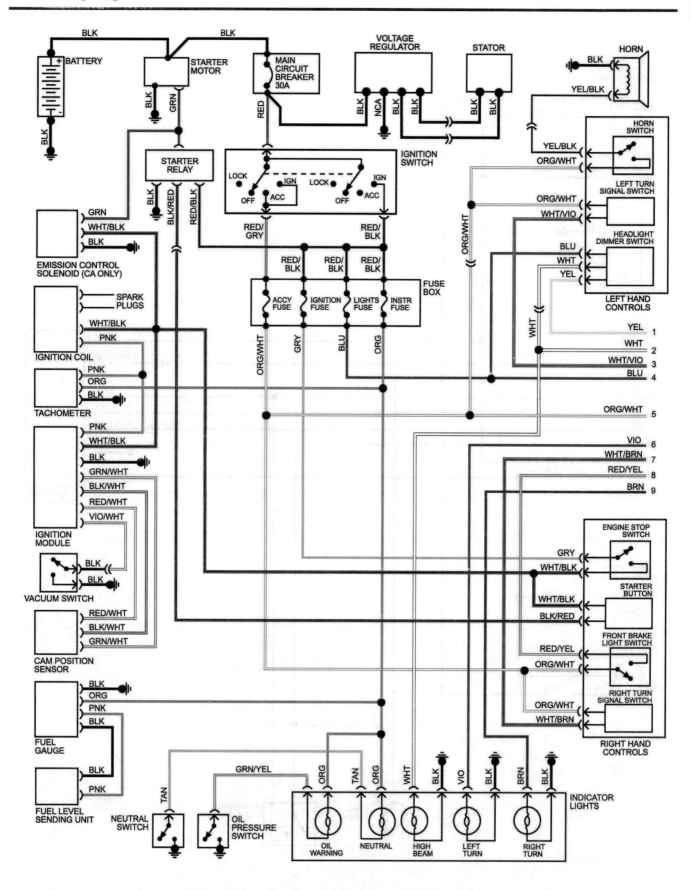

1995 and later Dyna Glide and Softail - typical (page 1 of 2)

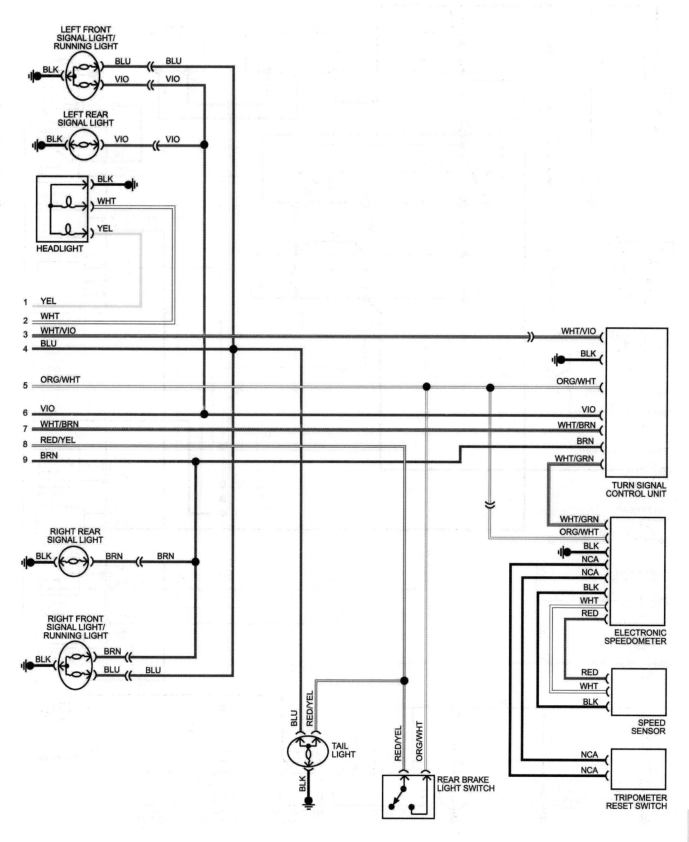

1995 and later Dyna Glide and Softail - typical (page 2 of 2)

8

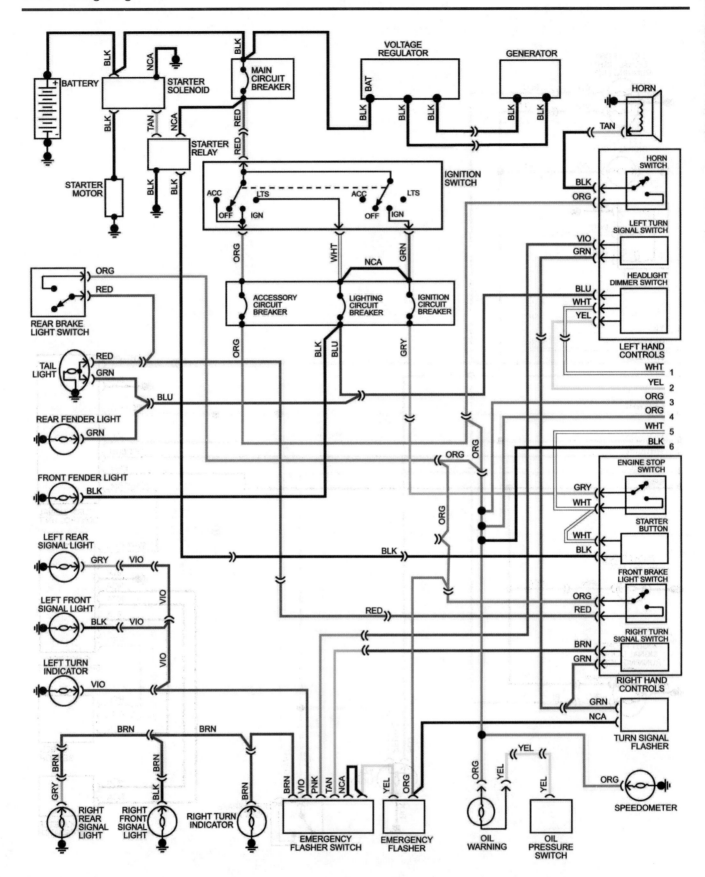

1980 through 1983 FLT models - typical (page 1 of 2)

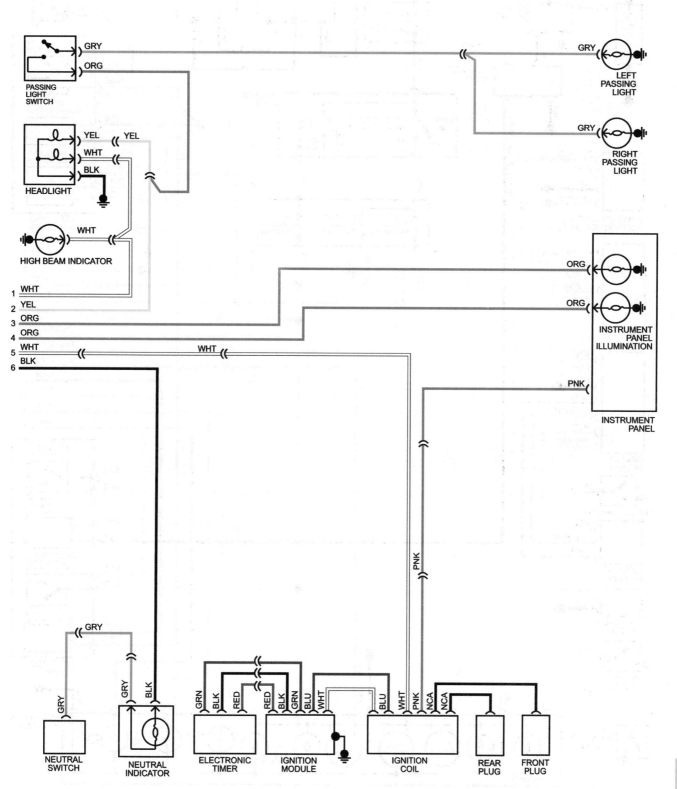

1980 through 1983 FLT models - typical (page 2 of 2)

8

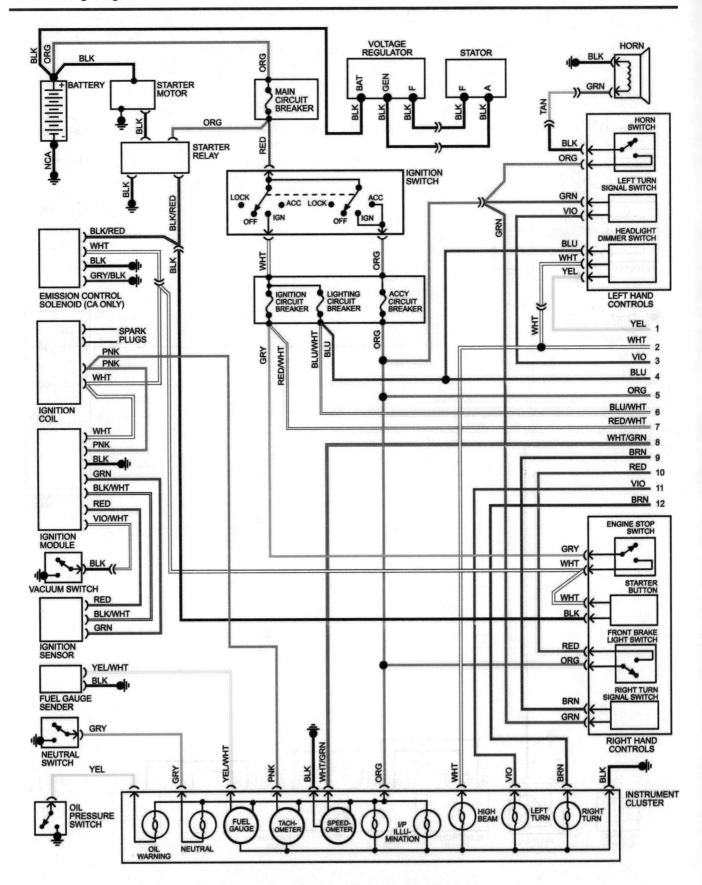

1988 through 1994 FLT models - typical (page 1 of 2)

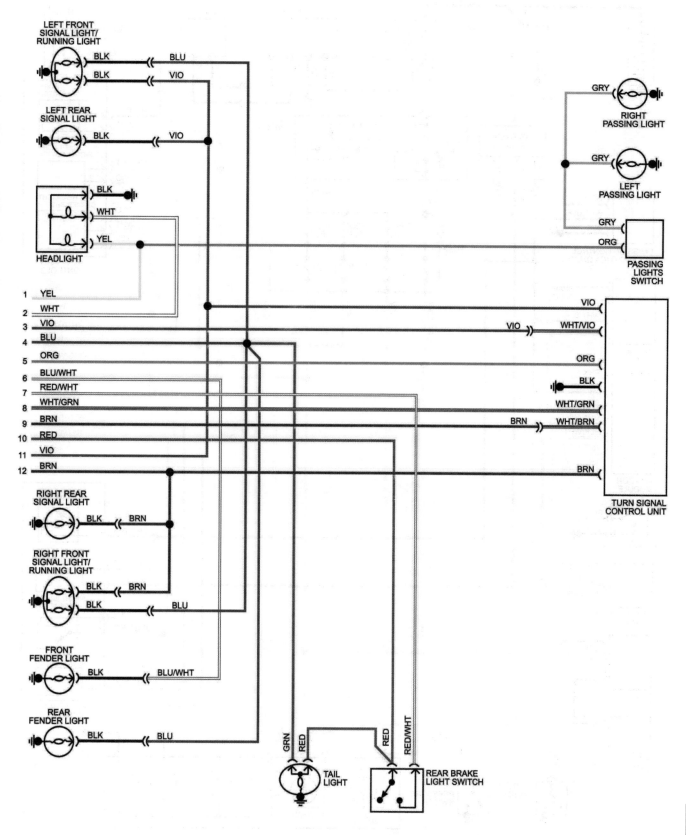

1988 through 1994 FLT models - typical (page 2 of 2)

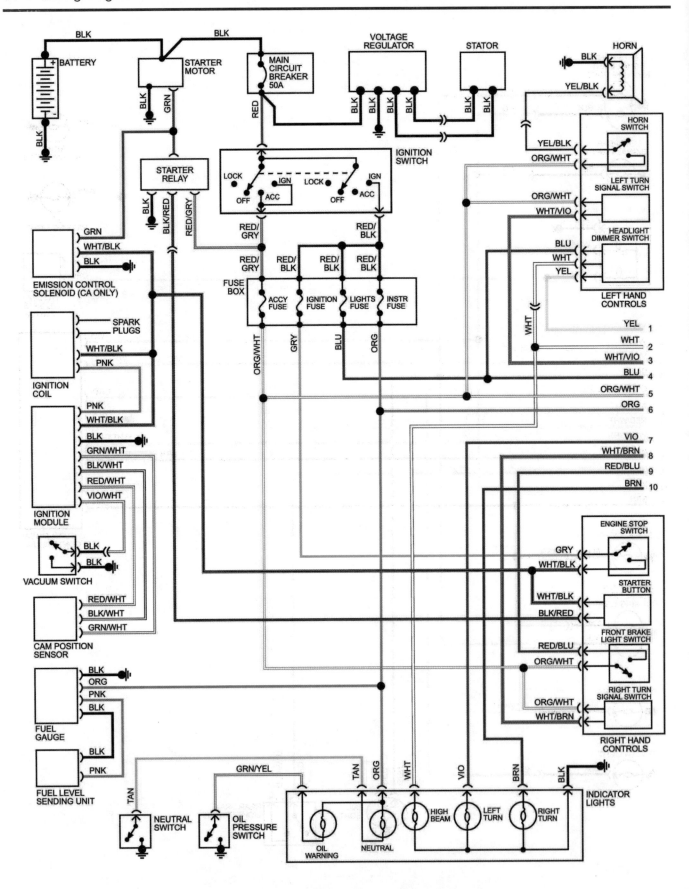

1995 and later carbureted FLT models - typical (page 1 of 2)

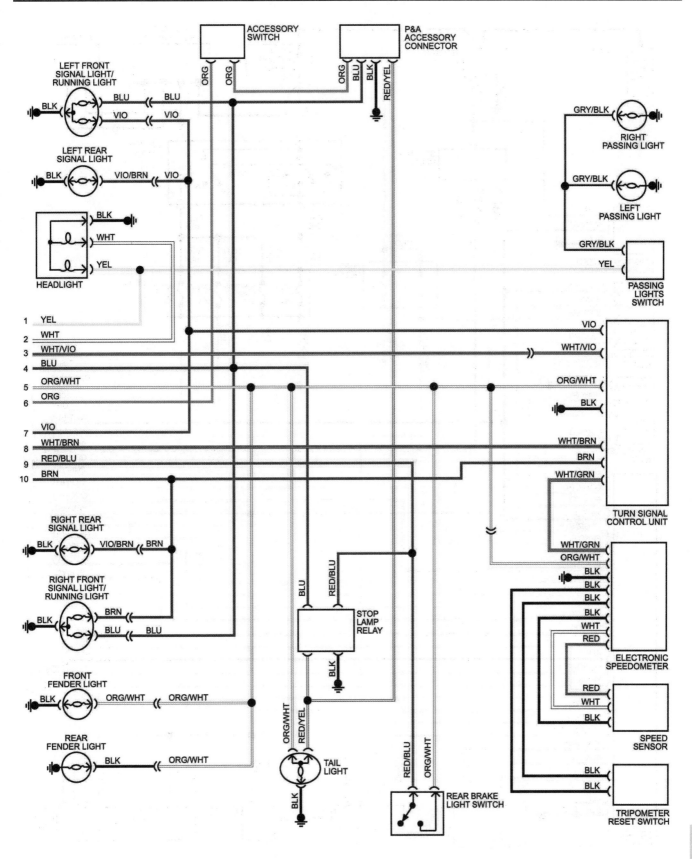

1995 and later carbureted FLT models - typical (page 2 of 2)

8

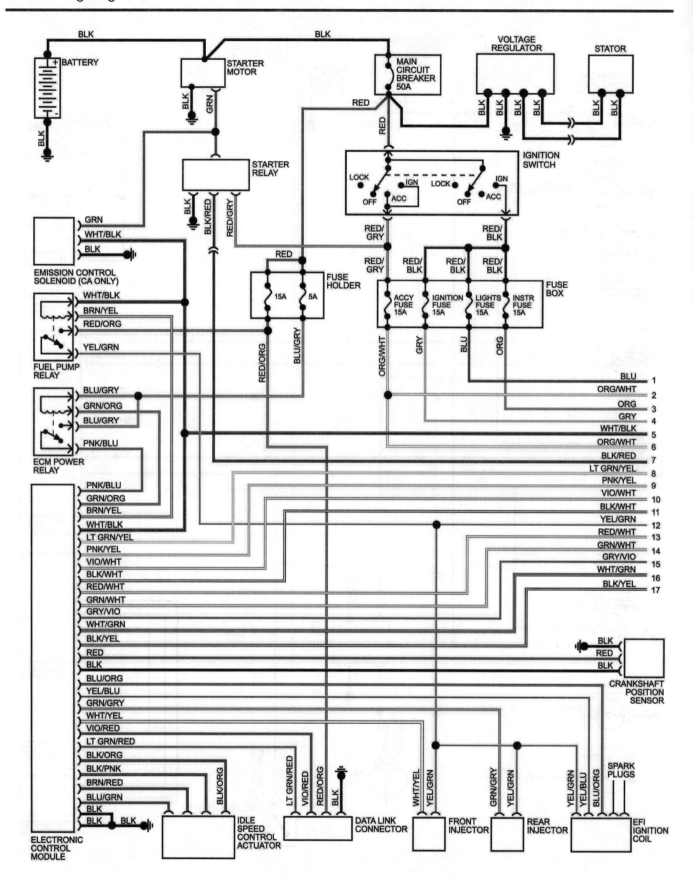

1995 and later fuel injected FLT models - typical (page 1 of 3)

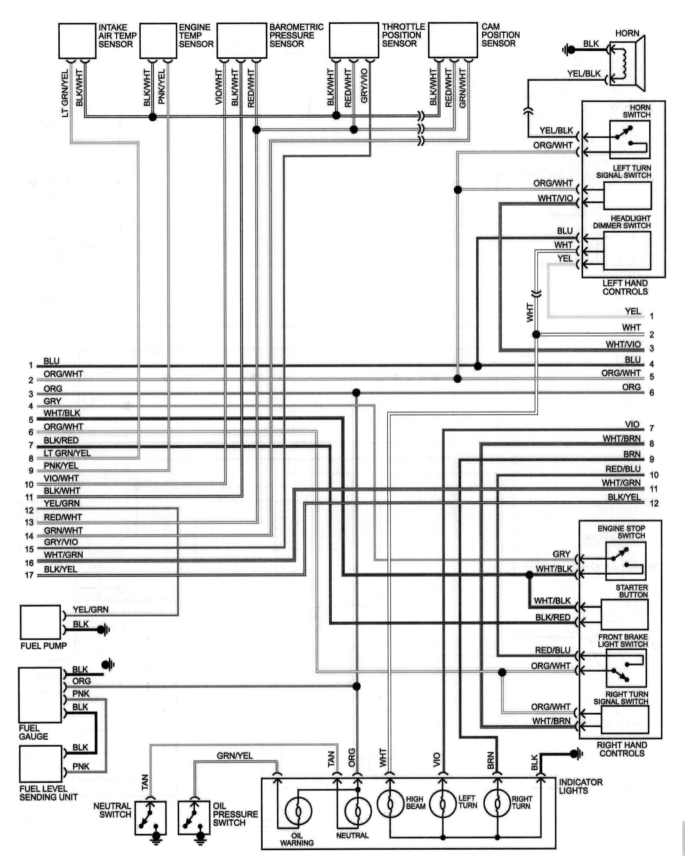

1995 and later fuel injected FLT models - typical (page 2 of 3)

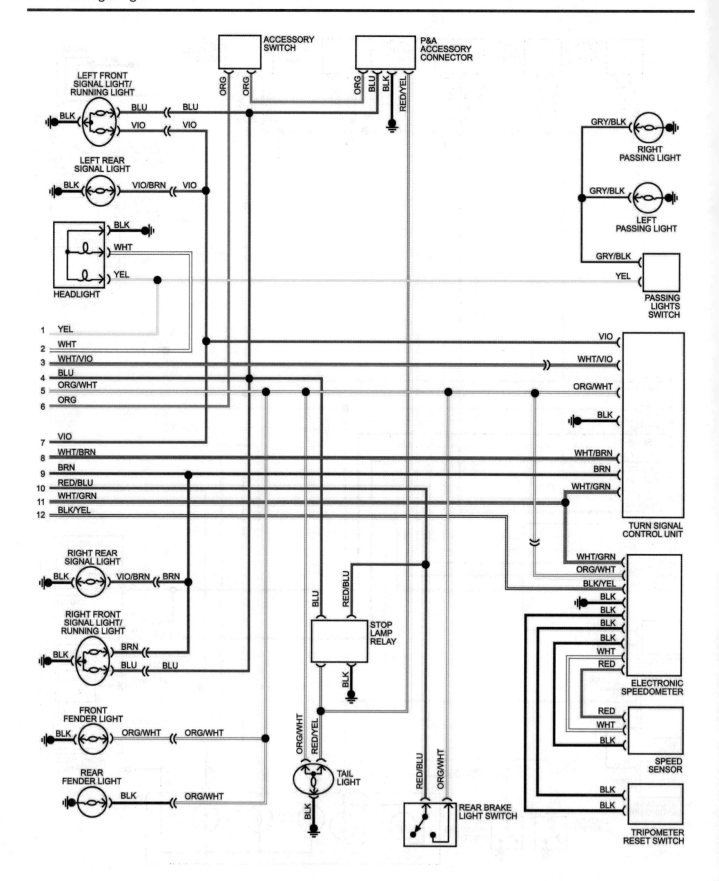

1995 and later fuel injected FLT models - typical (page 3 of 3)

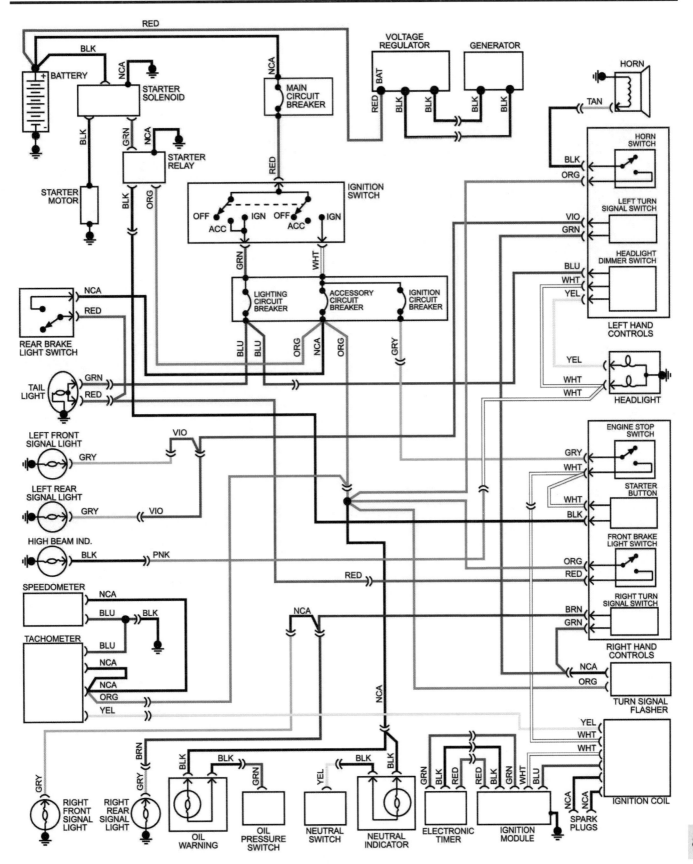

1980 through 1983 FX models - typical (except FXR)

8

Notes

Dimensions and weights

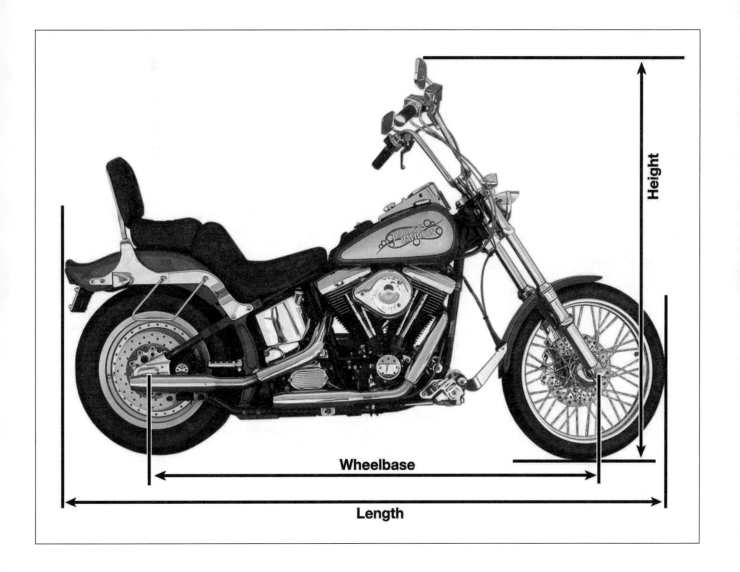

1970 through early 1978 FL

FL/FLH
Wheelbase . . . . 61.0 inches
Overall length . . . . 89.0 inches
Overall width . . . . 39.0 inches
Overall height . . . . 43.5 inches
Minimum ground clearance . . . . . . Not specified
Dry weight . . . . Not specified
Seat height . . . . Not specified

Mid-1978 through 1984 FL

FLH
Wheelbase . . . . 61.12 inches
Overall length . . . . 92.88 inches
Overall width . . . . 42.5 inches
Overall height . . . . 63.25 inches
Minimum ground clearance . . . . . . Not specified
Dry weight . . . . 722 lbs
Seat height . . . . Not specified

FLHS
Wheelbase . . . . 61.12 inches
Overall length . . . . 92.88 inches
Overall width . . . . 33.75 inches
Overall height . . . . 48.12 inches
Minimum ground clearance . . . . . . Not specified
Dry weight . . . . 626 lbs
Seat height . . . . Not specified

1970 through early 1978 FX

FX
Wheelbase . . . . 63.0 inches
Overall length . . . . 92.0 inches
Overall width . . . . 34.0 inches
Overall height . . . . 45.75 inches
Minimum ground clearance . . . . . . Not specified
Dry weight . . . . Not specified
Seat height . . . . Not specified

FXS
Wheelbase . . . . 63.5 inches
Overall length . . . . 92.0 inches
Overall width . . . . 29.0 inches
Overall height . . . . 41.75 inches
Minimum ground clearance . . . . . . Not specified
Dry weight . . . . Not specified
Seat height . . . . Not specified

Mid-1978 through 1984 FX

FXB/FXSB
Wheelbase . . . . 63.5 inches
Overall length . . . . 92.0 inches
Overall width . . . . 29.0 inches
Overall height . . . . 41.75 inches
Minimum ground clearance . . . . . . Not specified
Dry weight . . . . 572 lbs
Seat height . . . . Not specified

FXE/FXEF
Wheelbase . . . . 63.0 inches
Overall length . . . . 91.5 inches
Overall width . . . . 33.75 inches
Overall height . . . . 45.75 inches
Minimum ground clearance . . . . . . Not specified
Dry weight . . . . 572 lbs
Seat height . . . . Not specified

FXS
Wheelbase . . . . 63.5 inches
Overall length . . . . 92.0 inches
Overall width . . . . 29.0 inches
Overall height . . . . 41.75 inches
Minimum ground clearance . . . . . . Not specified
Dry weight . . . . 572 lbs
Seat height . . . . Not specified

FXST
Wheelbase . . . . 66.3 inches
Overall length . . . . 93.0 inches
Overall width . . . . 27.5 inches
Overall height . . . . 47.0 inches
Minimum ground clearance . . . . . . Not specified
Dry weight . . . . 612 lbs
Seat height . . . . Not specified

FXWG
Wheelbase . . . . 65.0 inches
Overall length . . . . 93.0 inches
Overall width . . . . 27.5 inches
Overall height . . . . 47.00 inches
Minimum ground clearance . . . . . . Not specified
Dry weight . . . . 572 lbs
Seat height . . . . Not specified

1984 and 1985 FLT

FLHT/C
Wheelbase . . . . 62.9 inches
Overall length . . . . 94.2 inches
Overall width . . . . 37.0 inches
Overall height . . . . 60.5 inches
Minimum ground clearance . . . . 5.1 inches
Dry weight . . . . 712 lbs
Seat height . . . . 28.0 inches

FLT/C
Wheelbase . . . . 62.9 inches
Overall length . . . . 94.2 inches
Overall width . . . . 37.0 inches
Overall height . . . . 59.0 inches
Minimum ground clearance . . . . 5.1 inches
Dry weight . . . . 712 lbs
Seat height . . . . 28.1 inches

1986 through 1990 FLT

FLTC
Wheelbase . . . . 62.94 inches
Overall length . . . . 94.25 inches
Overall width . . . . 37.0 inches

Overall height . . . . 58.75 inches
Minimum ground clearance . . . . 5.12 inches
Dry weight . . . . 741 lbs
Seat height . . . . 29.6 inches

FLHS, FLHT/C
Wheelbase . . . . 62.94 inches
Overall length . . . . 94.25 inches
Overall width . . . . 39.0 inches
Overall height . . . . 61.0 inches
Minimum ground clearance . . . . 5.12 inches
Dry weight . . . . 722 lbs
Seat height . . . . 28.0 inches

1991 and 1992 FLT

FLTC
Wheelbase . . . . 62.94 inches
Overall length . . . . 94.25 inches
Overall width . . . . 37.0 inches
Overall height . . . . 58.75 inches
Minimum ground clearance . . . . 5.12 inches
Dry weight . . . . 741 lbs
Seat height . . . . 29.6 inches

FLHT/C, FLHS
Wheelbase . . . . 62.94 inches
Overall length . . . . 94.25 inches
Overall width . . . . 39.0 inches
Overall height . . . . 61.0 inches
Minimum ground clearance . . . . 5.12 inches
Dry weight . . . . 722 lbs
Seat height . . . . 28.0 inches

1993 and 1994 FLT

FLTC
Wheelbase . . . . 62.94 inches
Overall length . . . . 94.25 inches
Overall width . . . . 37.0 inches
Overall height . . . . 58.75 inches
Minimum ground clearance . . . . 5.12 inches
Dry weight . . . . 741 lbs
Seat height . . . . 29.62 inches

FLHS
Wheelbase . . . . 62.94 inches
Overall length . . . . 94.25 inches
Overall width . . . . 39.0 inches
Overall height . . . . 61.0 inches
Minimum ground clearance . . . . 5.12 inches
Dry weight . . . . 692 lbs
Seat height . . . . 27.0 inches

FLHT/C, FLHTC/U
Wheelbase . . . . 62.94 inches
Overall length . . . . 94.25 inches
Overall width . . . . 39.0 inches
Overall height . . . . 61.0 inches
Minimum ground clearance . . . . 5.12 inches
Dry weight . . . . 765 lbs
Seat height . . . . 28.0 inches

1995 and 1996 FLT

FLHR
Wheelbase . . . . 63.5 inches
Overall length . . . . 94.25 inches
Overall width . . . . 34.45 inches
Overall height . . . . 55.06 inches
Minimum ground clearance . . . . 5.12 inches
Dry weight . . . . 692 lbs
Seat height . . . . 28.2 inches

FLTC/U
Wheelbase . . . . 62.68 inches
Overall length . . . . 94.25 inches
Overall width . . . . 37.0 inches
Overall height . . . . 58.75 inches
Minimum ground clearance . . . . 5.12 inches
Dry weight . . . . 765 lbs
Seat height . . . . 28.5 inches

FLHT/C/U
Wheelbase . . . . 62.68 inches
Overall length . . . . 94.25 inches
Overall width . . . . 39.0 inches
Overall height . . . . 61.0 inches
Minimum ground clearance . . . . 5.12 inches
Dry weight
  FLHT . . . . 711 lbs
  FLHT/U . . . . 741 lbs
  FLHT/C/U . . . . 765 lbs
Seat height . . . . 28.0 inches

1997 FLT

FLHR
Wheelbase . . . . 63.5 inches
Overall length . . . . 94.25 inches
Overall width . . . . 34.45 inches
Overall height . . . . 55.06 inches
Minimum ground clearance . . . . 5.12 inches
Dry weight . . . . 730 lbs
Seat height . . . . 27.25 inches

FLHTC/U
Wheelbase . . . . 63.5 inches
Overall length . . . . 94.25 inches
Overall width . . . . 39.0 inches
Overall height . . . . 61.0 inches
Minimum ground clearance . . . . 5.12 inches
Dry weight
  FLHT . . . . 742 lbs
  FLHT/U . . . . 760 lbs
  FLHT/C/U . . . . 785 lbs
Seat height . . . . 27.25 inches

1998 FLT

FLHR/C
Wheelbase . . . . 63.5 inches
Overall length . . . . 93.7 inches
Overall width . . . . 34.45 inches
Overall height . . . . 55.06 inches

Minimum ground clearance .... 5.12 inches
Dry weight
   FLHR .... 707 lbs
   FLHRC .... 694 lbs
Seat height
   FLHR .... 27.25 inches
   FLHRC .... 26.94 inches
FLHT/C/U
  Wheelbase .... 63.5 inches
  Overall length
   FLHT .... 93.7 inches
   FLHTC .... 97.5 inches
   FLHTCU .... 98.3 inches
  Overall width .... 39.0 inches;
  Overall height .... 61.0 inches
  Minimum ground clearance .... 5.12 inches
  Dry weight
   FLHT .... 742 lbs
   FLHT/U .... 760 lbs
   FLHT/C/U .... 772 lbs
  Seat height .... 27.25 inches

1984 and 1985 FXR
FXRT
  Wheelbase .... 64.7 inches
  Overall length .... 94.2 inches
  Overall width .... 34.5 inches
  Overall height .... 59.5 inches
  Minimum ground clearance .... 6.0 inches
  Dry weight .... 640 lbs
  Seat height .... 28.0 inches
FXRS
  Wheelbase .... 63.13 inches
  Overall length .... 91.65 inches
  Overall width .... 31.0 inches
  Overall height .... 48.0 inches
  Minimum ground clearance .... 5.25 inches
  Dry weight .... 575 lbs
  Seat height .... 28.1 inches

1986 through 1990 FXR
FXR/FXRS
  Wheelbase .... 63.13 inches
  Overall length .... 91.65 inches
  Overall width .... 31.0 inches
  Overall height .... 48.0 inches
  Minimum ground clearance .... 5.25 inches
  Dry weight .... 575 lbs
  Seat height .... 26.5 inches
FXLR
  Wheelbase .... 63.2 inches
  Overall length .... 91.6 inches
  Overall width .... 31.0 inches
  Overall height .... 48.0 inches
  Minimum ground clearance .... 5.25 inches
  Dry weight .... 575 lbs
  Seat height .... 27.5 inches

FXRD
  Wheelbase .... 64.7 inches
  Overall length .... 98.0 inches
  Overall width .... 34.5 inches
  Overall height .... 59.5 inches
  Minimum ground clearance .... 6.0 inches
  Dry weight .... 672 lbs
  Seat height .... 28.25 inches
FXRT
  Wheelbase .... 64.7 inches
  Overall length .... 94.2 inches
  Overall width .... 34.5 inches
  Overall height .... 59.5 inches
  Minimum ground clearance .... 6.0 inches
  Dry weight .... 640 lbs
  Seat height .... 27.75 inches
FXRS SE, SP
  Wheelbase .... 64.7 inches
  Overall length .... 93.2 inches
  Overall width .... 31.0 inches
  Overall height .... 50.0 inches
  Minimum ground clearance .... 6.0 inches
  Dry weight .... 585 lbs
  Seat height .... 27.5 inches

1991 and 1992 FXR
FXR, FXRS
  Wheelbase .... 63.13 inches
  Overall length .... 91.65 inches
  Overall width .... 31.0 inches
  Overall height .... 48.0 inches
  Minimum ground clearance .... 5.25 inches
  Dry weight .... 575 lbs
  Seat height .... 26.5 inches
FXLR
  Wheelbase .... 63.13 inches
  Overall length .... 91.6 inches
  Overall width .... 31.0 inches
  Overall height .... 48.0 inches
  Minimum ground clearance .... 5.25 inches
  Dry weight .... 575 lbs
  Seat height .... 26.5 inches
FXRS-SP, FXRS-CONV
  Wheelbase .... 64.7 inches
  Overall length .... 93.2 inches
  Overall width .... 31.0 inches
  Overall height .... 50.0 inches
  Minimum ground clearance .... 6.0 inches
  Dry weight .... 575 lbs
  Seat height .... 27.5 inches

1993 and 1994 FXR
FXR
  Wheelbase .... 63.13 inches
  Overall length .... 91.63 inches
  Overall width .... 31.0 inches
  Overall height .... 48.0 inches

Minimum ground clearance . . . . 5.25 inches
Dry weight . . . . 575 lbs
Seat height . . . . 26.0 inches

FXLR
Wheelbase . . . . 63.13 inches
Overall length . . . . 91.63 inches
Overall width . . . . 31.0 inches
Overall height . . . . 48.0 inches
Minimum ground clearance . . . . 5.25 inches
Dry weight . . . . 575 lbs
Seat height . . . . 26.5 inches

FXRS-SP, FXRS-CONV
Wheelbase . . . . 64.7 inches
Overall length . . . . 93.2 inches
Overall width . . . . 31.0 inches
Overall height . . . . 50.0 inches
Minimum ground clearance . . . . 6.0 inches
Dry weight . . . . 585 lbs
Seat height . . . . 27.5 inches

1985 through 1990 FX/Softail

FXEF
Wheelbase . . . . 63.0 inches
Overall length . . . . 91.5 inches
Overall width . . . . 33.75 inches
Overall height . . . . 45.75 inches
Minimum ground clearance . . . . . . Not specified
Dry weight . . . . 572 lbs
Seat height . . . . Not specified

FXSB
Wheelbase . . . . 63.5 inches
Overall length . . . . 92.0 inches
Overall width . . . . 29.0 inches
Overall height . . . . 41.75 inches
Minimum ground clearance . . . . . . Not specified
Dry weight . . . . 572 lbs
Seat height . . . . Not specified

FXWG
Wheelbase . . . . 65.0 inches
Overall length . . . . 93.0 inches
Overall width . . . . 27.5 inches
Overall height . . . . 47.0 inches
Minimum ground clearance . . . . . . Not specified
Dry weight . . . . 572 lbs
Seat height . . . . Not specified

FXST/C
Wheelbase . . . . 66.3 inches
Overall length . . . . 94.3 inches
Overall width . . . . 29.0 inches
Overall height . . . . 47.0 inches
Minimum ground clearance . . . . . . Not specified
Dry weight . . . . 618 lbs
Seat height . . . . Not specified

FLST/F
Wheelbase . . . . 62.5 inches
Overall length . . . . 93.8 inches

Overall width . . . . 38.0 inches
Overall height . . . . 49.0 inches
Minimum ground clearance . . . . . . Not specified
Dry weight . . . . 650 lbs
Seat height . . . . Not specified

FLSTC
Wheelbase . . . . 62.5 inches
Overall length . . . . 93.8 inches
Overall width . . . . 38.0 inches
Overall height . . . . 59.4 inches
Minimum ground clearance . . . . . . Not specified
Dry weight . . . . 710 lbs
Seat height . . . . Not specified

FXSTS
Wheelbase . . . . 66.3 inches
Overall length . . . . 94.3 inches
Overall width . . . . 29.0 inches
Overall height . . . . 47.0 inches
Minimum ground clearance . . . . . . Not specified
Dry weight . . . . 625 lbs
Seat height . . . . Not specified

1991 and 1992 Softail

FLSTC
Wheelbase . . . . 62.5 inches
Overall length . . . . 93.8 inches
Overall width . . . . 38.0 inches
Overall height . . . . 59.4 inches
Minimum ground clearance . . . . . . Not specified
Dry weight . . . . 710 lbs
Seat height . . . . Not specified

FLSTF
Wheelbase . . . . 62.5 inches
Overall length . . . . 93.8 inches
Overall width . . . . 38.0 inches
Overall height . . . . 49.0 inches
Minimum ground clearance . . . . . . Not specified
Dry weight . . . . 650 lbs
Seat height . . . . Not specified

FXSTC
Wheelbase . . . . 66.3 inches
Overall length . . . . 94.3 inches
Overall width . . . . 29.0 inches
Overall height . . . . 47.0 inches
Minimum ground clearance . . . . . . Not specified
Dry weight . . . . 618 lbs
Seat height . . . . Not specified

FXSTS
Wheelbase . . . . 66.3 inches
Overall length . . . . 94.3 inches
Overall width . . . . 29.0 inches
Overall height . . . . 47.0 inches
Minimum ground clearance . . . . . . Not specified
Dry weight . . . . 625 lbs
Seat height . . . . Not specified

1993 through 1995 Softail

FLSTC
Wheelbase . . . . 63.9 inches
Overall length . . . . 94.02 inches
Overall width . . . . 38.0 inches
Overall height . . . . 59.4 inches
Minimum ground clearance . . . . . . Not specified
Dry weight . . . . 710 lbs
Seat height . . . . Not specified

FLSTF/N
Wheelbase . . . . 63.89 inches
Overall length . . . . 93.85 inches
Overall width . . . . 38.0 inches
Overall height . . . . 49.0 inches
Minimum ground clearance . . . . . . Not specified
Dry weight . . . . 710 lbs
Seat height . . . . Not specified

FXSTC
Wheelbase . . . . 66.5 inches
Overall length . . . . 94.92 inches
Overall width . . . . 29.0 inches
Overall height . . . . 47.0 inches
Minimum ground clearance . . . . . . Not specified
Dry weight . . . . 618 lbs
Seat height . . . . Not specified

FXSTS/SB
Wheelbase . . . . 64.41 inches
Overall length . . . . 95.52 inches
Overall width . . . . 29.0 inches
Overall height . . . . 47.0 inches
Minimum ground clearance . . . . . . Not specified
Dry weight . . . . 625 lbs
Seat height . . . . Not specified

1996 Softail

FLSTC
Wheelbase . . . . 63.9 inches
Overall length . . . . 94.02 inches
Overall width . . . . 38.0 inches
Overall height . . . . 59.4 inches
Minimum ground clearance . . . . . . Not specified
Dry weight . . . . 704 lbs
Seat height . . . . Not specified

FLSTF/N
Wheelbase . . . . 63.89 inches
Overall length . . . . 93.85 inches
Overall width . . . . 38.0 inches
Overall height . . . . 49.0 inches
Minimum ground clearance . . . . . . Not specified
Dry weight
    FLSTF . . . . 631 lbs
    FLSTN . . . . 638 lbs
Seat height . . . . Not specified

FXSTC
Wheelbase . . . . 66.5 inches
Overall length . . . . 94.92 inches
Overall width . . . . 29.0 inches

Overall height . . . . 47.0 inches
Minimum ground clearance . . . . . . Not specified
Dry weight . . . . 613 lbs
Seat height . . . . Not specified

FXSTS/SB
Wheelbase . . . . 64.41 inches
Overall length . . . . 95.52 inches
Overall width . . . . 29.0 inches
Overall height . . . . 47.0 inches
Minimum ground clearance . . . . . . Not specified
Dry weight
    FXSTS . . . . 625 lbs
    FXSTSB . . . . 620 lbs
Seat height . . . . Not specified

1997 through 1999 Softail

FLSTC
Wheelbase . . . . 63.9 inches
Overall length . . . . 94.0 inches
Overall width . . . . Not specified
Overall height . . . . 59.4 inches
Minimum ground clearance . . . . . . Not specified
Dry weight . . . . 704 lbs
Seat height . . . . 26.7 inches

FLSTF
Wheelbase . . . . 63.9 inches
Overall length . . . . 93.9 inches
Overall width . . . . Not specified
Overall height . . . . 48.0 inches
Minimum ground clearance . . . . . . Not specified
Dry weight . . . . 631 lbs
Seat height . . . . 26.5 inches

FLSTS
Wheelbase . . . . 63.1 inches
Overall length . . . . 94.0 inches
Overall width . . . . Not specified
Overall height . . . . 44.0 inches
Minimum ground clearance . . . . . . Not specified
Dry weight . . . . 690 lbs
Seat height . . . . 25.8 inches

FXST
Wheelbase . . . . 66.5 inches
Overall length . . . . 94.92 inches
Overall width . . . . Not specified
Overall height . . . . 47.5 inches
Minimum ground clearance . . . . . . Not specified
Dry weight . . . . 596 lbs
Seat height . . . . 26.16 inches

FXSTB
Wheelbase . . . . 66.5 inches
Overall length . . . . 94.92 inches
Overall width . . . . Not specified
Overall height . . . . 45.7 inches
Minimum ground clearance . . . . . . Not specified
Dry weight . . . . 606 lbs
Seat height . . . . 25.35 inches

FXSTC
- Wheelbase .... 66.5 inches
- Overall length .... 94.92 inches
- Overall width .... Not specified
- Overall height .... 47.0 inches
- Minimum ground clearance ...... Not specified
- Dry weight .... 613 lbs
- Seat height .... 26.7 inches

FXSTS/SB
- Wheelbase .... 64.4 inches
- Overall length .... 95.52 inches
- Overall width .... Not specified
- Overall height .... 47.0 inches
- Minimum ground clearance ...... Not specified
- Dry weight
  - FXSTS .... 625 lbs
  - FXSTSB .... 620 lbs
- Seat height
  - FXSTS .... 26.1 inches
  - FXSTSB .... 25.7 inches

1991 and 1992 Dyna Glide

All models
- Wheelbase .... 65.5 inches
- Overall length .... 94.0 inches
- Overall width .... 28.5 inches
- Overall height .... 47.5 inches
- Minimum ground clearance ...... 5.62 inches
- Dry weight .... 598 lbs
- Seat height .... 26.62 inches

1993 and 1994 Dyna Glide

FXDL
- Wheelbase .... 66.1 inches
- Overall length .... 94.0 inches
- Overall width .... 28.5 inches
- Overall height .... 47.5 inches
- Minimum ground clearance ...... 5.62 inches
- Dry weight .... 598 lbs
- Seat height .... 26.62 inches

FXDWG
- Wheelbase .... 65.6 inches
- Overall length .... 94.0 inches
- Overall width .... 28.5 inches
- Overall height .... 47.5 inches
- Minimum ground clearance ...... 5.62 inches
- Dry weight .... 598 lbs
- Seat height .... 26.60 inches

1995 and 1996 Dyna Glide

FXD
- Wheelbase .... 62.5 inches
- Overall length .... 91.0 inches
- Overall width .... 28.5 inches
- Overall height .... 47.5 inches
- Minimum ground clearance ...... Not specified
- Dry weight .... 593 lbs
- Seat height .... 27.0 inches

FXDL
- Wheelbase .... 65.6 inches
- Overall length .... 94.0 inches
- Overall width .... 28.5 inches
- Overall height .... 47.5 inches
- Minimum ground clearance ...... Not specified
- Dry weight .... 598 lbs
- Seat height .... 27.0 inches

FXDS-CONV
- Wheelbase .... 63.88 inches
- Overall length .... 92.88 inches
- Overall width .... 28.5 inches
- Overall height .... 47.5 inches
- Minimum ground clearance ...... Not specified
- Dry weight .... 621 lbs
- Seat height .... 28.75 inches

FXDWG
- Wheelbase .... 66.1 inches
- Overall length .... 94.5 inches
- Overall width .... 31.7 inches
- Overall height .... 47.5 inches
- Minimum ground clearance ...... Not specified
- Dry weight .... 598 lbs
- Seat height .... 27.80 inches

1997 and 1998 Dyna Glide

FXD
- Wheelbase .... 62.5 inches
- Overall length .... 91.0 inches
- Overall width .... Not specified
- Overall height .... 47.5 inches
- Minimum ground clearance ...... Not specified
- Dry weight .... 593 lbs
- Seat height .... 26.5 inches

FXDL
- Wheelbase .... 65.5 inches
- Overall length .... 94.0 inches
- Overall width .... Not specified
- Overall height .... 47.5 inches
- Minimum ground clearance ...... Not specified
- Dry weight .... 598 lbs
- Seat height .... 26.5 inches

FXDS-CONV
- Wheelbase .... 63.88 inches
- Overall length .... 92.88 inches
- Overall width .... Not specified
- Overall height .... 59.25 inches
- Minimum ground clearance ...... Not specified
- Dry weight .... 621 lbs
- Seat height .... 27.75 inches

FXDWG
- Wheelbase .... 66.1 inches
- Overall length .... 94.5 inches
- Overall width .... Not specified
- Overall height .... 47.5 inches
- Minimum ground clearance ...... Not specified
- Dry weight .... 598 lbs
- Seat height .... 26.75 inches

Buying tools

A good set of tools is a fundamental requirement for servicing and repairing a motorcycle. Although there will be an initial expense in building up enough tools for servicing, this will soon be offset by the savings made by doing the job yourself. As experience and confidence grow, additional tools can be added to enable the repair and overhaul of the motorcycle. Many of the special tools are expensive and not often used so it may be preferable to rent them, or for a group of friends or motorcycle club to join in the purchase.

As a rule, it is better to buy more expensive, good quality tools. Cheaper tools are likely to wear out faster and need to be replaced more often, nullifying the original savings.

> **Warning: To avoid the risk of a poor quality tool breaking in use, causing injury or damage to the component being worked on, always aim to purchase tools which meet the relevant national safety standards.**

The following lists of tools do not represent the manufacturer's service tools, but serve as a guide to help the owner decide which tools are needed for this level of work. In addition, items such as an electric drill, hacksaw, files, soldering iron and a workbench equipped with a vise, may be needed. Although not classed as tools, a selection of bolts, screws, nuts, washers and pieces of tubing always come in useful.

For more information about tools, refer to the Haynes *Motorcycle Workshop Practice Techbook* (Bk. No. 3470).

Manufacturer's service tools

Inevitably certain tasks require the use of a service tool. Where possible an alternative tool or method of approach is recommended, but sometimes there is no option if personal injury or damage to the component is to be avoided. Where required, service tools are referred to in the relevant procedure.

Service tools can be purchased from JIMS Tools (www.JIMUSA.com) or Motion Pro (www.MotionPro.com). Some of the commonly-used tools, such as rotor pullers, are available in aftermarket form from mail-order motorcycle tool and accessory suppliers.

Maintenance and minor repair tools

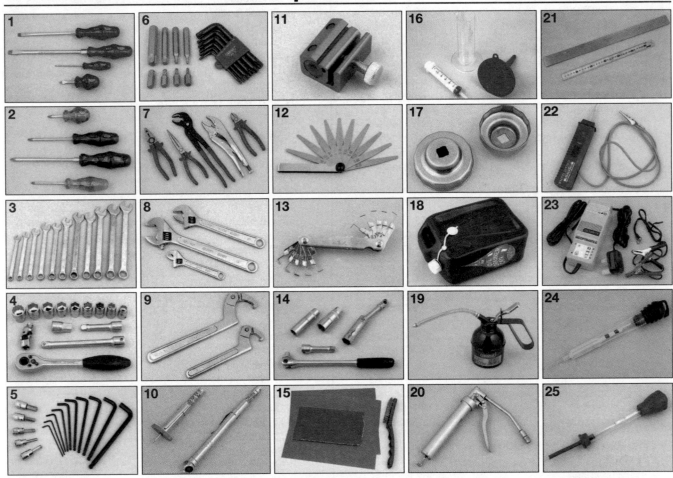

1. Set of flat-bladed screwdrivers
2. Set of Phillips head screwdrivers
3. Combination open-end and box wrenches
4. Socket set (3/8 inch or 1/2 inch drive)
5. Set of Allen keys or bits

6. Set of Torx keys or bits
7. Pliers, cutters and self-locking grips (vise grips)
8. Adjustable wrenches
9. C-spanners
10. Tread depth gauge and tire pressure gauge

11. Cable oiler clamp
12. Feeler gauges
13. Spark plug gap measuring tool
14. Spark plug wrench or deep plug sockets
15. Wire brush and emery paper

16. Calibrated syringe, measuring cup and funnel
17. Oil filter adapters
18. Oil drainer can or tray
19. Pump type oil can
20. Grease gun

21. Straight-edge and steel ruler
22. Continuity tester
23. Battery charger
24. Hydrometer (for battery specific gravity check)
25. Anti-freeze tester (for liquid-cooled engines)

Repair and overhaul tools

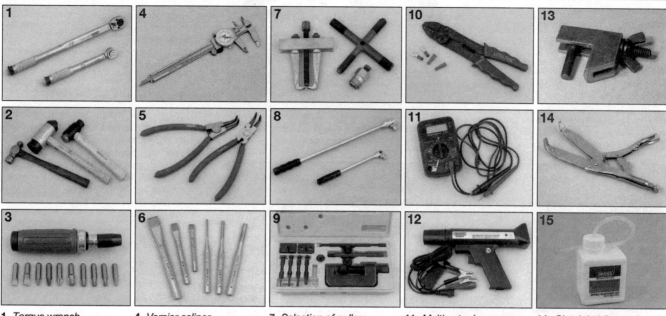

1 Torque wrench
(small and mid-ranges)
2 Conventional, plastic or
soft-faced hammers
3 Impact driver set

4 Vernier caliper
5 Snap-ring pliers (internal
and external, or
combination)
6 Set of cold chisels
and punches

7 Selection of pullers
8 Breaker bars
9 Chain breaking/
riveting tool set
10 Wire stripper and
crimper tool

11 Multimeter (measures
amps, volts and ohms)
12 Stroboscope (for
dynamic timing checks)
13 Hose clamp
(wingnut type shown)

14 Clutch holding tool
15 One-man brake/clutch
bleeder kit

Special tools

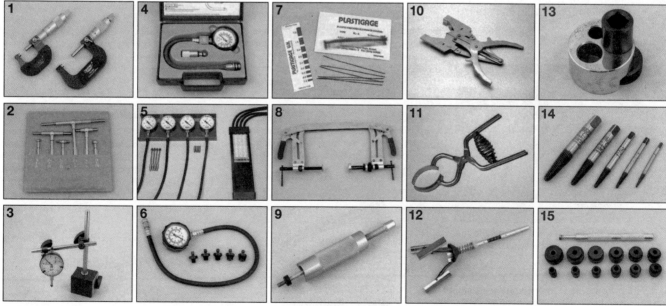

1 Micrometers
(external type)
2 Telescoping gauges
3 Dial gauge

4 Cylinder
compression gauge
5 Vacuum gauges (left) or
manometer (right)
6 Oil pressure gauge

7 Plastigage kit
8 Valve spring compressor
(4-stroke engines)
9 Piston pin drawbolt tool

10 Piston ring removal and
installation tool
11 Piston ring clamp
12 Cylinder bore hone
(stone type shown)

13 Stud extractor
14 Screw extractor set
15 Bearing driver set

1	**Workshop equipment and facilities**

The workbench

● Work is made much easier by raising the bike up on a ramp - components are much more accessible if raised to waist level. The hydraulic or pneumatic types seen in the dealer's workshop are a sound investment if you undertake a lot of repairs or overhauls **(see illustration 1.1)**.

1.1 Hydraulic motorcycle ramp

● If raised off ground level, the bike must be supported on the ramp to avoid it falling. Most ramps incorporate a front wheel locating clamp which can be adjusted to suit different diameter wheels. When tightening the clamp, take care not to mark the wheel rim or damage the tire - use wood blocks on each side to prevent this.
● Secure the bike to the ramp using tie-downs **(see illustration 1.2)**. If the bike has only a sidestand, and hence leans at a dangerous angle when raised, support the bike on an auxiliary stand.

1.2 Tie-downs are used around the passenger footrests to secure the bike

● Auxiliary (paddock) stands are widely available from mail order companies or motorcycle dealers and attach either to the wheel axle or swingarm pivot **(see illustration 1.3)**. If the motorcycle has a centerstand, you can support it under the crankcase to prevent it toppling while either wheel is removed **(see illustration 1.4)**.

1.3 This auxiliary stand attaches to the swingarm pivot

1.4 Always use a block of wood between the engine and jack head when supporting the engine in this way

Fumes and fire

● Refer to the Safety first! page at the beginning of the manual for full details. Make sure your workshop is equipped with a fire extinguisher suitable for fuel-related fires (Class B fire - flammable liquids) - it is not sufficient to have a water-filled extinguisher.
● Always ensure adequate ventilation is available. Unless an exhaust gas extraction system is available for use, ensure that the engine is run outside of the workshop.
● If working on the fuel system, make sure the workshop is ventilated to avoid a build-up of fumes. This applies equally to fume build-up when charging a battery. Do not smoke or allow anyone else to smoke in the workshop.

Fluids

● If you need to drain fuel from the tank, store it in an approved container marked as suitable for the storage of gasoline **(see illustration 1.5)**. Do not store fuel in glass jars or bottles.

1.5 Use an approved can only for storing gasoline

● Use proprietary engine degreasers or solvents which have a high flash-point, such as kerosene, for cleaning off oil, grease and dirt - never use gasoline for cleaning. Wear rubber gloves when handling solvent and engine degreaser. The fumes from certain solvents can be dangerous - always work in a well-ventilated area.

Dust, eye and hand protection

● Protect your lungs from inhalation of dust particles by wearing a filtering mask over the nose and mouth. Many frictional materials still contain asbestos which is dangerous to your health. Protect your eyes from spouts of liquid and sprung components by wearing a pair of protective goggles **(see illustration 1.6)**.

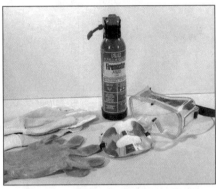

1.6 A fire extinguisher, goggles, mask and protective gloves should be at hand in the workshop

● Protect your hands from contact with solvents, fuel and oils by wearing rubber gloves. Alternatively apply a barrier cream to your hands before starting work. If handling hot components or fluids, wear suitable gloves to protect your hands from scalding and burns.

What to do with old fluids

● Old cleaning solvent, fuel, coolant and oils should not be poured down domestic drains or onto the ground. Package the fluid up in old oil containers, label it accordingly, and take it to a garage or disposal facility. Contact your local disposal company for location of such sites.

Note: It is illegal to dump oil down the drain. Check with your local auto parts store, disposal facility or environmental agency to see if they accept the oil for recycling.

2 Fasteners -
screws, bolts and nuts

Fastener types and applications

Bolts and screws

● Fastener head types are either of hexagonal, Torx or splined design, with internal and external versions of each type **(see illustrations 2.1 and 2.2)**; splined head fasteners are not in common use on motorcycles. The conventional slotted or Phillips head design is used for certain screws. Bolt or screw length is always measured from the underside of the head to the end of the item **(see illustration 2.11)**.

2.1 Internal hexagon/Allen (A), Torx (B) and splined (C) fasteners, with corresponding bits

2.2 External Torx (A), splined (B) and hexagon (C) fasteners, with corresponding sockets

● Certain fasteners on the motorcycle have a tensile marking on their heads, the higher the marking the stronger the fastener. High tensile fasteners generally carry a 10 or higher marking. Never replace a high tensile fastener with one of a lower tensile strength.

Washers **(see illustration 2.3)**

● Plain washers are used between a fastener head and a component to prevent damage to the component or to spread the load when torque is applied. Plain washers can also be used as spacers or shims in certain assemblies. Copper or aluminum plain washers are often used as sealing washers on drain plugs.

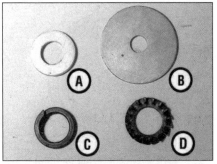

2.3 Plain washer (A), penny washer (B), spring washer (C) and serrated washer (D)

● The split-ring spring washer works by applying axial tension between the fastener head and component. If flattened, it is fatigued and must be replaced. If a plain (flat) washer is used on the fastener, position the spring washer between the fastener and the plain washer.

● Serrated star type washers dig into the fastener and component faces, preventing loosening. They are often used on electrical ground connections to the frame.

● Cone type washers (sometimes called Belleville) are conical and when tightened apply axial tension between the fastener head and component. They must be installed with the dished side against the component and often carry an OUTSIDE marking on their outer face. If flattened, they are fatigued and must be replaced.

● Tab washers are used to lock plain nuts or bolts on a shaft. A portion of the tab washer is bent up hard against one flat of the nut or bolt to prevent it loosening. Due to the tab washer being deformed in use, a new tab washer should be used every time it is removed.

● Wave washers are used to take up endfloat on a shaft. They provide light springing and prevent excessive side-to-side play of a component. Can be found on rocker arm shafts.

Nuts and cotter pins

● Conventional plain nuts are usually six-sided **(see illustration 2.4)**. They are sized by thread diameter and pitch. High tensile nuts carry a number on one end to denote their tensile strength.

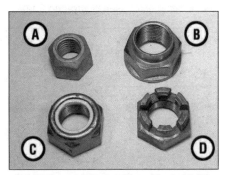

2.4 Plain nut (A), shouldered locknut (B), nylon insert nut (C) and castellated nut (D)

● Self-locking nuts either have a nylon insert, two spring metal tabs, or a shoulder which is staked into a groove in the shaft - their advantage over conventional plain nuts is a resistance to loosening due to vibration. The nylon insert type can be used a number of times, but must be replaced when the friction of the nylon insert is reduced, i.e. when the nut spins freely on the shaft. The spring tab type can be reused unless the tabs are damaged. The shouldered type must be replaced every time it is removed.

● Cotter pins are used to lock a castellated nut to a shaft or to prevent loosening of a plain nut. Common applications are wheel axles and brake torque arms. Because the cotter pin arms are deformed to lock around the nut a new cotter pin must always be used on installation - always use the correct size cotter pin which will fit snugly in the shaft hole. Make sure the cotter pin arms are correctly located around the nut **(see illustrations 2.5 and 2.6)**.

2.5 Bend cotter pin arms as shown (arrows) to secure a castellated nut

2.6 Bend cotter pin arms as shown to secure a plain nut

Caution: If the castellated nut slots do not align with the shaft hole after tightening to the torque setting, tighten the nut until the next slot aligns with the hole - never loosen the nut to align its slot.

● R-pins (shaped like the letter R), or slip pins as they are sometimes called, are sprung and can be reused if they are otherwise in good condition. Always install R-pins with their closed end facing forwards **(see illustration 2.7)**.

**2.7 Correct fitting of R-pin.
Arrow indicates forward direction**

Snap-rings (see illustration 2.8)

● Snap-rings are used to retain components on a shaft or in a housing and have corresponding external or internal ears to permit removal. Parallel-sided (machined) snap-rings can be installed either way round in their groove, whereas stamped snap-rings (which have a chamfered edge on one face) must be installed with the chamfer facing away from the direction of thrust load **(see illustration 2.9)**.

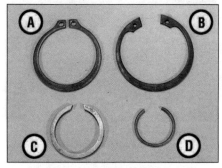

**2.8 External stamped snap-ring (A),
internal stamped snap-ring (B), machined
snap-ring (C) and wire snap-ring (D)**

● Always use snap-ring pliers to remove and install snap-rings; expand or compress them just enough to remove them. After installation, rotate the snap-ring in its groove to ensure it is securely seated. If installing a snap-ring on a splined shaft, always align its opening with a shaft channel to ensure the snap-ring ends are well supported and unlikely to catch **(see illustration 2.10)**.

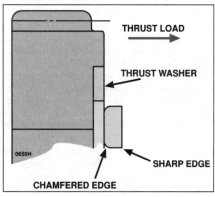

2.9 Correct fitting of a stamped snap-ring

THRUST LOAD

THRUST WASHER

SHARP EDGE

CHAMFERED EDGE

0650H

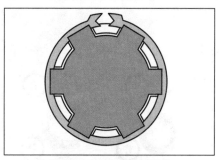

**2.10 Align snap-ring opening
with shaft channel**

● Snap-rings can wear due to the thrust of components and become loose in their grooves, with the subsequent danger of becoming dislodged in operation. For this reason, replacement is advised every time a snap-ring is disturbed.
● Wire snap-rings are commonly used as piston pin retaining clips. If a removal tang is provided, long-nosed pliers can be used to dislodge them, otherwise careful use of a small flat-bladed screwdriver is necessary. Wire snap-rings should be replaced every time they are disturbed.

Thread diameter and pitch

● Diameter of a male thread (screw, bolt or stud) is the outside diameter of the threaded portion **(see illustration 2.11)**. Most motorcycle manufacturers use the ISO (International Standards Organization) metric system expressed in millimeters. For example, M6 refers to a 6 mm diameter thread. Sizing is the same for nuts, except that the thread diameter is measured across the valleys of the nut.
● Pitch is the distance between the peaks of the thread **(see illustration 2.11)**. It is expressed in millimeters, thus a common bolt size may be expressed as 6.0 x 1.0 mm (6 mm thread diameter and 1 mm pitch). Generally pitch increases in proportion to thread diameter, although there are always exceptions.
● Thread diameter and pitch are related for conventional fastener applications and the accompanying table can be used as a guide. Additionally, the AF (Across Flats), wrench or socket size dimension of the bolt or nut **(see illustration 2.11)** is linked to thread and pitch specification. Thread pitch can be measured with a thread gauge **(see illustration 2.12)**.

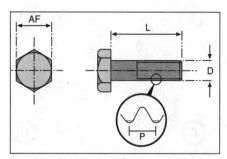

AF

L

D

P

**2.11 Fastener length (L), thread diameter
(D), thread pitch (P) and head size (AF)**

**2.12 Using a thread gauge
to measure pitch**

AF size	Thread diameter x pitch (mm)
8 mm	M5 x 0.8
8 mm	M6 x 1.0
10 mm	M6 x 1.0
12 mm	M8 x 1.25
14 mm	M10 x 1.25
17 mm	M12 x 1.25

● The threads of most fasteners are of the right-hand type, i.e. they are turned clockwise to tighten and counterclockwise to loosen. The reverse situation applies to left-hand thread fasteners, which are turned counterclockwise to tighten and clockwise to loosen. Left-hand threads are used where rotation of a component might loosen a conventional right-hand thread fastener.

Seized fasteners

● Corrosion of external fasteners due to water or reaction between two dissimilar metals can occur over a period of time. It will build up sooner in wet conditions or in countries where salt is used on the roads during the winter. If a fastener is severely corroded it is likely that normal methods of removal will fail and result in its head being ruined. When you attempt removal, the fastener thread should be heard to crack free and unscrew easily - if it doesn't, stop there before damaging something.
● A smart tap on the head of the fastener will often succeed in breaking free corrosion which has occurred in the threads **(see illustration 2.13)**.
● An aerosol penetrating fluid (such as WD-40) applied the night beforehand may work its way down into the thread and ease removal. Depending on the location, you may be able to make up a modeling-clay well around the fastener head and fill it with penetrating fluid.

**2.13 A sharp tap on the head of a fastener
will often break free a corroded thread**

● If you are working on an engine internal component, corrosion will most likely not be a problem due to the well lubricated environment. However, components can be very tight and an impact driver is a useful tool in freeing them **(see illustration 2.14)**.

2.14 Using an impact driver to free a fastener

● Where corrosion has occurred between dissimilar metals (e.g. steel and aluminum alloy), the application of heat to the fastener head will create a disproportionate expansion rate between the two metals and break the seizure caused by the corrosion. Whether heat can be applied depends on the location of the fastener - any surrounding components likely to be damaged must first be removed **(see illustration 2.15)**. Heat can be applied using a paint stripper heat gun or clothes iron, or by immersing the component in boiling water - wear protective gloves to prevent scalding or burns to the hands.

2.15 Using heat to free a seized fastener

● As a last resort, it is possible to use a hammer and cold chisel to work the fastener head unscrewed **(see illustration 2.16)**. This will damage the fastener, but more importantly extreme care must be taken not to damage the surrounding component.

Caution: Remember that the component being secured is generally of more value than the bolt, nut or screw - when the fastener is freed, do not unscrew it with force, instead work the fastener back and forth when resistance is felt to prevent thread damage.

2.16 Using a hammer and chisel to free a seized fastener

Broken fasteners and damaged heads

● If the shank of a broken bolt or screw is accessible you can grip it with self-locking grips. The knurled wheel type stud extractor tool or self-gripping stud puller tool is particularly useful for removing the long studs which screw into the cylinder mouth surface of the crankcase or bolts and screws from which the head has broken off **(see illustration 2.17)**. Studs can also be removed by locking two nuts together on the threaded end of the stud and using a wrench on the lower nut **(see illustration 2.18)**.

2.17 Using a stud extractor tool to remove a broken crankcase stud

2.18 Two nuts can be locked together to unscrew a stud from a component

● A bolt or screw which has broken off below or level with the casing must be extracted using a screw extractor set. Centerpunch the fastener to centralize the drill bit, then drill a hole in the fastener **(see illustration 2.19)**. Select a drill bit which is approximately half to three-quarters the

2.19 When using a screw extractor, first drill a hole in the fastener . . .

diameter of the fastener and drill to a depth which will accommodate the extractor. Use the largest size extractor possible, but avoid leaving too small a wall thickness otherwise the extractor will merely force the fastener walls outwards wedging it in the casing thread.

● If a spiral type extractor is used, thread it counterclockwise into the fastener. As it is screwed in, it will grip the fastener and unscrew it from the casing **(see illustration 2.20)**.

2.20 . . . then thread the extractor counterclockwise into the fastener

● If a taper type extractor is used, tap it into the fastener so that it is firmly wedged in place. Unscrew the extractor (counterclockwise) to draw the fastener out.

 Warning: Stud extractors are very hard and may break off in the fastener if care is not taken - ask a machine shop about spark erosion if this happens.

● Alternatively, the broken bolt/screw can be drilled out and the hole retapped for an oversize bolt/screw or a diamond-section thread insert. It is essential that the drilling is carried out squarely and to the correct depth, otherwise the casing may be ruined - if in doubt, entrust the work to a machine shop.
● Bolts and nuts with rounded corners cause the correct size wrench or socket to slip when force is applied. Of the types of wrench/socket available always use a six-point type rather than an eight or twelve-point type - better grip

2.21 Comparison of surface drive box wrench (left) with 12-point type (right)

is obtained. Surface drive wrenches grip the middle of the hex flats, rather than the corners, and are thus good in cases of damaged heads **(see illustration 2.21)**.

● Slotted-head or Phillips-head screws are often damaged by the use of the wrong size screwdriver. Allen-head and Torx-head screws are much less likely to sustain damage. If enough of the screw head is exposed you can use a hacksaw to cut a slot in its head and then use a conventional flat-bladed screwdriver to remove it. Alternatively use a hammer and cold chisel to tap the head of the fastener around to loosen it. Always replace damaged fasteners with new ones, preferably Torx or Allen-head type.

HAYNES HiNT

A dab of valve grinding compound between the screw head and screw-driver tip will often give a good grip.

Thread repair

● Threads (particularly those in aluminum alloy components) can be damaged by overtightening, being assembled with dirt in the threads, or from a component working loose and vibrating. Eventually the thread will fail completely, and it will be impossible to tighten the fastener.

● If a thread is damaged or clogged with old locking compound it can be renovated with a thread repair tool (thread chaser) **(see illustrations 2.22 and 2.23)**; special thread

2.22 A thread repair tool being used to correct an internal thread

2.23 A thread repair tool being used to correct an external thread

chasers are available for spark plug hole threads. The tool will not cut a new thread, but clean and true the original thread. Make sure that you use the correct diameter and pitch tool. Similarly, external threads can be cleaned up with a die or a thread restorer file **(see illustration 2.24)**.

2.24 Using a thread restorer file

● It is possible to drill out the old thread and retap the component to the next thread size. This will work where there is enough surrounding material and a new bolt or screw can be obtained. Sometimes, however, this is not possible - such as where the bolt/screw passes through another component which must also be suitably modified, also in cases where a spark plug or oil drain plug cannot be obtained in a larger diameter thread size.

● The diamond-section thread insert (often known by its popular trade name of Heli-Coil) is a simple and effective method of replacing the thread and retaining the original size. A kit can be purchased which contains the tap, insert and installing tool **(see illustration 2.25)**. Drill out the damaged thread with the size drill specified **(see illustration 2.26)**. Carefully retap the thread **(see illustration 2.27)**. Install the

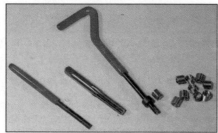

2.25 Obtain a thread insert kit to suit the thread diameter and pitch required

2.26 To install a thread insert, first drill out the original thread . . .

2.27 . . . tap a new thread . . .

2.28 . . . fit insert on the installing tool . . .

2.29 . . . and thread into the component . . .

2.30 . . . break off the tang when complete

insert on the installing tool and thread it slowly into place using a light downward pressure **(see illustrations 2.28 and 2.29)**. When positioned between a 1/4 and 1/2 turn below the surface withdraw the installing tool and use the break-off tool to press down on the tang, breaking it off **(see illustration 2.30)**.

● There are epoxy thread repair kits on the market which can rebuild stripped internal threads, although this repair should not be used on high load-bearing components.

Thread locking and sealing compounds

● Locking compounds are used in locations where the fastener is prone to loosening due to vibration or on important safety-related items which might cause loss of control of the motorcycle if they fail. It is also used where important fasteners cannot be secured by other means such as lockwashers or cotter pins.

● Before applying locking compound, make sure that the threads (internal and external) are clean and dry with all old compound removed. Select a compound to suit the component being secured - a non-permanent general locking and sealing type is suitable for most applications, but a high strength type is needed for permanent fixing of studs in castings. Apply a drop or two of the compound to the first few threads of the fastener, then thread it into place and tighten to the specified torque. Do not apply excessive thread locking compound otherwise the thread may be damaged on subsequent removal.

● Certain fasteners are impregnated with a dry film type coating of locking compound on their threads. Always replace this type of fastener if disturbed.

● Anti-seize compounds, such as copper-based greases, can be applied to protect threads from seizure due to extreme heat and corrosion. A common instance is spark plug threads and exhaust system fasteners.

3 Measuring tools and gauges

Feeler gauges

● Feeler gauges (or blades) are used for measuring small gaps and clearances (see illustration 3.1). They can also be used to measure endfloat (sideplay) of a component on a shaft where access is not possible with a dial gauge.

● Feeler gauge sets should be treated with care and not bent or damaged. They are etched with their size on one face. Keep them clean and very lightly oiled to prevent corrosion build-up.

3.1 Feeler gauges are used for measuring small gaps and clearances - thickness is marked on one face of gauge

● When measuring a clearance, select a gauge which is a light sliding fit between the two components. You may need to use two gauges together to measure the clearance accurately.

Micrometers

● A micrometer is a precision tool capable of measuring to 0.01 or 0.001 of a millimeter. It should always be stored in its case and not in the general toolbox. It must be kept clean and never dropped, otherwise its frame or measuring anvils could be distorted resulting in inaccurate readings.

● External micrometers are used for measuring outside diameters of components and have many more applications than internal micrometers. Micrometers are available in different size ranges, typically 0 to 25 mm, 25 to 50 mm, and upwards in 25 mm steps; some large micrometers have interchangeable anvils to allow a range of measurements to be taken. Generally the largest precision measurement you are likely to take on a motorcycle is the piston diameter.

● Internal micrometers (or bore micrometers) are used for measuring inside diameters, such as valve guides and cylinder bores. Telescoping gauges and small hole gauges are used in conjunction with an external micrometer, whereas the more expensive internal micrometers have their own measuring device.

External micrometer

Note: *The conventional analogue type instrument is described. Although much easier to read, digital micrometers are considerably more expensive.*

● Always check the calibration of the micrometer before use. With the anvils closed (0 to 25 mm type) or set over a test gauge (for

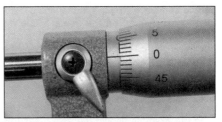

3.2 Check micrometer calibration before use

the larger types) the scale should read zero (see illustration 3.2); make sure that the anvils (and test piece) are clean first. Any discrepancy can be adjusted by referring to the instructions supplied with the tool. Remember that the micrometer is a precision measuring tool - don't force the anvils closed, use the ratchet (4) on the end of the micrometer to close it. In this way, a measured force is always applied.

● To use, first make sure that the item being measured is clean. Place the anvil of the micrometer (1) against the item and use the thimble (2) to bring the spindle (3) lightly into contact with the other side of the item (see illustration 3.3). Don't tighten the thimble down because this will damage the micrometer - instead use the ratchet (4) on the end of the micrometer. The ratchet mechanism applies a measured force preventing damage to the instrument.

● The micrometer is read by referring to the linear scale on the sleeve and the annular scale on the thimble. Read off the sleeve first to obtain the base measurement, then add the fine measurement from the thimble to obtain the overall reading. The linear scale on the sleeve represents the measuring range of the micrometer (eg 0 to 25 mm). The annular scale

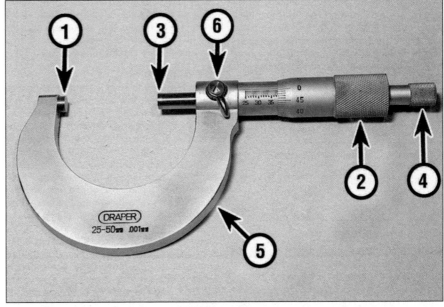

3.3 Micrometer component parts

1	Anvil	3	Spindle	5	Frame
2	Thimble	4	Ratchet	6	Locking lever

on the thimble will be in graduations of 0.01 mm (or as marked on the frame) - one full revolution of the thimble will move 0.5 mm on the linear scale. Take the reading where the datum line on the sleeve intersects the thimble's scale. Always position the eye directly above the scale otherwise an inaccurate reading will result.

In the example shown the item measures 2.95 mm **(see illustration 3.4)**:

Linear scale	2.00 mm
Linear scale	0.50 mm
Annular scale	0.45 mm
Total figure	**2.95 mm**

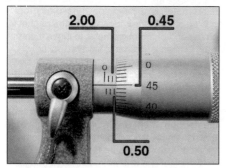

3.4 Micrometer reading of 2.95 mm

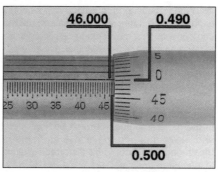

3.5 Micrometer reading of 46.99 mm on linear and annular scales . . .

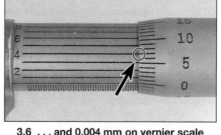

3.6 . . . and 0.004 mm on vernier scale

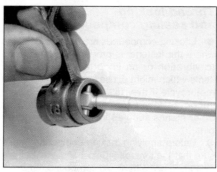

3.7 Expand the telescoping gauge in the bore, lock its position . . .

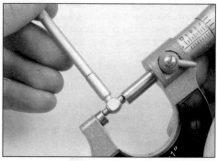

3.8 . . . then measure the gauge with a micrometer

3.9 Expand the small hole gauge in the bore, lock its position . . .

3.10 . . . then measure the gauge with a micrometer

Most micrometers have a locking lever (6) on the frame to hold the setting in place, allowing the item to be removed from the micrometer.
● Some micrometers have a vernier scale on their sleeve, providing an even finer measurement to be taken, in 0.001 increments of a millimeter. Take the sleeve and thimble measurement as described above, then check which graduation on the vernier scale aligns with that of the annular scale on the thimble **Note:** *The eye must be perpendicular to the scale when taking the vernier reading - if necessary rotate the body of the micrometer to ensure this.* Multiply the vernier scale figure by 0.001 and add it to the base and fine measurement figures.

In the example shown the item measures 46.994 mm **(see illustrations 3.5 and 3.6)**:

Linear scale (base)	46.000 mm
Linear scale (base)	00.500 mm
Annular scale (fine)	00.490 mm
Vernier scale	00.004 mm
Total figure	**46.994 mm**

Internal micrometer

● Internal micrometers are available for measuring bore diameters, but are expensive and unlikely to be available for home use. It is suggested that a set of telescoping gauges and small hole gauges, both of which must be used with an external micrometer, will suffice for taking internal measurements on a motorcycle.
● Telescoping gauges can be used to measure internal diameters of components. Select a gauge with the correct size range, make sure its ends are clean and insert it into the bore. Expand the gauge, then lock its position and withdraw it from the bore **(see illustration 3.7)**. Measure across the gauge ends with a micrometer **(see illustration 3.8)**.
● Very small diameter bores (such as valve guides) are measured with a small hole gauge. Once adjusted to a slip-fit inside the component, its position is locked and the gauge withdrawn for measurement with a micrometer **(see illustrations 3.9 and 3.10)**.

Vernier caliper

Note: *The conventional linear and dial gauge type instruments are described. Digital types are easier to read, but are far more expensive.*
● The vernier caliper does not provide the precision of a micrometer, but is versatile in being able to measure internal and external diameters. Some types also incorporate a depth gauge. It is ideal for measuring clutch plate friction material and spring free lengths.
● To use the conventional linear scale vernier, loosen off the vernier clamp screws (1) and set its jaws over (2), or inside (3), the item to be measured **(see illustration 3.11)**. Slide the jaw into contact, using the thumbwheel (4) for fine movement of the sliding scale (5) then tighten the clamp screws (1). Read off the main scale (6) where the zero on the sliding scale (5) intersects it, taking the whole number to the left of the zero; this provides the base measurement. View along the sliding scale and select the division which lines up exactly with any of the divisions on the main scale, noting that the divisions usually represents 0.02 of a millimeter. Add this fine measurement to the base measurement to obtain the total reading.

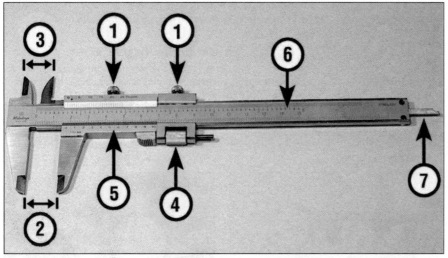

3.11 Vernier component parts (linear gauge)

1	Clamp screws	3	Internal jaws	5	Sliding scale	7	Depth gauge
2	External jaws	4	Thumbwheel	6	Main scale		

In the example shown the item measures 55.92 mm **(see illustration 3.12)**:

Base measurement	55.00 mm
Fine measurement	00.92 mm
Total figure	**55.92 mm**

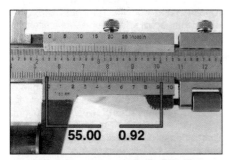

3.12 Vernier gauge reading of 55.92 mm

● Some vernier calipers are equipped with a dial gauge for fine measurement. Before use, check that the jaws are clean, then close them fully and check that the dial gauge reads zero. If necessary adjust the gauge ring accordingly. Slacken the vernier clamp screw (1) and set its jaws over (2), or inside (3), the item to be measured **(see illustration 3.13)**. Slide the jaws into contact, using the thumbwheel (4) for fine movement. Read off the main scale (5) where the edge of the sliding scale (6) intersects it, taking the whole number to the left of the zero; this provides the base measurement. Read off the needle position on the dial gauge (7) scale to provide the fine measurement; each division represents 0.05 of a millimeter. Add this fine measurement to the base measurement to obtain the total reading.

In the example shown the item measures 55.95 mm **(see illustration 3.14)**:

Base measurement	55.00 mm
Fine measurement	00.95 mm
Total figure	**55.95 mm**

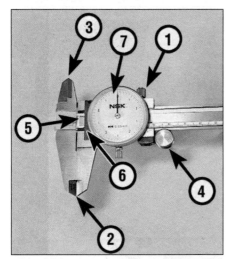

3.13 Vernier component parts (dial gauge)

1	Clamp screw	5	Main scale
2	External jaws	6	Sliding scale
3	Internal jaws	7	Dial gauge
4	Thumbwheel		

3.14 Vernier gauge reading of 55.95 mm

Plastigage

● Plastigage is a plastic material which can be compressed between two surfaces to measure the oil clearance between them. The width of the compressed Plastigage is measured against a calibrated scale to determine the clearance.

● Common uses of Plastigage are for measuring the clearance between crankshaft journal and main bearing inserts, between crankshaft journal and big-end bearing inserts, and between camshaft and bearing surfaces. The following example describes big-end oil clearance measurement.

● Handle the Plastigage material carefully to prevent distortion. Using a sharp knife, cut a length which corresponds with the width of the bearing being measured and place it carefully across the journal so that it is parallel with the shaft **(see illustration 3.15)**. Carefully install both bearing shells and the connecting rod. Without rotating the rod on the journal tighten its bolts or nuts (as applicable) to the specified torque. The connecting rod and bearings are then disassembled and the crushed Plastigage examined.

3.15 Plastigage placed across shaft journal

● Using the scale provided in the Plastigage kit, measure the width of the material to determine the oil clearance **(see illustration 3.16)**. Always remove all traces of Plastigage after use using your fingernails.

Caution: Arriving at the correct clearance demands that the assembly is torqued correctly, according to the settings and sequence (where applicable) provided by the motorcycle manufacturer.

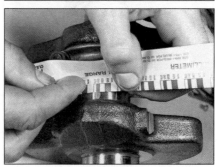

3.16 Measuring the width of the crushed Plastigage

Dial gauge or DTI (Dial Test Indicator)

● A dial gauge can be used to accurately measure small amounts of movement. Typical uses are measuring shaft runout or shaft endfloat (sideplay) and setting piston position for ignition timing on two-strokes. A dial gauge set usually comes with a range of different probes and adapters and mounting equipment.

● The gauge needle must point to zero when at rest. Rotate the ring around its periphery to zero the gauge.

● Check that the gauge is capable of reading the extent of movement in the work. Most gauges have a small dial set in the face which records whole millimeters of movement as well as the fine scale around the face periphery which is calibrated in 0.01 mm divisions. Read off the small dial first to obtain the base measurement, then add the measurement from the fine scale to obtain the total reading.

In the example shown the gauge reads 1.48 mm (see illustration 3.17):

Base measurement	1.00 mm
Fine measurement	0.48 mm
Total figure	**1.48 mm**

3.17 Dial gauge reading of 1.48 mm

● If measuring shaft runout, the shaft must be supported in vee-blocks and the gauge mounted on a stand perpendicular to the shaft. Rest the tip of the gauge against the center of the shaft and rotate the shaft slowly while watching the gauge reading (see illustration 3.18). Take several measurements along the length of the shaft and record the

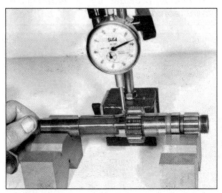

3.18 Using a dial gauge to measure shaft runout

maximum gauge reading as the amount of runout in the shaft. **Note:** The reading obtained will be total runout at that point - some manufacturers specify that the runout figure is halved to compare with their specified runout limit.

● Endfloat (sideplay) measurement requires that the gauge is mounted securely to the surrounding component with its probe touching the end of the shaft. Using hand pressure, push and pull on the shaft noting the maximum endfloat recorded on the gauge (see illustration 3.19).

3.19 Using a dial gauge to measure shaft endfloat

● A dial gauge with suitable adapters can be used to determine piston position BTDC on two-stroke engines for the purposes of ignition timing. The gauge, adapter and suitable length probe are installed in the place of the spark plug and the gauge zeroed at TDC. If the piston position is specified as 1.14 mm BTDC, rotate the engine back to 2.00 mm BTDC, then slowly forwards to 1.14 mm BTDC.

Cylinder compression gauges

● A compression gauge is used for measuring cylinder compression. Either the rubber-cone type or the threaded adapter type can be used. The latter is preferred to ensure a perfect seal against the cylinder head. A 0 to 300 psi (0 to 20 Bar) type gauge (for gasoline engines) will be suitable for motorcycles.

● The spark plug is removed and the gauge either held hard against the cylinder head (cone type) or the gauge adapter screwed into the cylinder head (threaded type) (see illustration 3.20). Cylinder compression is measured with the engine turning over, but not running - carry out the compression test as described in

3.20 Using a rubber-cone type cylinder compression gauge

Troubleshooting Equipment. The gauge will hold the reading until manually released.

Oil pressure gauge

● An oil pressure gauge is used for measuring engine oil pressure. Most gauges come with a set of adapters to fit the thread of the take-off point (see illustration 3.21). If the take-off point specified by the motorcycle manufacturer is an external oil pipe union, make sure that the specified replacement union is used to prevent oil starvation.

3.21 Oil pressure gauge and take-off point adapter (arrow)

● Oil pressure is measured with the engine running (at a specific rpm) and often the manufacturer will specify pressure limits for a cold and hot engine.

Straight-edge and surface plate

● If checking the gasket face of a component for warpage, place a steel rule or precision straight-edge across the gasket face and measure any gap between the straight-edge and component with feeler gauges (see illustration 3.22). Check diagonally across the component and between mounting holes (see illustration 3.23).

3.22 Use a straight-edge and feeler gauges to check for warpage

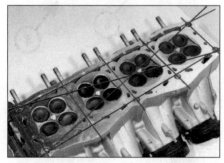

3.23 Check for warpage in these directions

4 Torque and leverage

What is torque?

● Torque describes the twisting force around a shaft. The amount of torque applied is determined by the distance from the center of the shaft to the end of the lever and the amount of force being applied to the end of the lever; distance multiplied by force equals torque.

● The manufacturer applies a measured torque to a bolt or nut to ensure that it will not loosen in use and to hold two components securely together without movement in the joint. The actual torque setting depends on the thread size, bolt or nut material and the composition of the components being held.

● Too little torque may cause the fastener to loosen due to vibration, whereas too much torque will distort the joint faces of the component or cause the fastener to shear off. Always stick to the specified torque setting.

Using a torque wrench

● Check the calibration of the torque wrench and make sure it has a suitable range for the job. Torque wrenches are available in Nm (Newton-meters), kgf m (kilograms-force meter), lbf ft (pounds-feet), lbf in (inch-pounds). Do not confuse lbf ft with lbf in.

● Adjust the tool to the desired torque on the scale (see illustration 4.1). If your torque wrench is not calibrated in the units specified, carefully convert the figure (see *Conversion Factors*). A manufacturer sometimes gives a torque setting as a range (8 to 10 Nm) rather than a single figure - in this case set the tool midway between the two settings. The same torque may be expressed as 9 Nm ± 1 Nm. Some torque wrenches have a method of locking the setting so that it isn't inadvertently altered during use.

4.1 Set the torque wrench index mark to the setting required, in this case 12 Nm

● Install the bolts/nuts in their correct location and secure them lightly. Their threads must be clean and free of any old locking compound. Unless specified the threads and flange should be dry - oiled threads are necessary in certain circumstances and the manufacturer will take this into account in the specified torque figure. Similarly, the manufacturer may also specify the application of thread-locking compound.

● Tighten the fasteners in the specified sequence until the torque wrench clicks, indicating that the torque setting has been reached. Apply the torque again to double-check the setting. Where different thread diameter fasteners secure the component, as a rule tighten the larger diameter ones first.

● When the torque wrench has been finished with, release the lock (where applicable) and fully back off its setting to zero - do not leave the torque wrench tensioned. Also, do not use a torque wrench for loosening a fastener.

Angle-tightening

● Manufacturers often specify a figure in degrees for final tightening of a fastener. This usually follows tightening to a specific torque setting.

● A degree disc can be set and attached to the socket (see illustration 4.2) or a protractor can be used to mark the angle of movement on the bolt/nut head and the surrounding casting (see illustration 4.3).

4.2 Angle tightening can be accomplished with a torque-angle gauge . . .

4.3 . . . or by marking the angle on the surrounding component

Loosening sequences

● Where more than one bolt/nut secures a component, loosen each fastener evenly a little at a time. In this way, not all the stress of the joint is held by one fastener and the components are not likely to distort.

● If a tightening sequence is provided, work in the REVERSE of this, but if not, work from the outside in, in a criss-cross sequence (see illustration 4.4).

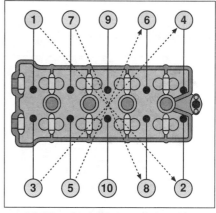

4.4 When loosening, work from the outside inwards

Tightening sequences

● If a component is held by more than one fastener it is important that the retaining bolts/nuts are tightened evenly to prevent uneven stress build-up and distortion of sealing faces. This is especially important on high-compression joints such as the cylinder head.

● A sequence is usually provided by the manufacturer, either in a diagram or actually marked in the casting. If not, always start in the center and work outwards in a criss-cross pattern (see illustration 4.5). Start off by securing all bolts/nuts finger-tight, then set the torque wrench and tighten each fastener by a small amount in sequence until the final torque is reached. By following this practice,

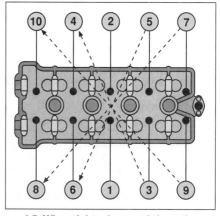

4.5 When tightening, work from the inside outwards

● Checking individual components for warpage, such as clutch plain (metal) plates, requires a perfectly flat plate or piece of plate glass and feeler gauges.

the joint will be held evenly and will not be distorted. Important joints, such as the cylinder head and big-end fasteners often have two- or three-stage torque settings.

Applying leverage

● Use tools at the correct angle. Position a socket or wrench on the bolt/nut so that you pull it towards you when loosening. If this can't be done, push the wrench without curling your fingers around it **(see illustration 4.6)** - the wrench may slip or the fastener loosen suddenly, resulting in your fingers being crushed against a component.

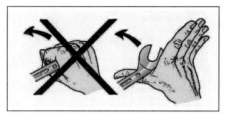

4.6 If you can't pull on the wrench to loosen a fastener, push with your hand open

● Additional leverage is gained by extending the length of the lever. The best way to do this is to use a breaker bar instead of the regular length tool, or to slip a length of tubing over the end of the wrench or socket.
● If additional leverage will not work, the fastener head is either damaged or firmly corroded in place (see *Fasteners*).

5 Bearings

Bearing removal and installation

Drivers and sockets

● Before removing a bearing, always inspect the casing to see which way it must be driven out - some casings will have retaining plates or a cast step. Also check for any identifying markings on the bearing and, if installed to a certain depth, measure this at this stage. Some roller bearings are sealed on one side - take note of the original installed position.
● Bearings can be driven out of a casing using a bearing driver tool (with the correct size head) or a socket of the correct diameter. Select the driver head or socket so that it contacts the outer race of the bearing, not the balls/rollers or inner race. Always support the casing around the bearing housing with wood blocks, otherwise there is a risk of fracture. The bearing is driven out with a few blows on the driver or socket from a heavy mallet. Unless access is severely restricted (as with wheel bearings), a pin-punch is not recommended unless it is moved around the bearing to keep it square in its housing.

● The same equipment can be used to install bearings. Make sure the bearing housing is supported on wood blocks and line up the bearing in its housing. Install the bearing as noted on removal - generally they are installed with their marked side facing outwards. Tap the bearing squarely into its housing using a driver or socket which bears only on the bearing's outer race - contact with the bearing balls/rollers or inner race will destroy it **(see illustrations 5.1 and 5.2)**.
● Check that the bearing inner race and balls/rollers rotate freely.

5.1 Using a bearing driver against the bearing's outer race

5.2 Using a large socket against the bearing's outer race

Pullers and slide-hammers

● Where a bearing is pressed on a shaft a puller will be required to extract it **(see illustration 5.3)**. Make sure that the puller clamp or legs fit securely behind the bearing and are unlikely to slip out. If pulling a bearing

5.3 This bearing puller clamps behind the bearing and pressure is applied to the shaft end to draw the bearing off

off a gear shaft for example, you may have to locate the puller behind a gear pinion if there is no access to the race and draw the gear pinion off the shaft as well **(see illustration 5.4)**.

> **Caution: Ensure that the puller's center bolt locates securely against the end of the shaft and will not slip when pressure is applied. Also ensure that puller does not damage the shaft end.**

5.4 Where no access is available to the rear of the bearing, it is sometimes possible to draw off the adjacent component

● Operate the puller so that its center bolt exerts pressure on the shaft end and draws the bearing off the shaft.
● When installing the bearing on the shaft, tap only on the bearing's inner race - contact with the balls/rollers or outer race will destroy the bearing. Use a socket or length of tubing as a drift which fits over the shaft end **(see illustration 5.5)**.

5.5 When installing a bearing on a shaft use a piece of tubing which bears only on the bearing's inner race

● Where a bearing locates in a blind hole in a casing, it cannot be driven or pulled out as described above. A slide-hammer with knife-edged bearing puller attachment will be required. The puller attachment passes through the bearing, and when tightened, expands to fit firmly behind the bearing **(see illustration 5.6)**. By operating the slide-hammer part of the tool the bearing is jarred out of its housing **(see illustration 5.7)**.
● It is possible, if the bearing is of reasonable weight, for it to drop out of its housing if the casing is heated as described opposite. If this

5.6 Expand the bearing puller so that it locks behind the bearing . . .

5.7 . . . attach the slide hammer to the bearing puller

method is attempted, first prepare a work surface which will enable the casing to be tapped face down to help dislodge the bearing - a wood surface is ideal since it will not damage the casing's gasket surface. Wearing protective gloves, tap the heated casing several times against the work surface to dislodge the bearing under its own weight **(see illustration 5.8)**.

5.8 Tapping a casing face down on wood blocks can often dislodge a bearing

● Bearings can be installed in blind holes using the driver or socket method described above.

Drawbolts

● Where a bearing or bushing is set in the eye of a component, such as a suspension linkage arm or connecting rod small-end, removal by drift may damage the component. Furthermore, a rubber bushing in a shock absorber eye cannot successfully be driven out of position. If access is available to a hydraulic press, the task is straightforward. If not, a drawbolt can be fabricated to extract the bearing or bushing.

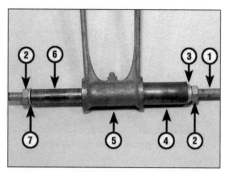

5.9 Drawbolt component parts assembled on a suspension arm

1 Bolt or length of threaded bar
2 Nuts
3 Washer (external diameter greater than tubing internal diameter)
4 Tubing (internal diameter sufficient to accommodate bearing)
5 Suspension arm with bearing
6 Tubing (external diameter slightly smaller than bearing)
7 Washer (external diameter slightly smaller than bearing)

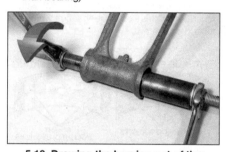

5.10 Drawing the bearing out of the suspension arm

● To extract the bearing/bushing you will need a long bolt with nut (or piece of threaded bar with two nuts), a piece of tubing which has an internal diameter larger than the bearing/bushing, another piece of tubing which has an external diameter slightly smaller than the bearing/bushing, and a selection of washers **(see illustrations 5.9 and 5.10)**. Note that the pieces of tubing must be of the same length, or longer, than the bearing/bushing.
● The same kit (without the pieces of tubing) can be used to draw the new bearing/bushing back into place **(see illustration 5.11)**.

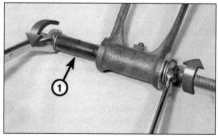

5.11 Installing a new bearing (1) in the suspension arm

Temperature change

● If the bearing's outer race is a tight fit in the casing, the aluminum casing can be heated to release its grip on the bearing. Aluminum will expand at a greater rate than the steel bearing outer race. There are several ways to do this, but avoid any localized extreme heat (such as a blow torch) - aluminum alloy has a low melting point.
● Approved methods of heating a casing are using a domestic oven (heated to 100°C/200°F) or immersing the casing in boiling water **(see illustration 5.12)**. Low temperature range localized heat sources such as a paint stripper heat gun or clothes iron can also be used **(see illustration 5.13)**. Alternatively, soak a rag in boiling water, wring it out and wrap it around the bearing housing.

> ⚠ **Warning: All of these methods require care in use to prevent scalding and burns to the hands. Wear protective gloves when handling hot components.**

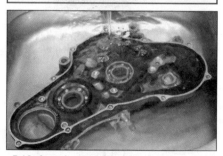

5.12 A casing can be immersed in a sink of boiling water to aid bearing removal

5.13 Using a localized heat source to aid bearing removal

● If heating the whole casing note that plastic components, such as the neutral switch, may suffer - remove them beforehand.
● After heating, remove the bearing as described above. You may find that the expansion is sufficient for the bearing to fall out of the casing under its own weight or with a light tap on the driver or socket.
● If necessary, the casing can be heated to aid bearing installation, and this is sometimes the recommended procedure if the motorcycle manufacturer has designed the housing and bearing fit with this intention.

● Installation of bearings can be eased by placing them in a freezer the night before installation. The steel bearing will contract slightly, allowing easy insertion in its housing. This is often useful when installing steering head outer races in the frame.

Bearing types and markings

● Plain shell bearings, ball bearings, needle roller bearings and tapered roller bearings will all be found on motorcycles (see illustrations 5.14 and 5.15). The ball and roller types are usually caged between an inner and outer race, but uncaged variations may be found.

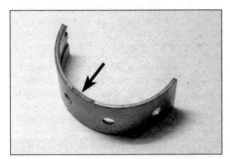

5.14 Shell bearings are either plain or grooved. They are usually identified by color code (arrow)

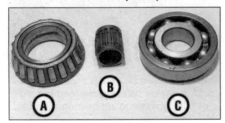

5.15 Tapered roller bearing (A), needle roller bearing (B) and ball journal bearing (C)

● Shell bearings (often called inserts) are usually found at the crankshaft main and connecting rod big-end where they are good at coping with high loads. They are made of a phosphor-bronze material and are impregnated with self-lubricating properties.
● Ball bearings and needle roller bearings consist of a steel inner and outer race with the balls or rollers between the races. They require constant lubrication by oil or grease and are good at coping with axial loads. Taper roller bearings consist of rollers set in a tapered cage set on the inner race; the outer race is separate. They are good at coping with axial loads and prevent movement along the shaft - a typical application is in the steering head.
● Bearing manufacturers produce bearings to ISO size standards and stamp one face of the bearing to indicate its internal and external diameter, load capacity and type (see illustration 5.16).
● Metal bushings are usually of phosphor-bronze material. Rubber bushings are used in suspension mounting eyes. Fiber bushings have also been used in suspension pivots.

5.16 Typical bearing marking

Bearing troubleshooting

● If a bearing outer race has spun in its housing, the housing material will be damaged. You can use a bearing locking compound to bond the outer race in place if damage is not too severe.
● Shell bearings will fail due to damage of their working surface, as a result of lack of lubrication, corrosion or abrasive particles in the oil (see illustration 5.17). Small particles of dirt in the oil may embed in the bearing material whereas larger particles will score the bearing and shaft journal. If a number of short journeys are made, insufficient heat will be generated to drive off condensation which has built up on the bearings.

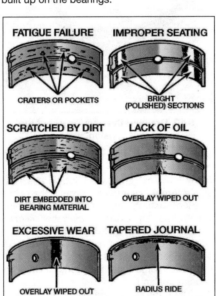

5.17 Typical bearing failures

● Ball and roller bearings will fail due to lack of lubrication or damage to the balls or rollers. Tapered-roller bearings can be damaged by overloading them. Unless the bearing is sealed on both sides, wash it in kerosene to remove all old grease then allow it to dry. Make a visual inspection looking to dented balls or rollers, damaged cages and worn or pitted races (see illustration 5.18).
● A ball bearing can be checked for wear by listening to it when spun. Apply a film of light oil to the bearing and hold it close to the ear - hold the outer race with one hand and spin the inner

5.18 Example of ball journal bearing with damaged balls and cages

5.19 Hold outer race and listen to inner race when spun

race with the other hand (see illustration 5.19). The bearing should be almost silent when spun; if it grates or rattles it is worn.

6 Oil seals

Oil seal removal and installation

● Oil seals should be replaced every time a component is dismantled. This is because the seal lips will become set to the sealing surface and will not necessarily reseal.
● Oil seals can be pried out of position using a large flat-bladed screwdriver (see illustration 6.1). In the case of crankcase seals, check first that the seal is not lipped on the inside, preventing its removal with the crankcases joined.

6.1 Pry out oil seals with a large flat-bladed screwdriver

● New seals are usually installed with their marked face (containing the seal reference code) outwards and the spring side towards the fluid being retained. In certain cases, such as a two-stroke engine crankshaft seal, a double lipped seal may be used due to there being fluid or gas on each side of the joint.

● Use a bearing driver or socket which bears only on the outer hard edge of the seal to install it in the casing - tapping on the inner edge will damage the sealing lip.

Oil seal types and markings

● Oil seals are usually of the single-lipped type. Double-lipped seals are found where a liquid or gas is on both sides of the joint.
● Oil seals can harden and lose their sealing ability if the motorcycle has been in storage for a long period - replacement is the only solution.
● Oil seal manufacturers also conform to the ISO markings for seal size - these are molded into the outer face of the seal (see illustration 6.2).

6.2 These oil seal markings indicate inside diameter, outside diameter and seal thickness

7   Gaskets and sealants

Types of gasket and sealant

● Gaskets are used to seal the mating surfaces between components and keep lubricants, fluids, vacuum or pressure contained within the assembly. Aluminum gaskets are sometimes found at the cylinder joints, but most gaskets are paper-based. If the mating surfaces of the components being joined are undamaged the gasket can be installed dry, although a dab of sealant or grease will be useful to hold it in place during assembly.
● RTV (Room Temperature Vulcanizing) silicone rubber sealants cure when exposed to moisture in the atmosphere. These sealants are good at filling pits or irregular gasket faces, but will tend to be forced out of the joint under very high torque. They can be used to replace a paper gasket, but first make sure that the width of the paper gasket is not essential to the shimming of internal components. RTV sealants should not be used on components containing gasoline.
● Non-hardening, semi-hardening and hard setting liquid gasket compounds can be used with a gasket or between a metal-to-metal joint. Select the sealant to suit the application: universal non-hardening sealant can be used on virtually all joints; semi-hardening on joint faces which are rough or damaged; hard setting sealant on joints which require a permanent bond and are subjected to high temperature and pressure. **Note:** *Check first if the paper gasket has a bead of sealant*

impregnated in its surface before applying additional sealant.
● When choosing a sealant, make sure it is suitable for the application, particularly if being applied in a high-temperature area or in the vicinity of fuel. Certain manufacturers produce sealants in either clear, silver or black colors to match the finish of the engine. This has a particular application on motorcycles where much of the engine is exposed.
● Do not over-apply sealant. That which is squeezed out on the outside of the joint can be wiped off, whereas an excess of sealant on the inside can break off and clog oilways.

Breaking a sealed joint

● Age, heat, pressure and the use of hard setting sealant can cause two components to stick together so tightly that they are difficult to separate using finger pressure alone. Do not resort to using levers unless there is a pry point provided for this purpose (see illustration 7.1) or else the gasket surfaces will be damaged.
● Use a soft-faced hammer (see illustration 7.2) or a wood block and conventional hammer to strike the component near the mating surface. Avoid hammering against cast extremities since they may break off. If this method fails, try using a wood wedge between the two components.

> **Caution: If the joint will not separate, double-check that you have removed all the fasteners.**

7.1 If a pry point is provided, apply gentle pressure with a flat-bladed screwdriver

7.2 Tap around the joint with a soft-faced mallet if necessary - don't strike cooling fins

Removal of old gasket and sealant

● Paper gaskets will most likely come away complete, leaving only a few traces stuck on

Most components have one or two hollow locating dowels between the two gasket faces. If a dowel cannot be removed, do not resort to gripping it with pliers - it will almost certainly be distorted. Install a close-fitting socket or Phillips screwdriver into the dowel and then grip the outer edge of the dowel to free it.

the sealing faces of the components. It is imperative that all traces are removed to ensure correct sealing of the new gasket.
● Very carefully scrape all traces of gasket away making sure that the sealing surfaces are not gouged or scored by the scraper (see illustrations 7.3, 7.4 and 7.5). Stubborn deposits can be removed by spraying with an aerosol gasket remover. Final preparation of

7.3 Paper gaskets can be scraped off with a gasket scraper tool . . .

7.4 . . . a knife blade . . .

7.5 . . . or a household scraper

7.6 Fine abrasive paper is wrapped around a flat file to clean up the gasket face

7.7 A kitchen scourer can be used on stubborn deposits

the gasket surface can be made with very fine abrasive paper or a plastic kitchen scourer **(see illustrations 7.6 and 7.7)**.

● Old sealant can be scraped or peeled off components, depending on the type originally used. Note that gasket removal compounds are available to avoid scraping the components clean; make sure the gasket remover suits the type of sealant used.

8 Chains

Breaking and joining final drive chains

● Drive chains for all but small bikes are continuous and do not have a clip-type connecting link. The chain must be broken using a chain breaker tool and the new chain securely riveted together using a new soft rivet-type link. Never use a clip-type connecting link instead of a rivet-type link, except in an emergency. Various chain breaking and riveting tools are available, either as separate tools or combined as illustrated in the accompanying photographs - read the instructions supplied with the tool carefully.

> ⚠ **Warning: The need to rivet the new link pins correctly cannot be overstressed - loss of control of the motorcycle is very likely to result if the chain breaks in use.**

● Rotate the chain and look for the soft link. The soft link pins look like they have been

8.1 Tighten the chain breaker to push the pin out of the link . . .

8.2 . . . withdraw the pin, remove the tool . . .

8.3 . . . and separate the chain link

deeply center-punched instead of peened over like all the other pins **(see illustration 8.9)** and its sideplate may be a different color. Position the soft link midway between the sprockets and assemble the chain breaker tool over one of the soft link pins **(see illustration 8.1)**. Operate the tool to push the pin out through the chain **(see illustration 8.2)**. On an O-ring chain, remove the O-rings **(see illustration 8.3)**. Carry out the same procedure on the other soft link pin.

> *Caution: Certain soft link pins (particularly on the larger chains) may require their ends to be filed or ground off before they can be pressed out using the tool.*

● Check that you have the correct size and strength (standard or heavy duty) new soft link - do not reuse the old link. Look for the size marking on the chain sideplates **(see illustration 8.10)**.

● Position the chain ends so that they are engaged over the rear sprocket. On an O-ring

8.4 Insert the new soft link, with O-rings, through the chain ends . . .

8.5 . . . install the O-rings over the pin ends . . .

8.6 . . . followed by the sideplate

chain, install a new O-ring over each pin of the link and insert the link through the two chain ends **(see illustration 8.4)**. Install a new O-ring over the end of each pin, followed by the sideplate (with the chain manufacturer's marking facing outwards) **(see illustrations 8.5 and 8.6)**. On an unsealed chain, insert the link through the two chain ends, then install the sideplate with the chain manufacturer's marking facing outwards.

● Note that it may not be possible to install the sideplate using finger pressure alone. If using a joining tool, assemble it so that the plates of the tool clamp the link and press the sideplate over the pins **(see illustration 8.7)**. Otherwise, use two small sockets placed over

8.7 Push the sideplate into position using a clamp

8.8 Assemble the chain riveting tool over one pin at a time and tighten it fully

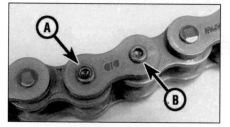

8.9 Pin end correctly riveted (A), pin end unriveted (B)

the rivet ends and two pieces of the wood between a C-clamp. Operate the clamp to press the sideplate over the pins.

● Assemble the joining tool over one pin (following the manufacturer's instructions) and tighten the tool down to spread the pin end securely **(see illustrations 8.8 and 8.9)**. Do the same on the other pin.

> ⚠ **Warning: Check that the pin ends are secure and that there is no danger of the sideplate coming loose. If the pin ends are cracked the soft link must be replaced.**

Final drive chain sizing

● Chains are sized using a three digit number, followed by a suffix to denote the chain type **(see illustration 8.10)**. Chain type is either standard or heavy duty (thicker sideplates), and also unsealed or O-ring/X-ring type.

● The first digit of the number relates to the pitch of the chain, ie the distance from the center of one pin to the center of the next pin **(see illustration 8.11)**. Pitch is expressed in eighths of an inch, as follows:

8.10 Typical chain size and type marking

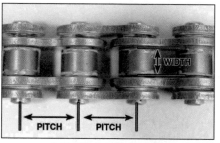

8.11 Chain dimensions

Sizes commencing with a 4 (for example 428) have a pitch of 1/2 inch (12.7 mm)
Sizes commencing with a 5 (for example 520) have a pitch of 5/8 inch (15.9 mm)
Sizes commencing with a 6 (for example 630) have a pitch of 3/4 inch (19.1 mm)

● The second and third digits of the chain size relate to the width of the rollers, for example the 525 shown has 5/16 inch (7.94 mm) rollers **(see illustration 8.11)**.

9 Hoses

Clamping to prevent flow

● Small-bore flexible hoses can be clamped to prevent fluid flow while a component is worked on. Whichever method is used, ensure that the hose material is not permanently distorted or damaged by the clamp.

a) A brake hose clamp available from auto parts stores **(see illustration 9.1)**.
b) A wingnut type hose clamp **(see illustration 9.2)**.

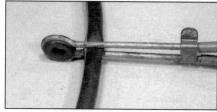

9.1 Hoses can be clamped with an automotive brake hose clamp . . .

9.2 . . . a wingnut type hose clamp . . .

c) Two sockets placed on each side of the hose and held with straight-jawed self-locking pliers **(see illustration 9.3)**.
d) Thick card stock on each side of the hose held between straight-jawed self-locking pliers **(see illustration 9.4)**.

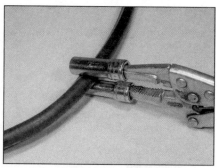

9.3 . . . two sockets and a pair of self-locking grips . . .

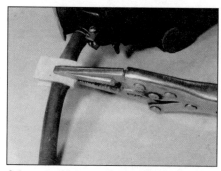

9.4 . . . or thick card and self-locking grips

Freeing and fitting hoses

● Always make sure the hose clamp is moved well clear of the hose end. Grip the hose with your hand and rotate it while pulling it off the union. If the hose has hardened due to age and will not move, slit it with a sharp knife and peel its ends off the union **(see illustration 9.5)**.

● Resist the temptation to use grease or soap on the unions to aid installation; although it helps the hose slip over the union it will equally aid the escape of fluid from the joint. It is preferable to soften the hose ends in hot water and wet the inside surface of the hose with water or a fluid which will evaporate.

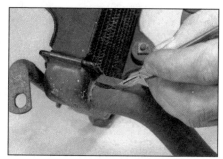

9.5 Cutting a coolant hose free with a sharp knife

Conversion Factors

Length (distance)				
Inches (in)	X 25.4	= Millimeters (mm)	X 0.0394	= Inches (in)
Feet (ft)	X 0.305	= Meters (m)	X 3.281	= Feet (ft)
Miles	X 1.609	= Kilometers (km)	X 0.621	= Miles
Volume (capacity)				
Cubic inches (cu in; in^3)	X 16.387	= Cubic centimeters (cc; cm^3)	X 0.061	= Cubic inches (cu in; in^3)
Imperial pints (Imp pt)	X 0.568	= Liters (l)	X 1.76	= Imperial pints (Imp pt)
Imperial quarts (Imp qt)	X 1.137	= Liters (l)	X 0.88	= Imperial quarts (Imp qt)
Imperial quarts (Imp qt)	X 1.201	= US quarts (US qt)	X 0.833	= Imperial quarts (Imp qt)
US quarts (US qt)	X 0.946	= Liters (l)	X 1.057	= US quarts (US qt)
Imperial gallons (Imp gal)	X 4.546	= Liters (l)	X 0.22	= Imperial gallons (Imp gal)
Imperial gallons (Imp gal)	X 1.201	= US gallons (US gal)	X 0.833	= Imperial gallons (Imp gal)
US gallons (US gal)	X 3.785	= Liters (l)	X 0.264	= US gallons (US gal)
Mass (weight)				
Ounces (oz)	X 28.35	= Grams (g)	X 0.035	= Ounces (oz)
Pounds (lb)	X 0.454	= Kilograms (kg)	X 2.205	= Pounds (lb)
Force				
Ounces-force (ozf; oz)	X 0.278	= Newtons (N)	X 3.6	= Ounces-force (ozf; oz)
Pounds-force (lbf; lb)	X 4.448	= Newtons (N)	X 0.225	= Pounds-force (lbf; lb)
Newtons (N)	X 0.1	= Kilograms-force (kgf; kg)	X 9.81	= Newtons (N)
Pressure				
Pounds-force per square inch (psi; lbf/in^2; lb/in^2)	X 0.070	= Kilograms-force per square centimeter (kgf/cm^2; kg/cm^2)	X 14.223	= Pounds-force per square inch (psi; lbf/in^2; lb/in^2)
Pounds-force per square inch (psi; lbf/in^2; lb/in^2)	X 0.068	= Atmospheres (atm)	X 14.696	= Pounds-force per square inch (psi; lbf/in^2; lb/in^2)
Pounds-force per square inch (psi; lbf/in^2; lb/in^2)	X 0.069	= Bars	X 14.5	= Pounds-force per square inch (psi; lbf/in^2; lb/in^2)
Pounds-force per square inch (psi; lbf/in^2; lb/in^2)	X 6.895	= Kilopascals (kPa)	X 0.145	= Pounds-force per square inch (psi; lbf/in^2; lb/in^2)
Kilopascals (kPa)	X 0.01	= Kilograms-force per square centimeter (kgf/cm^2; kg/cm^2)	X 98.1	= Kilopascals (kPa)
Torque (moment of force)				
Pounds-force inches (lbf in; lb in)	X 1.152	= Kilograms-force centimeter (kgf cm; kg cm)	X 0.868	= Pounds-force inches (lbf in; lb in)
Pounds-force inches (lbf in; lb in)	X 0.113	= Newton meters (Nm)	X 8.85	= Pounds-force inches (lbf in; lb in)
Pounds-force inches (lbf in; lb in)	X 0.083	= Pounds-force feet (lbf ft; lb ft)	X 12	= Pounds-force inches (lbf in; lb in)
Pounds-force feet (lbf ft; lb ft)	X 0.138	= Kilograms-force meters (kgf m; kg m)	X 7.233	= Pounds-force feet (lbf ft; lb ft)
Pounds-force feet (lbf ft; lb ft)	X 1.356	= Newton meters (Nm)	X 0.738	= Pounds-force feet (lbf ft; lb ft)
Newton meters (Nm)	X 0.102	= Kilograms-force meters (kgf m; kg m)	X 9.804	= Newton meters (Nm)
Vacuum				
Inches mercury (in. Hg)	X 3.377	= Kilopascals (kPa)	X 0.2961	= Inches mercury
Inches mercury (in. Hg)	X 25.4	= Millimeters mercury (mm Hg)	X 0.0394	= Inches mercury
Power				
Horsepower (hp)	X 745.7	= Watts (W)	X 0.0013	= Horsepower (hp)
Velocity (speed)				
Miles per hour (miles/hr; mph)	X 1.609	= Kilometers per hour (km/hr; kph)	X 0.621	= Miles per hour (miles/hr; mph)
Fuel consumption*				
Miles per gallon, Imperial (mpg)	X 0.354	= Kilometers per liter (km/l)	X 2.825	= Miles per gallon, Imperial (mpg)
Miles per gallon, US (mpg)	X 0.425	= Kilometers per liter (km/l)	X 2.352	= Miles per gallon, US (mpg)

Temperature

Degrees Fahrenheit = (°C x 1.8) + 32

Degrees Celsius (Degrees Centigrade; °C) = (°F - 32) x 0.56

****It is common practice to convert from miles per gallon (mpg) to liters/100 kilometers (l/100km), where mpg (Imperial) x l/100 km = 282 and mpg (US) x l/100 km = 235***

A number of chemicals and lubricants are available for use in motorcycle maintenance and repair. They include a wide variety of products ranging from cleaning solvents and degreasers to lubricants and protective sprays for rubber, plastic and vinyl.

• **Contact point/spark plug cleaner** is a solvent used to clean oily film and dirt from points, grime from electrical connectors and oil deposits from spark plugs. It is oil free and leaves no residue. It can also be used to remove gum and varnish from carburetor jets and other orifices.

• **Carburetor cleaner** is similar to contact point/spark plug cleaner but it usually has a stronger solvent and may leave a slight oily residue. It is not recommended for cleaning electrical components or connections.

• **Brake system cleaner** is used to remove brake dust, grease and brake fluid from the brake system, where clean surfaces are absolutely necessary. It leaves no residue and often eliminates brake squeal caused by contaminants.

• **Silicone-based lubricants** are used to protect rubber parts such as hoses and grommets, and are used as lubricants for hinges and locks.

• **Multi-purpose grease** is an all purpose lubricant used wherever grease is more practical than a liquid lubricant such as oil. Some multi-purpose grease is colored white and specially formulated to be more resistant to water than ordinary grease.

• **Gear oil** (sometimes called gear lube) is a specially designed oil used in transmissions and final drive units, as well as other areas where high friction, high temperature lubrication is required. It is available in a number of viscosities (weights) for various applications.

• **Motor oil**, of course, is the lubricant specially formulated for use in the engine. It normally contains a wide variety of additives to prevent corrosion and reduce foaming and wear. Motor oil comes in various weights (viscosity ratings) from 5 to 80. The recommended weight of the oil depends on the seasonal temperature and the demands on the engine. Light oil is used in cold climates and under light load conditions; heavy oil is used in hot climates where high loads are encountered. Multi-viscosity oils are designed to have characteristics of both light and heavy oils and are available in a number of weights from 5W-20 to 20W-50.

• **Gasoline additives** perform several functions, depending on their chemical makeup. They usually contain solvents that help dissolve gum and varnish that build up on carburetor and inlet parts. They also serve to break down carbon deposits that form on the inside surfaces of the combustion chambers. Some additives contain upper cylinder lubricants for valves and piston rings.

• **Brake and clutch fluid** is a specially formulated hydraulic fluid that can withstand the heat and pressure encountered in break/clutch systems. Care must be taken that this fluid does not come in contact with painted surfaces or plastics. An opened container should always be resealed to prevent contamination by water or dirt.

• **Chain lubricants** are formulated especially for use on motorcycle final drive chains. A good chain lube should adhere well and have good penetrating qualities to be effective as a lubricant inside the chain and on the side plates, pins and rollers. Most chain lubes are either the foaming type or quick drying type and are usually marketed as sprays. Take care to use a lubricant marked as being suitable for O-ring chains.

• **Degreasers** are heavy duty solvents used to remove grease and grime that may accumulate on the engine and frame components. They can be sprayed or brushed on and, depending on the type, are rinsed with either water or solvent.

• **Solvents** are used alone or in combination with degreasers to clean parts and assemblies during repair and overhaul. The home mechanic should use only solvents that are non-flammable and that do not produce irritating fumes.

• **Gasket sealing compounds** may be used in conjunction with gaskets, to improve their sealing capabilities, or alone, to seal metal-to-metal joints. Many gasket sealers can withstand extreme heat, some are impervious to gasoline and lubricants, while others are capable of filling and sealing large cavities. Depending on the intended use, gasket sealers either dry hard or stay relatively soft and pliable. They are usually applied by hand, with a brush or are sprayed on the gasket sealing surfaces.

• **Thread locking compound** is an adhesive locking compound that prevents threaded fasteners from loosening because of vibration. It is available in a variety of types for different applications.

• **Moisture dispersants** are usually sprays that can be used to dry out electrical components such as the fuse block and wiring connectors. Some types an also be used as treatment for rubber and as a lubricant for hinges, cables and locks.

• **Waxes and polishes** are used to help protect painted and plated surfaces from the weather. Different types of paint may require the use of different types of wax polish. Some polishes utilize a chemical or abrasive cleaner to help remove the top layer of oxidized (dull) paint on older vehicles. In recent years, many non-wax polishes (that contain a wide variety of chemicals such as polymers and silicones) have been introduced. These non-wax polishes are usually easier to apply and last longer than conventional waxes and polishes.

Preparing for storage

Before you start

If repairs or an overhaul is needed, see that this is carried out now rather than left until you want to ride the bike again.

Give the bike a good wash and scrub all dirt from its underside. Make sure the bike dries completely before preparing for storage.

Engine

● Remove the spark plug(s) and lubricate the cylinder bores with approximately a teaspoon of motor oil using a spout-type oil can **(see illustration 1)**. Reinstall the spark plug(s). Crank the engine over a couple of times to coat the piston rings and bores with oil. If the bike has a kickstart, use this to turn the engine over. If not, flick the kill switch to the OFF position and crank the engine over on the starter **(see illustration 2)**. If the nature of the ignition system prevents the starter operating with the kill switch in the OFF position, remove the spark plugs and fit them back in their caps; ensure that the plugs are grounded against the cylinder head when the starter is operated **(see illustration 3)**.

> ⚠️ **Warning: It is important that the plugs are grounded away from the spark plug holes otherwise there is a risk of atomized fuel from the cylinders igniting.**

> **HAYNES HINT** *On a single cylinder four-stroke engine, you can seal the combustion chamber completely by positioning the piston at TDC on the compression stroke.*

● Drain the carburetor(s) otherwise there is a risk of jets becoming blocked by gum deposits from the fuel **(see illustration 4)**.

● If the bike is going into long-term storage, consider adding a fuel stabilizer to the fuel in the tank. If the tank is drained completely, corrosion of its internal surfaces may occur if left unprotected for a long period. The tank can be treated with a rust preventative especially for this purpose. Alternatively, remove the tank and pour half a liter of motor oil into it, install the filler cap and shake the tank to coat its internals with oil before draining off the excess. The same effect can also be achieved by spraying WD-40 or a similar water-dispersant around the inside of the tank via its flexible nozzle.

● Make sure the cooling system contains the correct mix of antifreeze. Antifreeze also contains important corrosion inhibitors.

● The air intakes and exhaust can be sealed off by covering or plugging the openings. Ensure that you do not seal in any condensation; run the engine until it is hot, then switch off and allow to cool. Tape a piece

Squirt a drop of motor oil into each cylinder

Flick the kill switch to OFF . . .

. . . and ensure that the metal bodies of the plugs (arrows) are grounded against the cylinder head

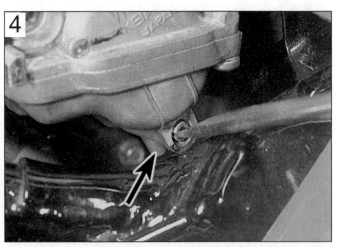

Connect a hose to the carburetor float chamber drain stub (arrow) and unscrew the drain screw

Exhausts can be sealed off with a plastic bag

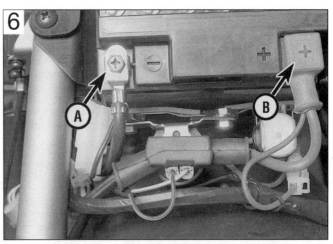

Disconnect the negative lead (A) first, followed by the positive lead (B)

of thick plastic over the silencer end(s) **(see illustration 5)**. Note that some advocate pouring a tablespoon of motor oil into the silencer(s) before sealing them off.

Battery

● Remove it from the bike - in extreme cases of cold the battery may freeze and crack its case **(see illustration 6)**.
● Check the electrolyte level and top up if necessary (conventional refillable batteries). Clean the terminals.
● Store the battery off the motorcycle and away from any sources of fire. Position a wooden block under the battery if it is to sit on the ground.
● Give the battery a trickle charge for a few hours every month **(see illustration 7)**.

Tires

● Place the bike on its centerstand or an auxiliary stand which will support the motorcycle in an upright position. Position wood blocks under the tires to keep them off the ground and to provide insulation from damp. If the bike is being put into long-term storage, ideally both tires should be off the

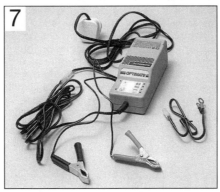

Use a suitable battery charger - this kit also assesses battery condition

ground; not only will this protect the tires, but will also ensure that no load is placed on the steering head or wheel bearings.
● Deflate each tire by 5 to 10 psi, no more or the beads may unseat from the rim, making subsequent inflation difficult on tubeless tires.

Pivots and controls

● Lubricate all lever, pedal, stand and

footrest pivot points. If grease nipples are fitted to the rear suspension components, apply lubricant to the pivots.
● Lubricate all control cables.

Cycle components

● Apply a wax protectant to all painted and plastic components. Wipe off any excess, but don't polish to a shine. Where fitted, clean the screen with soap and water.
● Coat metal parts with Vaseline (petroleum jelly). When applying this to the fork tubes, do not compress the forks otherwise the seals will rot from contact with the Vaseline.
● Apply a vinyl cleaner to the seat.

Storage conditions

● Aim to store the bike in a shed or garage which does not leak and is free from damp.
● Drape an old blanket or bedspread over the bike to protect it from dust and direct contact with sunlight (which will fade paint). Beware of tight-fitting plastic covers which may allow condensation to form and settle on the bike.

Getting back on the road

Engine and transmission

● Change the oil and replace the oil filter. If this was done prior to storage, check that the oil hasn't emulsified - a thick whitish substance which occurs through condensation.
● Remove the spark plugs. Using a spout-type oil can, squirt a few drops of oil into the cylinder(s). This will provide initial lubrication as the piston rings and bores comes back into contact. Service the spark plugs, or buy new ones, and install them in the engine.

● Check that the clutch isn't stuck on. The plates can stick together if left standing for some time, preventing clutch operation. Engage a gear and try rocking the bike back and forth with the clutch lever held against the handlebar. If this doesn't work on cable-operated clutches, hold the clutch lever back against the handlebar with a strong rubber band or cable tie for a couple of hours **(see illustration 8)**.
● If the air intakes or silencer end(s) were blocked off, remove the plug or cover used.
● If the fuel tank was coated with a rust

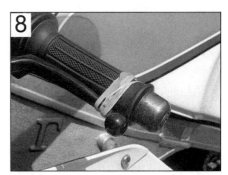

Hold the clutch lever back against the handlebar with rubber bands or a cable tie

preventative, oil or a stabilizer added to the fuel, drain and flush the tank and dispose of the fuel sensibly. If no action was taken with the fuel tank prior to storage, it is advised that the old fuel is disposed of since it will go bad over a period of time. Refill the fuel tank with fresh fuel.

Frame and running gear

● Oil all pivot points and cables.
● Check the tire pressures. They will definitely need inflating if pressures were reduced for storage.
● Lubricate the final drive chain (where applicable).
● Remove any protective coating applied to the fork tubes (stanchions) since this may well destroy the fork seals. If the fork tubes weren't protected and have picked up rust spots, remove them with very fine abrasive paper and refinish with metal polish.
● Check that both brakes operate correctly. Apply each brake hard and check that it's not possible to move the motorcycle forwards, then check that the brake frees off again once released. Brake caliper pistons can stick due to corrosion around the piston head, or on the sliding caliper types, due to corrosion of the slider pins. If the brake doesn't free after repeated operation, take the caliper off for examination. Similarly drum brakes can stick

due to a seized operating cam, cable or rod linkage.
● If the motorcycle has been in long-term storage, replace the brake fluid and clutch fluid (where applicable).
● Depending on where the bike has been stored, the wiring, cables and hoses may have been nibbled by rodents. Make a visual check and investigate disturbed wiring loom tape.

Battery

● If the battery has been previously removed and given top up charges it can simply be reconnected. Remember to connect the positive cable first and the negative cable last.
● On conventional refillable batteries, if the battery has not received any attention, remove it from the motorcycle and check its electrolyte level. Top up if necessary then charge the battery. If the battery fails to hold a charge and a visual check show heavy white sulfation of the plates, the battery is probably defective and must be replaced. This is particularly likely if the battery is old. Confirm battery condition with a specific gravity check.
● On sealed (MF) batteries, if the battery has not received any attention, remove it from the motorcycle and charge it according to the information on the battery case - if the battery fails to hold a charge it must be replaced.

Starting procedure

● If a kickstart is fitted, turn the engine over a couple of times with the ignition OFF to distribute oil around the engine. If no kickstart is fitted, flick the engine kill switch OFF and the ignition ON and crank the engine over a couple of times to work oil around the upper cylinder components. If the nature of the ignition system is such that the starter won't work with the kill switch OFF, remove the spark plugs, fit them back into their caps and ground their bodies on the cylinder head. Reinstall the spark plugs afterwards.
● Switch the kill switch to RUN, operate the choke and start the engine. If the engine won't start don't continue cranking the engine - not only will this flatten the battery, but the starter motor will overheat. Switch the ignition off and try again later. If the engine refuses to start, go through the troubleshooting procedures in this manual. **Note:** *If the bike has been in storage for a long time, old fuel or a carburetor blockage may be the problem. Gum deposits in carburetors can block jets - if a carburetor cleaner doesn't prove successful the carburetors must be dismantled for cleaning.*

● Once the engine has started, check that the lights, turn signals and horn work properly.

● Treat the bike gently for the first ride and check all fluid levels on completion. Settle the bike back into the maintenance schedule.

This Section provides an easy reference-guide to the more common faults that are likely to afflict your machine. Obviously, the opportunities are almost limitless for faults to occur as a result of obscure failures, and to try and cover all eventualities would require a book. Indeed, a number have been written on the subject.

Successful troubleshooting is not a mysterious 'black art' but the application of a bit of knowledge combined with a systematic and logical approach to the problem. Approach any troubleshooting by first accurately identifying the symptom and then checking through the list of possible causes, starting with the simplest or most obvious and progressing in stages to the most complex. Take nothing for granted, but above all apply liberal quantities of common sense.

The main symptom of a fault is given in the text as a major heading below which are listed the various systems or areas which may contain the fault. Details of each possible cause for a fault and the remedial action to be taken are given. Further information should be sought in the relevant Chapter.

1 Engine doesn't start or is difficult to start

- ☐ Starter motor doesn't rotate
- ☐ Starter motor rotates but engine does not turn over
- ☐ Starter works but engine won't turn over (seized)
- ☐ No fuel flow
- ☐ Engine flooded
- ☐ No spark or weak spark
- ☐ Compression low
- ☐ Stalls after starting
- ☐ Rough idle

2 Poor running at low speed

- ☐ Spark weak
- ☐ Fuel/air mixture incorrect
- ☐ Compression low
- ☐ Poor acceleration

3 Poor running or no power at high speed

- ☐ Firing incorrect
- ☐ Fuel/air mixture incorrect
- ☐ Compression low
- ☐ Knocking or pinging
- ☐ Miscellaneous causes

4 Overheating

- ☐ Engine overheats
- ☐ Firing incorrect
- ☐ Fuel/air mixture incorrect
- ☐ Compression too high
- ☐ Engine load excessive
- ☐ Lubrication inadequate
- ☐ Miscellaneous causes

5 Clutch problems

- ☐ Clutch slipping
- ☐ Clutch not disengaging completely

6 Gearchanging problems

- ☐ Doesn't go into gear, or lever doesn't return
- ☐ Jumps out of gear
- ☐ Overselects

7 Abnormal engine noise

- ☐ Knocking or pinging
- ☐ Piston slap or rattling
- ☐ Valve noise
- ☐ Other noise

8 Abnormal driveline noise

- ☐ Clutch noise
- ☐ Transmission noise
- ☐ Final drive noise

9 Abnormal frame and suspension noise

- ☐ Front end noise
- ☐ Shock absorber noise
- ☐ Brake noise

10 Oil pressure warning light comes on

- ☐ Engine lubrication system
- ☐ Electrical system

11 Excessive exhaust smoke

- ☐ White smoke
- ☐ Black smoke

12 Poor handling or stability

- ☐ Handlebar hard to turn
- ☐ Handlebar shakes or vibrates excessively
- ☐ Handlebar pulls to one side
- ☐ Poor shock absorbing qualities

13 Braking problems

- ☐ Brakes are spongy, don't hold
- ☐ Brake lever or pedal pulsates
- ☐ Brakes drag

14 Electrical problems

- ☐ Battery dead or weak
- ☐ Battery overcharged

1 Engine doesn't start or is difficult to start

Starter motor doesn't rotate

- [ ] Engine kill switch OFF.
- [ ] Fuse blown. Check main circuit breaker (Chapter 8).
- [ ] Battery voltage low. Check and recharge battery (Chapter 8).
- [ ] Starter motor defective. Make sure the wiring to the starter is secure. Make sure the starter solenoid clicks when the start button is pushed. If the solenoid clicks, then the fault is in the wiring or motor.
- [ ] Starter solenoid faulty. Check it according to the procedure in Chapter 8.
- [ ] Starter switch not contacting. The contacts could be wet, corroded or dirty. Disassemble and clean the switch (Chapter 8).
- [ ] Wiring open or shorted. Check all wiring connections and harnesses to make sure that they are dry, tight and not corroded. Also check for broken or frayed wires that can cause a short to ground (see wiring diagram, Chapter 8).
- [ ] Ignition (main) switch defective. Check the switch according to the procedure in Chapter 8. Replace the switch with a new one if it is defective.
- [ ] Engine kill switch defective. Check for wet, dirty or corroded contacts. Clean or replace the switch as necessary (Chapter 8).

Starter motor rotates but engine does not turn over

- [ ] Starter pinion gear defective. Inspect and repair or replace (Chapter 8).
- [ ] Damaged starter jackshaft. Inspect and replace the damaged parts (Chapter 8).

Starter works but engine won't turn over (seized)

- [ ] Seized engine caused by one or more internally damaged components. Failure due to wear, abuse or lack of lubrication. Damage can include seized valves, rocker arms, lifters, camshafts, pistons, crankshaft or connecting rod bearings. Refer to Chapter 2 for engine disassembly.

No fuel flow

- [ ] No fuel in tank.
- [ ] Fuel tank breather hose obstructed.
- [ ] Fuel filter is blocked (see Chapter 1).

Engine flooded

- [ ] Starting technique incorrect. Under normal circumstances the machine should start with little or no throttle. When the engine is cold, the choke should be operated (carburetor models) and the engine started without opening the throttle. When the engine is at operating temperature, only a very slight amount of throttle should be necessary.

No spark or weak spark

- [ ] Ignition switch OFF.
- [ ] Engine kill switch turned to the OFF position.
- [ ] Battery voltage low. Check and recharge the battery as necessary (Chapter 8).
- [ ] Spark plugs dirty, defective or worn out. Locate reason for fouled plugs using spark plug condition chart and follow the plug maintenance procedures (Chapter 1).
- [ ] Spark plug caps or secondary (HT) wiring faulty. Check condition. Replace either or both components if cracks or deterioration are evident (Chapter 4).

- [ ] Spark plug caps not making good contact. Make sure that the plug caps fit snugly over the plug ends.
- [ ] Ignition HT coils defective. Check the coils, referring to Chapter 4.
- [ ] ECM defective. Refer to Chapter 4 for details.
- [ ] Crankshaft or camshaft position sensor defective. Check the unit, referring to Chapter 4 for details.
- [ ] Ignition or kill switch shorted. This is usually caused by water, corrosion, damage or excessive wear. The switches can be disassembled and cleaned with electrical contact cleaner. If cleaning does not help, replace the switches (Chapter 8).
- [ ] Wiring shorted or broken between:

a) Ignition (main) switch and engine kill switch (or blown fuse)
b) ECM and engine kill switch
c) ECM and ignition HT coils
d) Ignition HT coils and spark plugs
e) ECM and crankshaft position sensor.

- [ ] Make sure that all wiring connections are clean, dry and tight. Look for chafed and broken wires (Chapters 4 and 8).

Compression low

- [ ] Spark plugs loose. Remove the plugs and inspect their threads. Reinstall and tighten to the specified torque (Chapter 1).
- [ ] Cylinder head not sufficiently tightened down. If the cylinder head is suspected of being loose, then there's a chance that the gasket or head is damaged if the problem has persisted for any length of time. The head bolts should be tightened to the proper torque in the correct sequence (Chapter 2).
- [ ] Cylinder and/or piston worn. Excessive wear will cause compression pressure to leak past the rings. This is usually accompanied by worn rings as well. A top-end overhaul is necessary (Chapter 2).
- [ ] Piston rings worn, weak, broken, or sticking. Broken or sticking piston rings usually indicate a lubrication or fuelling problem that causes excess carbon deposits or seizures to form on the pistons and rings. Top-end overhaul is necessary (Chapter 2).
- [ ] Piston ring-to-groove clearance excessive. This is caused by excessive wear of the piston ring lands. Piston replacement is necessary (Chapter 2).
- [ ] Cylinder head gasket damaged. If a head is allowed to become loose, or if excessive carbon build-up on the piston crown and combustion chamber causes extremely high compression, the head gasket may leak. Retorquing the head is not always sufficient to restore the seal, so gasket replacement is necessary (Chapter 2).
- [ ] Cylinder head warped. This is caused by overheating or improperly tightened head bolts. Machine shop resurfacing or head replacement is necessary (Chapter 2).
- [ ] Valve spring broken or weak. Caused by component failure or wear; the springs must be replaced (Chapter 2).
- [ ] Valve not seating properly. This is caused by a bent valve (from over-revving burned valve or seat (improper fuelling) or an accumulation of carbon deposits on the seat (from fuelling or lubrication problems). The valves must be cleaned and/or replaced and the seats serviced if possible (Chapter 2).

1 Engine doesn't start or is difficult to start (continued)

Stalls after starting

☐ Improper choke action (carburetor models). Make sure the choke linkage shaft is getting a full stroke and staying in the out position (Chapter 3).
☐ Ignition malfunction. See Chapter 4.
☐ Carburetor malfunction. See Chapter 3.
☐ Fuel contaminated. The fuel can be contaminated with either dirt or water, or can change chemically if the machine is allowed to sit for several months or more. Drain the tank (Chapter 3).
☐ Intake air leak. Check for loose intake manifold and damaged/disconnected vacuum hoses (Chapter 3).
☐ Engine idle speed incorrect. On carburetor models, turn idle adjusting screw until the engine idles at the specified rpm (Chapter 1).

Rough idle

☐ Ignition malfunction. See Chapter 4.
☐ Idle speed incorrect. See Chapter 1.
☐ Carburetor or EFI malfunction. See Chapter 3.
☐ Fuel contaminated. The fuel can be contaminated with either dirt or water, or can change chemically if the machine is allowed to sit for several months or more. Drain the tank (Chapter 3).
☐ Intake air leak. Check for loose intake manifold and damaged/disconnected vacuum hoses. Replace the intake ducts if they are split or deteriorated (Chapter 3).
☐ Air filter clogged. Replace the air filter element (Chapter 1).

2 Poor running at low speeds

Spark weak

☐ Battery voltage low. Check and recharge battery (Chapter 8).
☐ Spark plugs fouled, defective or worn out. Refer to Chapter 1 for spark plug maintenance.
☐ Spark plug cap or HT wiring defective. Refer to Chapters 1 and 4 for details on the ignition system.
☐ Spark plug caps not making contact.
☐ Incorrect spark plugs. Wrong type, heat range or cap configuration. Check and install correct plugs listed in Chapter 1.
☐ ECM faulty. See Chapter 3.
☐ Pick-up coil defective. See Chapter 3.
☐ Ignition coil defective. See Chapter 4.

Fuel/air mixture incorrect

☐ Pilot jet or air passage blocked. Remove and overhaul the carburetor (if equipped) (Chapter 3).
☐ Air filter clogged, poorly sealed or missing (Chapter 1).
☐ Air filter housing poorly sealed. Look for cracks, holes or loose clamps and replace or repair defective parts.
☐ Fuel tank breather hose obstructed.
☐ Intake air leak. Check for loose intake manifold and damaged/disconnected vacuum hoses. Replace the intake ducts if they are split or deteriorated (Chapter 3).

Compression low

☐ Spark plugs loose. Remove the plugs and inspect their threads. Reinstall and tighten to the specified torque (Chapter 1).
☐ Cylinder head not sufficiently tightened down. If the cylinder head is suspected of being loose, then there's a chance that the gasket and head are damaged if the problem has persisted for any length of time. The head bolts should be tightened to the proper torque in the correct sequence (Chapter 2).
☐ Cylinder and/or piston worn. Excessive wear will cause compression pressure to leak past the rings. This is usually accompanied by worn rings as well. A top-end overhaul is necessary (Chapter 2).

☐ Piston rings worn, weak, broken, or sticking. Broken or sticking piston rings usually indicate a lubrication or fuelling problem that causes excess carbon deposits or seizures to form on the pistons and rings. Top-end overhaul is necessary (Chapter 2).
☐ Piston ring-to-groove clearance excessive. This is caused by excessive wear of the piston ring lands. Piston replacement is necessary (Chapter 2).
☐ Cylinder head gasket damaged. If a head is allowed to become loose, or if excessive carbon build-up on the piston crown and combustion chamber causes extremely high compression, the head gasket may leak. Retorquing the head is not always sufficient to restore the seal, so gasket replacement is necessary (Chapter 2).
☐ Cylinder head warped. This is caused by overheating or improperly tightened head bolts. Machine shop resurfacing or head replacement is necessary (Chapter 2).
☐ Valve spring broken or weak. Caused by component failure or wear; the springs must be replaced (Chapter 2).
☐ Valve not seating properly. This is caused by a bent valve (from over-revving or improper valve adjustment), burned valve or seat (improper fuelling) or an accumulation of carbon deposits on the seat (from fuelling, lubrication problems). The valves must be cleaned and/or replaced and the seats serviced if possible (Chapter 2).

Poor acceleration

☐ Carburetor fault. Remove and overhaul the carburetor (Chapter 3).
☐ Electronic fuel injection system fault. Inspect the components (Chapter 3).
☐ Engine oil viscosity too high. Using a heavier oil than that recommended in Chapter 1 can damage the oil pump or lubrication system and cause drag on the engine.
☐ Brakes dragging. Usually caused by debris which has entered the brake piston seals, or from a warped disc or bent axle. Repair as necessary (Chapter 6).

3 Poor running or no power at high speed

Firing incorrect

☐ Air filter restricted. Clean or replace filter (Chapter 1).
☐ Spark plugs fouled, defective or worn out. See Chapter 1 for spark plug maintenance.
☐ Spark plug caps or HT wiring defective. See Chapters 1 and 4 for details of the ignition system.
☐ Spark plug caps not in good contact. See Chapter 4.
☐ Incorrect spark plugs. Wrong type, heat range or cap configuration. Check and install correct plugs listed in Chapter 1.
☐ ECM defective. See Chapter 4.
☐ Crankshaft or camshaft position sensor defective. See Chapter 4.
☐ Ignition coils defective. See Chapter 4.

Fuel/air mixture incorrect

☐ Carburetor fault. Remove and overhaul the carburetor (Chapter 3).
☐ Electronic fuel injection system fault. Inspect the components (Chapter 3).
☐ Air filter clogged, poorly sealed, or missing (Chapter 1).
☐ Air filter housing poorly sealed. Look for cracks, holes or loose clamps, and replace or repair defective parts.
☐ Fuel tank breather hose obstructed.
☐ Intake air leak. Check for loose intake manifold and damaged/disconnected vacuum hoses. Replace the intake ducts if they are split or deteriorated (Chapter 4).

Compression low

☐ Spark plugs loose. Remove the plugs and inspect their threads. Reinstall and tighten to the specified torque (Chapter 1).
☐ Cylinder head not sufficiently tightened down. If the cylinder head is suspected of being loose, then there's a chance that the gasket and head are damaged if the problem has persisted for any length of time. The head bolts should be tightened to the proper torque in the correct sequence (Chapter 2).
☐ Cylinder and/or piston worn. Excessive wear will cause compression pressure to leak past the rings. This is usually accompanied by worn rings as well. A top-end overhaul is necessary (Chapter 2).
☐ Piston rings worn, weak, broken, or sticking. Broken or sticking piston rings usually indicate a lubrication or fuelling problem that causes excess carbon deposits or seizures to form on the pistons and rings. Top-end overhaul is necessary (Chapter 2).
☐ Piston ring-to-groove clearance excessive. This is caused by excessive wear of the piston ring lands. Piston replacement is necessary (Chapter 2).

☐ Cylinder head gasket damaged. If a head is allowed to become loose, or if excessive carbon build-up on the piston crown and combustion chamber causes extremely high compression, the head gasket may leak. Retorquing the head is not always sufficient to restore the seal, so gasket replacement is necessary (Chapter 2).
☐ Cylinder head warped. This is caused by overheating or improperly tightened head bolts. Machine shop resurfacing or head replacement is necessary (Chapter 2).
☐ Valve spring broken or weak. Caused by component failure or wear; the springs must be replaced (Chapter 2).
☐ Valve not seating properly. This is caused by a bent valve (from over-revving), burned valve or seat (improper fuelling) or an accumulation of carbon deposits on the seat (from fuelling or lubrication problems). The valves must be cleaned and/or replaced and the seats serviced if possible (Chapter 2).

Knocking or pinging

☐ Carbon build-up in combustion chamber. Use of a fuel additive that will dissolve the adhesive bonding the carbon particles to the crown and chamber is the easiest way to remove the build-up. Otherwise, the cylinder head will have to be removed and decarbonized (Chapter 2).
☐ Incorrect or poor quality fuel. Old or improper grades of fuel can cause detonation. This causes the piston to rattle, thus the knocking or pinging sound. Drain old fuel and always use the recommended fuel grade.
☐ Spark plug heat range incorrect. Uncontrolled detonation indicates the plug heat range is too hot. The plug in effect becomes a glow plug, raising cylinder temperatures. Install the proper heat range plug (Chapter 1).
☐ Improper air/fuel mixture. This will cause the cylinders to run hot, which leads to detonation. An intake air leak can cause this imbalance. See Chapter 3.

Miscellaneous causes

☐ Throttle valve doesn't open fully. Adjust the throttle grip freeplay (Chapter 1).
☐ Clutch slipping. May be caused by loose or worn clutch components. Refer to Chapter 2 for clutch overhaul procedures.
☐ Engine oil viscosity too high. Using a heavier oil than the one recommended in Chapter 1 can damage the oil pump or lubrication system and cause drag on the engine.
☐ Brakes dragging. Usually caused by debris which has entered the brake piston seals, or from a warped disc or bent axle. Repair as necessary.

4 Overheating

Firing incorrect

☐ Spark plugs fouled, defective or worn out. See Chapter 1 for spark plug maintenance.
☐ Incorrect spark plugs.
☐ ECM defective. See Chapter 4.
☐ Crankshaft or camshaft position sensor faulty. See Chapter 4.
☐ Faulty ignition coil. See Chapter 4.

Fuel/air mixture incorrect

☐ Carburetor fault. Remove and overhaul the carburetor (Chapter 3).
☐ Air filter clogged, poorly sealed, or missing (Chapter 1).
☐ Air filter housing poorly sealed. Look for cracks, holes or loose clamps, and replace or repair defective parts.
☐ Fuel tank breather hose obstructed.
☐ Intake air leak. Check for loose carburetor intake duct retaining clips and damaged/disconnected vacuum hoses. Replace the intake ducts if they are split or deteriorated (Chapter 3).

Compression too high

☐ Carbon build-up in combustion chamber. Use of a fuel additive that will dissolve the adhesive bonding the carbon particles to the piston crown and chamber is the easiest way to remove the build-up. Otherwise, the cylinder head will have to be removed and decarbonized (Chapter 2).
☐ Improperly machined head surface or installation of incorrect gasket during engine assembly.

Engine load excessive

☐ Clutch slipping. Can be caused by damaged, loose or worn clutch components. Refer to Chapter 2 for overhaul procedures.
☐ Engine oil level too high. The addition of too much oil will cause pressurization of the crankcase and inefficient engine operation. Check Specifications and drain to proper level (Chapter 1).
☐ Engine oil viscosity too high. Using a heavier oil than the one recommended in Chapter 1 can damage the oil pump or lubrication system as well as cause drag on the engine.
☐ Brakes dragging. Usually caused by debris which has entered the brake piston seals, or from a warped disc or bent axle. Repair as necessary.

Lubrication inadequate

☐ Engine oil level too low. Friction caused by intermittent lack of lubrication or from oil that is overworked can cause overheating. The oil provides a definite cooling function in the engine. Check the oil level (Chapter 1).
☐ Poor quality engine oil or incorrect viscosity or type. Oil is rated not only according to viscosity but also according to type. Some oils are not rated high enough for use in this engine. Check the Specifications section and change to the correct oil (Chapter 1).

Miscellaneous causes

☐ Modification to exhaust system. Most aftermarket exhaust systems cause the engine to run leaner, which makes it run hotter.

5 Clutch problems

Clutch slipping

☐ Clutch cable freeplay incorrectly adjusted (Chapter 1).
☐ Friction plates worn or warped. Overhaul the clutch assembly (Chapter 2).
☐ Metal plates warped (Chapter 2).
☐ Clutch diaphragm spring broken or weak. An old or heat-damaged (from slipping clutch) spring should be replaced with a new one (Chapter 2).
☐ Clutch pushrod bent. Check and, if necessary, replace (Chapter 2).
☐ Clutch center or housing unevenly worn. This causes improper engagement of the plates. Replace the damaged or worn parts (Chapter 2).

Clutch not disengaging completely

☐ Clutch cable freeplay incorrectly adjusted (Chapter 1).

☐ Clutch plates warped or damaged. This will cause clutch drag, which in turn will cause the machine to creep. Overhaul the clutch assembly (Chapter 2).
☐ Clutch spring tension uneven. Usually caused by a sagged or broken spring. Check and replace the diaphragm spring (Chapter 2).
☐ Engine oil deteriorated. Old, thin, worn out oil will not provide proper lubrication for the plates, causing the clutch to drag. Replace the oil and filter (Chapter 1).
☐ Engine oil viscosity too high. Using a heavier oil than recommended in Chapter 1 can cause the plates to stick together, putting a drag on the engine. Change to the correct weight oil (Chapter 1).
☐ Clutch housing bearing seized. Lack of lubrication, severe wear or damage can cause the bearing to seize on the input shaft. Overhaul of the clutch, and perhaps transmission, may be necessary to repair the damage (Chapter 2).

6 Gearchanging problems

Doesn't go into gear or lever doesn't return

☐ Clutch not disengaging. See above.
☐ Shift fork(s) bent or seized. Often caused by dropping the machine or from lack of lubrication. Overhaul the transmission (Chapter 2).
☐ Gear(s) stuck on shaft. Most often caused by a lack of lubrication or excessive wear in transmission bearings and bushings. Overhaul the transmission (Chapter 2).
☐ Gear shift drum binding. Caused by lubrication failure or excessive wear. Replace the drum and bearing (Chapter 2).
☐ Gear shift lever pawl spring weak or broken (Chapter 2).
☐ Gear shift lever broken. Splines stripped out of lever or shaft, caused by allowing the lever to get loose or from dropping the machine. Replace necessary parts (Chapter 2).
☐ Gear shift mechanism stopper arm broken or worn. Full engagement and rotary movement of shift drum results. Replace the arm (Chapter 2).

☐ Stopper arm spring broken. Allows arm to float, causing sporadic shift operation. Replace spring (Chapter 2).

Jumps out of gear

☐ Shift fork(s) worn. Overhaul the transmission (Chapter 2).
☐ Gear groove(s) worn. Overhaul the transmission (Chapter 2).
☐ Gear dogs or dog slots worn or damaged. The gears should be inspected and replaced. No attempt should be made to service the worn parts.

Overselects

☐ Stopper arm spring weak or broken (Chapter 2).
☐ Return spring post broken or distorted (Chapter 2).

7 Abnormal engine noise

Knocking or pinging

☐ Carbon build-up in combustion chamber. Use of a fuel additive that will dissolve the adhesive bonding the carbon particles to the piston crown and chamber is the easiest way to remove the build-up. Otherwise, the cylinder head will have to be removed and decarbonized (Chapter 2).
☐ Incorrect or poor quality fuel. Old or improper fuel can cause detonation. This causes the pistons to rattle, thus the knocking or pinging sound. Drain the old fuel and always use the recommended grade fuel (Chapter 3).
☐ Spark plug heat range incorrect. Uncontrolled detonation indicates that the plug heat range is too hot. The plug in effect becomes a glow plug, raising cylinder temperatures. Install the proper heat range plug (Chapter 1).
☐ Improper air/fuel mixture. This will cause the cylinders to run hot and lead to detonation. Blocked carburetor jets or an air leak can cause this imbalance. See Chapter 3.

Piston slap or rattling

☐ Cylinder-to-piston clearance excessive. Caused by improper assembly. Inspect and overhaul top-end parts (Chapter 2).
☐ Connecting rod bent. Caused by over-revving, trying to start a badly flooded engine or from ingesting a foreign object into the combustion chamber. Replace the damaged parts (Chapter 2).
☐ Piston pin or piston pin bore worn or seized from wear or lack of lubrication. Replace damaged parts (Chapter 2).
☐ Piston ring(s) worn, broken or sticking. Overhaul the top-end (Chapter 2).
☐ Piston seizure damage. Usually from lack of lubrication or overheating. Replace the pistons and cylinders, as necessary (Chapter 2).

☐ Connecting rod bearing clearance excessive. Caused by excessive wear or lack of lubrication. Replace worn parts.

Valve noise

☐ Hydraulic lifter worn or damaged. Inspect and replace as necessary (Chapter 2).
☐ Valve spring broken or weak. Check and replace weak valve springs (Chapter 2).
☐ Camshaft or rocker arms worn or damaged. Lack of lubrication at high rpm is usually the cause of damage. Insufficient oil or failure to change the oil at the recommended intervals are the chief causes. Inspect and replace as necessary. Rocker arm bushings can be replaced separately (Chapter 2).

Other noise

☐ Cylinder head gasket leaking.
☐ Exhaust pipe leaking at cylinder head connection. Caused by improper fit of pipe(s) or loose exhaust nuts. All exhaust fasteners should be tightened evenly and carefully. Failure to do this will lead to a leak.
☐ Crankshaft runout excessive. Caused by a bent crankshaft (from over-revving) or damage from an upper cylinder component failure. Can also be attributed to dropping the machine on either of the crankshaft ends.
☐ Engine mounting bolts loose. Tighten all engine mount bolts (Chapter 2).
☐ Crankshaft bearings worn (Chapter 2).
☐ Camchain, tensioner or guides worn. Replace according to the procedure in Chapter 2.

8 Abnormal driveline noise

Clutch and primary drive noise

☐ Clutch outer drum/friction plate clearance excessive (Chapter 2).
☐ Loose or damaged clutch pressure plate and/or bolts (Chapter 2).
☐ Loose or damaged primary chain (Chapter 1).

Transmission noise

☐ Bearings worn. Also includes the possibility that the shafts are worn. Overhaul the transmission (Chapter 2).
☐ Gears worn or chipped (Chapter 2).
☐ Metal chips jammed in gear teeth. Probably pieces from a broken gear or shift mechanism that were picked up by the gears. This will cause early bearing failure (Chapter 2).

☐ Transmission oil level too low. Causes a howl from transmission (Chapter 1).

Final drive noise

☐ Belt not adjusted properly (Chapter 1).
☐ Front or rear sprocket loose. Tighten fasteners (Chapter 6).
☐ Sprockets worn. Replace sprockets (Chapter 6).
☐ Rear sprocket warped. Replace sprockets (Chapter 6).

9 Abnormal frame and suspension noise

Front end noise

☐ Low fluid level or improper viscosity oil in forks. This can sound like spurting and is usually accompanied by irregular fork action (Chapter 5).
☐ Spring weak or broken. Makes a clicking or scraping sound. Fork oil, when drained, will have a lot of metal particles in it (Chapter 5).
☐ Steering head bearings loose or damaged. Clicks when braking. Check and adjust or replace as necessary (Chapters 1 and 5).
☐ Triple clamps loose. Make sure all clamp bolts are tightened to the specified torque (Chapter 5).
☐ Fork tube bent. Good possibility if machine has been dropped. Replace tube with a new one (Chapter 5).
☐ Front axle bolt or axle pinch bolts loose. Tighten them to the specified torque (Chapter 6).
☐ Loose or worn wheel bearings. Check and replace as needed (Chapter 6).

Shock absorber noise

☐ Fluid level incorrect. Indicates a leak caused by defective seal. Shock will be covered with oil. Replace shock (Chapter 5).
☐ Defective shock absorber with internal damage. This is in the body of the shock and can't be remedied. The shock must be replaced with a new one (Chapter 5).

☐ Bent or damaged shock body. Replace the shock with a new one (Chapter 5).

Brake noise

☐ Squeal caused by dust on brake pads. Usually found in combination with glazed pads. Clean using brake cleaning solvent (Chapter 6).
☐ Contamination of brake pads. Oil, brake fluid or dirt causing brake to chatter or squeal. Clean or replace pads (Chapter 6).
☐ Pads glazed. Caused by excessive heat from prolonged use or from contamination. Do not use sandpaper/emery cloth or any other abrasive to roughen the pad surfaces as abrasives will stay in the pad material and damage the disc. A very fine flat file can be used, but pad replacement is suggested as a cure (Chapter 6).
☐ Disc warped. Can cause a chattering, clicking or intermittent squeal. Usually accompanied by a pulsating lever and uneven braking. Replace the disc (Chapter 6).
☐ Loose or worn wheel bearings. Check and replace as needed (Chapter 6).

10 Oil pressure warning light comes on

Engine lubrication system

☐ Engine oil pump defective or failed relief valve. Inspect (Chapter 2).
☐ Engine oil level low. Inspect for leak or other problem causing low oil level and add recommended oil (Chapter 1).
☐ Engine oil viscosity too low. Very old, thin oil or an improper weight of oil used in the engine. Change to correct oil (Chapter 1).

Electrical system

☐ Oil pressure switch defective. Check the switch according to the procedure in Chapter 8. Replace it if it is defective.
☐ Oil pressure indicator light circuit defective. Check for pinched, shorted, disconnected or damaged wiring (Chapter 8).

11 Excessive exhaust smoke

White smoke

☐ Piston oil ring worn. The ring may be broken or damaged, causing oil from the crankcase to be pulled past the piston into the combustion chamber. Replace the rings with new ones (Chapter 2).

☐ Cylinders worn, cracked, or scored. Caused by overheating or oil starvation. Install a new cylinder (Chapter 2).

☐ Valve oil seal damaged or worn. Replace oil seals with new ones (Chapter 2).

☐ Valve guide worn. Perform a complete valve job (Chapter 2).

☐ Engine oil level too high, which causes the oil to be forced past the rings. Drain oil to the proper level (Chapter 1).

☐ Head gasket broken between oil return and cylinder. Causes oil to be pulled into the combustion chamber. Replace the head gasket and check the head for warpage (Chapter 2).

☐ Abnormal crankcase pressurization, which forces oil past the rings. Clogged breather is usually the cause.

Black smoke

☐ Air filter clogged. Clean or replace the element (Chapter 1).

☐ Carburetor flooding. Remove and overhaul the carburetor (Chapter 3).

☐ Main jet too large. Remove and overhaul the carburetor(s) (Chapter 3).

☐ Choke cable stuck (Chapter 3).

☐ Fuel level too high. Check the fuel level (Chapter 3).

12 Poor handling or stability

Handlebar hard to turn

☐ Steering head bearing adjuster nut too tight. Check adjustment as described in Chapter 5.

☐ Bearings damaged. Roughness can be felt as the bars are turned from side-to-side. Replace bearings and races (Chapter 5).

☐ Races dented or worn. Denting results from wear in only one position (e.g., straight ahead), from a collision or hitting a pothole or from dropping the machine. Replace races and bearings (Chapter 5).

☐ Steering stem lubrication inadequate. Causes are grease getting hard from age or being washed out by high pressure car washes. Disassemble steering head and repack bearings (Chapter 5).

☐ Steering stem bent. Caused by a collision, hitting a pothole or by dropping the machine. Replace damaged part. Don't try to straighten the steering stem (Chapter 5).

☐ Front tire air pressure too low (Chapter 1).

Handlebar shakes or vibrates excessively

☐ Tires worn or out of balance (Chapter 6).

☐ Swingarm bearings worn. Replace worn bearings (Chapter 5).

☐ Wheel rim(s) warped or damaged. Inspect wheels for runout (Chapter 6).

☐ Wheel bearings worn. Worn front or rear wheel bearings can cause poor tracking. Worn front bearings will cause wobble (Chapter 6).

☐ Handlebar clamp bolts loose (Chapter 5).

☐ Fork yoke bolts loose. Tighten them to the specified torque (Chapter 5).

☐ Engine mounting bolts loose. Will cause excessive vibration with increased engine rpm (Chapter 2).

Handlebar pulls to one side

☐ Frame bent. Definitely suspect this if the machine has been dropped. May or may not be accompanied by cracking near the bend. Replace the frame (Chapter 7).

☐ Wheels out of alignment. Caused by improper location of axle spacers or from bent steering stem or frame (Chapters 5 and 7).

☐ Swingarm bent or twisted. Caused by age (metal fatigue) or impact damage. Replace the arm (Chapter 5).

☐ Steering stem bent. Caused by impact damage or by dropping the motorcycle. Replace the steering stem (Chapter 5).

☐ Fork tube bent. Disassemble the forks and replace the damaged parts (Chapter 5).

☐ Fork oil level uneven. Check and add or drain as necessary (Chapter 1).

Poor shock absorbing qualities

Too hard:
a) *Fork oil level excessive (Chapter 1).*
b) *Fork oil viscosity too high. Use a lighter oil (see the Specifications in Chapter 1).*
c) *Fork tube bent. Causes a harsh, sticking feeling (Chapter 5).*
d) *Shock shaft or body bent or damaged (Chapter 5).*
e) *Fork internal damage (Chapter 5).*
f) *Shock internal damage.*
g) *Tire pressure too high (Chapter 1).*
Too soft:
a) *Fork or shock oil insufficient and/or leaking (Chapter 1).*
b) *Fork oil level too low (Chapter 5).*
c) *Fork oil viscosity too light (Chapter 5).*
d) *Fork springs weak or broken (Chapter 5).*
e) *Shock internal damage or leakage (Chapter 5).*

13 Braking problems

Brakes are spongy, don't hold

- [ ] Air in brake line. Caused by inattention to master cylinder fluid level or by leakage. Locate problem and bleed brakes (Chapter 6).
- [ ] Pad or disc worn (Chapters 1 and 6).
- [ ] Brake fluid leak. See paragraph 1.
- [ ] Contaminated pads. Caused by contamination with oil, grease, brake fluid, etc. Clean or replace pads. Clean disc thoroughly with brake cleaner (Chapter 7).
- [ ] Brake fluid deteriorated. Fluid is old or contaminated. Drain system, replenish with new fluid and bleed the system (Chapter 6).
- [ ] Master cylinder internal parts worn or damaged causing fluid to bypass (Chapter 6).
- [ ] Master cylinder bore scratched by foreign material or broken spring. Repair or replace master cylinder (Chapter 6).
- [ ] Disc warped. Replace disc (Chapter 6).

Brake lever or pedal pulsates

- [ ] Disc warped. Replace disc (Chapter 6).

- [ ] Axle bent. Replace axle (Chapter 6).
- [ ] Brake caliper bolts loose (Chapter 6).
- [ ] Wheel warped or otherwise damaged (Chapter 6).
- [ ] Wheel bearings damaged or worn (Chapter 6).

Brakes drag

- [ ] Master cylinder piston seized. Caused by wear or damage to piston or cylinder bore (Chapter 6).
- [ ] Lever binding. Check pivot and lubricate (Chapter 6).
- [ ] Brake caliper piston seized in bore. Caused by wear or ingestion of dirt past deteriorated seal (Chapter 6).
- [ ] Brake caliper mounting bracket pins corroded. Clean off corrosion and lubricate (Chapter 6).
- [ ] Brake pad damaged. Material separated from backing plate. Usually caused by faulty manufacturing process or from contact with chemicals. Replace pads (Chapter 6).
- [ ] Pads improperly installed (Chapter 6).

14 Electrical problems

Battery dead or weak

- [ ] Battery faulty. Caused by sulfated plates which are shorted through sedimentation. Also, broken battery terminal making only occasional contact (Chapter 8).
- [ ] Battery cables making poor contact (Chapter 8).
- [ ] Load excessive. Caused by addition of high wattage lights or other electrical accessories.
- [ ] Ignition (main) switch defective. Switch either grounds internally or fails to shut off system. Replace the switch (Chapter 8).
- [ ] Regulator/rectifier defective (Chapter 8).
- [ ] Alternator stator coil open or shorted (Chapter 8).
- [ ] Wiring faulty. Wiring grounded or connections loose in ignition, charging or lighting circuits (Chapter 8).

Battery overcharged

- [ ] Regulator/rectifier defective. Overcharging is noticed when battery gets excessively warm (Chapter 8).
- [ ] Battery defective. Replace battery with a new one (Chapter 8).
- [ ] Battery amperage too low, wrong type or size. Install manufacturer's specified amp-hour battery to handle charging load (Chapter 8).

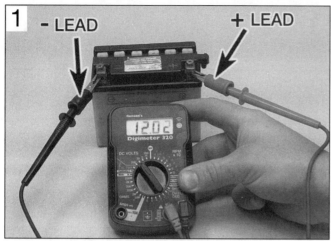

Measuring open-circuit battery voltage

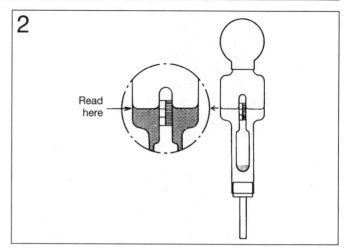

Float-type hydrometer for measuring battery specific gravity

Checking engine compression

● Low compression will result in exhaust smoke, heavy oil consumption, poor starting and poor performance. A compression test will provide useful information about an engine's condition and if performed regularly, can give warning of trouble before any other symptoms become apparent.

● A compression gauge will be required, along with an adapter to suit the spark plug hole thread size. Note that the screw-in type gauge/adapter set up is preferable to the rubber cone type.

● Compression testing procedures for the motorcycles covered in this manual are described in Chapter 2.

Checking battery open-circuit voltage

 Warning: The gases produced by the battery are explosive - never smoke or create any sparks in the vicinity of the battery. Never allow the electrolyte to contact your skin or clothing - if it does, wash it off and seek immediate medical attention.

● Before any electrical fault is investigated the battery should be checked.

● You'll need a dc voltmeter or multimeter to check battery voltage. Check that the leads are inserted in the correct terminals on the meter, red lead to positive (+), black lead to

negative (-). Incorrect connections can damage the meter.

● A sound, fully-charged 12 volt battery should produce between 12.3 and 12.6 volts across its terminals (12.8 volts for a maintenance-free battery). On machines with a 6 volt battery, voltage should be between 6.1 and 6.3 volts.

1 Set a multimeter to the 0 to 20 volts dc range and connect its probes across the battery terminals. Connect the meter's positive (+) probe, usually red, to the battery positive (+) terminal, followed by the meter's negative (-) probe, usually black, to the battery negative terminal (-) **(see illustration 1)**.

2 If battery voltage is low (below 10 volts on a 12 volt battery or below 4 volts on a six volt battery), charge the battery and test the voltage again. If the battery repeatedly goes flat, investigate the motorcycle's charging system.

Checking battery specific gravity (SG)

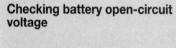 *Warning: The gases produced by the battery are explosive - never smoke or create any sparks in the vicinity of the battery. Never allow the electrolyte to contact your skin or clothing - if it does, wash it off and seek immediate medical attention.*

● The specific gravity check gives an indication of a battery's state of charge.

● A hydrometer is used for measuring specific gravity. Make sure you purchase one which has a small enough hose to insert in the aperture of a motorcycle battery.

● Specific gravity is simply a measure of the electrolyte's density compared with that of water. Water has an SG of 1.000 and fully-

charged battery electrolyte is about 26% heavier, at 1.260.

● Specific gravity checks are not possible on maintenance-free batteries. Testing the open-circuit voltage is the only means of determining their state of charge.

1 To measure SG, remove the battery from the motorcycle and remove the first cell cap. Draw some electrolyte into the hydrometer and note the reading **(see illustration 2)**. Return the electrolyte to the cell and install the cap.

2 The reading should be in the region of 1.260 to 1.280. If SG is below 1.200 the battery needs charging. Note that SG will vary with temperature; it should be measured at 20°C (68°F). Add 0.007 to the reading for every 10°C above 20°C, and subtract 0.007 from the reading for every 10°C below 20°C. Add 0.004 to the reading for every 10°F above 68°F, and subtract 0.004 from the reading for every 10°F below 68°F.

3 When the check is complete, rinse the hydrometer thoroughly with clean water.

Checking for continuity

● The term continuity describes the uninterrupted flow of electricity through an electrical circuit. A continuity check will determine whether an **open-circuit** situation exists.

● Continuity can be checked with an ohmmeter, multimeter, continuity tester or battery and bulb test circuit **(see illustrations 3, 4 and 5)**.

● All of these instruments are self-powered by a battery, therefore the checks are made with the ignition OFF.

● As a safety precaution, always disconnect the battery negative (-) lead before making checks, particularly if ignition switch checks are being made.

● If using a meter, select the appropriate

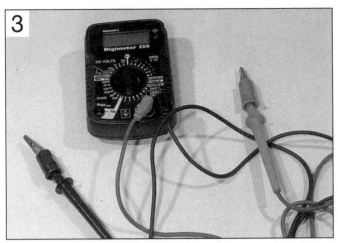

Digital multimeter can be used for all electrical tests

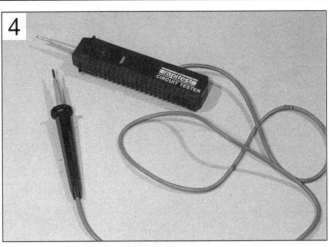

Battery-powered continuity tester

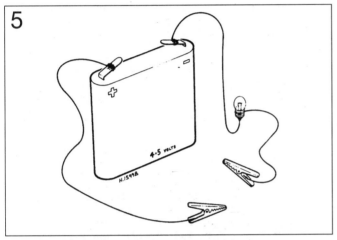

Battery and bulb test circuit

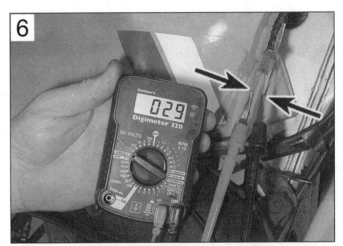

Continuity check of front brake light switch using a meter - note cotter pins used to access connector terminals

ohms scale and check that the meter reads infinity (∞). Touch the meter probes together and check that meter reads zero; where necessary adjust the meter so that it reads zero.

● After using a meter, always switch it OFF to conserve its battery.

Switch checks

1 If a switch is at fault, trace its wiring up to the wiring connectors. Separate the wire connectors and inspect them for security and condition. A build-up of dirt or corrosion here will most likely be the cause of the problem - clean up and apply a water dispersant such as WD40.

2 If using a test meter, set the meter to the ohms x 10 scale and connect its probes across the wires from the switch **(see illustration 6)**. Simple ON/OFF type switches, such as brake light switches, only have two wires whereas combination switches, like the ignition switch, have many internal links.

Study the wiring diagram to ensure that you are connecting across the correct pair of wires. Continuity (low or no measurable resistance - 0 ohms) should be indicated with the switch ON and no continuity (high resistance) with it OFF.

3 Note that the polarity of the test probes doesn't matter for continuity checks, although care should be taken to follow specific test procedures if a diode or solid-state component is being checked.

4 A continuity tester or battery and bulb circuit can be used in the same way. Connect its probes as described above **(see illustration 7)**. The light should come on to indicate continuity in the ON switch position, but should extinguish in the OFF position.

Wiring checks

● Many electrical faults are caused by damaged wiring, often due to incorrect routing or chaffing on frame components.

● Loose, wet or corroded wire connectors

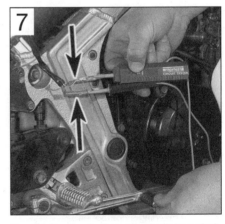

Continuity check of rear brake light switch using a continuity tester

can also be the cause of electrical problems, especially in exposed locations.

Continuity check of front brake light switch sub-harness

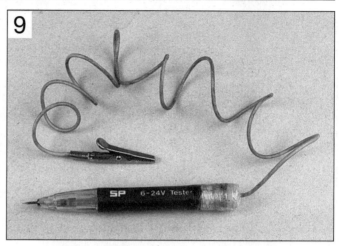

A simple test light can be used for voltage checks

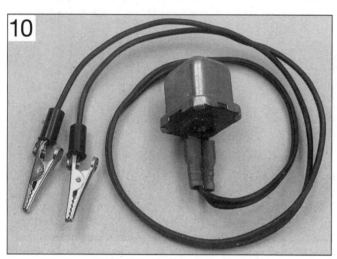

A buzzer is useful for voltage checks

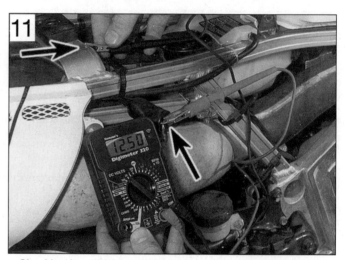

Checking for voltage at the rear brake light power supply wire using a meter . . .

1 A continuity check can be made on a single length of wire by disconnecting it at each end and connecting a meter or continuity tester across both ends of the wire **(see illustration 8)**.

2 Continuity (low or no resistance - 0 ohms) should be indicated if the wire is good. If no continuity (high resistance) is shown, suspect a broken wire.

Checking for voltage

● A voltage check can determine whether current is reaching a component.

● Voltage can be checked with a dc voltmeter, multimeter set on the dc volts scale, test light or buzzer **(see illustrations 9 and 10)**. A meter has the advantage of being able to measure actual voltage.

● When using a meter, check that its leads are inserted in the correct terminals on the meter, red to positive (+), black to negative (-). Incorrect connections can damage the meter.

● A voltmeter (or multimeter set to the dc volts scale) should always be connected in parallel (across the load). Connecting it in series will destroy the meter.

● Voltage checks are made with the ignition ON.

1 First identify the relevant wiring circuit by referring to the wiring diagram at the end of this manual. If other electrical components share the same power supply (ie are fed from the same fuse), take note whether they are working correctly - this is useful information in deciding where to start checking the circuit.

2 If using a meter, check first that the meter leads are plugged into the correct terminals on the meter (see above). Set the meter to the dc volts function, at a range suitable for the battery voltage. Connect the meter red probe (+) to the power supply wire and the black probe to a good metal ground on the motor-cycle's frame or directly to the battery negative (-) terminal **(see illustration 11)**. Battery voltage should be shown on the meter with the ignition switched ON.

3 If using a test light or buzzer, connect its positive (+) probe to the power supply terminal and its negative (-) probe to a good ground on the motorcycle's frame or directly to the battery negative (-) terminal **(see illustration 12)**. With the ignition ON, the test light should illuminate or the buzzer sound.

4 If no voltage is indicated, work back towards the fuse continuing to check for voltage. When you reach a point where there is voltage, you know the problem lies between that point and your last check point.

Checking the ground

● Ground connections are made either

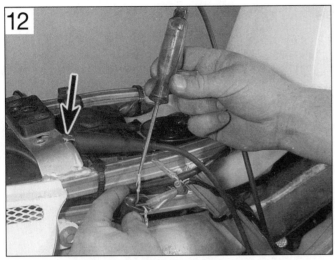

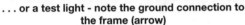

. . . or a test light - note the ground connection to the frame (arrow)

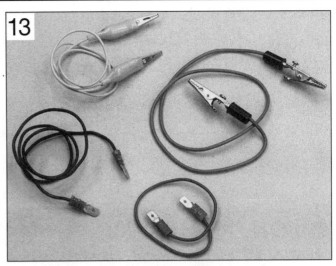

A selection of jumper wires for making ground checks

directly to the engine or frame (such as sensors, neutral switch etc. which only have a positive feed) or by a separate wire into the ground circuit of the wiring harness. Alternatively a short ground wire is sometimes run directly from the component to the motorcycle's frame.

● Corrosion is often the cause of a poor ground connection.

● If total failure is experienced, check the security of the main ground lead from the negative (-) terminal of the battery and also the main ground point on the wiring harness. If corroded, dismantle the connection and clean all surfaces back to bare metal.

1 To check the ground on a component, use an insulated jumper wire to temporarily bypass its ground connection **(see illustration 13)**. Connect one end of the jumper wire between the ground terminal or metal body of the component and the other end to the motorcycle's frame.

2 If the circuit works with the jumper wire installed, the original ground circuit is faulty. Check the wiring for open-circuits or poor connections. Clean up direct ground connections, removing all traces of corrosion and remake the joint. Apply petroleum jelly to the joint to prevent future corrosion.

Tracing a short-circuit

● A short-circuit occurs where current shorts to ground bypassing the circuit components. This usually results in a blown fuse.

● A short-circuit is most likely to occur where the insulation has worn through due to wiring chafing on a component, allowing a direct path to ground on the frame.

1 Remove any body panels necessary to access the circuit wiring.

2 Check that all electrical switches in the circuit are OFF, then remove the circuit fuse and connect a test light, buzzer or voltmeter (set to the dc scale) across the fuse terminals. No voltage should be shown.

3 Move the wiring from side to side while observing the test light or meter. When the test light comes on, buzzer sounds or meter shows voltage, you have found the cause of the short. It will usually shown up as damaged or burned insulation.

4 Note that the same test can be performed on each component in the circuit, even the switch.

Notes

A

ABS (Anti-lock braking system) A system, usually electronically controlled, that senses incipient wheel lockup during braking and relieves hydraulic pressure at wheel which is about to skid.

Aftermarket Components suitable for the motorcycle, but not produced by the motorcycle manufacturer.

Allen key A hexagonal wrench which fits into a recessed hexagonal hole.

Alternating current (ac) Current produced by an alternator. Requires converting to direct current by a rectifier for charging purposes.

Alternator Converts mechanical energy from the engine into electrical energy to charge the battery and power the electrical system.

Ampere (amp) A unit of measurement for the flow of electrical current. Current = Volts ÷ Ohms.

Ampere-hour (Ah) Measure of battery capacity.

Angle-tightening A torque expressed in degrees. Often follows a conventional tightening torque for cylinder head or main bearing fasteners **(see illustration)**.

Angle-tightening cylinder head bolts

Antifreeze A substance (usually ethylene glycol) mixed with water, and added to the cooling system, to prevent freezing of the coolant in winter. Antifreeze also contains chemicals to inhibit corrosion and the formation of rust and other deposits that would tend to clog the radiator and coolant passages and reduce cooling efficiency.

Anti-dive System attached to the fork lower leg (slider) to prevent fork dive when braking hard.

Anti-seize compound A coating that reduces the risk of seizing on fasteners that are subjected to high temperatures, such as exhaust clamp bolts and nuts.

API American Petroleum Institute. A quality standard for 4-stroke motor oils.

Asbestos A natural fibrous mineral with great heat resistance, commonly used in the composition of brake friction materials. Asbestos is a health hazard and the dust created by brake systems should never be inhaled or ingested.

ATF Automatic Transmission Fluid. Often used in front forks.

ATU Automatic Timing Unit. Mechanical device for advancing the ignition timing on early engines.

ATV All Terrain Vehicle. Often called a Quad.

Axial play Side-to-side movement.

Axle A shaft on which a wheel revolves. Also known as a spindle.

B

Backlash The amount of movement between meshed components when one component is held still. Usually applies to gear teeth.

Ball bearing A bearing consisting of a hardened inner and outer race with hardened steel balls between the two races.

Bearings Used between two working surfaces to prevent wear of the components and a build-up of heat. Four types of bearing are commonly used on motorcycles: plain shell bearings, ball bearings, tapered roller bearings and needle roller bearings.

Bevel gears Used to turn the drive through 90°. Typical applications are shaft final drive and camshaft drive **(see illustration)**.

BHP Brake Horsepower. The British measure-ment for engine power output. Power output is now usually expressed in kilowatts (kW).

Bevel gears are used to turn the drive through 90°

Bias-belted tire Similar construction to radial tire, but with outer belt running at an angle to the wheel rim.

Big-end bearing The bearing in the end of the connecting rod that's attached to the crankshaft.

Bleeding The process of removing air from a hydraulic system via a bleed nipple or bleed screw.

Bottom-end A description of an engine's crankcase components and all components contained therein.

BTDC Before Top Dead Center in terms of piston position. Ignition timing is often expressed in terms of degrees or millimeters BTDC.

Bush A cylindrical metal or rubber component used between two moving parts.

Burr Rough edge left on a component after machining or as a result of excessive wear.

C

Cam chain The chain which takes drive from the crankshaft to the camshaft(s).

Canister The main component in an evaporative emission control system (California market only); contains activated charcoal granules to trap vapors from the fuel system rather than allowing them to vent to the atmosphere.

Castellated Resembling the parapets along the top of a castle wall. For example, a castellated wheel axle or spindle nut.

Catalytic converter A device in the exhaust system of some machines which

Cush drive rubber segments dampen out transmission shocks

converts certain pollutants in the exhaust gases into less harmful substances.

Charging system Description of the components which charge the battery, ie the alternator, rectifier and regulator.

Clearance The amount of space between two parts. For example, between a piston and a cylinder, between a bearing and a journal, etc.

Coil spring A spiral of elastic steel found in various sizes throughout a vehicle, for example as a springing medium in the suspension and in the valve train.

Compression Reduction in volume, and increase in pressure and temperature, of a gas, caused by squeezing it into a smaller space.

Compression damping Controls the speed the suspension compresses when hitting a bump.

Compression ratio The relationship between cylinder volume when the piston is at top dead center and cylinder volume when the piston is at bottom dead center.

Continuity The uninterrupted path in the flow of electricity. Little or no measurable resistance.

Continuity tester Self-powered bleeper or test light which indicates continuity.

Cp Candlepower. Bulb rating commonly found on US motorcycles.

Crossply tire Tire plies arranged in a criss-cross pattern. Usually four or six plies used, hence 4PR or 6PR in tire size codes.

Cush drive Rubber damper segments fitted between the rear wheel and final drive sprocket to absorb transmission shocks **(see illustration)**.

D

Degree disc Calibrated disc for measuring piston position. Expressed in degrees.

Dial gauge Clock-type gauge with adapters for measuring runout and piston position. Expressed in mm or inches.

Diaphragm The rubber membrane in a master cylinder or carburetor which seals the upper chamber.

Diaphragm spring A single sprung plate often used in clutches.

Direct current (dc) Current produced by a dc generator.

Decarbonization The process of removing carbon deposits - typically from the combustion chamber, valves and exhaust port/system.

Detonation Destructive and damaging explosion of fuel/air mixture in combustion chamber instead of controlled burning.

Diode An electrical valve which only allows current to flow in one direction. Commonly used in rectifiers and starter interlock systems.

Disc valve (or rotary valve) An induction system used on some two-stroke engines.

Double-overhead camshaft (DOHC) An engine that uses two overhead camshafts, one for the intake valves and one for the exhaust valves.

Drivebelt A toothed belt used to transmit drive to the rear wheel on some motorcycles. A drivebelt has also been used to drive the camshafts. Drivebelts are usually made of Kevlar.

Driveshaft Any shaft used to transmit motion. Commonly used when referring to the final driveshaft on shaft drive motorcycles.

E

ECU (Electronic Control Unit) A computer which controls (for instance) an ignition system, or an anti-lock braking system.

EGO Exhaust Gas Oxygen sensor. Some-times called a Lambda sensor.

Electrolyte The fluid in a lead-acid battery.

EMS (Engine Management System) A computer controlled system which manages the fuel injection and the ignition systems in an integrated fashion.

Endfloat The amount of lengthways movement between two parts. As applied to a crankshaft, the distance that the crankshaft can move side-to-side in the crankcase.

Endless chain A chain having no joining link. Common use for cam chains and final drive chains.

EP (Extreme Pressure) Oil type used in locations where high loads are applied, such as between gear teeth.

Evaporative emission control system Describes a charcoal filled canister which stores fuel vapors from the tank rather than allowing them to vent to the atmosphere. Usually only fitted to California models and referred to as an EVAP system.

Expansion chamber Section of two-stroke engine exhaust system so designed to improve engine efficiency and boost power.

F

Feeler blade or gauge A thin strip or blade of hardened steel, ground to an exact thickness, used to check or measure clearances between parts.

Final drive Description of the drive from the transmission to the rear wheel. Usually by chain or shaft, but sometimes by belt.

Firing order The order in which the engine cylinders fire, or deliver their power strokes, beginning with the number one cylinder.

Flooding Term used to describe a high fuel level in the carburetor float chambers, leading to fuel overflow. Also refers to excess fuel in the combustion chamber due to incorrect starting technique.

Free length The no-load state of a component when measured. Clutch, valve and fork spring lengths are measured at rest, without any preload.

Freeplay The amount of travel before any action takes place. The looseness in a linkage, or an assembly of parts, between the initial application of force and actual movement. For example, the distance the rear brake pedal moves before the rear brake is actuated.

Fuel injection The fuel/air mixture is metered electronically and directed into the engine intake ports (indirect injection) or into the cylinders (direct injection). Sensors supply information on engine speed and conditions.

Fuel/air mixture The charge of fuel and air going into the engine. See Stoichiometric ratio.

Fuse An electrical device which protects a circuit against accidental overload. The typical fuse contains a soft piece of metal which is calibrated to melt at a predetermined current flow (expressed as amps) and break the circuit.

G

Gap The distance the spark must travel in jumping from the center electrode to the side electrode in a spark plug. Also refers to the distance between the ignition rotor and the pickup coil in an electronic ignition system.

Gasket Any thin, soft material - usually cork, cardboard, asbestos or soft metal - installed between two metal surfaces to ensure a good seal. For instance, the cylinder head gasket seals the joint between the block and the cylinder head.

Gauge An instrument panel display used to monitor engine conditions. A gauge with a movable pointer on a dial or a fixed scale is an analog gauge. A gauge with a numerical readout is called a digital gauge.

Gear ratios The drive ratio of a pair of gears in a gearbox, calculated on their number of teeth.

Glaze-busting see **Honing**

Grinding Process for renovating the valve face and valve seat contact area in the cylinder head.

Ground return The return path of an electrical circuit, utilizing the motorcycle's frame.

Gudgeon pin The shaft which connects the connecting rod small-end with the piston. Often called a piston pin or wrist pin.

H

Helical gears Gear teeth are slightly curved and produce less gear noise that straight-cut gears. Often used for primary drives.

Helicoil A thread insert repair system. Commonly used as a repair for stripped spark plug threads **(see illustration)**.

Installing a Helicoil thread insert in a cylinder head

Honing A process used to break down the glaze on a cylinder bore (also called glaze-busting). Can also be carried out to roughen a rebored cylinder to aid ring bedding-in.

HT (High Tension) Description of the electrical circuit from the secondary winding of the ignition coil to the spark plug.

Hydraulic A liquid filled system used to transmit pressure from one component to another. Common uses on motorcycles are brakes and clutches.

Hydrometer An instrument for measuring the specific gravity of a lead-acid battery.

Hygroscopic Water absorbing. In motorcycle applications, braking efficiency will be reduced if DOT 3 or 4 hydraulic fluid absorbs water from the air - care must be taken to keep new brake fluid in tightly sealed containers.

I

lbf ft Pounds-force feet. An imperial unit of torque. Sometimes written as ft-lbs.

lbf in Pound-force inch. An imperial unit of torque, applied to components where a very low torque is required. Sometimes written as inch-lbs.

IC Abbreviation for Integrated Circuit.

Ignition advance Means of increasing the timing of the spark at higher engine speeds. Done by mechanical means (ATU) on early engines or electronically by the ignition control unit on later engines.

Ignition timing The moment at which the spark plug fires, expressed in the number of crankshaft degrees before the piston reaches the top of its stroke, or in the number of millimeters before the piston reaches the top of its stroke.

Infinity (∞) Description of an open-circuit electrical state, where no continuity exists.

Inverted forks (upside down forks) The sliders or lower legs are held in the yokes and the fork tubes or stanchions are connected to the wheel axle (spindle). Less unsprung weight and stiffer construction than conventional forks.

J

JASO Japan Automobile Standards Organization. JASO MA is a standard for motorcycle oil equivalent to API SJ, but designed to prevent problems with wet-type motorcycle clutches.

Joule The unit of electrical energy.

Journal The bearing surface of a shaft.

K

Kickstart Mechanical means of turning the engine over for starting purposes.

Only usually fitted to mopeds, small capacity motorcycles and off-road motorcycles.

Kill switch Handlebar-mounted switch for emergency ignition cut-out. Cuts the ignition circuit on all models, and additionally prevent starter motor operation on others.

km Symbol for kilometer.

kmh Abbreviation for kilometers per hour.

L

Lambda sensor A sensor fitted in the exhaust system to measure the exhaust gas oxygen content (excess air factor). Also called oxygen sensor.

Lapping see **Grinding.**

LCD Abbreviation for Liquid Crystal Display.

LED Abbreviation for Light Emitting Diode.

Liner A steel cylinder liner inserted in an aluminum alloy cylinder block.

Locknut A nut used to lock an adjustment nut, or other threaded component, in place.

Lockstops The lugs on the lower triple clamp (yoke) which abut those on the frame, preventing handlebar-to-fuel tank contact.

Lockwasher A form of washer designed to prevent an attaching nut from working loose.

LT Low Tension Description of the electrical circuit from the power supply to the primary winding of the ignition coil.

M

Main bearings The bearings between the crankshaft and crankcase.

Maintenance-free (MF) battery A sealed battery which cannot be topped up.

Manometer Mercury-filled calibrated tubes used to measure intake tract vacuum. Used to synchronize carburetors on multi-cylinder engines.

Tappet shims are measured with a micrometer

Micrometer A precision measuring instrument that measures component outside diameters **(see illustration).**

MON (Motor Octane Number) A measure of a fuel's resistance to knock.

Monograde oil An oil with a single viscosity, eg SAE80W.

Monoshock A single suspension unit linking the swingarm or suspension linkage to the frame.

mph Abbreviation for miles per hour.

Multigrade oil Having a wide viscosity range (eg 10W40). The W stands for Winter, thus the viscosity ranges from SAE10 when cold to SAE40 when hot.

Multimeter An electrical test instrument with the capability to measure voltage, current and resistance. Some meters also incorporate a continuity tester and buzzer.

N

Needle roller bearing Inner race of caged needle rollers and hardened outer race. Examples of uncaged needle rollers can be found on some engines. Commonly used in rear suspension applications and in two-stroke engines.

Nm Newton meters.

NOx Oxides of Nitrogen. A common toxic pollutant emitted by gasoline engines at higher temperatures.

O

Octane The measure of a fuel's resistance to knock.

OE (Original Equipment) Relates to components fitted to a motorcycle as standard or replacement parts supplied by the motorcycle manufacturer.

Ohm The unit of electrical resistance. Ohms = Volts 4 Current.

Ohmmeter An instrument for measuring electrical resistance.

Oil cooler System for diverting engine oil outside of the engine to a radiator for cooling purposes.

Oil injection A system of two-stroke engine lubrication where oil is pump-fed to the engine in accordance with throttle position.

Open-circuit An electrical condition where there is a break in the flow of electricity - no continuity (high resistance).

O-ring A type of sealing ring made of a special rubber-like material; in use, the O-ring is compressed into a groove to provide the sealing action.

Oversize (OS) Term used for piston and ring size options fitted to a rebored cylinder.

Overhead cam (sohc) engine An engine with single camshaft located on top of the cylinder head.

Overhead valve (ohv) engine An engine with the valves located in the cylinder head, but with the camshaft located in the engine block or crankcase.

Oxygen sensor A device installed in the exhaust system which senses the oxygen content in the exhaust and converts this information into an electric current. Also called a Lambda sensor.

P

Plastigage A thin strip of plastic thread, available in different sizes, used for measuring clearances. For example, a strip of Plastigage is laid across a bearing journal. The parts are assembled and dismantled; the width of the crushed strip indicates the clearance between journal and bearing.

Polarity Either negative or positive ground, determined by which battery lead is connected to the frame (ground return). Modern motorcycles are usually negative ground.

Pre-ignition A situation where the fuel/air mixture ignites before the spark plug fires. Often due to a hot spot in the combustion chamber caused by carbon build-up. Engine has a tendency to 'run-on'.

Pre-load (suspension) The amount a spring is compressed when in the unloaded state. Preload can be applied by gas, spacer or mechanical adjuster.

Premix The method of engine lubrication on some gasoline two-stroke engines. Engine oil is mixed with the gasoline in the fuel tank in a specific ratio. The fuel/oil mix is sometimes referred to as "petrol".

Primary drive Description of the drive from the crankshaft to the clutch. Usually by gear or chain.

PS Pferdestärke - a German interpretation of BHP.

PSI Pounds-force per square inch. Imperial measurement of tire pressure and cylinder pressure measurement.

PTFE Polytetrafluoroethylene. A low friction substance.

Pulse secondary air injection system A process of promoting the burning of excess fuel present in the exhaust gases by routing fresh air into the exhaust ports.

Q

Quartz halogen bulb Tungsten filament surrounded by a halogen gas. Typically used for the headlight **(see illustration)**.

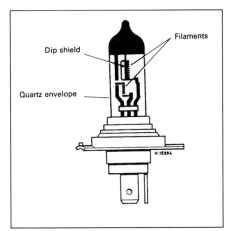

Quartz halogen headlight bulb construction

R

Rack-and-pinion A pinion gear on the end of a shaft that mates with a rack (think of a geared wheel opened up and laid flat). Sometimes used in clutch operating systems.

Radial play Up and down movement about a shaft.

Radial ply tires Tire plies run across the tire (from bead to bead) and around the circumference of the tire. Less resistant to tread distortion than other tire types.

Radiator A liquid-to-air heat transfer device designed to reduce the temperature of the coolant in a liquid cooled engine.

Rake A feature of steering geometry - the angle of the steering head in relation to the vertical **(see illustration)**.

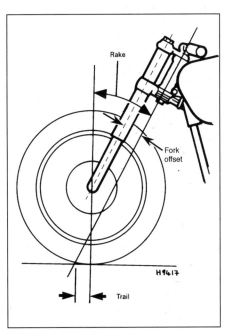

Steering geometry

Rebore Providing a new working surface to the cylinder bore by boring out the old surface. Necessitates the use of oversize piston and rings.

Rebound damping A means of controlling the oscillation of a suspension unit spring after it has been compressed. Resists the spring's natural tendency to bounce back after being compressed.

Rectifier Device for converting the ac output of an alternator into dc for battery charging.

Reed valve An induction system commonly used on two-stroke engines.

Regulator Device for maintaining the charging voltage from the generator or alternator within a specified range.

Relay A electrical device used to switch heavy current on and off by using a low current auxiliary circuit.

Resistance Measured in ohms. An electrical component's ability to pass electrical current.

RON (Research Octane Number) A measure of a fuel's resistance to knock.

rpm revolutions per minute.

Runout The amount of wobble (in-and-out movement) of a wheel or shaft as it's rotated. The amount a shaft rotates 'out-of-true'. The out-of-round condition of a rotating part.

S

SAE (Society of Automotive Engineers) A standard for the viscosity of a fluid.

Sealant A liquid or paste used to prevent leakage at a joint. Sometimes used in conjunction with a gasket.

Service limit Term for the point where a component is no longer useable and must be replaced.

Shaft drive A method of transmitting drive from the transmission to the rear wheel.

Shell bearings Plain bearings consisting of two shell halves. Most often used as big-end and main bearings in a four-stroke engine. Often called bearing inserts.

Shim Thin spacer, commonly used to adjust the clearance or relative positions between two parts. For example, shims inserted into or under tappets or followers to control valve clearances. Clearance is adjusted by changing the thickness of the shim.

Short-circuit An electrical condition where current shorts to ground bypassing the circuit components.

Skimming Process to correct warpage or repair a damaged surface, eg on brake discs or drums.

Slide-hammer A special puller that screws into or hooks onto a component such as a shaft or bearing; a heavy sliding handle on the shaft bottoms against the end of the shaft to knock the component free.

Small-end bearing The bearing in the upper end of the connecting rod at its joint with the gudgeon pin.

Snap-ring A ring-shaped clip used to prevent endwise movement of cylindrical parts and shafts. An internal snap-ring is installed in a groove in a housing; an external snap-ring fits into a groove on the outside of a cylindrical piece such as a shaft. Also known as a snap-ring.

Spalling Damage to camshaft lobes or bearing journals shown as pitting of the working surface.

Specific gravity (SG) The state of charge of the electrolyte in a lead-acid battery. A measure of the electrolyte's density compared with water.

Straight-cut gears Common type gear used on gearbox shafts and for oil pump and water pump drives.

Stanchion The inner sliding part of the front forks, held by the yokes. Often called a fork tube.

Stoichiometric ratio The optimum chemical air/fuel ratio for a gasoline engine, said to be 14.7 parts of air to 1 part of fuel.

Sulphuric acid The liquid (electrolyte) used in a lead-acid battery. Poisonous and extremely corrosive.

Surface grinding (lapping) Process to correct a warped gasket face, commonly used on cylinder heads.

T

Tapered-roller bearing Tapered inner race of caged needle rollers and separate tapered outer race. Examples of taper roller bearings can be found on steering heads.

Tappet A cylindrical component which transmits motion from the cam to the valve stem, either directly or via a pushrod and rocker arm. Also called a cam follower.

TCS Traction Control System. An electronically-controlled system which senses wheel spin and reduces engine speed accordingly.

TDC Top Dead Center denotes that the piston is at its highest point in the cylinder.

Thread-locking compound Solution applied to fastener threads to prevent loosening. Select type to suit application.

Thrust washer A washer positioned between two moving components on a shaft. For example, between gear pinions on gearshaft.

Timing chain See **Cam Chain**.

Timing light Stroboscopic lamp for carrying out ignition timing checks with the engine running.

Top-end A description of an engine's cylinder block, head and valve gear components.

Torque Turning or twisting force about a shaft.

Torque setting A prescribed tightness specified by the motorcycle manufacturer to ensure that the bolt or nut is secured correctly. Undertightening can result in the bolt or nut coming loose or a surface not being sealed. Overtightening can result in stripped threads, distortion or damage to the component being retained.

Torx key A six-point wrench.

Tracer A stripe of a second color applied to a wire insulator to distinguish that wire from another one with the same color insulator. For example, Br/W is often used to denote a brown insulator with a white tracer.

Trail A feature of steering geometry. Distance from the steering head axis to the tire's central contact point.

Triple clamps The cast components which extend from the steering head and support the fork stanchions or tubes. Often called fork yokes.

Turbocharger A centrifugal device, driven by exhaust gases, that pressurizes the intake air. Normally used to increase the power output from a given engine displacement.

TWI Abbreviation for Tire Wear Indicator. Indicates the location of the tread depth indicator bars on tires.

U

Universal joint or U-joint (UJ) A double-pivoted connection for transmitting power from a driving to a driven shaft through an angle. Typically found in shaft drive assemblies.

Unsprung weight Anything not supported by the bike's suspension (ie the wheel, tires, brakes, final drive and bottom (moving) part of the suspension).

V

Vacuum gauges Clock-type gauges for measuring intake tract vacuum. Used for carburetor synchronization on multi-cylinder engines.

Valve A device through which the flow of liquid, gas or vacuum may be stopped, started or regulated by a moveable part that opens, shuts or partially obstructs one or more ports or passageways. The intake and exhaust valves in the cylinder head are of the poppet type.

Valve clearance The clearance between the valve tip (the end of the valve stem) and the rocker arm or tappet/follower. The valve clearance is measured when the valve is closed. The correct clearance is important - if too small the valve won't close fully and will burn out, whereas if too large noisy operation will result.

Valve lift The amount a valve is lifted off its seat by the camshaft lobe.

Valve timing The exact setting for the opening and closing of the valves in relation to piston position.

Vernier caliper A precision measuring instrument that measures inside and outside dimensions. Not quite as accurate as a micrometer, but more convenient.

VIN Vehicle Identification Number. Term for the bike's engine and frame numbers.

Viscosity The thickness of a liquid or its resistance to flow.

Volt A unit for expressing electrical "pressure" in a circuit. Volts = current x ohms.

W

Water pump A mechanically-driven device for moving coolant around the engine.

Watt A unit for expressing electrical power. Watts = volts x current.

Wet liner arrangement

Wear limit see **Service limit**

Wet liner A liquid-cooled engine design where the pistons run in liners which are directly surrounded by coolant **(see illustration)**.

Wheelbase Distance from the center of the front wheel to the center of the rear wheel.

Wiring harness or loom Describes the electrical wires running the length of the motorcycle and enclosed in tape or plastic sheathing. Wiring coming off the main harness is usually referred to as a sub harness.

Woodruff key A key of semi-circular or square section used to locate a gear to a shaft. Often used to locate the alternator rotor on the crankshaft.

Wrist pin Another name for gudgeon or piston pin.

Notes

Note: *References throughout this index are in the form - "Chapter number"•"Page number"*

Notes